A CONCISE H

MW00860718

The small and densely populated nation of Belgium has played an important role in the history of Europe and other continents, especially Africa. It was a pioneering force in industry, trade, and finance during the Middle Ages, through early modern times and into the nineteenth and twentieth centuries. It introduced innovative political regimes and played a leading role in the creative arts. Yet this rich past is not widely known. This introductory history offers an accessible and rigorous overview of this small but important West-European country, synthesizing Belgium's main economic, social, political, and cultural developments from pre-Roman times until today. Today, this nation-state, born in 1830, is well known for the rivalries between its two main language communities, and as a result is often considered a fragile or even an artificial political construct. This systematic chronological analysis of both present-day Belgium and the polities that preceded it throws fresh light on this controversial issue and demonstrates Belgium's enduring importance and influence.

Guy Vanthemsche is Professor Emeritus at the Free University Brussels, where he taught contemporary history for over three decades. He is the secretary of the Belgian Royal Historical Commission and a member of the Belgian Royal Academy of Overseas Sciences. He is the author of several books on nineteenth- and twentieth-century social, economic, and political Belgian history, including *Belgium and the Congo, 1885–1980* (Cambridge University Press, 2012).

Roger De Peuter was a lecturer in economic and social history at Utrecht University and taught late medieval and early modern history of the Low Countries at the Free University Brussels until his retirement in 2011. His publications include articles and a book on early modern Belgian history.

CAMBRIDGE CONCISE HISTORIES

This is a series of illustrated 'concise histories' of selected individual countries, intended both as university and college textbooks and as general historical introductions for general readers, travellers, and members of the business community.

A full list of titles in the series can be found at:
www.cambridge.org/concisehistories

A Concise History of Belgium

GUY VANTHEMSCHE
Free University Brussels

ROGER DE PEUTER
Free University Brussels and Utrecht University

CAMBRIDGE
UNIVERSITY PRESS

CAMBRIDGE
UNIVERSITY PRESS

Shaftesbury Road, Cambridge CB2 8EA, United Kingdom

One Liberty Plaza, 20th Floor, New York, NY 10006, USA

477 Williamstown Road, Port Melbourne, VIC 3207, Australia

314–321, 3rd Floor, Plot 3, Splendor Forum, Jasola District Centre,
New Delhi – 110025, India

103 Penang Road, #05–06/07, Visioncrest Commercial, Singapore 238467

Cambridge University Press is part of Cambridge University Press & Assessment,
a department of the University of Cambridge.

We share the University's mission to contribute to society through the pursuit of
education, learning and research at the highest international levels of excellence.

www.cambridge.org
Information on this title: www.cambridge.org/9780521192415

DOI: 10.1017/9781139018005

First published 2023

A catalogue record for this publication is available from the British Library.

A Cataloging-in-Publication data record for this book is available from the Library of Congress.

ISBN 978-0-521-19241-5 Hardback
ISBN 978-0-521-12737-0 Paperback

To my mother, Mariette Medo, born in 1926 and still going strong — a witness to almost half of modern Belgium's history — GV

In memory of my parents, Antoine De Peuter and Marie De Peuter-Luyts. The stories they told me as a youngster about their experiences in the 1930s and 1940s taught me a lot about history — RDP

Contents

Contents

Contents

Contents

Contents

Figures

Maps

Acknowledgments

.

Guy Vanthemsche wrote the Introduction, Chapters 1 and 2, 7 to 10, and
the final Conclusion, while Roger De Peuter authored Chapters 3 to 6.
We would like to thank the following colleagues for reading and com-
menting on parts of this book: Marc Boone, Jean Bourgeois, Martin
Conway, Alain Dierkens, Janet Polasky, Dries Tys, and Els Witte. We are
also grateful to Laure De Cock and Philippe De Maeyer who drew the
map reproduced at the end of the Introduction. Many thanks finally also
to William Chew III, who made linguistic corrections to the
Introduction, Chapters 1 and 2, 7 to 10 and the Conclusion.

Note on the Text

Names of places and persons will be written in the original French or Dutch, unless an English equivalent is currently used (for instance Ghent and Brussels, and not *Gent* or *Bruxelles*; or Charles the Bold and not *Charles le Téméraire* or *Karel de Stoute*). We will also use the continental metric system (for instance kilometers and not miles).

Introduction

Until well into the twentieth century, writing "national history" hardly required any justification. On the contrary: for more than a century and a half, it was generally considered a supreme achievement in a successful historian's career. However, the last few decades have profoundly changed the game, with the breakthrough of new and thrilling approaches to the human past, for instance global, connected, or trans-national history. Today, this "old" branch of historiography hardly yields academic glory; it has even fallen into deep disrepute. According to the French historian Nicolas Offenstadt national history is "an ideological instrument, similar to the discourse on national identity. This type of synthesis seems problematic to me, it always sounds false" (cited by the newspaper *Le Monde [des Livres]*, 30 November 2012). This is just one (harsh) expression of the critical stance of many contemporary scholars toward this genre. Obviously, the present *Concise History of Belgium* needs some clarification – if not an apology.

Size is not what matters here. To be sure, Belgium is one of the smallest nations of the planet: in the relevant world ranking, it occupies the 139th place. With its 30,530 km² – a surface area more or less that of Maryland (32,133 km²), or one and a half times that of Wales (20,735 km²) – the country is hardly noticeable on a European, let alone a world map. In 2020, about 11.5 million people were estimated to live in this modest nation-state. Belgium therefore belongs to the group of small countries with a high population density: it occupies the twenty-second position in the relevant global ranking.

But is quantity the right criterion with which to evaluate a nation's importance? In the case of Belgium, it is not difficult to prove that this country, however small, undoubtedly left important marks on European and even on world history. Let us quickly mention just a few examples, which we will of course elaborate in due time.

- The "Belgian" principalities and cities played an important role in the European Middle Ages and pioneered – together with the English *Magna Carta* – the mechanisms of political representation and "liberties."
- From the fourteenth to the sixteenth centuries, cities like Bruges, Ghent and Antwerp were among the main economic centers of their time.
- In the seventeenth and eighteenth centuries, the Southern Netherlands (the predecessor of contemporary Belgium) were often the battleground of rivaling powers.
- When it was created in 1830, Belgium introduced one of the most liberal constitutions of its time, a model – or a spectre – for many citizens and politicians abroad.
- In the nineteenth century, it was labelled the "second industrial nation of the world," being in the vanguard of capitalist development. Belgian entrepreneurs were active all over the planet.
- Between 1885 and 1908, King Leopold II ruled over the Independent Congo State, a colony that was heavily criticized in Europe and the US, and Congolese decolonization in 1960 was an important factor in the Cold War.
- Belgium's involvement in the First and Second World War was far from unimportant – in 1914 the resistance of Belgian troops even played a decisive role in the outcome of the struggle between the allied armies and the German invader.
- "Belgians" feature among the most prominent painters in Western art history, from Jan Van Eyck, to Brueghel and Rubens, and to Magritte.

Clearly, all these – and other – facts and developments deserve a mention in world history textbooks. From this point of view, a synthesis of Belgian history is therefore far from irrelevant. But the crucial issue here is not so much justifying a national history of *Belgium*, but rather arguing the validity of a *national* history of Belgium and clarifying the perspective from which the present book was written.

The attentive reader will have noticed that in some instances the word "Belgian" has been put between inverted commas. In the forthcoming chapters these punctuation marks will often reappear, surrounding the same word. Far from being fortuitous, they refer to several fundamental questions confronting any author of a "national history of Belgium." Is it legitimate to use the words Belgium and Belgian before 1830, the year when the present nation-state was born? How far in the past can we identify its roots? Did some embryonic form of modern Belgium exist (long) before the nineteenth century? And cautiously adopting the nationalistic vocabulary still in use today, to the great displeasure of Nicolas Offenstadt and so many historians, when did the "Belgian identity" come into existence? Or, more correctly, does (or did) a "Belgian identity" (ever) exist in the first place?

These questions have haunted Belgian historiography and politics since the early nineteenth century. They are intimately linked with a key feature of modern Belgian history, the coexistence, within the same nation, of two language communities, French and Dutch, the first somewhat smaller than the second. Of course, this is far from being a unique feature; many modern countries also host different linguistic groups and some even have two or more official languages (for instance Switzerland). However, Belgium differs from other multilingual countries in that its linguistic duality has exerted, and still exerts, a heavy strain on the national state – even to the point of calling into question the latter's very existence. This singularity alone makes a book on Belgian history worthwhile. The growing confrontation between the two language communities dominates the country's history in the second half of the twentieth century and will therefore be a key element in our final chapter, but it also determines the way Belgium's past is interpreted. Consequently, it must be mentioned in these introductory pages as well.

Indeed, Belgium's "historical depth" was, and still is, the object of diverging readings. Many proponents of Flemish nationalism – a political and cultural current born in the early twentieth century, as we shall see – largely deny any historicity (and "legitimacy") to the Belgian nation-state. They present it as an artificial creation of the Great Powers in 1830, bringing together two different "peoples," the Dutch-speaking Flemings and the French-speaking Walloons, in an institutional framework dominated by the latter, and oppressing the former. Romantic nineteenth-century Belgian nationalists held a totally opposite view. For them, the roots of "Belgian identity" lay in a remote past. According to them, the heroic (but ultimately defeated) *Belgae* mentioned by the Roman conqueror Julius Caesar in his *De Bello Gallico*, already displayed some essential characteristics of the glorious Belgian "race" that finally gained independence in 1830 after centuries of "foreign oppression." In between these radically contrasting visions, many other interpretations of Belgium's genesis have been formulated. It is therefore one of the tasks of this book to clarify this issue on the basis of recent scholarly insights.

Of course, nobody in earnest still defends the nineteenth-century patriotic image claiming high antiquity for the Belgian "nation" or "identity." Our first chapter will nevertheless start with these oldest times, not only to examine the origins and significance of this now completely discredited view, but also to explain what these *Belgae* and the Romans exactly represented in the flow of time, beyond the mythic discourse produced by erstwhile Belgian patriots. This early starting point also helps to clarify the origins and significance of the medieval principalities, an important issue in the debate concerning Belgium's historical depth. Resulting from the dissolution of the Carolingian Empire (Chapter 2), a series of quasi-autonomous polities emerged in the area that, many centuries later, would become Belgium. Some were within the sphere of influence of the nascent French kingdom, others within that of the Holy Roman (Germanic) Empire (Chapter 3). Did they already herald some "Belgian" specificity? The great historian Henri Pirenne (1862–1935) thought so. According to his views, mainly elaborated in his multi-volume *Histoire de Belgique* (1900-1932) the medieval principalities in this part of Western Europe already displayed some specific traits leading to later Belgium – in particular the unique mix of so-called Romanic and Germanic elements. Pirenne's long shadow is still perceptible in historiography today, but contemporary scholars no longer accept his vision of Belgium's medieval origins – we will of course explain why.

In the course of the fourteenth and fifteenth centuries, all these principalities – with the notable exception of the prince-bishopric of Liège – came to be ruled by the *same* sovereigns, first the Burgundians, then the Habsburgs, and these rulers initiated a process of submission and centralization of the territories they governed, limiting their autonomy and imposing upon them some sort of common political destiny (Chapter 4). However, this process did not yet lead to modern Belgium in a straightforward manner. The "Netherlands" or "Low Countries" (or "Seventeen Provinces"), as they were called (*Pays-Bas* in French; *Nederlanden* or *Lage Landen* in Dutch), still included the polities that, from the late sixteenth and early seventeenth centuries onward, would ultimately form today's nation-state "The Netherlands," modern

Belgium's northern neighbor. The protracted and bloody wars resulting from the religious divide between Catholics and Protestants would indeed mark the fate of both countries, since they led to the independence of the (Protestant) Dutch Republic, the ancestor of the contemporary kingdom of The Netherlands. Some of the former Seventeen Provinces, ruled by the emperor Charles V in the early sixteenth century, remained under the sovereignty of the (Catholic) Habsburg dynasty, first the Spanish and then the Austrian branch, respectively, in the seventeenth and eighteenth century (Chapters 5 and 6).

Henceforth called the "Spanish," then the "Austrian Netherlands," or also the "Southern Netherlands," the principalities remaining under Habsburg authority were, however, not yet automatically "destined" to become modern Belgium. Moreover, the principality of Liège still existed independently from the Southern Netherlands. In a short period, a mere forty years (1789–1830), the fate of the latter seemed to be sealed in very different ways. After a brief experiment of "independence" (1789–1790), they were first absorbed by France (1794–1814), together with Liège – the realization of a dream already pursued by the French Bourbon kings since the seventeenth century – then amalgamated with the former Dutch Republic into the United Kingdom of the Netherlands (1814–1830). The vagaries of history (to be explained in Chapter 7) finally led to the failure of both solutions, and to the emergence of Belgium as an independent country in 1830.

Underneath these (apparently chaotic) chronological sequences lies a pattern that gives some coherence to the developments analyzed in this book. Different layers of power can be observed from the Middle Ages until the present. First the local communities, especially the cities; then the regions (from the medieval principalities, over the modern provinces, to the contemporary institutions of federalized Belgium); above these regions then comes a "national" level, budding since the rule of the Burgundians and fully blooming with the creation of Belgium proper in 1830; and finally some "supranational" levels, represented by such diverse phenomena as the medieval Holy Roman Empire or the suzerainty of the French kingdom in medieval times, the Habsburg Empires in the early modern era, and finally the European Economic Community and Union in the second half of the twentieth century. Despite their enormous contrasts, these entities all encompassed, at some time and in very different ways, the previous power levels. We therefore invite the reader to carefully watch the changing relationships between these four levels – they are a kind of red thread that binds together many elements that would otherwise seem unconnected.

*

* *

A flag; an anthem; a well-defined and internationally recognized territory; a set of stable political institutions governed by local politicians; a single legal system – Belgium seemingly possessed all the ingredients of a genuine nation-state. However, this young and thriving bourgeois regime, analyzed in Chapter 8, was inevitably confronted with a nagging problem, that of its so-called national identity. What did it mean, exactly, to be "a Belgian"? What differentiated this European citizen from other inhabitants of the Old Continent? Was it religion? From the seventeenth century, the authorities, intellectuals, and the Church itself, all presented Catholicism as a defining element of the Southern Netherlands, transformed into a bastion of the Counter-Reformation. Indeed, after the eradication, forced conversion or emigration of the many Protestants present there in the sixteenth century, the population of "Belgium" remained devoutly and almost exclusively Catholic – a striking contrast with the Protestant faith of most citizens of the newly created Dutch Republic. But this adherence to Rome did not differentiate the residents of the Southern Netherlands from other Europeans who also remained faithful to Catholicism (France, Spain, the Italian principalities, etc.). In the nineteenth century, Catholic politicians also presented their faith as *the* constituent feature of the new Belgian nation. But this "identity" was contested from the start by a large number of politicians and intellectuals – and also public opinion – and the public role of the Roman Catholic Church remained a bone of contention until far into the twentieth century. Moreover, although the vast majority of the Belgians indeed adhered to its faith and practices, part of the population gradually lost contact with religion or even abruptly broke with it. In other words, while the Catholic religion undoubtedly played a key role in both public and private life in the Southern Netherlands, it could not (and cannot) be considered a defining element of "Belgianness." Throughout the following chapters, we will address the successive phases of Catholic presence in the history of these regions.

Perhaps language was, or could become, the key defining element of "all things Belgian"? This was not the case either, since the population consisted of

Francophones and Flemish speakers (i.e. people using one of the many Dutch dialects spoken in this area). Both languages, as it were, already "had their own nation-state" – respectively France and The Netherlands. Although language could not become a defining character of "Belgian identity," the patriotic leaders and intellectuals of young Belgium nevertheless produced, as we just saw, different discourses "proving" the reality and even the antiquity of this "identity." The creation of "Belgianness" was however accompanied by a specific cultural and institutional policy, namely a thorough Gallicization of public life. Only French was used in Belgian public administrative life. This was also the case in the northern part of the country, where it was imposed upon a population that predominantly spoke Flemish. Moreover, language acted as a marker of social hierarchy. Elite figures (landlords, industrialists, rich traders, etc.), and even the petty bourgeoisie spoke French to differentiate themselves from common people using a Flemish dialect, an idiom they considered obscure and unfit for civilized persons.

In the course of the late nineteenth and the first half of the twentieth century (Chapter 9), social, political, and cultural discrimination against the Flemish population generated the "Flemish movement," which gradually developed a sense of "Flemish identity." Its followers also forged the notion of "Flanders," a region that encompassed all Flemish speakers in Belgium. Defined this way, Flanders was previously non-existent, both in politics and in people's minds, since it differed notably from the medieval principality of the same name. The Flemish movement gradually obtained equality, before the law and in public life, of the Flemish language (meanwhile standardized into "correct" Dutch). As a reaction against these advances, some French speakers launched the Walloon movement. They created their own "identity" discourse, crystallized around the notion of "Wallonia" – a region encompassing the French-speaking inhabitants of Belgium (or, at least, the vast majority of them, i.e. those living outside the bilingual capital, Brussels). This movement, born at the end of the nineteenth century, was far less powerful than its Flemish counterpart, but it nevertheless produced its own interpretation of the past, now from the Francophone viewpoint.

During the twentieth century (Chapters 9 and 10), Belgium became even more complex. After the First World War, the Treaty of Versailles transferred some 850 km^2 from Germany to Belgium, the so-called East cantons (*cantons de l'Est*), introducing a new, German-speaking community into an already linguistically divided country. Since the 1970s, although quantitatively modest (60,000 persons in 1928, 78,000 in 2019), this population has enjoyed a specific set of institutions in Belgium's new federal state structure. Moreover, after the Second World War, successive waves of immigrant workers came from Italy, then from Morocco and Turkey. They were soon followed by growing numbers of refugees and immigrants from African, Latin-American or Asian countries – not to mention the many "Eurocrats" and expats working for international institutions or companies. Of course, their languages have not been accorded official status, but this multitude of people of different origins has turned Belgium, and especially its capital city Brussels, into a linguistic and cultural kaleidoscope, a multicultural environment that has not only profoundly reshaped the social fabric, but also generated new kinds of tensions, including various forms of "identity politics," as we shall see in Chapter 10.

Producing a homogenous narrative of the past in such a complex country is far from evident. A century or more after Belgium's birth, three conflicting interpretations of this particular area's past had developed: a Belgian, a Flemish, and a Walloon version. One could also add a fourth version, a "Great-Netherlandic" view, which stressed the common political and cultural destiny of all Dutch speakers; that is, of both The Netherlands and Flanders, whose natural fate it seemingly was to live together in one polity, without the Francophones dominating the "artificial" state of Belgium. During the twentieth century, some ambitious historiographical syntheses were published, inspired by these conflicting views. But whether they were entitled *Histoire de Belgique*, *Geschiedenis van Vlaanderen*, *Histoire de la Wallonie*, or even *Geschiedenis van de Nederlandse stam* (inspired by the Great-Netherlandic view), the authors of all these works had something in common. They generally interpreted the past from a teleological point of view – they considered their preferred political construct as the inexorable product of historical evolution. In the case of Belgium, the "legitimate" outcome existed and had to be promoted, both abroad and within the country itself. In the other instances, the desired nation-state had not yet taken form – an injustice that needed reparation in the eyes of respective proponents. All these historiographical endeavors tried to demonstrate that the defining features, or "identity," of Belgium – or Flanders, or Wallonia, or the Great-Netherlands – were already present in the past. This almost "natural" identity, the product of a linear past to be proud of, had to express itself in a nation-state, existing or yet to come.

For sure, not all these views are equally vibrant today. In twenty-first-century Belgium, undermined by a long struggle between its two main

8

language communities (Chapter 10), hardly anyone interprets the past from a nationalistic "Belgicist" point of view. The defenders of Walloon identity, for their part, very rarely strive for Wallonia's full-fledged independence – in a less finalistic approach, they rather promote the existence of a purely *regional identity*, within the framework of a larger nation-state (whether Belgium or, far less often, France). Proponents of the Great-Netherlands, encompassing both the inhabitants of The Netherlands and modern Flanders, are also very few nowadays – although this political project enjoyed some resonance in the interwar period. It is essentially within Flemish nationalism that the idea of an independent Flanders lives on; since the start of the twenty-first century, it is being vocally supported by a large fraction of Flemish public opinion. This position is underpinned by a finalistic view, projecting the modern region of Flanders into the past as an ever-existing entity with a well-defined and immutable "identity."

Our approach to the "Belgian" past is entirely different. This synthesis does not want to "justify" one or the other polity or project. It not only eschews teleological biases; it also tries, on the contrary, to deconstruct some myths concerning Belgian, Flemish, or Walloon history. It tries to do so by highlighting the main historical developments that took place within the geographical scope of contemporary Belgium – while being well aware that this spatial framework, based on the borders defined in 1830–1831, is often deficient if one wants to capture the processes at work in bygone times. The regions constituting today's nation-state were previously embedded in specific, original configurations that differed from the present ones. For instance, until the seventeenth century parts of northern France fully belonged to the Southern Netherlands, and the country's historical trajectory can only be understood if these regions are integrated into our narrative.

Therefore, we must always bear in mind that the fate of the "Belgian" territories was not determined by the later outcome – Belgium – but by other political, economic, and cultural relationships, in particular those resulting from the emergence of the Low Countries as a more or less coherent political reality from the late fourteenth century. The position adopted here, namely to explore the past starting from the modern Belgian space, is indeed arbitrary and artificial (in the sense that it imposes a framework that was not *necessarily* relevant before). But it is not more so than if one chooses Flanders or Wallonia as a starting point. Writing the "history of Flanders" or the "history of Wallonia" raises the same kinds of problems of retro-analysis. Taking the Low Countries as a framework to describe past developments in this part of Western Europe also has its shortcomings. The so-called Seventeen Provinces did not exist at all in the Early Middle Ages; between approximately the fourteenth to the sixteenth century they indeed constituted a more or less coherent spatial and political framework; but they largely lose their relevance for developments in the "Belgian" territories from the seventeenth century onward.

Any *Concise History of Belgium* must also avoid another pitfall. However important during the most recent decades, the struggles between both language communities should not become its sole point of reference. It would indeed be wrong to assume that this specific dimension of *modern* Belgian history was automatically relevant in all times past. Clearly, it was not. Before the end of the eighteenth century, the fact that some principalities consisted of French speakers and others of Dutch speakers, or even that both languages were used simultaneously *within* some principalities, was not a real problem. Indeed, the use of languages was determined by other mechanisms than those dominant in modern Belgium. Prior to Belgium's birth in 1830, and even thereafter, politics of course meant far more than language issues. Moreover, economic, social, and cultural developments, both in the "Belgian" territories and in Belgium proper, are important in their own right. We shall therefore pay due attention to these as well.

This panoramic view obviously requires some knowledge of the geographical setting: after having travelled quickly through time, we will also do so through space (see map 1.1, p. 15). We therefore invite the foreign reader to imagine him- or herself as a fellow traveller of the German aristocrat Leopold of Saxe-Coburg, the widower of the heiress to the British throne, the late Princess Charlotte. In 1831, he had accepted the invitation of the young Belgian authorities to become their king. To reach Brussels, where he was to swear a solemn oath on the brand-new Belgian constitution on July 21, 1831 – Belgium's national holiday since 1890 – the future Leopold I crossed the North Sea from Dover to Calais. At the French town of Dunkirk, he continued, via the beach, to Belgium's north-westernmost commune of De Panne (*La Panne* in French), where he first set foot on Belgian soil. On the king's trail, we will travel from north to south to introduce Belgium's main physical and topographical traits.

Belgium's short coast, stretching a mere 60 km in a north-easterly direction, presents itself as a long sandy beach bordered by dunes, only interrupted first by the mouth of the (modest) river Yser (that was to play an important role in the First World War), then by the ports of Ostend and Zeebrugge (the latter created as late as the beginning of the twentieth century). Today's seashore is largely covered with concrete, strewn with large apartment buildings and villas, and therefore looks immutable. This is of course a false impression, not only with regard to the perilous future of global warming, but also when looking back in time. Indeed, in antiquity and during the Middle Ages the limits between sea and land often fluctuated, marked by a changing landscape of small islands, marshes, and salty meadows. By the nineteenth century, however, the inhabitants had long since won their age-old struggle with the sea: behind the tiny area occupied by the dunes, tireless efforts of land reclamation had created a landscape of polders.

Here begins Low Belgium, the first of the country's three components traditionally distinguished by geographical textbooks. Its main feature is aptly described by its adjective. It presents an open and flat landscape, with no relief. Leopold, passing through this region, still saw some sparse forests on his way to the city of Bruges, in the east, some 15 km from the Dutch border. Nowadays, these wooded zones have almost completely disappeared. Deforestation was practiced from the Middle Ages, not only in this part of the country, but also elsewhere. Land was increasingly cleared for agriculture or husbandry, although the sub-soil, consisting of sandy soils and sandy loam, is not ideally fertile for farming. Some 60 km south from the coast, one crosses the first of the two big rivers flowing through Belgium, the Scheldt (*Schelde*, in Dutch, *Escaut* in French). Leaving Bruges on his way to Brussels, Leopold and his entourage reached Ghent, one of Flanders' main cities. It is located on the exact point where the Scheldt is met by its main tributary, the Lys (in Dutch *Leie*). The Scheldt runs northeast but does not reach the sea on Belgian soil: its delta is located in The Netherlands. Before leaving Belgian territory this river borders the other important Flemish city, Antwerp, whose port has played a key role since the fifteenth century.

A few kilometres south of the Scheldt begins Middle Belgium, the second of Belgium's three geographical regions. The rolling landscape now consists of gentle hills, molded by a series of modest waterways that ultimately flow into the Scheldt. Among them are the Senne and the Dyle, on whose banks are located, respectively, the Brabant cities of Brussels and Leuven (Louvain). The soil here consists of loam, making this part of the country more fertile and fit for agriculture. Forests are somewhat more present here – even if deforestation has also taken a heavy toll. The *Forêt de Soignes*, for instance, the green lung on the southern side of Brussels, the capital located right in the centre of Belgium, was once part of the much larger Coal Forest, which we will mention in Chapter 2.

In July 1831, Leopold of course halted in Brussels for his inauguration ceremony, but we will continue our journey to discover the southern part of the country. About 50 km southeast of Brussels, one reaches the second of Belgium's main rivers, the Meuse. The city of Namur – today the capital of Wallonia – is located on the confluence of this waterway and its tributary, the Sambre. The important city of Liège is also located on the banks of the Meuse, some 55 km downstream, near the Dutch border. Indeed, the Meuse, like the Scheldt, continues its course through the territory of The Netherlands before flowing into the North Sea. The Meuse more or less marks the beginning of Belgium's third physical part, High Belgium. This is a somewhat misleading name. This southern region is certainly known for its more accentuated relief, but Belgium's highest point, the *Signal de Botrange* in the east, culminates at a modest 694 m. Its soils are less conducive to agriculture, and dense forests and large pastures dominate the area. Here is located the vast wooded and thinly populated area of the Belgian Ardennes that imperceptibly continues into the neighboring countries of France (the French Ardennes) and the Grand-Duchy of Luxemburg. Belgium's south-easternmost city, Arlon, is only 25 km from the city of Luxemburg, the Grand-Duchy's capital. The distance between De Panne to Arlon is about the longest one can travel on Belgian territory, about 300 km as the crow flies. By car, the journey takes about five hours. This gives one an idea of the exiguity of Belgium's territory, a small part of Western Europe that nevertheless carries a rich history spanning two millennia.

Before embarking on this narrative, it is however important to clarify some terminological issues. Certain words may indeed seem confusing to non-specialist readers, since they refer to different realities according to context or period. Some of these shifting notions have already been mentioned before, but a summary appears useful to avoid fatal anachronisms.

- The term "Belgium" itself requires some clarification. As mentioned before, it dates from Roman times, but it then referred to realities that were very different from the present. The word disappears at the beginning of the Middle Ages, before being picked up again by the Humanists in the sixteenth century. However, *Belgica* then referred to the Seventeen Provinces; that is the territories of both future Belgium and The Netherlands. The famous maps showing the *Leo Belgicus* graphically demonstrate this. When the northern provinces seceded from Habsburg rule, the remaining provinces, or Southern (or Spanish, later Austrian) Netherlands were increasingly designated, especially in the eighteenth century, with the adjective *belgique* (*les territoires belgiques*, or *l'Église belgique*, etc.) or even (but rarely) with the noun *Belgique*, the name finally given to the country that became independent in 1830 (in Dutch *België*, in French *la Belgique*).

- The term "Low Countries" (*Nederlanden* in Dutch; *Pays-Bas* in French) can be used in two different ways. It not only designates the two modern nation-states Belgium and The Netherlands, but also the collection of principalities that were ruled first by the Burgundian and then the Habsburg sovereigns (the Seventeen Provinces). Consequently, the reader must not confuse "the Netherlands" (another wording in English for "Low Countries" in the old acceptation) and "The Netherlands" (the modern kingdom, smaller than the first). The Dutch language introduces a nuance to distinguish both realities: the word *Nederlanden* refers to the former principalities, while *Nederland* (without the final "en" indicating the plural) designates the modern kingdom. The French language, alas, uses *les Pays-Bas* to express both significations.

- The word "Dutch" also might produce confusion. Both as an adjective and a noun, it refers to things relating to the modern kingdom of The Netherlands (for instance the Dutch territory, the Dutch economy, or "the Dutch," i.e. the citizens of this country). In theory, these meanings are irrelevant for Belgium. But "Dutch" also designates a language of Germanic origin that is spoken not only by the Dutch themselves, but also by the Flemings, the people living in the northern part of modern Belgium. They represent about 60 percent of the total Belgian population and live in the modern region of Flanders (see below). However, they are sometimes also referred to as speaking "Flemish" (*Vlaams*, in the Dutch language; *le flamand* in French). This is not a language of its own; it generally indicates one of the many different local dialectical variants of Dutch. In the following pages we will, however, use the word "Flemish" to designate the idiom spoken by the inhabitants of the northern part of Belgium and its predecessors until the second half of the nineteenth century; for subsequent periods, we will switch to the word "Dutch" (*Nederlands*, in Dutch; *le néerlandais* in French), because the leaders of the Flemish movement then chose to standardize their language according to the norms used in The Netherlands (see Chapter 8).

- This brings us to the term "Flanders," whose meaning drastically changed over time. Originally, it refers to a small Carolingian *pagus* located near the North Sea coast that evolved into a medieval county with a much larger surface area. But this county did not encompass all speakers of Flemish languages. When Belgium was created in 1830, two of its original nine provinces were given that name: West and East Flanders. But taken together, these provinces still did not encompass all Flemish (or Dutch) speakers living in Belgium. Gradually, due to the growing sense of identity created by the Flemish movement, all people speaking Flemish/Dutch were called "Flemings" (*Vlamingen*, in Dutch; *Flamands* in French), and they were seen as members of one and the same community and region: Flanders (*Vlaanderen* in Dutch; *la Flandre* in French). In the late twentieth century, Belgium's state reforms officially created the region (and community) "Flanders," a public body endowed with ever-increasing competences managing the lives of all Dutch-speaking Belgians.

- One of the medieval principalities where Flemish was spoken, outside the county of Flanders, was the duchy of Brabant. This ancient polity, however, was much larger than nineteenth-century Brabant, one of constitutive provinces of modern Belgium. The former included the modern province of Antwerp and even some parts of The Netherlands (one of the modern Dutch provinces is indeed still named "Noord-Brabant"). The Belgian province (as the ancient principality), however, consisted of both Dutch and French speakers. Consequently, in 1993, one of the Belgian state reforms split this entity into two new provinces, *Vlaams-Brabant* and *Brabant wallon*.

- The word "Liège" refers to three different geographical and political entities: first, it is an important city on the Meuse. Second, it was a medieval principality governed by a bishop (the so-called prince-bishopric of Liège). Finally, it is one of the modern Belgian provinces in the east of Belgium. The spatial definition of the ancient principality was very different from that of the modern province. Moreover, the prince-bishopric was not part of the Seventeen Provinces (or the ancient Netherlands); only from the late eighteenth century did this polity merge with the destiny of the Southern Netherlands to lead to modern Belgium.

- Etymologically, the words "Wallonia" and "Walloon" derive from the old Germanic "*walha*" or "*welsch*," designating in (post-) Roman times the Celtic- and Romance-speaking populations and neighboring Germanic ones (this also explains the origin of the words "Wales," "Welsh," and "Cornwall" in the United Kingdom, and of the term *Welsch* used in Switzerland by German-speaking Swiss to designate their Romance-speaking fellow compatriots). More generally, the word also meant "foreigners," or "strangers." Despite some sporadic references dating from the fifteenth century, the word "Wallonia" takes on its modern definition – that is, the region encompassing all Francophones living in Belgium (except those living in Brussels) – only in the final decades of the nineteenth century. Wallonia became a political reality – an official region – from 1970, after the first Belgian state reform. The word "Walloon" also refers to a series of Romance dialects spoken in the southern parts of Belgium, characterized by a degree of Germanic influence. These dialects gradually waned as standard French took over (a process somewhat similar to that of Flemish and Dutch).

Map 1.1 Belgium in 2022 (© Laure De Cock, Ghent University)

I

Earliest Times

From Prehistory to the End of the Roman Period

Introduction

Dating back to Celtic times, the words "Belgium" and "Belgians" are indeed very ancient, but this antiquity is wholly fallacious if one wants to understand the genesis of the contemporary nation-state that carries this name. These terms do not, in any way, reflect some remote historical antecedents of the country founded in 1830. In the nineteenth and early twentieth centuries, however, many Belgian patriots – historians, politicians, artists, teachers, and other opinion makers – were enthralled by the abundant mentions of these "Belgians" in Julius Caesar's *De Bello Gallico*, the well-known report of his bloody conquest of Gaul. In their eyes, these references clearly proved the age-old existence of a "Belgian identity," or at least of some of its constitutive elements. Of course, nowadays no one seriously refers to "Ancient Belgians" as the "ancestors" of the contemporary people of this nation. But that does not mean that these early times are irrelevant. On the contrary: the prehistoric, Celtic, and Roman legacies played a role in shaping the territories that were to form today's Belgium.

Before the Celts

The people known as "Belgians" were not the first inhabitants of these territories, and human presence in the region was of course much older. At first sight, however, Belgium's prehistory does not seem particularly engaging. A contemporary tourist eager to admire spectacular relics of early mankind is not likely to choose Belgium as a priority destination. Here, she or he will find no equivalents of the caves of Lascaux or Altamira, nor monumental sites such as Carnac, Stonehenge, or the Maltese temples of Gozo and Tarxien. But prehistoric remains are not (necessarily) relevant because of their aesthetic qualities or impressive dimensions, for even tiny bone fragments or crude stone objects can reveal crucial information concerning mankind's early development. An example taken from Belgian soil illustrates this in a striking way. In the 1820s, a young physician, Philippe-Charles Schmerling (1790–1836), was interested in "old stones" and fossils. His explorations in several caves in the province of Liège led to the discovery of bone fragments that obviously did not belong to modern human beings. Moreover, these fragments were linked to remains of extinct, "antediluvian" animals and to primitive stone tools. Unfortunately, Schmerling's work, published in 1833–1834, went largely unnoticed, and so its author became a forgotten pioneer of the study of Prehistory, predating by a decade and more the work of the Frenchman Jacques Boucher de Perthes and other founding fathers of this scientific discipline.

Among Schmerling's discoveries, made in the cave of Engis number 2, was part of a child's skull, subsequently identified as belonging to *Homo neanderthalensis*. More than half a century later, in 1886, two incomplete skeletons came to light in another cave, located in Spy, also in the southern part of Belgium. They belonged to the same species that was discovered in Neanderthal in 1856 – but the discoveries in Spy (near Namur) indisputably proved the existence of a different kind of *Homo* long before the arrival of modern *Homo sapiens sapiens* in Europe. According to recent ^{14}C analysis, these remains dated from 44,000 to 40,500 years Before Present (BP).

But even Neanderthal man was not the first hominid to set foot in this part of north-western Europe. The earliest traces of human presence in "Belgium," as evident in finds of rudimentary stone tools made by *Homo erectus*, go back to *c.*500,000 or 400,000 BP. This is much later than in other parts of Europe. In Spain and France, hominid activity is demonstrable 1.2 million years ago; and recent finds in Happisburgh, Great Britain (a place much closer to Belgium), go back in time from 800 to 900,000 years. In general, evidence from the Early Palaeolithic is rare in Belgium. The Middle Palaeolithic is better documented, especially in its later phases, through the presence of Neanderthals, from *c*.90,000 BP (the dating of a child's mandible found in Sclayn, yet another cave in southern Belgium) to *c*.40,000 BP. *Homo sapiens sapiens* appeared in Belgium around 37,500 BP. These anatomically modern humans produced the first, albeit very modest, figurative objects found in the country (an engraved reindeer antler, a small anthropomorphic ivory sculpture, etc.) – but the relics of the cultural activity of early societies found in Belgium are rather modest compared to the artifacts discovered in other parts of Europe.

After a long period almost devoid of human presence (from 26,500 to 15,000 BP), due to the extreme cold of the last glaciation, Belgium was peopled by new groups of hunter-gatherers. They were bearers of the Magdalenian industry that also produced the admirable paintings of the Lascaux cave. The most notable, aesthetically significant artifact they left in Belgium – a stone plaque of about 80 by 47 cm now on display in the Brussels Museum of Natural Sciences, dating to about 12,300 Before the Common Era (BCE) and vividly representing a walking auroch – in fact reveals a striking resemblance to the animals painted on the walls of the so-called Sistine chapel of Prehistory. It would, however, be wrong to infer from all these examples that the significant prehistoric sites in Belgium are exclusively located in the southern part of the country (where caves are indeed numerous); the less hilly regions constituting today's Flanders also yielded significant finds. In Kanne (in the province of Limburg), for example, archaeologists unearthed a Magdalenian hunters' camp (dated 13,000 BCE), identified as the most northern site belonging to this culture ever found in Europe (together with a site in the nearby Netherlands). During the subsequent Mesolithic period (9000–5300 BCE) the density of sites in Flanders even ranked among the highest in north-western Europe.

The next crucial step in human evolution was the emergence of agriculture. The first farmers – not only cultivating grains and vegetables, but also raising domesticated animals such as cattle, pigs, sheep, and goats – arrived in Belgium *c*.5300 years BCE, coming from the northeast and following the Meuse valley upstream. These people, named after the typical form of their pottery (*Rubané* or Linear Pottery), mostly established themselves on the loess soils of the centrally located Hesbaye region and in northern Hainaut. Around the same time, another type of Neolithic culture, the so-called Blicquy culture, also settled there. This culture was a hybrid between the Linear Pottery culture that originated east of the Rhine, and a Neolithic culture that came from southern Europe (the so-called Impresso-Cardial culture).

For unidentified reasons, these first agriculturalists left almost no traces from *c.*4800 BCE. This most probably points to an important population decline. New types of settlement and, with them, indications of a growing population, emerged only half a millennium later, at *c.*4300 BCE. These farmers now covered a much larger area of Belgium and significantly changed the landscape, in particular through forest clearances. Henceforth, agriculture also rapidly progressed in the northern part of the country. A specific feature of this so-called Michelsberg culture (named after the German site where these cultural traits were prominently identified) was the existence of fortified structures, consisting of earth walls, sometimes surrounded by ditches and topped with wooden palisades. These structures (already present during the final phase of the Linear Pottery culture) need not necessarily be interpreted as defensive settlements, protecting farmers from hostile attack. Modern archaeologists tend to identify them as ceremonial spaces with little or no permanent habitation, or as symbolic markers of territory. In the Late Neolithic period (2900–2200 BCE), the erection of dolmens and menhirs also reveal the emergence of new (but alas largely unknown) funeral practices and symbolic beliefs. These megaliths, located in the southern part of the country (for example in Wéris, near the commune of Durbuy), are quite modest when compared with the spectacular megalithic sites found in other European countries. But the "Belgian" megaliths prove that this region was part of a wider cultural and social space ranging from Brittany to Germany, and from Great Britain to Malta.

The Neolithic period also shows the first signs of specialized economic activity. Flint, a key production tool (next to wood), was dug in many places, but some spots developed into outright specialized mining centers. The most notable, located at Spiennes (Hainaut province) – now ranked a UNESCO World Heritage Site – was exploited for more than two thousand years (4350–2300 BCE). This intricate set of galleries, some reaching 16 m deep, may have produced a total of 100 to 200,000 tons of flint. The extracted stones underwent a first, rudimentary, processing before being "exported" to distant places where they were given their final form. Spiennes tools were found within a range of 160 km from their original locus.

Taken together, all the features of the Neolithic period we have just mentioned reveal a society marked by a growing complexity: agricultural surplus fed specialized workers; trade networks linked distant places; collective and exhausting labor schemes created the first monuments ever; a hierarchy of places (scattered dwellings existing next to permanent farming settlements, specialized camps and ceremonial spaces) reflected a multifaceted social structure – of which, alas, little is known. Moreover, Neolithic settlements most probably coexisted with surviving groups of hunter-gatherers – since this way of living did not suddenly disappear, and (hostile or peaceful?) relations with sedentary farmers were perhaps maintained for an undetermined time span.

Far from being abrupt and clear-cut, the transition to the Metal Ages was also slow and gradual. The first copper objects marginally penetrated late Neolithic societies – known as the Bell-beaker culture, named after the specific form of their pottery (2600–2000 BCE). Due to the absence of essential ores, the rise of Early and Middle Bronze Age societies in Belgium was rather protracted (2000–1100 BCE). Tin and copper, the basic ores for bronze production, were absent in this part of Europe: bronze artefacts were imported either from the Atlantic regions or from Central Europe. These changes went hand-in-hand with the spread of new funeral rites. Cremated bodies were henceforth buried in urns deposited in funeral fields, the so-called urnfields. Simultaneously, social differentiation increased: elites were interred in burial mounds, of which some examples are still visible in the landscape. However, the material relics of the Late Bronze Age no longer express this social differentiation. Bronze Age cultural traits were not necessarily caused by the arrival of new population groups from the east but could also be explained by the slow adoption of new technologies and ways of living by people already present and open to different influences. Gradually, bronze objects were also produced locally, with specific, "regional" traits. A striking characteristic of this period is the (possibly religiously inspired) tradition of depositing precious bronze objects in rivers.

The Celtic Era

The Iron Age (from 800 BCE) not only represented a change in technology (the mastering of a new type of metallurgy) but also, and foremost, the rise of new political structures and increased social differentiation (or, at least, different and more explicit expressions of contrasts in wealth and power between social groups). Within this period, archaeologists traditionally distinguish two phases: Hallstatt (800–450 BCE) and La Tène (450–50 BCE). These names refer to the eponymous (respectively Austrian and Swiss) places where the specific traits of these cultures were originally identified. Yet unlike the people of the Linear Pottery, or Michelsberg, or Urnfield, etc., "cultures," only defined by a place name or a cultural trait, the men and women living then and there can now, for the first time, be designated with a specific name: the Celts.

This name, first given to them by Greek sources of the late sixth century relating to specific populations living in a wide area north of the Alps, which they called Κελτοι, could induce some false inferences. It would indeed be wrong to see the Celtic world as a homogenous and static bloc. A "Celtic realm," let alone a "Celtic nation," of course never existed. Although they spoke related languages and shared certain cultural, artistic, and religious features, the Celts primarily consisted of autonomous, often rival, political entities characterized by moving boundaries and contrasting levels of power, influence, and wealth.

This is clear, for instance, if one looks at the regions that would later form Belgium. Archaeologists have noted that the break between the Late Bronze and the Early Iron Age is not clear-cut in this part of north-western Europe. Here, Bronze Age traditions persisted throughout the first phases of the Hallstatt culture. Moreover, it is far from certain that the populations living here were all of a sudden "new" ones, originating from the primordial Celtic core and "invading" this new periphery. The local inhabitants might well have gradually adopted some Celtic traits (such as language, habits, material culture, etc.). Local funeral gifts do point to increasing social differentiation, or, at least, they reflect more spectacular ways of expressing them. However, splendid "princely" tombs are less numerous in Belgium than, for example, in Baden-Württemberg or Burgundy, with such famous sites as, respectively, Hochdorf and Vix. Such elite grave finds in Belgium also date from a later period.

As discovered elsewhere in the Celtic world, fortified places, generally located on hilltops, have also been identified in Belgium. These places were the seats of aristocrats, who possibly controlled local trade networks. These elites both consolidated and expressed their power through the acquisition and display of foreign (i.e. Italic or Greek) prestige goods.

The fortification on the Kemmelberg (province of West Flanders), dating from the early La Tène period (fifth–fourth century BCE), for instance, was probably linked to the salt trade, since the nearby North Sea shores produced and exported large quantities of this precious commodity. But the "Belgian" fortified places were clearly located at the periphery of the Hallstatt and La Tène heartland. One striking example is that the Kemmelberg excavations yielded, among many other objects, a small fragment of Attic pottery – the most northern example of this prestigious Greek ware ever found in Europe. Some rare, typically Etruscan objects were also found in Belgium. In the eyes of Mediterranean traders who maintained commercial contacts with northern Europe, the land bordering the North Sea probably was a sort of *finis terrae*, even if precious products such as amber came from further north still. The wealthiest and most powerful parts of the early Celtic world clearly lay south of contemporary Belgium.

During the La Tène phase of the Iron Age (450–50 BCE), important waves of migration directly affected later Belgium. While population movements had already occurred before, now, for the first time, they left a trace in a written source: the account written by the Roman general Julius Caesar. We have of course to stress the biased, probably distorted or even erroneous nature of Caesar's view of a local situation wholly unfamiliar to him. Given its unique nature, we will however briefly summarize his description of the "ethnic" and linguistic landscape in this part of Western Europe. At the beginning of his conquest of Gaul (58–51 BCE), Caesar had heard that the north-eastern part of this region was inhabited by *Belgae*. His Gallic informers told him "most *Belgae* originated in Germany and had crossed the Rhine long ago" (*De Bello Gallico [BG]*, II, 4). Defeating, driving away, and/or absorbing the pre-existing populations, they had settled in the territories delimited by the Seine and Marne rivers, the North Sea and the Rhine–Meuse delta. Some even crossed the Channel to Britain. Nowadays, we believe that these migrations took place during the third or second century BCE. Consequently, Caesar clearly distinguished these *Belgae* from the other inhabitants of Gaul; that is, the *Aquitani* and the Celts (or Gauls): according to him, they all "differ from each other in language, customs and law" (*BG*, I, 1). But Caesar never used the word *Belgica* as a proper noun to designate this part of Gaul. Nor did he use it as an adjective (the term *Gallia belgica*, for instance, dates from later Roman times).

To complicate things further, Caesar also sporadically mentioned a specific region that he called *Belgium* (in Latin), which he situated in the regions now known as Picardie and Haute-Normandie (in France); that is, the western part of the (much larger) region inhabited by the *Belgae*. Needless to say, Caesar's *Belgium* has nothing to do with present-day "Belgium" (in English). Etymologically, the word *Belgae* appears to be linked to the old Indo-European root *belg-*, which means "to swell" (cf. the English verb "to bulge") as well as "being angry" (the meaning of the present Dutch word "ver*bolg*en"). Thus, the name of the *Belgae* presents them as "those who are swelled [by anger]," "the angry people," or perhaps, figuratively, "the proud ones."

But who exactly were these *Belgae*? More precisely, did they speak a Celtic or a Germanic language? This question triggered a long-lasting debate. For nineteenth- and twentieth-century Belgians, it was a highly sensitive issue, both politically and psychologically. By stressing the "Celtic" nature of the *Belgae*, contemporary Belgians wanted to under-line their "kinship" with the contemporary French, "heirs of the Gauls"; by saying that the *Belgae* were "Germans," they distanced themselves from their southern neighbor and emphasized their connection with contemporary Germany. In his widely read *Histoire de la Belgique* (1881, 5th ed., 13), for instance, the romantic nineteenth-century Belgian historian Henri-Guillaume Moke firmly stated that the *Belgae* "were of German blood," belonging "to a race as blond as the Gaëls [Celts], but stronger than them." In the mid-nineteenth century, this "racial" definition of the *Belgae* made clear that young Belgium was independent from expansionist France, and that Brussels was not a subsidiary of Paris.

Based on archaeological, toponymic, and linguistic evidence, modern scholars generally conclude that most *Belgae* actually belonged to the Celtic sphere. When Caesar mentioned their "German" origin, he most probably referred to the region where they came from, namely the territories east of the Rhine, but not to an "ethnic" or linguistic group. The differences in language between the *Belgae* and the other inhabitants of Gaul, mentioned by Caesar in the cited passage (*BG*, I, 1), probably referred to regional variants of Celtic. But this does not imply that *all* inhabitants of the territories occupied by the *Belgae* belonged to the Celtic cultural and linguistic sphere. People speaking a Germanic lan-guage most probably also lived there. Caesar himself – somewhat contradictorily – even made a distinction between the different tribes inhabiting the territory of the *Belgae*. Only some of them, most notably the *Condrusi* and the *Eburones*, were explicitly identified as *Germani* (*BG*, II, 4), while yet another tribe, the *Aduatuci*, was presented as the offspring of the Germanic tribes *Cimbri* and *Teutoni*, that had passed through these territories earlier, on their way to Italy (*BG*, II, 29).

Contrary to the worldview of nineteenth- and early twentieth-century scientists and politicians – obsessed by sharp borders, static "races" and homogenous "identities" – these early times were characterized by moving and mingling populations, and complex shifting zones of inter-action between groups of different linguistic and "ethnic" origin. Tribes were far from fixed, so that different groups could easily mix and coalesce to form new entities. Local populations could moreover adopt cultural elements (such as language or artistic traditions) introduced or simply used by "foreign" ("invading" or adjacent) groups. It is therefore, in brief, impossible to reconstruct the exact linguistic map of the terri-tories inhabited by the ancient *Belgae*. Both Celtic- and German-speaking people were probably present in different mixtures, and a kaleidoscopic and moving picture, with mutual cultural and linguistic exchanges, is far more plausible than a homogenous and static one.

Belgae society was characterized by the existence of aristocrats who ruled the mass of free people, consisting of farmers; in contrast to other parts of the Celtic world, where their presence is clearly attested, there is no evidence of the religious specialists known as druids. As in other parts of Gaul, their polity was fragmented, consisting of different autonomous tribes. Some of these, smaller or less mighty, were subordinated as "clients" to another, more powerful tribe. Once again, Caesar's *Commentaries* mentions some essential details of the tribal landscape. The most important tribes present on the territory of later Belgium were the *Menapii* (living near the North Sea coast and in Flanders, next to the *Morini*, essentially dwelling in what today is northern France), the *Nervii* (in the central part of contemporary Belgium, mostly in the provinces of Hainaut and Brabant), the *Eburones* (mostly in today's province of Limburg), the *Aduatuci* and the *Condrusi* (along the Meuse river) and the *Treveri* (in the south of the Ardennes).

While both archaeology and Caesar's text prove the existence of fortified places, or strongholds of tribes, in Belgium there are no traces of *oppida* in the strict sense of the term. These pre-urban agglomerations – with residential, political, economic, and religious functions – had developed in other parts of the Celtic world, but not in the regions inhabited by the above-mentioned tribes (with the exception of the Titelberg, an *oppidum* of the *Treveri*, but this site is located in the contemporary Grand-Duchy of Luxemburg). Money was also introduced late in comparison to other parts of Gaul, that is, not until the second half of the second century BCE. Since the nineteenth century, many Celtic hoards have come to light in Belgium but ordinary people did not use these gold coins for daily economic transactions. Celtic money most likely had a political and diplomatic function and only circulated among tribal aristocrats. This corroborates Caesar's famous description of the *Belgae* as the "bravest" (*fortissimi*) of all the populations of Gaul, because they were "farthest from the civilisation and refinement of [our] Province, and merchants less frequently resort to them and import things which tend to effeminate the mind" (*BG*, I, 1). The social and political effects of commercial and cultural contact with the Mediterranean world were far less pronounced in the territories of the *Belgae*, and especially in its most northern margins. Political power was less crystalized, social differentiation less pronounced, and commerce less active.

The Establishment of Roman Rule

The history of the Roman conquest of Gaul has been told many times over; moreover, Caesar's own narration of his feats of arms – essentially a book expressing his political and military propaganda – is both widely read and easily accessible. Hence, our description of Roman military operations in the lands of the *Belgae* will be very brief. After Caesar's first incursion in southern Gaul, the Belgian tribes feared that their lands would be among the next targets of the Roman legions. At a general assembly they decided combine forces in order to resist the invader. Not all Belgian tribes joined the coalition – some even helped Caesar with troops and logistics – but Caesar considered this (shaky) alliance to be a threat. Acting swiftly, he decided to invade the territory of the *Belgae*. In 57 BCE the *Nervii* were decimated at the Sabis river (whose precise location is still unclear and heavily debated) because, among other reasons, their allies the *Aduatuci* arrived too late to help. The latter then took refuge in their fortress. Caesar's troops besieged and took the place, massacring the fighters and abducting the women and children as slaves. The following year the Romans waged destructive campaigns against the *Morini* and *Menapii* but failed to completely defeat them. The indefatigable Caesar then also briefly invaded Britain and *Germania*, but this did not mean that the lands of the *Belgae* were entirely "pacified." On the contrary, a major uprising nearly jeopardized all the previous conquests. Roman legions, spending the winter of 54 BCE amidst the territories of the *Belgae*, suffered a surprise attack, mainly by the *Eburones* and the *Treveri* (who had been Caesar's allies during the battle at the Sabis, but had now changed sides). Many Romans lost their lives and Caesar found it difficult to restore his military supremacy (54–52 BCE). Caesar explicitly mentions the leader of the *Eburones*, Ambiorix. Except for these few references in *De Bello Gallico*, nothing is known about him; but nineteenth-century Belgian patriots did not hesitate to turn him into a "national hero": the symbol of Belgian resistance to foreign domination – in fact, a striking example of nationalistic myth construction. However, one thing is certain: in the next years, Belgian tribes continued to resist the Roman conquerors. Some of them, for example the *Atrebates* and the *Menapii*, even participated in the great Gallic uprising led by Vercingetorix, who was finally defeated in 51 BCE at Alesia, south of the territory of the *Belgae*.

That year marked the official end of the Roman conquest of Gaul. Caesar could now pursue his higher ambitions in Roman politics. But at that moment, the Roman presence in the lands of the *Belgae* was still very superficial. The main and immediate effect of Caesar's campaigns was most likely demographic. The *Eburones* seems to have been almost wiped out; other tribes also suffered heavy losses. Should we take Caesar's propagandistic writings at face value? This of course remains unclear, since we have no other source to corroborate his claims. Archaeological sources also remain silent on the matter, since Caesar's legions left not a single material trace of their presence in today's Belgium, with one possible exception. In 2012, a large quantity of leaden Roman sling stones was found near the city of Thuin (in the province of Hainaut), possibly the location of the fortified place of the *Aduatuci*. Even today, virtually all geographical place names mentioned by Caesar remain unidentified in Belgium. Many researchers, both scholars and amateurs, still tenaciously try to locate his whereabouts in the country, fiercely rejecting identifications proposed by others and advocating their own findings.

Notwithstanding Caesar's extensive massacres and his destruction of farmsteads, fields, and fortified places, the lands inhabited by the *Belgae* were not yet completely brought to submission. While the Roman legions pursued successive military operations in Germany, east of the Rhine, uprisings continued for decades on the west bank of the river – also, but not exclusively, on the territory of later Belgium. The Romans put down revolts of the *Treveri* in 31–30 BCE and the *Morini* in 30–29 BCE. *Belgae* also participated in a broader rebellion of Gallic tribes in 21 CE, and one of their leaders, the *Treveri* chief Julius Florus, was defeated by Roman legions in the Ardennes, where he committed suicide. A few decades later, yet another uprising shook Roman Gaul. In 69–70 CE, the *Batavi* (a tribe established in what is now The Netherlands) took the lead, under their chief Caius Julius Civilis. These developments also involved the people and territories of later Belgium. Gaul was on the brink of breaking away from the Empire, but Roman rule was finally restored.

These events show that Caesar's conquest was not a clear-cut break in the history of these northern regions. While it certainly marked the beginning of Roman rule, for many years the bulk of the "conquered" people continued their lives largely unchanged. Part of the Celtic aristocracy had allied itself with the new masters, and some members of this local elite were even Romanized to a certain extent, as indicated by the names of the insurgent leaders just mentioned. But it was also clear that large segments of society, from top to bottom, were disgruntled by foreign rule. Heavy taxation and other abuses, for instance, had triggered the revolt of 21 CE. During the four decades or so following Caesar's victory in 51 BCE, the Roman imprint on the newly conquered north-eastern regions of Gaul was rather modest – apart from destruction and plunder. It is quite significant that the first material evidence of Roman presence in later Belgium, except the above-mentioned finds near Thuin, dates from about 15 BCE. This is no coincidence, since real organizational and structural change only started under the first Roman emperor, Augustus (r. 27 BCE–14 CE). The founder of the Principate had close links with the regions conquered by his adoptive father, Julius Caesar, residing there on several occasions. This interest was largely due to his military ambitions beyond the Rhine, and his legions waged several bloody campaigns in *Germania*. When Augustus finally abandoned his dream of conquering and annexing these lands, the frontier or *limes* was definitively established on the Rhine.

The military campaigns east of that river, and the subsequent stabilization of this border of the Roman world, profoundly influenced the fate of north-eastern Gaul by fundamentally changing its political, social, and cultural status. This part of Western Europe, formerly an outskirt of the world known to Greco-Roman civilization, now became the hinterland of one its most strategic frontiers. Several crucial actions undertaken by Emperor Augustus and his immediate successors profoundly transformed these regions, and the results of these decisions and enterprises – sometimes conscious, sometimes unplanned – were to last for centuries; in some respects, they even survived the Roman Empire itself. Administrative and legal changes went hand-in-hand with visible modifications of the landscape. We will start by examining the political framework imposed on conquered Gaul.

The Romans first exercised power through purely military means, and army camps were obviously its quintessential and tangible expression. One of the earliest examples of these sites on Belgian territory, dating back to Augustan times, was excavated in the village of Velzeke (in the province of East Flanders). However, given the permanent state of confrontation, and later face-off, with the Germanic tribes, the main Roman forces were naturally stationed further east near the Rhine. In this way, most legions were established permanently on the territories of contemporary Germany, while later Belgium evolved into a zone focused on logistics and supply for the military guarding the *limes*. However, at about the same time – the transitional decades from BCE to CE – the exercise of Roman power also gradually took on political, legal, and administrative forms. This was reflected in the creation of a hierarchical network of territorial entities or districts named *provinciae* and *civitates*.

Between *c.* 16 and 13 BCE, Augustus divided recently conquered Gaul into three large provinces: *Aquitania*, *Gallia Lugdunensis*, and *Gallia Belgica*. Needless to say, Belgium belonged to the latter but it is worthwhile stressing that this Roman province also stretched far beyond the boundaries of the modern nation; it covered vast regions of modern northern France, as well as the whole of today's Grand-Duchy of Luxemburg. The territories west of the Rhine also belonged to *Gallia Belgica* until 82–90 CE, from which date they were integrated into the newly created provinces of *Germania Superior* and *Germania Inferior*.

During the reign of Emperor Diocletian and his co-rulers, *c.*297 CE, *Gallia Belgica* was split into two new provinces – *Belgica Prima* and *Belgica Secunda* – while at the same time, the two Germanic provinces were respectively renamed *Germania Prima* and *Germania Secunda*. This means that at the end of the third century CE, contemporary Belgium did not belong to one single province, but to three, namely *Belgica Secunda* (in the west), *Germania Secunda* (in the east) and finally, for a very limited part, to *Belgica Prima* (in the south of the Ardennes).

Each province was further subdivided in a varying number of *civitates*, themselves consisting of districts called *pagi* (singular *pagus*), a territorial entity that had a fiscal and religious role, but of which very little is known. The *pagi* would, however, play an important role in post-Roman times (see Chapter 2). The *civitates* were more or less based on the areas occupied by the pre-existing Gallic tribes. Consequently, the following *civitates* were established in the territory of later Belgium. The *civitas Menapiorum* and *civitas Nerviorum* belonged to *Belgica Secunda*, while the *civitas Tungrorum* probably belonged to *Germania Inferior* from the start. The *civitas Treverorum* was part of *Belgica Prima*, and its territory mainly stretched outside the borders of contemporary Belgium. Contrary to the *Menapii*, *Nervii*, and *Treveri*, Caesar never mentioned the *Tungri* in *De Bello Gallico*. They were probably a small tribe already present that now resettled into the territories left "vacant" after Caesar's massacres, together with survivors of the slaughtered *Eburones*, *Condrusi*, and *Aduatuci*, and with Germanic peoples coming from over the Rhine.

This administrative organization materialized through the foundation of cities, a major innovation in this specific part of the former Celtic world. As we have seen, these north-eastern regions of Gaul had not yet produced permanent (pre-) urban settlements, and tribesmen and - women gathered temporarily in existing fortified places, mainly for ceremonial or military reasons. A few decades after Caesar's conquest, the power of Rome expressed itself not only through military camps, but also through newly founded towns that acted as "capitals" (singular *caput*, plural *capita*) of the *provinciae* and *civitates*. However, due to the vagaries of history, Reims, Trier, and Cologne (the capitals of respectively *Gallia Belgica / Belgica Secunda*, *Belgica Prima*, and *Germania Inferior / Secunda*) are not located on the territory of contemporary Belgium. The same largely goes for the central places of the underlying administrative level of the *civitates*, since Bavay and Cassel, the capitals of the *civitas*

Nerviorum and the *civitas Menapiorum*, are now located in France. The sole exception is Atuatuca Tungrorum, the central place of the *civitas Tungrorum*, founded around 10 BCE and now the city of Tongeren in the province of Limburg. "Roman Belgium" was moreover strewn with urban settlements, though these were mostly small. This was largely due to yet another fundamental vector of Roman rule; that is, the road system, a remarkable achievement that reshaped space in recently conquered Gaul.

In all likelihood, the *Belgae* had already developed pathways across their territories, but these trails left almost no traces. However, Roman domination required a more elaborate and sophisticated communication and transport system – the logical extension of that already developed in Italy and in other Mediterranean regions under Roman occupation. The first road in *Gallia Belgica* was built under Augustus, and by the reign of Emperor Claudius (middle of the first century CE) this network, equipped with way stations, was largely operational. The main axis on contemporary Belgian territory ran from west to east, linking the port of Boulogne (on the Channel) to Cologne (on the Rhine) via the *civitates* capitals Bavay and Tongeren. The latter city was linked to Arlon by a road running from north to south. Many subsidiary and secondary roads stretched in other directions and completed this spider's web of Roman power. The resultant crossroads, together with the spots bridging rivers and smaller waterways, quickly generated new permanent settlements. Some developed into communities of some importance called *vici* (singular *vicus*). These places did not enjoy the legal status of *municipium*, that not only bestowed Roman law but other advantages as well on the respective urban area. In the territory of later Belgium, only Tongeren obtained this position, probably in the second century CE. Nevertheless, the *vici* unquestionably exercised a local or even regional influence. Indeed, as nodal points in the road system they rapidly fulfilled a crucial economic and social role, as we shall see when examining the new society that resulted from Roman domination.

Gallo-Roman Society during the *Pax Romana*

The instruments of Roman power – army, administration, cities, and roads – jointly triggered an all-round and profound transformation of society. This process was complex, since foreign and local elements combined in a subtle way. As elsewhere in the Empire, the introduction of seemingly "flawless" Roman features was accompanied by the more or less incomplete adoption (or adaptation) of these foreign ingredients by the local population, or even by the persistence of pre-Roman traditions and structures. In Gaul this process gave rise to the so-called Gallo-Roman society. *Gallia Belgica*, including later Belgium, was of course no exception to this rule. Recent scholarship has emphasized the spatial and social variations of this process, so that in marginal rural territories and lower social groups the impact of Rome was less pronounced, and Celtic traditions persisted.

This Roman imprint was most clearly visible in the *municipia* and in the most important *vici*. We have already mentioned Atuatuca Tungrorum (Tongeren), the only *municipium* and undoubtedly the leading city in the territory of future Belgium. Its first stone edifices, replacing the previous wooden and clay constructions, were built in the second half of the first century CE. The city displayed the essential features of Roman urbanism: a grid pattern; a forum or central marketplace (not yet excavated); religious edifices; *thermae*, that is, public or private bathing facilities; more or less luxurious houses for the well-to-do; funeral monuments on the outskirts of the town; and of course the more modest dwellings of ordinary townspeople (for instance the houses and workshops of artisans). A vast *horreum* (warehouse) shows that the city played a significant role in the supply of the troops stationed near the *limes*. The city's population is estimated at about 8,000 around 150 CE. In the south of the Belgian Ardennes, Orolaunum (now Arlon, capital of the Belgian province of Luxemburg), due to its strategic location at the intersection of two important roads, developed into one of the most important *vici*. This place possibly had some 3,000–4,000 inhabitants.

Unfortunately, few remnants of Roman architecture are extant in Belgium today. This country cannot boast spectacular monuments such as the *Porta Nigra* and the Basilica of Constantine in Trier, or the well-preserved theaters of Nîmes or Arles in France. Apart from some unimpressive building foundations here and there, aficionados of Roman ruins visiting Belgium will have to settle for parts of the old city walls of Tongeren and Arlon. Nevertheless, a series of fine funerary monuments from the latter town partially compensate for this meagre offering. The bas-reliefs of these *stelae* provide a lively glimpse of daily life in the first

Figure 1.1 Bas-relief representing a *vallus*, or Gallo-Roman
harvesting machine, used by Treveri peasants, second century AD
(Virton, Musée gaumais)

centuries CE, for example a teacher and his pupils; a peasant harvesting
grain; merchants selling or transporting their goods; a tax official collecting money, etc. (Figure 1.1)

Indeed, these sculpted stone slabs vividly illustrate one of the most
important aspects of Gallo-Roman society, namely that it was far more
complex than its Celtic predecessor. For one, *Gallia Belgica* was now
much more connected to the rest of the world. Foreigners arrived there
from Rome, Italy, or other Mediterranean regions in their capacity as
administrative officials, military personnel, merchants, men of letters,
artists, and craftsmen, etc., and sometimes settled for good. This was also
the case for persons of modest social background, like Roman soldiers.
After having accomplished their tour of duty, they received a diploma
and a land grant, and some of them chose not to return to their *patria*.
But since no legions were stationed in the territory of later Belgium, this
probably happened rarely in these regions. All these newcomers of
course introduced their habits, beliefs, and – last but not least – their
language. Still, the number of these southerners was very limited.

The autochthonous population adapted to the new situation in varying
degrees and rates, and this phenomenon largely accounts for the massive

character of Gallo-Romanization. Soldiers of local origin and serving in the legions as *auxilia* (literally, "auxiliary troops") were among the very first vectors of Romanization, even if they also maintained some aspects of their traditional habits and culture. As mentioned earlier, the surviving aristocracy of the *Belgae* was also rapidly integrated into the Roman power structure. They remained or became mighty landowners; some of them settled in the new cities where they also held public offices. Roman citizenship was bestowed upon former soldiers and city magistrates; this was a powerful tool of upward social mobility. Other natives grasped the opportunities offered by the "globalized" Roman economy, and became specialized producers and traders, linked to regions far beyond local horizons. Their primary commodities were exported to distant markets, sometimes as far as Rome and the Mediterranean. As we saw, salt produced on the shores of the North Sea was already marketed during the Iron Age; this activity continued during the Roman era. The *Menapii*, for instance, were renowned for their smoked ham, a valued gastronomic item transported over large distances. Iron ore was mined and stone quarries supplied building materials, mainly for the cities. Wine, oil, and *garum*, the famous fish sauce, figured prominently among imported consumer goods. The Romans also introduced the plum and the peach tree.

A wide variety of crafts also emerged in *Gallia Belgica*, as in other parts of the Roman world. Originally, fine pottery such as the renowned *terra sigillata* was imported from Italy or southern Gaul as early as the second decade BCE. The same goes for sophisticated manufactured objects, such as bronzes, jewels, and other artistic artifacts. Soon, local arts and crafts also flourished in the Roman Belgian provinces. Some of these activities continued existing traditions; others were stimulated and modernized by imported Roman technologies (for instance the pottery wheel, unknown to the Celts); still others were entirely new, for example crafts linked to stone buildings, architecture, and public facilities. A wide variety of artisans thus emerged from the first century CE: fullers, dyers, tanners, weavers, shoemakers, potters, blacksmiths, sculptors, glassmakers, etc. They did not merely replicate Roman standards, but often produced artifacts with a distinctive "local" character. These industrious people – mostly of modest status, but some more prosperous – lived in or around the neighborhoods of large and small agglomerations (the *municipia*, the *vici*, the crossroads, etc.), marketing their goods or skills locally or regionally, and in some cases even on a wider scale. The *birrus*, for instance, a warm, hooded woollen cloak, was a valued export product of the *Nervii*. Transport workers dispatched these goods far and wide – not only carters, but also boatmen since waterways also played an important role in communication networks.

Within this world of specialized market production, one aspect is particularly striking: the development of large-scale production of grains and other basic foodstuffs for the legions and the large cities located on the Rhine. Huge rural estates known as *villae* took care of this important activity. The reorganization of agriculture was preceded by yet another Roman administrative innovation, known as the *centuriatio*. Parts of the conquered territories were divided into separate land plots, generally based on a grid pattern, and allotted to deserving persons. Many *villae* have been excavated in the last few decades, and their formal aspects and typology are by now well known. The center of these estates consisted of a set of more or less extensive buildings, consisting partly of sometimes lavishly equipped and decorated residential homes (the *pars urbana*), and partly of structures for economic use (the *pars rustica*). Their geographical location is also well known. Most *villae*, often grouped near the *vici*, were situated on the fertile lands stretching right through central Belgium, from west to east. But unfortunately, far less is known about their social meaning. It is unclear, for instance, whether the labor force was servile or free, although scholars assume that slavery was not essential to the rural economy of this part of the Empire. Were parts of the estates rented out? Were the *villae* engaged in some sort of relationship with smallholders? These questions remain unanswered. And who were the masters of these domains? Some might have been newcomers, but the vast majority of powerful landowners were probably the descendants of previous Celtic aristocratic families. While some *villae* were based on pre-Roman estates, others were new exploitations. Production intensified with the introduction of new agricultural methods, but total output also rose through the extension of cultivated land. Mighty landowners sometimes lived in the cities, where they also carried out public duties, in which case an overseer ran the villa. Deceased rich proprietors were buried in large *tumuli*, often along an important road, some of which still mark the landscape.

It would, however, be wrong to equate the Gallo-Roman rural world with these big market-oriented estates. A more traditional type of agriculture, with a greater presence of animal husbandry, existed north of the *villae* area. Numerous modest farms producing for nearby consumers also existed, as well as small subsistence farms run by independent families living in (almost complete) autarky. It goes without saying that the latter left fewer traces, but it is nevertheless clear (and logical) that the Roman imprint was less important as farm size diminished. In these modest rural units, located on less fertile ground and in isolated regions, Celtic traditions survived for an unknown time span.

Of course, life for the Gallo-Romans was not limited to producing, trading, or consuming goods. Cultural and religious activities also left a wealth of traces abundantly illustrating the process of Gallo-Romanization. The introduction of writing was another major innovation of Roman times. Many aspects of daily life now generated written documents: administrative texts, tax registers, military orders, correspondence between individuals, etc. Unfortunately, this written heritage was almost completely lost to us. Even epigraphic evidence – inscriptions on pottery, stone or metal – is rather scarce in this distant part of the Roman Empire. The most recent collection of Roman inscriptions found on the soil of contemporary Belgium, the *Nouveau recueil des inscriptions latines de Belgique* (*ILB* 2nd ed., 2002), consists of a mere 192 items, many of which are very brief and repetitive. Fortunately, inscriptions originating from other countries but relating to this part of *Gallia Belgica* complement this meagre harvest. These writings – on funerary steles, dedicatory texts, etc. – can help reconstruct daily life, social practices, and so on; they even make it possible to reconstruct (part of) the life course of certain individuals. The literary evidence relating to Belgium in Roman times is also rather scant. Contemporary historians and writers only incidentally mentioned places located in, or events relating to, that remote part of the Empire.

Religious life, for its part, is rather well documented. The archaeological museums of Brussels, Tongeren, and Arlon (to mention only the most important) display many statues and other artefacts representing figures of the classical Roman pantheon and mythology. Temples were erected in Tongeren and the main *vici* to honour these deities, and of course the emperor himself, in the framework of Roman civic religion. But many sanctuaries were also erected in the countryside, outside the urban and semi-urban centers. *Fana* (singular *fanum*) were shrines often dating back to Celtic times and constructed according to local, pre-Roman traditions (a square sanctuary surrounded by a portico). These temples were not only dedicated to Roman gods, but also to traditional Celtic deities. Indeed, as everywhere in their vast Empire, the Romans tolerated local cults. They never imposed their own religious views exclusively, nor did they try to eradicate established forms of worship. This means that in the Roman Belgian provinces the pre-existing Celtic gods, local spirits, or natural "forces" (such as sources, trees, etc.), continued to fulfill their ancient spiritual role. A well-known aspect of Gallo-Romanization was the equation of local divinities with Roman gods, the so-called *interpretatio romana*. This "translation" was flexible and dynamic; and the fact that local people venerated Celtic gods was not a sign of "opposition" to Roman dominance. City authorities were free to choose which deity or deities would be honoured locally.

This tolerant attitude produced a diversified, but also *changing* religious landscape. Indeed, significant transformations in religious practices occurred during Roman times. Funerary rites are one illustration of this dynamic situation: the incineration of bodies, already practised during Celtic times, persisted in Gallo-Roman *Belgica* before gradually giving way to inhumation from the third century onwards. Another example of religious change is the introduction of new cults in the later period of Roman rule, more specifically the Mithras cult and Christianity. The latter belief was rather marginal and essentially limited to cities. The first bishop ever consecrated on the territory of later Belgium, more precisely in Tongeren, was Servatius, probably from eastern (Armenian?) origins (in the mid-fourth century CE). Still, unequivocal evidence of this new faith dating from Roman times is rather limited. Among these traces are, for example, grave finds in Tongeren and the remains of a prayer room, dating from the fourth century CE, discovered beneath the basilica, in the same city. However, the main spread of Christianity dates from post-Roman times (see Chapter 2).

The Gradual Transformation and Demise of Roman Rule (Third–Fifth Centuries CE)

In Belgium, as in other parts of Europe, Roman dominance did not suddenly "disappear." Long before its definitive and irrevocable end, the Empire had already endured both severe shocks and slow transformations that radically changed the entire social fabric. For decades and even centuries, the regions west of the Rhine lived through periods of severe crisis alternating with years of relative restoration.

After the crushing of the Batavian revolt (70 CE), *Gallia Belgica* enjoyed a century of *Pax Romana*. This long period of quiet prosperity, unaffected by revolts or invasions, was interrupted in 172–174 by the bloody incursion of German tribes, especially the *Chauci*, attacking by land and sea, and the *Chatti*, invading the Roman Empire in the central Rhine region. These invasions, marked by large-scale plunder, caused grave destruction as evidenced by marks of fire at several urban or rural sites. But this was only the first of many ordeals to come. The third century CE was a general period of crisis for the Roman Empire. The weakening of central authority went hand in hand with increasing internal troubles, and both elements facilitated successive waves of Germanic invasion. All these elements were intimately linked. The end of the Severan dynasty in 235 marked the beginning of a long period of political and military chaos. Many emperors took (and lost) power in but a few years' time. Some Germanic raids had already occurred in 215 and 234 CE, before the onset of imperial anarchy. But the next damaging blow took place around 250 CE, with new invasions from over the Rhine, especially by the Franks. In fact, this name – which probably means "the brave ones" – refers to a federation of several Germanic peoples (*Chamavi, Bructeri*, etc.), and not to a single tribe. New Frankish invasions followed in around 275. Meanwhile, marauding bands of deserters and poor people, the so-called *bagaudae*, also affected this part of the Empire. Yet another crisis occurred in 286–293. Carausius, a military of Menapian origin and the commander of the Roman Channel fleet, proclaimed himself "Emperor of Britain." His influence also stretched across to the mainland of *Gallia Belgica*. This secession came to an end in 296, three years after his assassination.

Half a century after the beginning of this chaotic period, central imperial authority was finally restored in this part of the Empire. Emperor Diocletian (r. 284–305) undertook important reforms that also affected *Gallia Belgica*. We have already mentioned his reorganization of the *provinciae*. Administrative changes also took place on the level of the *civitates*. For instance Tornacum, now the Belgian city of Tournai in the province of Hainaut, became the capital of the *civitas Menapiorum*, at the expense of Cassel. This *vicus* was to play an important role in early Frankish times, as we shall see in Chapter 2. Yet these measures did not resolve the Germanic problem. New invasions occurred in 355, 367, 373, and 388. Along with the Saxons, the Franks once again played a crucial role in these events. This continuing pressure on the Rhine *limes* enhanced the strategic importance of the provinces of *Germania* and *Belgica*. Emperors often resided there for many years at some point of their lives.

But under the surface of political and military turmoil more profound changes were also taking place. The hinterland of the *limes* became increasingly militarized, and this evolution of course affected, above all, the territory of later Belgium. Cities were defended by the erection of walls. Tongeren, for instance, was fortified in the second half of the second century CE, possibly after the incursion of the *Chauci*. Moreover, military camps and smaller fortified posts were established far behind the Rhine region, especially along the important road from Bavay to Cologne. In the Ardennes, new fortifications were built on heights, or abandoned ones reconstructed. Since the shores of the North Sea were also threatened by Germanic incursions, a series of forts was built there, the so-called *Litus Saxonicum*. On Belgian soil the most important *castellum* was erected at Oudenburg, near Ostend, and was in service from the second to the early fifth century.

Normal social and economic life was severely affected by this growing insecurity and, even more so, by the outright chaos caused by successive invasions. Urban settlements decreased in population and area. Most bathing facilities outside the main cities disappeared by the end of the third century. The many hoards dating from the second, third, and fourth centuries CE also evidence dramatic disruptions. Not only cities, but also rural areas were affected by Germanic attacks. Archaeological evidence shows that several *villae* disappeared during the third century CE. Other estates of course survived, but the final centuries of Roman rule are characterized by a gradual withdrawal of agricultural production from large-scale market mechanisms, and a slow shift toward autarky. In craft production, a similar evolution is perceptible: long-distance trade gradually receded without disappearing altogether.

Another decisive development took place during the two final centuries of Roman rule. The so-called barbarian incursions of the third century broke the fragile equilibrium between the Roman Empire and the Germanic tribes. This marked the beginning of a new era, with an altered relationship between the Roman polity and adjacent populations. Before this critical juncture, Romans and Germans were not always at loggerheads; peaceful, commercial exchanges also existed, and tribes living near the *limes* had concluded alliances with the Empire, becoming "buffer states." In the mid-third and fourth century CE, these incursions – turning into migrations – created a new context. Henceforth, the Roman authorities had to deal with important new groups of foreigners *living on imperial territory.* First, defeated Germanic groups were not "expelled," but stayed within the boundaries of the Empire. Second, it also happened that Germanic groups were authorized to cross the border peacefully and to settle on Roman territory. The intruding and invited newcomers could obtain the status of *laeti* or *foederati.* Both categories were integrated into the Roman defence system. The first were peasant-soldiers established in scarcely populated regions, and these remained under Roman command; the second were "allies" – separate and relatively autonomous groups with their own authority.

In his *Res Gestae* (XVII, 8), the ancient historian Ammianus Marcellinus mentions a striking example of such events, directly affecting later Belgium. In 358, the (later) emperor Julian ("the Apostate") routed a group of Franks, formerly (but improperly) known as the "Salian" Franks. In fact, a specific homogeneous "sub-tribe" of "Salians" never existed, since recent scholarship has pointed out that the Romans probably misunderstood the old Germanic word *saljon*, which simply meant "*Gesell*en," or something like "fellow-tribesmen" (we shall therefore refer to this group as "Western Franks"). They had already occupied territories west of the Rhine for decades and the Roman authorities had reached an agreement with them in the course of the third century, within certain confines establishing them as auxiliaries. The Franks possibly breached this deal, causing Julian's intervention. After having defeated them, he authorized them to settle in the region known as Taxandria, a region probably located north of Tongeren, in the territory of the Belgian and Dutch provinces of Limburg. This was the starting point of crucial developments in the next century, as we shall see in Chapter 2.

This process had a dual effect. First, the nature of Roman authority was transformed, as Germanic elements were increasingly present in the military and political apparatus, even at top levels. Second, the basic composition of the population also changed. Archaeology indeed reveals the increasing presence of Germanic groups (especially through their pottery), but is alas unable to demonstrate the exact linguistic changes

that undoubtedly accompanied these demographic shifts – only toponymic analysis can shed some light on language shifts.

Neither the measures taken in the late second century, nor the
Diocletian reforms and those of his successors (at the turn of the third
and fourth centuries) could halt the gradual erosion of Roman power.
A massive attack of Germanic tribes on the Rhine at the end of 406 and
in early 407 could not be stopped. Roman legions were definitively
withdrawn from the *limes*. A few years later, in around 425, the last
Roman troops also abandoned the *Litus Saxonicum*. This signified the
end of *direct military* Roman presence in north-eastern Gaul, but even
these dramatic events did not produce an absolute break with existing
political and military structures. Indeed, the Frankish leaders stepped, so
to say, into the shoes of the Romans. One of them, Chlodio (*c.*390–*c.*450),
the commander of the Western Franks, took advantage of the Roman
retreat to break out of Taxandria, where his people had settled, and to
take over the control of the adjacent, more southern regions, thus laying
the foundations of the Frankish kingdom that would dominate for
centuries to come (see Chapter 2). One of his successors, Childerik
(*c.*436–481), was not only the king of the so-called Salian Franks, but
also bore the title of governor of the province of *Gallia Secunda* and wore
the insignia of a "Roman" general. Although the Belgian territories
gradually slipped into another age, that of the early medieval polities,
the reference to Rome – and parts of its legacy – would survive
for centuries.

Conclusion

As in many other parts of Western Europe, imperial Rome changed the
destiny of the territories that were to form Belgium many centuries later.
In Celtic times, this part of Gaul had only very limited (commercial and
cultural) contact with the Mediterranean world; money circulated marginally, as a tool of the elites; writing was absent altogether; cities were
unknown; a central state with a legislative corps and an administration
was non-existent. Roman rule boosted or even introduced all these
elements in north-eastern Gaul from the first *decennia* BCE. Intense links
were developed with southern Europe. The spread of Latin facilitated
these contacts and, together with the introduction of the alphabet,
triggered a cultural revolution. A form of market economy was introduced, in agriculture as well as in craftsmanship; henceforth money was

used far more widely than before Caesar's conquest; some people now lived together in permanent agglomerations; and a central polity, based on legislation, public taxation, and administrative structures ruled the lives of the people. Did this heritage survive the Roman Empire?

This was only partially the case. Commercial contacts with distant lands and the monetary system certainly receded in the Early Middle Ages, but they did not disappear. The same goes for writing: the written word remained in use in the coming decades and centuries but was far less widespread. Roman political organization gave way to a different sort of polity, but some essential parts of it survived, together with the memory of (and nostalgia for) the Empire; the Roman Empire lived on as a crucial, albeit largely imagined touchstone. Urbanization declined markedly. It would take centuries before cities blossomed again. The urban network that revived during the Middle Ages differed profoundly from the network established in the first decades and centuries CE. Nevertheless, some of the main cities of the future already existed as modest Roman *vici* (e.g. Ghent, Antwerp, Kortrijk, Namur, etc.) – even if the continuity between these (very small) Roman agglomerations and the later (big) cities is not always proven.

One of the main elements that would dominate medieval and modern society, Christianity, obviously also has roots in Roman times. The very first signs of this new faith date from the late imperial period. But it had only marginal importance when Roman rule came to an end. The real expansion of Catholicism began in the Early Middle Ages. Nevertheless, the Church preserved some essential features of the Roman Empire: its written culture and Latin language; its hierarchical administration; and even its spatial organization, since the first bishoprics more or less took over the boundaries of previous Roman *civitates.*

In many ways, therefore, Roman rule caused important, even spectacular breaks, though this observation does not extend to long-term and large-scale population movements. As we have seen, migrations had already taken place long before Caesar's conquest. For centuries and even millennia, people coming from the east crossed the Rhine and headed west. Of course, these movements were not (necessarily) violent and sudden "invasions": most were probably more or less peaceful and gradual. We also know that changes in archaeologically observable features do not automatically denote the arrival of "foreign people": they can also reflect the adoption of new cultural markers by locals. But despite these useful caveats, the basic fact remains: from ancient times, successive groups originating in the eastern part of Europe settled in its western part, including the regions that were to form Belgium. The Roman Empire temporarily succeeded in stopping this historic trend for almost two centuries (*c.*50 BCE to *c.*170 CE), but from the second half of the second century CE the trend resumed. It gradually overcame the physical, military, and institutional barriers erected by the Romans – even if the latter appeared to be quite inventive and resourceful when it came to dealing with these migrants, as shown by the *laeti* and *foederati* system. Seen from a broad temporal perspective, Roman rule was only a temporary parenthesis in the long-term history of migrations.

The Era of the Frankish Kingdoms

(Fifth–Tenth Centuries)

Introduction

Almost five hundred years separate the end of Roman rule and the formation of the medieval principalities whose gradual amalgamation would eventually lead, many centuries later, to contemporary Belgium. Traditionally, these so-called Barbarian or Dark Ages have been depicted in harsh contrast with the preceding so-called civilized Roman world. In recent decades, however, medievalists have thoroughly revised this gloomy picture. Rejecting the idea of an abrupt break between Roman and post-Roman times, they now rather observe complex transitions and some measure of continuity between both periods. Important changes undoubtedly took place during the epoch of the Frankish kingdoms. Urban life and monumental stone architecture receded (but did not disappear); artistic expression diverged from the classical canons; Christianity supplanted paganism, etc. But by focusing on spectacular changes such as these, one misses other crucial points: not all Roman institutions vanished suddenly; economic life was not uniformly miserable and trade was far from insignificant; Catholicism did not swiftly replace old creeds and cults; literacy did not disappear and was not limited to clerical elites. Written sources dating from the fifth to the tenth century are certainly far less numerous than those from the later Middle Ages, characterized by an impressive *révolution de l'écrit*; but for the "Belgian" territories they are unquestionably more abundant than those dating from Roman times. Chronicles, saints' lives, polyptychs (inventories of goods of large rural domains), charters, diplomas, and even correspondence offer far more than a superficial glimpse of life in the Frankish kingdoms – even if historians have to demonstrate great critical acumen to distinguish forged from authentic records, or to distil reliable "facts" from hagiographies replete with legendary tales. Archaeology also produced startling new insights. Cemeteries, in particular, have yielded a wealth of information: most fifth- to seventh-century objects that we know of today – weapons, jewels, clothing articles, utensils for everyday life, etc. – have been found in graves. New approaches to textual evidence, in combination with material culture studies and (landscape) archaeology have led to a thorough re-evaluation of the Early Middle Ages, a complex period deserving more than worn-out clichés.

Polities between Unity and Fragmentation

The views expressed above undoubtedly apply to large parts of Western Europe. But once this broad geographical setting gives way to a narrower spatial focus, analysis becomes less obvious. The writing of "national" histories of this distant past, in particular, is especially arduous and even perilous. In the nineteenth and twentieth century, however, nationalistic historiographers did not hesitate to project the modern nations back into the Early Middle Ages, claiming that the "seeds" of countries such as France or Germany were already sown in these remote times. According to this vision, a natural, inevitable and quasi-teleological trajectory links the post-Roman period to the contemporary states, as if their essential features or some invariable "national identity" existed throughout the ages. While this approach is already highly debatable for other nations, it is wholly untenable in the case of Belgium. Not the slightest sign of a "common Belgian destiny" is perceptible in the second half of the first millennium CE – even if some essential building blocks do go back that far.

After the end of Roman rule, the term *Belgica* rapidly fell into oblivion – only to reappear a millennium later, when Humanists retrieved it from ancient texts and gave it a new meaning. The first chapter has shown that this ancient *Belgica* did not, in any way, "herald" Belgium. From the fifth century, new terms emerged to label natural and political regions. As we shall see, some of them have not stood the test of time (especially Neustria and Austrasia); others have survived till today but without keeping their original spatial definition (for instance Flanders, Brabant, Hainaut, etc.). In fact, the political life of the later Belgian territories unfolded simultaneously on a much larger, quasi

West-European scale, and on a smaller, sub-regional level – but not in a spatial setting prefiguring modern Belgium in some way or another.

The confederation of Germanic-speaking tribes known as the Franks was to have an extraordinary historical destiny. A specific, western group of Franks (improperly known as the "Salian" Franks, as we have seen earlier) had settled in the extreme north-east of the Roman Empire, more precisely in Taxandria, a territory roughly corresponding to the contemporary Campine region (the north of the Belgian provinces of Limburg and Antwerp and the southern part of the Dutch province of North-Brabant), although this localization is still debated. The Romans had accepted them as *foederati* (see Chapter 1). Almost nothing is known of their first recorded leader, Chlodio, and even less of Merovech, probably his successor. But the latter's son and heir Childerik (*c.*436–481) resumed an expansion initiated under his grandfather – an endeavor that changed the face of Western Europe. From Taxandria, this group of Western Franks moved along the river Scheldt, and finally reached the Somme and the Seine, now on French territory. Childerik's sumptuous burial in the city of Tornacum (now Tournai, in the Belgian province of Hainaut), rediscovered in the seventeenth century, might suggest that his power base – "capital" would be an anachronistic term – was still located in this specific region.

It soon appeared, anyway, that the struggle for supremacy took place in a much broader geographical setting. Under Childerik's son and successor Chlodowig, better known as Clovis (465–511), Frankish expansion reached unseen heights. He defeated Syagrius, a Roman general who dominated the north of Gaul; beat other Germanic populations, such as the Visigoths and the Alamans; conquered Aquitaine; subdued the Burgundians, who became a tributary polity; and established his authority over the other Frankish groups. In brief: at Clovis' death, Gaul (except Provence) was almost entirely ruled by Merovech's heirs, in other words the Merovingian dynasty. Clovis' successors extended Frankish rule even further, in the south of Gaul and in territories east of the Rhine.

Clearly, the ascent to power of this specific branch of Frankish rulers was not the result of a sudden "invasion" of "barbarians" into the Roman Empire. On the contrary, Childerik and his son were the administrators of *Belgica secunda*; they considered themselves the legitimate heirs of Roman authority. Yet they also adopted the title of *rex* (king), unknown in the classical political hierarchy of Republican Rome, thereby claiming supremacy over other contenders.

To legitimize and consolidate this new royal power, Clovis converted to Christianity, symbolized by his solemn baptism in Reims by the hands of Bishop Remi in 496 or, more probably, 508. This decision fortified Clovis' authority both internally and externally. By embracing Catholicism, Clovis reassured – and allied himself with – the Gallo-Roman (urban) upper classes that had already accepted this brand of Christianity, and especially the bishops who by then had become key figures of local and even regional public life. It was a decisive step in the gradual fusion of the "new" Frankish elites and the "old" Gallo-Roman ones. This amalgamation ultimately led to the formation of a "unified" landed aristocracy, a small group of powerful families with extensive land holdings. As we shall see, this budding aristocracy was to play a crucial role in the political, social and economic history of the coming centuries. Clovis' conversion also had an important international dimension. By abandoning paganism and rejecting Arianism (a Christian "heresy" condemned by the first ecumenical Council of Nicaea in 325 but adopted by other Germanic populations), he made himself acceptable to both the bishop of Rome, i.e. the Pope, and the emperor of the eastern Roman Empire, two crucial actors on the European scene. Henceforth, the Franks were a power to be reckoned with. Finally, the adoption of Catholicism by the Merovingian dynasty was also essential to the Christianization of the rural masses.

Although they embraced some elements of previous Roman politics, the Merovingians also diverged from this model in crucial respects. Under their rule, public authority was not an abstract and depersonalized concept. Merovech's heirs, on the contrary, considered political power (and the wealth that goes with it) to be the "private" possession of the ruler: it was intimately attached to their person. Together with Frankish inheritance rules, based on the equal division of estates between direct male descendants, this patrimonial view of political power inevitably led to a potential fragmentation of monarchical rule. It was also an ideal recipe for bloody confrontations within (and beyond) the ruling family. Whenever a king died, internal division threatened. This already happened when Clovis died in 511. The *regnum Francorum*, or kingdom of the Franks, was then split between his four sons, and unity only re-emerged temporarily after that division. In brief, the Frankish kingdom was constantly torn between (fragile and temporary) unity and (deep and lasting) fragmentation – even if the concept of the *regnum Francorum* as an overarching reality survived, and even if the geographical borders of both this construct and its components changed over time.

This is not the place to dissect the intricacies of Merovingian politics, riven with bloody strife between royal fathers and sons, brothers and half-brothers, uncles and nephews, not to forget wives, widows, and mothers. To understand what happened to the territories that later became Belgium, it suffices to mention two essential "subkingdoms": Austrasia, the "kingdom of the east," and Neustria, the "new kingdom," in the northwest of former Gaul, emerging around the end of the sixth and the beginning of the seventh centuries. Both polities got involved in a fierce struggle and developed a specific "identity" which, however, had nothing to do with a struggle between "Germanic/German" (Austrasian) and "Latin/French" (Neustrian) elements, but which was rather fueled by the competition between aristocratic families.

At this point of our exposé, a new and crucial element emerges that would decisively influence the fate of the Merovingian dynasty: the rise to power of a family of grandees rooted in the Austrasian regions between the rivers Rhine, Moselle, and the Meuse, namely the Pippinids, later called the Carolingians. Pippin I (†640), also called "Pippin of Landen" (a Flemish commune near today's Liège and his supposed place of origin) was a mighty aristocrat with huge domains in, inter alia, the southern part of contemporary Belgium, especially along the Meuse valley. Step-by-step, he and his heirs – most notably his grandson Pippin II (†714), also known as "Pippin of Herstal" (yet another commune near Liège), and his great-grandson Charles Martel ("the Hammer," †741) – became key figures of the Frankish political scene. They owed their influence not only to their status of large landowners, but also to their position at the Merovingian courts. The (successive or simultaneous) kings had entrusted a series of tasks to specific dignitaries: looking after the royal horses, table, or treasury, or managing the official records, etc. The *major domus* ("mayor of the palace" or "leader of the household") was the most prominent figure of this embryonic royal "administration." For decades, the Pippinids occupied this key function at the court of numerous Merovingian kings.

Gradually the *majores domus* eclipsed the reigning kings – a process not unlike the ascendency of the *shoguns* over the emperors in ancient Japan. From about the middle of the seventh century, the Austrasian Pippinids exerted real political power in the Frankish realm (or they struggled to do so against opposing forces), reducing the Merovingian monarchs to mere instruments of their policy. However, they refrained from openly assuming kingship due to the enduring symbolic prestige of the Merovingians – until 751, when Pippin III "the Short" (or "the Younger"), Charles Martel's son, deposed the last Merovingian Childerik III and was proclaimed king by the Frankish grandees – a move prepared by Pippin himself. Three years later, in 754, the Pope conferred a sacred dimension to Pippin's kingship by anointing him in Reims, thereby inaugurating a tradition that would last until 1824.

The Carolingian dynasty, that is, the "heirs of Charles" (Martel), ruled over large parts of Western Europe during approximately two centuries. Frankish predominance reached its zenith under Pippin III's son, the famous Charlemagne (*c.*747–814). During his long reign, the *regnum Francorum* not only expanded even further, beyond northern Italy and the Pyrenees and in Central Europe; it also achieved a previously unseen (but still relative) degree of stability, organization, and efficiency. For nine decades, a single monarch ruled this vast realm: first Pippin III, then Charlemagne, and his son after him. *Carolus Magnus'* huge kingdom even became an empire, when he was crowned emperor by the Pope in Rome on Christmas day 800. This confirmed Charles' ambition to inscribe his reign in the continuity of the former *Imperium Romanum*.

Charlemagne's only surviving son, Louis "the Pious," inherited his father's empire, along with the imperial title. The unity of the *regnum Francorum* was thus preserved by biological accident. But this was no longer the case after Louis' death in 840. Political unity was now lost for good, and the subsequent division of his realm was to have long-lasting effects in most of Western Europe. A series of successive steps reshuffled the spatial framework of political power in the Carolingian Empire. First, Louis' three sons divided the realm among themselves (Treaty of Verdun, 843). Charles the Bald reigned over West Francia (that would gradually give birth to modern France), Louis the German over East Francia (ditto for later Germany), while Lothar I, who also inherited the imperial crown, ruled over *Francia Media*, a vast territory separating both kingdoms and stretching from Frisia (the northern part of today's Netherlands) to Provence and northern Italy. By now, the previous notions of Neustria and Austrasia (already less significant under the first Carolingians) had lost all relevance. But *Francia Media* also turned out to be an evanescent reality. At Lothar's death, in 855, his "middle realm" was again divided among his three sons (second step). Lothar II inherited the northern part, named (after him) Lotharingia. In a third step, after the latter's demise, this ephemeral kingdom was split in two by his uncles Charles the Bald and Louis the German (Treaty of Meerssen, 870). The first took the territories west of a north–south axis formed by the rivers Meuse, Ourthe, and Moselle, while the second annexed the regions east of that line. The fourth and final step, with the Treaty of Ribemont (880), delivered the whole of former Lotharingia to the Germanic kingdom.

This brief overview of general Frankish political history, with its repeated divisions and border shifts, allows us, at last, to tackle our main point: the position and role of "Belgium" within this framework. From the middle of the fifth to the beginning of the tenth century, these territories never played an autonomous and coherent role in Frankish history – contrary to other parts of the *regnum Francorum*, for example Aquitaine or Burgundy, as they formed specific (sub-)kingdoms. As we have seen, the Western Franks originally came from Taxandria and then settled in the surroundings of Tournai – two regions located in contemporary Belgium. But once Clovis ascended to power, the Merovingians showed no special interest in these regions: they established their constantly moving seats of power in northern France, more specifically in and around Paris and the Seine area. The territories that later became Belgium were not only marginalized; they were, moreover, part of different subkingdoms. Roughly defined, the territories west of the so-called Coal Forest (*Sylva carbonaria*, or *Forêt charbonnière* in French) belonged to Neustria, the rest to Austrasia. This forest (which has now disappeared) ran from the river Dyle in the north-east to the river Sambre in the south-west – right through the middle of modern Belgium, from north to south.

The rise of the Pippinids and Carolingians changed the realm's centre of gravity. While the exact birthplaces of these successive rulers cannot always be determined with certainty, their cradle was located in the Belgian part of the Meuse valley and in adjacent regions towards the Moselle (around the French town of Metz) and the Rhine (with the German town of Aachen). Does this make Charles Martel, or Charlemagne, or any other member of this dynasty a "Belgian" (or a "Frenchman," or a "German"), as many old-school nationalistic historians have claimed in a not so remote past? Of course not: the use of these labels is utterly anachronistic, as is the claim that Charlemagne is "the father of Europe." These present-day political definitions are wholly irrelevant to understanding Europe's Early Middle Ages. It is nevertheless worth noting that under the Carolingians, the southern part of modern Belgium, with adjacent Dutch, French, and German regions, effectively became the heart of the realm, and since 800, of the empire. As in Merovingian times, the monarchy had no fixed "capital": the centre of power was located wherever the monarch temporarily resided. When Charlemagne, for instance, was not conducting some military expedition, he regularly stayed in "Belgian" places such as Jupille and Herstal (near Liège), in the "Dutch" city of Nijmegen or, mostly, in the "German" city of Aachen, where he was also buried. Moreover, the nearby and woody Ardennes were one of the favorite hunting places of successive Carolingian monarchs.

We have just seen that in Merovingian times the territory of future Belgium belonged to different subkingdoms, namely Neustria and Austrasia. The many reshuffles of the Carolingian realm after Louis the Pious' death in 840 led to a similar result. The northernmost part of modern Belgium, roughly the territories stretching from the west bank of the river Scheldt to the North Sea coast, was allotted to the king of West Francia, Charles the Bald and his successors. The rest was successively part of *Francia Media* and the smaller kingdom of Lotharingia. The rulers of these kingdoms had their power bases elsewhere, which means that the "Belgian" regions once more lost the central status they had occupied under the first Carolingians. These territories were (again) borderlands, not heartlands. In brief, under Frankish rule (500–900), there was no geopolitical structure "waiting" (let alone "destined") to "become Belgium."

But the macro-level – the *regnum Francorum* and its different subkingdoms – reveals only one dimension of politics, and, for our story, it is not the most relevant one. Indeed, in the present case, the micro-level is essential to apprehending the real and lasting legacy of Frankish times for the region's subsequent political evolution. Like all other extensive polities, the Merovingian and Carolingian monarchies inevitably faced a difficult challenge: how to control the many (vast and sometimes distant) territories they ruled? The first Frankish sovereigns did not maintain the *civitates*, that is, the administrative subdivisions of the former Roman *provinciae* (see Chapter 1). Instead, they chose the *pagus*, the subdivision of the *civitates*, as the unit composing their kingdom. Their Carolingian successors used the same system.

In the regions that would later form Belgium, the Frankish kings constituted around ten *pagi*. Some of them bore names that have disappeared since then, for instance, the *Pagus Mempiscus*, north of the river

Leie (Lys), or the *Pagus Renensium*, near the present-day city of Antwerp. Other *pagi* had names still existing in modern Belgium, even if their exact definition has largely changed since Frankish times. Among them we will only mention, by way of example, the *Pagus Hainau* (a name still resonating in the contemporary Belgian province of Hainaut), the *Pagus Bracbatensis* (differing from both the later duchy of Brabant and the modern provinces with that name), the *Pagus Gandensis* (around the modern city of Ghent) and the *Pagus Flandrensis* (along the North Sea coast).

Given the importance of the name "Flanders" in the following developments, it is necessary to clarify the origin and significance of this geographical and political concept. This *pagus* was a modest region located between the shores of the North Sea and the surroundings of today's city of Bruges. Its name was derived from the word "*flam*" or "*floem*" which in old North Sea Germanic means "hill in a sea marsh." The words "Fleming" (Dutch *Vlaming*, French *Flamand*) and "Flanders" (*Vlaanderen*) thus originally refer to a small geographical area, not an ethnic origin (a "Flemish tribe" never existed). More important still, the quite limited area corresponding to the original *Pagus Flandrensis* was very different from the spaces covered by the same word in later times: from the medieval county of Flanders, over the later Belgian provinces of East and West Flanders, to today's political region Flanders, one of the constituent parts of the modern federal state of Belgium.

The king controlled each *pagus* through a representative called *grafio* in Germanic or *comes* in Latin ("count"). In the course of time, the term *comitatus* therefore became a synonym for *pagus* ("county"). The *comes* had broad powers, since he maintained law and order, commanded military forces, collected taxes, and presided over the regional court of justice – all this in the name of the monarch. He was not paid directly by the royal treasury but was remunerated by the produce of royal domains (or *fiscus*), and by part of the fines he had collected. The management of local affairs was soon complicated by the fact that one count could administer several *pagi*; or that a *pagus* could be divided into smaller territories, each entrusted to a different count; or also that several *pagi* could be supervised by yet another royal official, the commander of an army with the title of *dux* ("duke"). Moreover, the borders of the *pagi* were not immutable, and not always clearly defined.

Needless to say, the office of *comes* was crucial for the cohesion of the Merovingian and Carolingian polities. In theory, the monarch chose the counts freely, and he could revoke them at will; but in practice, this position was soon predominantly entrusted to aristocrats, and it gradually became hereditary. From the start, the history of the Frankish kingdoms was deeply influenced by the mighty landowning families. In their insatiable quest for landed wealth – the main source of riches in the Frankish world – the aristocratic grandees developed a complex and changing relationship with the monarchy. Proximity and even, if possible, marital alliances with strong rulers, vested with sacred aura, were essential for accumulating rural properties (through royal donations) and/or for accessing the *honores* (public offices and functions such as the *comitatus*). These offices also yielded more (local or regional) wealth and power, but they were still under royal authority. A mighty ruler like Charlemagne managed to firmly hold the reins, by supervising his *comites*, in particular through the system of *missi dominici*, or royal envoys inspecting the counts' actions and reporting back on them to the imperial court. But under weak monarchs such as the late Merovingians and the late Carolingians, increasing competition between aristocratic families, or between these families and the dynasty itself, produced entirely different results. The ascent of the Austrasian Pippinids was a spectacular example of such an aristocratic challenge to royal power, but this resulted not in the fragmentation but, on the contrary, in the unification of the Frankish realm. However, an entirely different scenario unfolded when the later Carolingian rulers gradually lost power, not only due to intra-dynastic rivalry, but also to increasing aristocratic pressure and growing external threats, especially the repeated attacks and incursions of the Vikings (from *c.*820 to *c.*891).

A final and crucial element undermined central authority from the late ninth century onward: feudalism. Since Charles Martel, and essentially under Charlemagne, the Carolingian rulers had developed a system of personal dependency, apart from "public" functions such as *comes* or *dux* – precisely to somehow counterbalance the always-menacing influence of the great aristocratic families. By swearing an oath of allegiance to the monarch, an individual – not necessarily an aristocratic grandee – became his liegeman or *vassus dominicus*, expected to contribute to military expeditions. In exchange for this personal submission and fidelity, the overlord, also known as the suzerain – in this case the Carolingian monarch – delivered protection and material support, for instance in the form of land. Originally, this support was strictly attached to the person that had sworn fidelity, and the relationship ended with the death of one of both parties. But as time went by (and as the Carolingian monarchs grew weaker), this "temporary" material help evolved toward hereditary tenure. Moreover, these feudal relations tended to blend with the official positions or *honores*. In practice, this meant that a count often also became the king's liegeman. Men of aristocratic families increasingly occupied both positions. Finally, the feudal relationship extended beyond the limited circle of the monarch and his direct liegemen; the latter, and also other grandees, in turn built their own relationships based on allegiance, trust, and protection – thus creating a hierarchy of feudal bonds.

All these elements stimulated centrifugal tendencies, heralding the definitive end of the Carolingian dream of a single unified empire, and even of multiple "unified" subkingdoms. More and more, *comites* and vassals considered the material benefits attached to their position as hereditary: the domains "temporarily" and "personally" put at their disposal by the monarch became assets that were transmissible to their own heirs. Likewise, as mentioned before, the counts and dukes increasingly considered their prominent position in the counties and duchies as definitive and destined to be transmitted to their descendants.

In the territories that later became Belgium, one specific *comitatus* emerged as early as the second half of the ninth century. Count Baldwin I (†879), who had forced himself into the Carolingian family by marrying (in fact abducting) Charles the Bald's daughter Judith, was the founder of a dynasty that ruled Flanders as a quasi-independent polity. This county was much larger than the ancient *pagus Flandrensis*: it covered all the lands stretching from the North Sea shore to the left bank of the river Scheldt – and this was only the beginning of later territorial expansion. The counts of Flanders were the vassals of the kings of West Francia, later of France proper. As we have seen, the rest of "Belgium" was part of the Lotharingian kingdom (later duchy) that eventually disintegrated into several quasi-autonomous polities in the eleventh century (especially the duchy of Brabant, the county of Hainaut and the county of Namur) (see Chapter 3). These entities theoretically remained under the sovereignty of East Francia, later of the Holy Roman Germanic Empire. These developments paved the way for the medieval principalities emerging from the slowly disintegrating Carolingian Empire; a new epoch was born.

The Dawn of Christianity

In the 1940s, the Belgian Catholic historian Léon van der Essen (1883–1963) labelled the Merovingian period as *Le siècle des Saints*: heroic missionaries and saints turned the pagan population into devout and fervent Catholics – a faith that was long considered, by many, as *the* hallmark of the Belgian population. The spread of Catholicism – indeed a profound change in mental and societal landscapes – undoubtedly dates back to Frankish times, and this brand of Christianity definitely influenced the minds and social practices of the vast majority of Belgians until quite recently. Nevertheless, the process of Christianization was far more complex than this angelic image suggests. First, modern historians have questioned the validity of a sharp contrast between paganism and Christianity. Second, religious developments can only be understood if one takes into account their political, social, and economic dimensions.

Indeed, in Frankish times (as in subsequent centuries), the Catholic religion, political power, and landed wealth were narrowly entangled. Church, monarchy, and aristocracy developed ties that were closer than in any later period. It would be wrong, in particular, to see Church and state as two separate entities. Being the guardian of all things earthly, the monarch's interventions in clerical life were considered normal. The Church, for its part, needed royal (and aristocratic) backing to maintain and expand both its material wealth and its spiritual ascendency over the people. Finally, the aristocrats, who occupied most of the leading clerical positions, were also deeply involved in Church affairs, especially through donations, because their religious zeal accrued to their material and spiritual position both in society and in the afterlife.

The close link between politics and Christian religion predated Frankish times. At the end of the fourth century, the Roman emperor Theodosius I (347–395) had turned Christianity into the state religion. This identification between political and spiritual power explains the adoption, by the nascent Church, of the Empire's basic administrative structure. The bishoprics (dioceses), the basic units of clerical organization, were modeled on the Roman *civitates*. This organization was maintained throughout the centuries, even if its pattern was redefined over the course of time: originally existing dioceses were reshuffled or abolished, and new ones were created. Due to its Roman origin, the clerical pattern rapidly differed from the (extremely volatile) pattern of post-Roman *political* organization: in no time, the boundaries of polities (kingdoms, empires, *pagi*, counties, duchies, etc., and finally nation-states) no longer corresponded with those of the clerical structures. In the long run, this duality would ultimately reinforce the diverging dynamics between the lay world and the clerical world.

At the end of Roman rule, the Christian presence in later Belgian territories was probably mainly limited to urban areas, but a rudimentary organization of the Church unquestionably existed at that time (see Chapter 1). As in other parts of the Roman Empire, Gallic dioceses corresponded with the existing *civitates*. Consequently, five dioceses covered later Belgium. The bishopric of Thérouanne administered but a small part of the territory near the river Yser. The dioceses of Tournai and Cambrai oversaw, respectively, the western and the middle part of the future country. The bishopric of Tongeren (whose seat was transferred to Maastricht before the early sixth century, and from there to Liège around 800) exerted its authority in the eastern part. Finally, a small part of today's province of Luxemburg fell within the jurisdiction of the diocese of Trier. These dioceses respectively matched the previous *civitates Morinorum, Menapiorum, Nerviorum, Tungrorum,* and *Treverorum* (please note that Thérouanne and Cambrai are located in modern France, Maastricht in The Netherlands, and Trier in Germany). This diocesan structure would prove to be long lasting: the next reform did not take place until the sixteenth century (1559), more than a millennium later (see Chapter 5).

What happened to the early Christian communities in the very first stages of Frankish domination is unclear, given the extreme rarity of material and textual evidence from the fifth century. For instance, the names of the bishops successively occupying the diocesan thrones are either unknown or uncertain, some exceptions notwithstanding. However, historians assume that there was no real vacancy: the seeds sown in Roman times probably survived the initial turmoil. When he converted to Catholicism (probably in 508), Clovis took over and reinforced the late Roman system of state religion. Running the affairs of the Catholic Church within his realm was thus a logical and almost natural thing, both for him and his successors. The choice of the bishops was of course a crucial element in royal policy, since controlling the dioceses was key to guaranteeing Merovingian (and later Carolingian) authority over the realm. Some bishops were also entrusted with political functions, for example as *missus dominicus*. Whether or not the kings succeeded in imposing "their" men (in the majority of cases they did), the bishops were almost always scions of aristocratic families. Indeed, the landowning grandees also wanted to control dioceses, since this helped them to establish, maintain, or extend their influence.

If the Christian framework had not disappeared after the end of Roman rule, it certainly needed repairing and strengthening. The rural masses still largely escaped control of the Church. They either adhered to one of the many forms of paganism, or to a Christian creed inconsistent with the Catholic canon. Consolidating or reshuffling the dioceses was essential in this respect – but also insufficient, since the episcopal seats, located in surviving Roman cities, were unable to control, on their own, the surrounding countryside and its inhabitants. From the sixth to the eighth century, missionary activity was therefore stepped up, with the crucial support, or even on the initiative, of both the Merovingian monarchs and leading aristocratic families. A remarkable aspect of this evangelization was the role of foreign clerics, either from Aquitaine or Ireland. They could be invested with episcopal power, thus becoming *episcopi ad praedicandum* (i.e. without a fixed seat). Some of these "imported" figures (for instance Saint Amandus or Saint Remaclus, two Aquitanian monks of aristocratic origin), together with "autochthonous" ones (for example Saint Hubert, probably close to the Pippinids), left a lasting imprint on the hearts and minds of local people: after their deaths, some of them were revered as saints and their graves and/or relics became objects of an intense and persisting cult.

This drive toward Christianization is also inseparable from two institutional aspects that would mark the social, economic, and cultural landscape of the centuries to come: first, the foundation of abbeys, and second, the establishment of a network of parishes. Monasticism – or the living together of religious men or women isolating themselves from worldly affairs to pursue a devout life – originated in the Mediterranean world but gradually spread over the whole of Western Europe in the first centuries CE. The Frankish realm fully participated in this movement, as did the regions under consideration here, from the seventh century onward. This phenomenon perfectly illustrates the links between religion, political power, and economic wealth. Diocesan bishops could of course establish abbeys, but kings and aristocrats, led by complex motivations, also played a decisive role. By establishing a community of monks or nuns, through generous land donations, they not only safeguarded their spiritual well-being on earth and in the afterlife; they also defended their political and economic interests. Through successive gifts and extensions, the abbeys soon became huge rural domains, rich centers of economic activity and loci dominating masses of peasants. Consequently, they were essential to establish or reinforce the political influence of the aristocratic families, and also to avoid the division of their estates through inheritance. Control over the abbeys was therefore a crucial issue. Since the donators had some direct or indirect influence on the appointment of the head of the religious community (abbot or abbess), they could turn the abbey into an instrument of power. If the abbot was invested with episcopal power (*episcopus de monasterio* or *abbas episcopus*), the lay founder and the abbots themselves could escape or counterbalance the influence of a diocesan bishop belonging to a rival elite group.

This complex interplay between religion, monarchy, and aristocracy explains the foundation, especially between 625 and 730, of an impressive series of abbeys, essentially along the basins of the rivers Scheldt and Meuse, and in the regions in-between. Many of them would play a crucial role in the centuries to come. A few examples are telling. With the help of the Merovingian king Dagobert I, Saint Amandus founded an abbey in Ghent, in the 640s, later known as Saint Peter's abbey. Not long thereafter another abbey was founded nearby, dedicated to one of Amandus' followers, Saint Bavo. But in 718, the Austrasian *major domus* Charles Martel deposed and exiled the abbot of Saint Peter's, who was an ally of Charles' rival, the Neustrian mayor of the palace. Between 640 and 647, the widow and the daughter of the late Pippin I, Austrasian mayor of the palace, founded an abbey in Nivelles, a place located not far from Neustria, the realm controlled by their opponents. It is noteworthy that in several other cases, aristocratic ladies also played an important role in establishing religious communities. Some of these prominent women even became the object of an enduring and lively cult; for instance Saint Gertrude, Pippin's daughter, and the abbess of the aforementioned monastery. The Pippinids also created (or took control of) several abbeys in the region between the rivers Sambre and Meuse (*Entre-Sambre-et-Meuse*), because they wanted to increase their power in yet another border region between Austrasia and Neustria (for instance the abbeys of Fosses, Lobbes, and Aulne). Likewise, in Neustria, pro-Pippinid aristocrats also founded several strongly linked abbeys (for instance Mons and Soignies, in contemporary Hainaut, and Maubeuge and Hautmont, now in France). These and other examples demonstrate that political motives often underpinned the creation of Merovingian abbeys.

The creation of abbeys continued under Carolingian rule, but the new dynasty also reinforced its control over the Church. The domains of some abbeys were confiscated and redistributed to allied aristocrats (a policy inaugurated by Charles Martel). But on the other hand, land donations to other institutions continued. Charlemagne and Louis the Pious were also keen on strengthening the uniformity of the realm: the rules governing the abbeys were therefore standardized along the Benedictine model. Finally, the Carolingian monarchs reinforced their hold on the monastic insti-tutions. On the one hand, the abbot-bishops disappeared at the end of the eighth century (under the late Merovingians they were important pawns in elite rivalry); on the other hand, the Carolingians generalized the system of lay abbots. Prominent members of the elite not belonging to the clerical order were directly appointed by the king to manage one or more religious communities (in some cases in cooperation with a clerical abbot). A well-known example was Einhard (*c.*770–840), a learned man and courtier, also the famed author of Charlemagne's biography, whom Louis the Pious appointed as the lay abbot of Saint Peter's and Saint Bavo's in Ghent, along with five other abbeys.

The Carolingian control and standardization of monasticism cannot be understood without referring to the pre-existing system of immunities. Since Merovingian times, abbeys had obtained important material and judicial privileges. They were not subject to taxes, and the count, the representative of central authority, could not intervene in their domains. From the point of view of the Carolingian rulers, it was therefore all the more necessary to control the activity (and the produce) of these mighty religious institutions. But once the power of the Carolingian monarchs weakened, the immunity enjoyed by the powerful abbeys led to a further decline of central rule – thus reinforcing the growing subversion of royal authority by the feudal system.

The voluntaristic religious policy of the Merovingian and Carolingian monarchs had revived the dioceses and created rich and mighty abbeys. Yet an in-depth, extensive, and lasting religious control of the population also required an institutional network on the lowest level, nearest to those dwelling in rural areas: the parishes. The parochial network was mainly extended under Carolingian rule. Local chapels and churches were first established in large domains; when the population grew – a clear sign of the economic dynamism perceptible in the ninth century and analyzed below – new hamlets developed in previously unsettled areas, and this expansion in turn led to the erection of new churches providing for the spiritual needs of the inhabitants and collecting tithes to sustain the parish's activities. New churches were not only established by the local bishop, but also by the lords of estates (whether the abbot or a lay grandee). In many cases, landlords founded churches on their own initiative, and also appointed the man who would be in charge of the parish after being ordained. Here again, we see the intimate bond between (landed aristocratic) wealth and religious activity.

The growing presence of missionaries and saints, the multiplication of miracles, the foundation of abbeys and churches, and the increasing pressure exercised by the mighty all contributed to a profound change in the spiritual and social habits of ordinary men and women. But as mentioned before, scholars have by now abandoned the idea of an abrupt and monolithic switch to pure Catholicism. They are therefore extremely cautious when it comes to dating the conversion of the inhabitants of the territory of future Belgium. Changes in religious conceptions and practices were, in all probability, gradual and complex. Even funerary evidence is not as clear-cut as previously thought. The switch from incineration to inhumation, generalizing since the end of Roman rule, for instance, does not prove the end of paganism; the same goes for the presence (or absence) of funeral gifts marked (or not) with Christian signs. Dating the conversion process is therefore extremely difficult. In most "Belgian" regions, clear and unambiguous signs of Christianity only emerged in the course of the seventh century, and Christian beliefs and practices probably generalized during the eighth century. However, so-called pagan elements (such as amulets, magical practices, etc.), combined with some measure of Christianity, certainly dominated the daily life of the population long after the Church had established itself. The persistence of such unorthodox traditions was perhaps not alien to the great popularity of relics, and to the cult of saints in general. Obtaining (or producing) material remnants of venerated and charismatic personalities, and exposing them to public adoration, was essential to establishing and increasing the authority of a specific church or monastery and, consequently, of the elite groups behind them. These sacred objects attracted many pilgrims, whose presence stimulated (or even created) local economic activity and markets. The aura and attractiveness of the locales concerned (and their leading figures) grew accordingly – another trump card in political rivalries.

These new forms of religiosity also engendered various forms of artistic activity: the construction of places of worship and shrines, and the production of sacred objects and religious representations in various forms. But alas, only few testimonies of Merovingian and Carolingian art have survived in the territories of later Belgium. Many churches, chapels, or monasteries were indeed built in these early times, but they hardly left any trace. Due to the continuity of worship, the original constructions have often been thoroughly renovated and extended in later times, or have even been completely superseded by larger buildings, especially in the first centuries of the second millennium CE, with the flowering of Romanesque art. The church at Lobbes (Hainaut province) is a rare exception, since parts of this building date back to the early ninth century. Consequently, careful excavations are needed to unearth the Frankish foundations of still-existing edifices of worship. Some religious buildings dating from Merovingian and early Carolingian times were also destroyed during the incursions of the Vikings (ninth century), although historians now often downplay the importance of this destruction: the monks who chronicled these events in later years apparently exaggerated the extent of "God's scourge" through the "terrible Norsemen." On the other hand, civilian buildings – ranging from ordinary villagers' huts to most of the "palaces" of the powerful – were not made of stone but of wood, and, in the best of cases, these wooden constructions only left some faintly visible traces in the soil. In Carolingian times palatial architecture sometimes attained monumental stone proportions, but these constructions are largely lost and what is left of them is, moreover, located outside Belgium (particularly in Aachen).

A visitor looking for Merovingian and Carolingian artifacts in Belgian museums will find weaponry and objects of daily life, retrieved from the many cemeteries scattered all over the country, but such grave finds were already less common in later Frankish times, since the spread of Christianity led to the gradual disappearance of objects accompanying the deceased. Sculpture was almost exclusively limited to religious and/ or funerary contexts. Some stone slabs decorated with sculpted vegetal motifs or fantastic animal figures have been preserved, but they are both extremely rare and fragmentary. The most spectacular example of Frankish artistic expression in the "Belgian" area was found in 1977: a stone sarcophagus representing – so the accompanying inscription tells us – *Sancta Chrodoara*, a holy aristocratic lady who died in the early seventh century. She was represented on the lid of her last resting place, dressed in a cloak, holding a big walking stick, and staring us right in the eyes – a unique but fine example of stylized human representation from the heartland of the Pippinids (the coffin was found in the small commune of Amay near Liège, where it is still on display, see Figure 2.1).

Figure 2.1 The Frankish aristocracy played a key role in the beginnings of Christianization: view of the Saint Chrodoara sacrophagus (*Amay – prov. Liège, Saint-Georges church*, drawing by Laure-Anne Finoulst, 2009)

However, cultural and artistic expression in the *regnum Francorum* reached its zenith some 150 years later, under Charlemagne and his son Louis the Pious. The political and religious centralization of the Empire went hand in hand with a voluntaristic cultural policy, commonly known as the "Carolingian renaissance." Antique models and texts were revived; education, at the imperial court and in the great monasteries, was stimulated; the script was reformed and standardized (contemporary students in palaeography sigh with relief at the legibility of the famous "Carolingian minuscule," compared with the more obscure Merovingian writing); high-quality manuscripts were produced and illustrated in the abbatial *scriptoria*. Carolingian miniatures and book illustrations compensate for the almost entirely lost (wall) paintings, of which only few remnants have survived in the Empire, and none at all on "Belgian" territory. Even the finest instances of manuscript production were realized outside modern Belgium. This cultural climax resulted not only from political factors – centralization, stability, and the quest for grandeur – but also from economic growth, an aspect to which we will turn soon.

Origins and Significance of the Linguistic Frontier

But before doing so, another crucial heritage of Frankish times demands our attention: the shifts in language use. In a multilingual nation-state like Belgium, this phenomenon has of course been scrutinized in great detail. It even became the object of an intense debate, where political, ideological, and scientific dimensions mingled in sometimes-unpalatable ways. Today, a linguistic fault line runs right through the middle of the Belgian territory, from east to west, dividing the nation in two more or less equal geographical parts. In the northern part, the dominant language is Dutch, a Germanic idiom (*Nederlands* is the correct word in this language, *néerlandais* is the French equivalent) also improperly known as Flemish (resp. *Vlaams* and *flamand*). In the southern part, people exclusively speak French, a Romance language stemming from Latin. Belgium also has a tiny German-speaking community in the east of the country, but this group became part of Belgium only after the First World War and is not relevant to the present discussion (see Chapter 9). Along this fault line, also called the linguistic frontier or language border (*frontière linguistique* in French or *taalgrens* in Dutch), some communes have a mixed population, speaking either Dutch or French (many individuals are, moreover, bilingual but bilingualism is not necessarily generalized in the areas concerned). But with the exception of these few places, the linguistic situation is (nowadays) generally homogenous, that is, the population speaks Dutch (in the north) and French (in the south) – with bilingualism far more common in the Dutch part. More importantly still for the present topic, this more or less "homogeneous" divide has *seemed* to exist since time immemorial. The country's recent political struggles also resulted in a *legal* definition of the linguistic frontier in 1962 (see Chapter 10), and this development has strengthened the (false) idea that the language border is "naturally" stable and that its origins are age old – even dating from the earliest Frankish times. In the nineteenth and twentieth centuries, some politicians, intellectuals, and even scholars established a link between languages and the "Germanic" or "Latin races," each supposedly endowed with specific immutable moral and physical features; the analysis of the origins and significance of this frontier therefore became all the more controversial.

The third- to fifth-century migrations of Germanic peoples, including the Franks, undoubtedly impacted the linguistic landscape of the northeastern parts of the former Roman Empire. But how and when these changes exactly occurred is still largely unclear. They were probably far more complex and gradual than previously assumed. As indicated in the first chapter, the linguistic situation in the later Roman Empire was already intricate and dynamic. Celtic languages persisted for centuries after Caesar's conquest. According to the testimony of Saint Hieronymous, who lived in Trier around 367 CE, Celtic was still spoken in this city, then the capital of *Belgica Prima*, some decades before the end of Roman rule. This was probably also the case in the regions of later Belgium, especially in the countryside. Unfortunately, it is impossible to know when the Celtic tongues disappeared altogether in *Gallia Belgica*, but it seems likely that they were already completely extinct in the Early Middle Ages. Henceforth, the two dominant tongues were Latin (and its local variants, which eventually evolved into Romance successor-languages such as French) on the one hand, and a variety of Germanic languages on the other. Indeed, we saw earlier that the latter idioms were already spoken in the territories of later Belgium before Caesar's conquest. But their presence undoubtedly increased from the third century CE, when Germanic populations, especially the Franks, were beginning to settle in these regions.

When Roman rule vanished altogether at the beginning of the fifth century, this Germanic group extended its dominance over the whole of

Gallia Belgica and beyond. But the crucial fact is that this new Frankish *political* supremacy did not generate a complete language shift in favor of Germanic idioms. Although it is impossible to know how many Germanic/Frankish men and women physically moved over the territories of the former Roman Empire, their numbers were, in all probability, fairly modest. They must have counted in the tens rather than in the hundreds of thousands. The more southwards the Franks went, the more their presence probably consisted of rather limited elite groups. Consequently, the Latin-speaking majority easily absorbed Germanic/Frankish linguistic elements. In most parts of the newly established *regnum Francorum*, Latin (and the subsequent Romance tongues) prevailed. This was the case in the vast majority of the territories belonging to contemporary France, and in today's region of Wallonia in Belgium. But in the northern part of the latter country, and in the northernmost regions of France, Germanic-origin idioms managed to become dominant.

This process has been intensely studied since the nineteenth century. How can one explain this divide? And why exactly along that line? According to the famous historian Godefroid Kurth (1847–1916), the apparently "neat" separation between Germanic and Latin speakers was due to the presence of a massive forest, the so-called *Forêt charbonnière* ("Coal Forest") already mentioned above. He thought that this natural "obstacle" had stopped the Frankish advance and the expansion of the Germanic languages. Unfortunately for him, it later appeared that this forest did not run from east to west, but from north to south. Another explanation referred to the existence of the ancient Roman road, with many fortified military posts, that stretched from Bavay in the west to Cologne in the east, right through the middle of later Belgium, and following more or less the same line as today's linguistic frontier. But could this road in any way have "stopped" the advance of Germanic populations? This is most unlikely. Today, explanations point to other elements, in particular the different population densities in the north and the south of later Belgium. Roman rule and, logically, the Latin language, were probably less deeply rooted in the northern regions *from the onset*, even before the Frankish expansion. In all likelihood, these territories were probably also less densely populated than those in the south. This might have facilitated the dominance of newcomers speaking a Germanic language in northern parts. Historians also think that the Germanic-speaking populations that established themselves in the somewhat inhospitable and isolated areas along the North Sea and its hinterland – consisting of sea marshes – were not Franks, but men and women of Saxon and Frisian origin (belonging to the group of so-called Maritime or North Sea Germans). The Franks, during the move to the south, seemed to have "passed through" contemporary Flanders without really settling there.

Finally, the stabilization of the linguistic divide and the homogenization of language use on both sides was a protracted process. The border did not crystallize once and for all, and all of a sudden, with early Frankish expansion in the fifth century. For centuries, a large zone of mixed Germanic–Latin use existed right in the middle of later Belgium. The linguist Maurits Gysseling proved this by analysing the double place names – both Dutch/Germanic and French/Romanic – so common in central Belgium. In the areas north and south of the present linguistic border some "pockets" of speakers of the other language also existed (Germanic enclaves in predominantly Romanic-speaking parts, and vice versa). These pockets slowly disappeared, being absorbed by the idiom spoken by the majority group. Historians now estimate that the linguistic frontier more or less stabilized, in its present form, in the course of the tenth or eleventh century. The respective adjacent regions linguistically homogenized at about the same time.

However, three important remarks will nuance this general picture. First, the specific issue of the "Belgian" linguistic border cannot be separated from the broader phenomenon of language contacts and shifts in the vast West European area stretching from the North Sea to the Alps. In other regions as well, for instance in Alsace-Lorraine and in Switzerland, Germanic and Romance tongues came into contact, interacted, and ultimately stabilized along a certain "border." Consequently, the quest for an explanation of the "origins" of the "Belgian" variant of this process will have to take into account the scientific explanations given for these other regions – a work still in progress. Second, language use of the local population was in fact irrelevant when it came to politics and, in a broad sense, public affairs. Both the medieval bishoprics and principalities stretched across the linguistic frontier: almost all had subjects speaking different languages, either ancient Netherlandic tongues (*Middelnederlands*, and its predecessors that later gave birth to contemporary Dutch), or one of the many Romance idioms spoken in the southern part of later Belgium. This linguistic diversity was not relevant to the official administration, since the clerical authorities always used

Latin, and the lay ones switched to the language of the majority of their subjects in the course of the medieval period. Third, after Frankish times, the language border gradually moved into what is now northern France. The Germanic languages slowly lost ground and were replaced by French, partly already in the Late Middle Ages. In the nineteenth century, only a steadily shrinking minority still used "Flemish" privately – but this is another story, of later times and relating to another country, France. This aspect of course falls outside the scope of the present book, but we will return later to yet another language shift which started in the late eighteenth century: the gradual spread of French in the Dutch-speaking regions of Belgium.

The Dynamics of Rural Society

The Frankish world was predominantly rural, and landed wealth was the cornerstone of power. It would however be wrong to assume that this basic pattern was static and uniformly gloomy. In the five centuries from 500 to 1000 CE, important changes occurred in social relationships and in the way products were made and exchanged. Contrasts with the glory years of the Roman Empire are undoubtedly striking and apparently disadvantageous for this period, but it would be reductive to judge Frankish economy and society from this sole perspective. This era must be considered on its own terms, and its dynamic features should not be underestimated.

For a start, there was no sudden and dramatic collapse at the beginning of the fifth century, when the last Roman troops left *Belgica*. Crucial changes were already underway in the two final centuries of Roman rule (see Chapter 1). From the third century, many market-oriented *villae* – large rural production units – disappeared. Towns big and small, respectively *civitates* and *vici*, also shrank and lost a number of their inhabitants. The repeated incursions of Germanic groups certainly wreaked havoc, but other wide-ranging causes, such as the general crisis of governance of the Roman Empire and long-term adverse environmental conditions, aggravated matters. The population probably declined, a trend that persisted well into early Frankish times. Precise demographical figures for Gaul and for the *regnum Francorum*, let alone for the later "Belgian" regions, are unfortunately lacking. Specialists even disagree on rough estimates. They nevertheless note the spread of epidemics and the ravages of malnutrition, as evidenced by bodily remains.

The conjuncture of these elements – the arrival and dominance of new population groups; the crisis of Roman methods of production and exchange; and negative biological and climatic conditions – led to profound changes in both the rural landscape and the agrarian system in early Frankish times. The area under cultivation diminished, and forests grew accordingly. Nature, so to say, took (some) revenge on man-made *(agri)cultura*. However, due to a lack of sources, the evolution of agrarian units and corresponding social relations is less clear. What exactly happened to the Gallo-Roman landlords: did some of them manage to preserve their estates, or parts of them, during and after the Germanic invasions? How extensive were the lands taken over by the Frankish chieftains and other strongmen? And how many small Frankish (or other Germanic) peasants succeeded in settling in the new regions? Were freeholders prevalent or not? All these questions still await answers. According to some scholars – though only a minority – the large Gallo-Roman domain somehow survived in post-Roman times. They assume some measure of continuity between the antique *villa* and later forms of rural exploitation. But most historians think otherwise and stress the discontinuity between both systems.

Indeed, in Merovingian times, modest individual farmsteads seem to have been fairly common, while the "large" domains occupied rather modest areas. These holdings, in the hands of minor aristocrats, were mostly exploited by servile or semi-servile labour. From the seventh century, however, landed wealth was increasingly concentrated. This process continued until the ninth century, when the large "Carolingian estate" reached its full bloom. During this long time span, great aristocratic families, the mayors of the palace, the monarchs and their kin, managed to accumulate landed property in hitherto unseen proportions. This was also the case for the abbeys, which grew both in number and in wealth, and we have seen the importance and meaning of the gifts made to monasteries by aristocrats and monarchs. These large domains, called *villae* (or *fisci*, singular *fiscus*, when the king was the proprietor), were also reorganized. In their classic form, essentially in the regions between the Seine and the Rhine (including later Belgium), the so-called bipartite manors were subdivided into two parts: the reserve (or demesne) on the one hand, and the tenures on the other. Some slaves or ordinary servants worked on the domain on behalf of the landlord, that is, a monarch, an aristocrat, or an abbot; while the *tenures* (also called *mansi*, singular *mansus*) were small plots of land also belonging to the *seigneur*, but provided to farmer families who cultivated these parcels for their own subsistence, but were obliged to work part-time on the *seigneur*'s reserve. The men and women exploiting tenures were either free people (*mansi ingenuiles*), whose land had been taken over, by force or legally, by the landlord; or former slaves set free but still dependent on the *seigneur* and theoretically bound to unlimited labour services for the latter's profit (*mansi serviles*). In some instances, individual peasants voluntarily sought the protection of a mighty landlord to avoid military or fiscal requirements, or just to escape prevailing insecurity. They therefore ceded their modest farmstead to the proprietor of an existing domain.

However, the significance of the large estates should not be misunderstood. These domains were not necessarily unsegmented. On the contrary, aristocratic families, abbeys, and a fortiori, monarchs held vast estates in often-distant places, scattered all over the Frankish realm(s). Moreover, not all rural estates corresponded to the "classic" model described above. In some instances, the occupants of the *mansi* were not compelled to work on the lord's reserve but had to deliver certain amounts of produce. Finally, small freeholders also existed. The classic bipartite manors mostly occupied the richer soils in the central parts of later Belgium, between and along the Scheldt and Meuse and their tributaries, while independent peasants were more present on less fertile soils, for example in the Campine region or in the coastal zones of Flanders. In other words, far from being monolithic, social relations and property patterns in the countryside were rather diversified.

Nor was the Carolingian rural world stagnating and withdrawn into itself. Some decades ago, scholars used to present the Carolingian demesnes as perfect examples of self-sufficient, even autarchic estates. Recent research has thoroughly modified this view. The late Frankish countryside manifested clear signs of dynamism. Contemporary written sources prove the existence of recurrent famines, but these periods of hardship did not prevent the population from growing. Both improving climatic conditions and rising productivity (for example the spread of watermills and heavy ploughs) made this evolution possible. Demographic pressure, in turn, led to the land clearances observed during the ninth century (and mentioned above (p. 56–57) when we evoked the multiplication of the parishes). Once again, man reshaped the rural landscape by pushing back "the wild."

Thanks to these trends, surpluses were far from inexistent. They took many forms and involved many destinations. Independent peasants sold small quantities of daily produce at modest but multiplying local markets. Large estates transported their output to places of monastic, aristocratic, or monarchical residence and consumption, where all sorts of people had to be fed and clothed: monks, nuns, courtiers, artists, privileged and idle family members, not to forget the subaltern personnel and the professional military. The large domains also created other forms of productive activity. Abbeys such as Lobbes and the Ghent monasteries of Saint Peter and Saint Bavo, for instance, controlled vast possessions in different, sometimes distant areas. The small plots of salt marsh in the Flemish plains near the North Sea owned by the latter abbeys are also noteworthy. Sheep were raised there, and part of their wool was transported to Ghent, where it was processed – forming the embryo of the industry that later thrived in this city. But many independent sheep breeders in fact dominated these northern pasturelands: they were actors in their own right in much larger economic networks. Recent archaeological research has revealed the relative wealth of this early Flemish peasant society.

Indeed, trade in the classical sense of the word, even long-distance commerce, was not unknown in the Frankish world. From Merovingian times, exchange links with the Mediterranean world gradually dwindled, but they were never completely severed. On the other hand, commercial relations increased with the Nordic world. Viking, Saxon, and Frisian merchants took the lead in the circulation of commodities such as slaves, furs, amber, etc. On the northern fringes of the Carolingian Empire, two places near modern Belgium developed into prosperous entrepôts (*emporia*), Dorestad (located in The Netherlands) and Quentovic (in France). These places were repeatedly destroyed by the Vikings in the ninth century and finally lost their relevance; however, they revealed that the Carolingian economy was not landlocked, but definitely had an important maritime component. While the Mediterranean was now far away, the North Sea was all the more present. All these commercial exchanges, great and small, furthered the persistence of a monetary economy. Coins continued to be minted both in Merovingian and Carolingian times. Next to many other initiatives, the Carolingians also introduced monetary reforms involving the circulation of new and qualitative silver currency. Mints were located in several places along the Meuse (on later Belgian territory in Huy, Dinant, etc.). However, money still played a very limited role in everyday life – it was mostly used either as a prestige item, or for paying taxes, fines or tribute (to the

Vikings, for instance), or also within the framework of long-distance trade. In Carolingian times there is also evidence of the use of money in a rural setting: services owed by tenants, or the wages of free labourers, could sometimes be paid in money.

This brings us to a final heritage of the Frankish period: the cities. While urban life indubitably receded compared with Roman times, it did not disappear in the Merovingian and Carolingian era. For sure, the aristocrats, including the Frankish monarchs, rarely resided in the former Roman cities; as we saw earlier, they generally preferred their rural manors, regularly switching between them. Charlemagne, however, increasingly stayed in Aachen – now in Germany – near the Belgian border. But the slow rebirth of urbanization was definitely not the result of dynastic or aristocratic rule. This phenomenon was caused by other evolutions. First, the bishops resided in the old Roman *civitas* that was the siege of their diocese. On later Belgian territory, this was the case at Tournai – also an important city in the later Middle Ages. Tongeren, on the other hand, almost completely disappeared and played an insignificant role in later centuries, since the bishop left the city before the beginning of the sixth century. He first moved to Maastricht, a strategic location on the Meuse, now on Dutch territory. From there, the seat of the diocese was transferred to Liège around 800, originally only a rural *villa* where Bishop (and later Saint) Lambert was murdered around 700 by a courtier of the Austrasian grandee Pippin II, and where his relics were kept and revered. This locale would become one of the main cities in the region. In some other places, the existence of abbeys also led to the creation of permanent settlements. Many pilgrims gathered there to worship the relics of saints, hoping for miracles; but producing, buying, and selling things was also common, as the monasteries were important centers of economic activity. In other words: religion caused some old Roman cities to survive (even if in a more modest manner) or generated new human agglomerations.

Trade and defence were other reasons for people to gather and dwell in certain places – sometimes also combined with religious motives. Ghent is a case in point: it was not only the seat of two important abbeys, but also a trading place at the confluence of Scheldt and Lys; moreover, the count's castle was built there. The economic importance of feudal forts, in general, should not be underestimated. Bruges, another key city in later centuries, also emerged in late Frankish times. It started on a very modest scale in the ninth century, but only acquired some importance in the middle of the tenth century. Some places (e.g. Ghent and Antwerp) had very modest Roman origins (probably military camps), and archaeologists now hypothesize some kind of (modest) continuous occupation. Viking attacks during the ninth century caused destruction but did not wipe out these seeds of urban life, and reconstruction seemed to have been rapid. In brief, several cities slowly emerged or re-emerged, mostly along the Scheldt and the Meuse. From the eleventh and twelfth centuries onward, they would not only blossom economically but also play a crucial political role, as the next chapter will make clear.

Conclusion

Half a millennium covered in just a few pages: at first sight, this book seems seriously imbalanced. Or is the Frankish heritage irrelevant? Both conclusions are wrong. First, it is not unjustified to devote just one short chapter to a period representing almost one-quarter of the total time span considered here. Indeed, our view of these five hundred years is impaired by the relative scarcity of sources. Although written and material sources definitely exist, as we stressed earlier, they are obviously far less abundant than in later periods. Consequently, many developments are simply beyond the reach of contemporary observers. Second, the basic patterns of Frankish times are not *specifically* relevant to later Belgium. The political system, the social fabric, the organization of the economy (for instance the Carolingian large demesne), the commercial networks, etc., all unfolded within a much larger geographical setting than the modern nation-state, and this broader framework falls outside the scope of the present book.

Nonetheless, these five centuries have left crucial imprints on the rest of our story. Catholicism is probably the most important and lasting one. The religious foundations built in Frankish times dominated public and private life for centuries to come, since parishes, abbeys, dioceses, churches and chapels, pilgrimages, devotional practices, sacred images, etc., all originated between 500 and 1000. Economically, the Carolingian era laid the foundations of later medieval growth, resulting from the dissolution of the large domains and the development of the urban seeds sown before the eleventh century. The political heritage, on the other hand, is more complex. The dream of many Merovingian and Carolingian monarchs, in particular Charlemagne's imperial ambition, ended in spectacular failure. Although it can be doubted that the latter ever envisaged and pursued long-term unity (he elaborated successive partition schemes between his sons), the basic fact remains that lasting unification of (large parts of) Western Europe under one scepter did not materialize. Instead, deep and enduring divisions henceforth character-ized public governance. The profoundly disruptive feudal system was a Carolingian invention. It took centuries to build modern, centralized nation-states such as France and Germany, while the intermediate regions (among them, later Belgium) would continue to exist as a "leftover," consisting of separate, independent principalities – some important, some more modest – in-between these two powerful entities. The fate of these principalities will be recounted in the next chapter.

3

The Origins of the Medieval Principalities

(Tenth-Fourteenth Centuries)

Introduction

After centuries of state formation, fourteenth-century "Belgium" consisted of three duchies (Brabant, Limburg, and Luxemburg), three counties (Flanders, Hainaut, and Namur), a prince-bishopric (Liège) and some smaller territories. The names and, in some measure, also the territories of the present-day Belgian provinces refer to these historical principalities. The dukes, counts, and prince-bishops were vassals of the French king or the German king-emperor (medieval German kings often bore the title of Holy Roman Emperor; for simplicity's sake we only use the title of (Holy Roman) Emperor in this and the following chapters). The counts of Flanders and Hainaut were vassals of both the French king and the emperor. The power of counts and dukes very much depended on the monarch's (in)ability to check their ambitions (see Map 3.1).

The geographical framework within which these principalities arose is broader than that of present-day Belgium. Located on the periphery of France and Germany, the Low Countries, the area where three important rivers (the Rhine, the Meuse, and the Scheldt) flow into the North Sea, also comprised today's Netherlands, Luxemburg, and parts of Northern France. The monumental *Histoire de Belgique* (7 volumes, 1900–1932) by the famous Belgian historian Henri Pirenne depicts the rise, during the Middle Ages, of a predominantly urban civilization, focused on trade and industry, in the area that would later become Belgium. In his view, this civilization linked Latin (read French) and Germanic (read Dutch) elements in such a way that the creation of an independent Belgian state was the logical consequence of this synthesis.

73

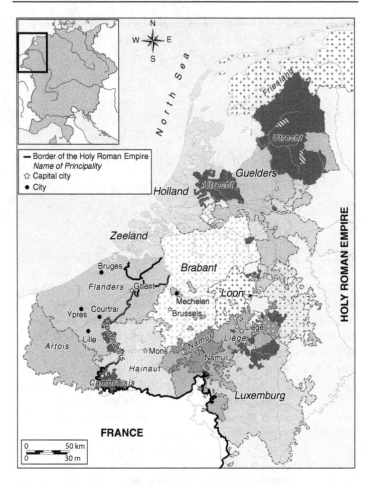

Map 3.1 The medieval principalities, *c.*1350.
Redrawn based on a map sourced from www.wikiwand.com/nl/
Geschiedenis van de opkomst van vorstendommen en steden in de
Lage Landen

Today, almost no historian still accepts Pirenne's thesis about the historical inevitability of the Belgian nation. The emergence of a predominantly urban civilization did play an important role in the political and socio-economic development of the main "Belgian" medieval principalities. But the present and the following chapters will make clear that

74

the birth of modern Belgium was by no means written in the stars. Other outcomes of the state formation process in the Low Countries would certainly have been possible, had it not been for factors such as religion and the influence of powerful neighboring states (see Chapters 4–7). It was mainly the latter that led to the final result: the three small, densely populated and highly developed states we just mentioned, surrounded by three large neighboring countries.

In this chapter we will answer three questions. First: how were the "Belgian" principalities born out of the dissolution of the Carolingian Empire and its aftermath? This complex history involved, first, many rivaling lords, noblemen and clergy and, later, also urban elites in multiple polities. In many ways, the county of Flanders was the frontrunner in this process. We will therefore pay due attention to it. Second: how did the "Belgian" part of the Low countries become one of the most economically advanced regions of medieval Europe north of the Alps? The third question concerns urbanization. How did urban growth and the changing urban social and economic fabric influence the functioning of the body politic, and when did some kind of balance of power emerge between the rulers, the nobility, and the urban elites?

The Carolingian Inheritance Shapes the International and Domestic Setting

The disintegration of the Carolingian empire marked the beginning of a process of political fragmentation. After the death of Louis the Pious (840), his empire was divided among his sons in 843 (the Treaty of Verdun). West Francia contained the greatest part of future France, while East Francia covered large areas of future Germany. Lothar received the imperial crown and Middle Francia, consisting of the Low Countries, eastern and south-eastern France, Switzerland and northern Italy. This division and the centrifugal force of feudalism (see Chapter 2) exposed the structural weaknesses of the Carolingian Empire. In 855, Middle Francia was divided among Lothar's sons. The northern part, consisting of the Low Countries, western Rhineland and the north-eastern part of present-day France, became a new kingdom, Lotharingia. When its ruler died without children in 869, his kingdom was divided between his uncles. But from 880 the king of East Francia or one of his siblings ruled the whole of Lotharingia as a separate kingdom. In 925 Lotharingia eventually became an integral part of East Francia as a duchy. In 959, it was divided in two: Upper Lorraine, which became the duchy of Lorraine in present-day France, and Lower Lorraine, the largest part of the Low Countries, which will be discussed later in this chapter. The other, smaller, part of the Low Countries belonged to West Francia from the first division of the Carolingian Empire. This region, west of the river Scheldt, would develop into the county of Flanders.

Until the last quarter of the twelfth century, the French kings were more or less like the *primus inter pares* among their great vassals, due to the modesty of their personal domains. The handling of three succession crises in Flanders demonstrates the changing balance of power between the crown and the county. In 1071 and 1128 the king had to accept the victory of claimants he had not supported. Moreover, in 1128 the victorious claimant was supported by the Flemish towns. However, in 1246–1256 the French king imposed his decision not only on Flanders but also on Hainaut, mostly a fief of the Holy Roman Empire. From the last quarter of the twelfth century onwards, the French monarchy would make full use of its military and political potential to strongly influence the course of events in the Low Countries.

Political developments took a different turn in East Francia. After the death of the last Carolingian king in 911, the Ottonian dynasty, named after their founder Otto I, ruled until 1024 with great authority. Germany consisted of some large duchies that were based on older Germanic tribes and, as such, may have provided the king with a solid base of power. To offset the decline of the royal domain and thus of royal power, Otto I founded the Imperial Church. Bishops and abbots of sizeable abbeys were appointed by the king and bestowed with secular authority in large parts of the empire. Lorraine hosted some of these spiritual principalities, with the bishoprics of Liège, Utrecht, and Cambrai. Since spiritual functions were not hereditary, the king was able to fill vacancies with his relatives and allies. However, the Imperial Church's function as the mainstay of royal authority could only function as long as the Church submitted to it.

After a long struggle, the Gregorian reform movement effectively ended imperial authority over the Church in the last quarter of the eleventh century. The Worms Concordat (1122) stipulated that bishops and abbots would no longer be appointed by the king. Only after their election by a chapter or their appointment by the Pope did the prince grant them secular power. Moreover, the emperor suffered an extra loss of power because local and regional rulers or even foreign monarchs could influence the appointment of bishops.

Contrary to France, where kingship quickly became hereditary, the great vassals of the crown elected the German king-emperor. The struggle between rival dynasties, between the emperor and the Pope, and the obsession of successive emperors for their power position in Italy resulted in a decline of imperial power in the thirteenth century. After 1250, imperial authority, unlike that of the French kings, was limited to their own, often small, territory.

The Emergence and Expansion of Flanders (Ninth–Twelfth Centuries)

The Carolingian Empire was divided into *pagi* (counties) led by a *comes* (count), representing the emperor. One of these counties was the *pagus Flandrensis* located in the area of present-day Bruges. In the turbulent period after the dissolution of the empire, a certain Baldwin (r. 864–879) became a prominent political figure. He acquired (quasi-) independence in a spectacular way, namely by abducting and subsequently marrying Judith, the eldest daughter of the French king. The latter eventually accepted the marriage and, consequently, the Carolingian descent of Baldwin's offspring conferred great prestige to his lineage.

Successive Flemish counts were very active in expanding their territory. In the ninth and tenth centuries, this expansion mainly went south, even as far as the river Somme in northern France. In the tenth century, expansion eastwards was prevented by the strong position of the Ottonian emperors who had established three "margraves," military commanders, to protect the western marches of the Empire. Baldwin IV (980–1035) conquered Western Zeeland, comprised of territories in the Scheldt estuary. This marked the beginning of expansion in the direction of the empire. During the reign of Baldwin V "the Great" or "of Lille" (r. 1035–1067) Flanders reached a first zenith in terms of administrative organization and expansion. At the end of his life, Baldwin definitively conquered the northern part of the margrave Ename of the Holy Roman Empire. As a result, he also became the emperor's vassal: Germanic "Imperial Flanders" was born, next to French "Crown Flanders." Baldwin also served for six years as regent of France.

Successive counts organized both the general and judicial administration from the late tenth century. The effective power of the count was greater in the northern "Belgian" part of the county, where he owned many private domains. In the southern part, the power of local nobility was still considerable. At the end of the tenth century, three viscounties (Ghent, Bruges, and Tournai-Kortrijk) were founded in the north. The viscount, a local nobleman, was the count's representative. In the viscounty of Bruges, for example, the administration of justice was performed by twelve aldermen appointed by the count, under the direction of the viscount.

Around 1050, the county enjoyed institutions comparable to a royal government. In the other principalities of the Low Countries this would only become the case at the end of the twelfth or in the thirteenth century. There was a *Curia*, a council of nobles and prelates, and a chancellor was in charge of the administration. In order to keep the often violently competing nobles in line, the Church, with the support of the count, tried to enforce the so-called *Pax Dei* (Peace of God). As the count's authority grew – around 1070 there were already twelve viscounties – the *Pax Dei* developed more and more into a *Pax Comitis*, law and order imposed by the count. The prestigious marriages of Baldwin V's children – his daughter Mathilde married William the Conqueror – reflected his status and were of great importance for later political and territorial developments.

After the short reign of Baldwin VI, who also ruled Hainaut through marriage, a conflict arose about his succession. His brother seized power and ousted the rightful heir. He swiftly succeeded in getting his position recognized by the king and the emperor, thereby demonstrating his power. In 1128 another major political crisis shook Flanders. Two claimants for the succession of the deceased count took up arms. Thierry (Dutch, Diederik) of Alsace who opposed the French king's candidate eventually prevailed, thanks to the support of both a part of the Flemish nobility and an important new player, the Flemish towns (see p. 88–91). During his reign (1128–1168) and that of his son Philip (1168–1191), the county of Flanders reached a second zenith and gained international renown. Thierry quickly succeeded in establishing his authority. After a few years, the king accepted his coup and Thierry was able to pay homage. Furthermore, the count was on good terms with the emperor and successfully navigated between the French and English rivals – thus serving the interests of the Flemish economy (see p. 85–87).

Philip of Alsace focused on expansion in north-western Europe. First, he settled his problems with Hainaut through the marriage of his sister to the count. Through his own marriage, Philip ruled an area stretching from Zeeland to the border of Île de France, the royal domain! In terms of power and wealth, he was almost equal to the English or French king. Though prestigious, this prominent position also provoked opposition from an unexpected side. After his appointment as counsel to the future Philip II August, he immediately arranged a marriage of the young king to his cousin and pledged an important part of his own county as a dowry – namely the region that was to become the county of Artois.

Philip's hopes did not materialize, on the contrary. The king was not grateful. He became an extraordinarily successful monarch, the first in a series of French rulers who, in the thirteenth to fifteenth centuries, expanded the royal domain and subjected vassals to the crown. The county of Flanders would also suffer the consequences. The count remained a powerful vassal, but in the final years of his reign he focused more on the administrative organization of the county. As Philip had no offspring, the count of Hainaut succeeded him, thereby restoring the union between the two counties that had been broken in 1071.

The Disintegration of Lorraine (Tenth–Twelfth Centuries)

Although Lotharingia became part of East Francia after 925, the kings of West Francia did not give up their claims to the area until the extinction of the Carolingian dynasty (987). This made sense, since Lotharingia, with its palaces, rich domains, and monasteries, was the core area of the Carolingian Empire (see Chapter 2). Many powerful nobles from the area were prepared to respond favorably to the advances of West Francia because they preferred the relationship between a weak king and mighty vassals that existed there. Moreover, from the end of the tenth century, the counts of Flanders also aspired to an eastward expansion. These factors made it difficult for the German king-emperors to maintain their authority in linguistically and ethnically divided Lotharingia.

In 959 the duchy was divided and renamed Lorraine. Upper Lorraine included (approximately) present-day Lorraine, Champagne-Ardennes in France, Luxemburg, and the German *Möselregion*. Lower Lorraine consisted of the rest of the Low Countries, territories east and north of the river Scheldt and the lower Rhineland.

From the end of the eleventh century onwards, things went downhill quickly for Lower Lorraine as a polity. The ducal title gave status to its bearer, but increasingly less so as several counts acted more and more as rulers of independent principalities. In 1087, the emperor gave the ducal title to Godfrey of Bouillon (*c.*1160–1100). Godfrey was one of the leaders of the first Crusade (1096–1099). After the conquest of Jerusalem (1099) his fellow crusaders made him king. During the nine-teenth century, romantic nationalist historians in young Belgium canon-ized him as a "Belgian" hero, although he was probably born in French Boulogne and his "government" of Lower Lorraine was not much to speak of.

In 1101–1139 the ducal title was granted no less than four times to members of two competing noble lineages, the counts of Limburg and Leuven. This clearly shows that none of the protagonists was able to gain control over the whole area. In 1190, one of Lower Lorraine's rulers changed the title in duke of Brabant and Lothier. Factually, Lower Lorraine ceased to exist as a polity. However, the possession of the ducal title remained attractive because it could legitimize its owner's territorial expansion in the Low Countries. Godfrey II of Leuven eventually became duke. Brabant was one of several major principalities that came into being in the "Belgian" part of Lower Lorraine, as we will see in the next paragraph.

Formation and Territorial Expansion of the Lotharingian Principalities (Tenth–Thirteenth Centuries)

The prince-bishopric of Liège was the first important Lotharingian principality. In 980, the emperor appointed the bishop as *comes*. This decision established the Imperial Church in the Holy Roman Empire. From the end of the tenth century onwards, (arch)bishops and abbots would acquire temporal power throughout the Empire through dona-tion, purchase, and political pressure.

A distinction must be made between the diocese of Liège and the prince-bishopric. The diocese was considerably larger and covered a large part of south-east Belgium and the south of today's Netherlands. The prince-bishopric, the territory where the bishop directly exercised his secular power, was a kind of patchwork of small and larger territories, acquired mainly during the eleventh century. In 985, the empress-dowager donated the huge county of Huy to bishop Notger. From 987, the latter settled permanently in Liège and transformed the city into a religious and political center. Rich abbeys such as Saint-Hubert, Lobbes and Gembloux also became possessions of the prince-bishop.

In 1180 the county of Loon, consisting of the greatest part of the present-day province of Limburg, became a fief of the prince-bishop. In 1361 Loon became an integral part of the prince-bishopric. Mechelen, a city far beyond the territory of Liège, as well as its surrounding villages, was formally under the authority of the prince-bishop, although he had to share power with a mighty Brabant family. By the thirteenth century, the prince-bishopric had developed into a polity with numerous enclaves and exclaves that stretched for about 160 km along the banks of the Meuse and Sambre rivers, from the present-day French border in the south to the north of present-day Belgian Limburg.

During the period of the Imperial Church, successive prince-bishops faithfully supported imperial authority. In 1081 the prince-bishop succeeded in imposing a *Paix de Dieu* (God's Peace) in the entire diocese with the help of neighboring counts. This *Paix de Dieu*, which was primarily intended to restrain noble violence, was maintained by synods of ecclesiastical and secular authorities under the leadership of the prince-bishop, the so-called *Tribunal de la Paix*. After the Worms Concordat (1122) the political position of the prince-bishop changed. From then on, he was to be nominated by the sixty canons of the chapter of the Liège Saint-Lambert Cathedral and appointed by the Pope. In this appointment process, the private interests of the canons, their "friends" and neighboring powers played an increasing role. From the thirteenth century onwards, the political influence of the prince-bishops ceased in the part of the diocese that did not belong to the prince-bishopric. Internally, prince-bishops were similarly increasingly confronted with the changing balance of power between nobility, the Saint-Lambert chapter and the towns (see p. 96–97).

The duchy of Brabant originated in the small county of Leuven. During the eleventh century, its successive counts acquired possessions in the area between the Scheldt and Meuse rivers, including the county of Brussels (1005–1012), the region around Tienen (1013, 1016) and Nivelles (*c.*1000). In 1085, the emperor elevated the count of Leuven (r. 1079–1095) to the rank of landgrave of Brabant, originally the region between the rivers Dender and Senne. Two decades later, his son became duke of Lower Lorraine and margrave of Antwerp (1106) but there was no longer any real exercise of authority throughout Lower Lorraine, as was shown above (p. 80). Around 1150, the duke acquired guardianship over all abbeys located in the area under his direct authority.

The most important expansion of Brabant took place between the end of the twelfth and thirteenth centuries in a northern and eastern direction. Territorial expansion in a western or southern direction, that is, at the expense of the powerful county of Flanders, was not an option. In the north, the scattered possessions were adjacent to territory owned by the count of Holland and the bishop of Utrecht. The territory was rounded off in the early thirteenth century, with the upper reaches of the Meuse and Rhine rivers as the northern boundary.

The eastward expansion led to a collision with the prince-bishopric of Liège. The duke conquered the county of Duras and from 1204 the prince-bishop had to share control of the strategically important city of Maastricht with the duke. In 1213, the duke suffered an important defeat against the prince-bishop and his allies at Steppes, after which relations with Liège stabilized for over a century and the eastern border of the duchy became permanent. Henry I was the first to be called duke of Brabant.

Limburg was a rather small polity consisting of scattered territories in the north-east of the present-day Belgian province of Liège and the southern part of the Dutch province of Limburg. John I of Brabant (r. 1268–1294) became the most important claimant for the succession of the childless duchess. In 1288 he won a great victory over his opponents. In Belgian historiography the battle of Wörringen, a village and castle of the left bank of the Rhine, north of Cologne was considered a milestone. Brabant succeeded in expanding its territory east of the Meuse by conquering Limburg. This made Brabant-Limburg, next to Flanders, a powerful "Belgian" polity in the making.

According to the same historiographical tradition (mainly expressed by Pirenne), Brabant, through its extension, loosened its feudal ties with the Holy Roman Empire and moved towards "Belgian" civilization and state building. According to others, the Brabant *Drang nach Osten* (push eastward) was mainly inspired by economic motives, namely controlling the trade route between Bruges and Cologne, which was also the route between England and the Rhineland. Arguments exist in defense of both visions. Protection and control of the trade route certainly played a role in the dukes' foreign policy. However, acquiring complete control of the mentioned route was an unlikely goal, as it was unfeasible. Nor was there any question of a diminished involvement of the dukes of Brabant in the affairs of the Holy Roman Empire. On the contrary, it seems that the successive dukes of Brabant took their position as a member of the *Reichsfürstenstand* very seriously. Through the guardianship of Aachen, the city of Charlemagne, and their numerous vassals in the Rhineland, they pursued status and prestige in the *Reich* even if this went against the interests of their subjects, as we shall see.

Demographic Growth and Economic Development

According to reliable estimates, Europe's population doubled between the tenth and thirteenth centuries. In the short term, crop failures, wars, and other calamities would temporarily reverse the positive trend. The most important economic challenge was the production of food for the growing population. The obvious solution was to cultivate more land. This process could continue until the area suitable for agriculture had been fully utilized. Once this point was reached, population growth theoretically came to an automatic halt due to either excess mortality caused by food shortage or emigration.

Much of the food supply depended on the social and economic dynamics of a region. Applying more efficient farming methods and breaking institutional relations that hindered change could raise agricultural productivity. The part of agricultural production that was skimmed off by secular and spiritual rulers – princes, aristocracy, Church, and landowners in general – was largely determined by institutional relationships. Due to the lack of a proper road network and the high cost of land transport, imports were mainly limited to areas accessible by sea or waterways. Taking these considerations into account, the challenges the growing population of the Low Countries faced in acquiring their livelihood were obviously impressive.

From a European perspective, the Low Countries, especially their "Belgian" part, developed into one of the most economically dynamic regions of the continent during the period 1000–1300. The classic large, self-sufficient Carolingian domain (see Chapter 2) disappeared under the pressure of population growth. Much of the land was cultivated through deforestation and reclamation. The average surface area of agricultural holdings fell to between 2 or 3 ha, that is, just enough to provide for the maintenance of a household. However, more than two-thirds of the total agricultural area consisted of farms with a surface of 10–20 ha that also produced for the market. This development, which occurred mainly in the county of Flanders, resulted in the creation of a numerous peasantry consisting of small farms that did not yield enough to maintain a household. These peasants contributed to their livelihood by working as laborers for the big farmers, the construction of dikes, peat digging, and especially the textile manufacturing industry (see p. 86–87).

The reclamation of land was achieved in two ways: from small cores in wooded areas, village communities gradually emerged in a spontaneous, quasi-organic way. This was the case, for instance, in the region between the rivers Leie, Scheldt, and Dender in Flanders and in the Campine region of Brabant in the eleventh and twelfth centuries. On the other hand, rulers such as the count of Flanders, noblemen, and abbeys played an important role in land reclamation when costly investments had to be made, for example through the construction of dikes and the reclamation of wetlands. With the exception of the surroundings of Bruges, the northernmost part of the county of Flanders was largely uninhabited in the eleventh century. It was only cultivated after 1200, mainly on the initiative of the count and large abbeys. From the thirteenth century onwards, rich city dwellers also increasingly invested in land ownership.

European agricultural productivity was low: two or three grains for every sowing seed of wheat, barley, or rye. The Low Countries, or at least parts of them, were undoubtedly one of the exceptions. In the Lille region, for example, a yield ratio of 22:1 was achieved at the end of thirteenth century. However, even within "Belgium" considerable productivity differences existed between regions. Apparently, the average production of staple foods (e.g. wheat and rye) per unit area doubled in the eleventh to thirteenth century.

The extent to which specific technical and organizational improvements contributed to the increase in production and productivity remains uncertain. Perhaps it was mainly due to the human factor, that is, the hard labor of farmers and farm workers, spurred on by growing demand and rising prices. However, the balance between supply and demand for the staple food, grain, was structurally unstable. Failed harvests, either due to climate or war, regularly led to famine and death. In spite of all these uncertainties, we can still conclude that between *c.*1000 and 1300 there was a considerable increase in population, especially in Flanders, and that this increased population was fed.

Two factors confirm the relative success of agriculture. First, arable farming did not focus exclusively on the production of basic food.

Production was diversified, with dye plants such as madder, weld and turnips for the cattle; from the end of thirteenth century onwards, flax and hops were increasingly grown. Second, population distribution had changed considerably. At the end of the tenth century, there were hardly any significant cities in the Low Countries and agriculture was mainly self-sufficient. Between 1000 and 1300 especially the county of Flanders developed into one of the most urbanized regions in Europe. As such, agriculture could meet the needs of a relatively large market and/or possible shortages could be remedied through imports.

Until the second half of the eighteenth century, the vast majority of Europe's population lived in the countryside and in countless small towns, often with only a few hundred inhabitants. In 1300, only one European in seven (14 percent) lived a city with more than 2,000 inhabitants. This ratio remained more or less stable until 1800 (17.5 percent). One of the peculiarities of the Low Countries, especially the "Belgian" part, was the creation of relatively numerous big cities in a relatively small area (between 1000 and 1300). The Low Countries were the most urbanized part of Europe: 18.5 percent of the population lived in big cities. In England and Wales this percentage was 3.1 percent and would not reach the level of the Low Countries until the eighteenth century.

After the end of the Viking invasions in the tenth century, cities first developed in the county of Flanders, especially along the rivers Scheldt and Lys and in the prince-bishopric of Liège along the Meuse. The intermediate area, which would become known as Brabant, followed from the end of eleventh century. Pirenne explained the creation and growth of these cities through the recovery of international trade and the essential role of merchants. International trade certainly played a role, but more significantly so at a later stage (in the twelfth century). As told in Chapter 2, cities arose from rural settlements in the vicinity of rich abbeys (Maastricht, Ghent, Arras) and bishop's seats or chapters (Tournai, Liège; see Figure 3.1). Similarly, the construction of castles as protection against the Vikings (ninth–tenth century), simultaneously serving as the residences of wealthy aristocrats and as seats of royal authority (e.g. of the Flemish count) was also at the basis of urban development. Thus, there was a market for the exchange of goods and services. During the eleventh–twelfth century these developments resulted in the emergence of a separate, new urban society with its own institutions and playing an increasing political, social, and cultural role.

Figure 3.1 The Cathedral Notre Dame of Tournai, twelfth-thirteenth century, is one of Belgium's biggest churches, with five Romanesque towers (83 m) and a Gothic choir (Unesco World Heritage, 2000)

The economic significance of cities was mainly due to the development of industry, especially textiles. In the eleventh century, in the maritime part of Flanders, sheep's wool was processed into fabrics intended exclusively for the local market. In the twelfth century, a technical improvement of the loom increased both the productivity of the industry and the quality of its product. Because of its high quality, Flemish cloth became an attractive export product. Cloth from Ypres is mentioned in Russian Novgorod around 1130–1136. Population growth in Flemish towns was closely linked to expansion of the woolen cloth industry. In the twelfth century, there were seven important cloth-producing towns in Flanders: Ghent, Bruges and Ypres in the Dutch-speaking part, and Arras, Douai, Lille, and Saint-Omer in the Romance part of the county (these cities are now in France).

As a result of the reclamation and desalinization of the polders, Flemish sheep farming declined. This resulted in a shortage of wool and especially high-quality wool. After 1200, the Flemish cloth industry mainly processed English wool. As we shall see, this economic link between Flanders and England became very important to the political relations within the county and between the county and the French king.

The Flemish cloth industry proved a powerful stimulus for the development of international trade in the Low Countries. In the twelfth century, merchants from Ghent, for instance, specialized in export to Cologne, Hamburg, and Lübeck in Germany. However, from the thirteenth century onwards, increasing competition and institutional restrictions weakened the position of Flemish merchants abroad. On the other hand, the role of foreign merchants in Flanders became increasingly important. An additional factor was the granting of charters to various cities by the count of Flanders. These charters formed the basis of a cycle of fairs that made it attractive for foreign merchants to come and do business there, especially as the count offered them legal protection. The most important of these fairs was established in Bruges in 1200.

Bruges became the major trading center of the Low Countries and held this position until the end of the fifteenth century. Merchants from Germany, England, Scotland, Gascony, and Galicia (Spain) brought wool, wine, salt, fish, and timber. During the last quarter of the thirteenth century, merchants from Venice and Genoa also sent galleys with silk, dyes, and spices to Bruges. The Italians were very active in banking and financial services. Some foreign merchants settled in Bruges permanently; if not, they visited the city regularly. According to a reliable estimate, there were about 400 foreign merchants permanently established in Bruges by the middle of the fifteenth century. Concerning its position, Bruges had but two worthy competitors: the fairs of Antwerp and Berg-op-Zoom in Brabant. These fairs originated at the beginning of the fourteenth century but were hampered in their ascent by the annexation of Antwerp (1356) by the count of Flanders, who protected the interests of Bruges (see p. 103).

The textile industry also played an important role in other parts of the southern Low Countries. Leuven, Brussels, and Mechelen were important production centers in Brabant. Brussels "scarlet," that is, very luxurious red dyed cloth, was exported all over Europe in the fourteenth century. The valley of the river Meuse was rich in coal, iron, lead, zinc, and stone quarries. The region was famous for its brass production in Dinant, Namur, Huy, and Liège in the twelfth century. Copper was imported from Cologne and from the mines in the Harz region in Germany, while tin was probably imported from England. Metal shrines, crucifixes, and small reliquaries were exported all over Europe. In the thirteenth century, brass production was concentrated in Dinant. The town was famous for its *dinanderie* cauldrons, brass candlesticks, and tableware. From the thirteenth century onwards, Liège, Huy, and Maastricht exported cloth to Central Europe. Merchants from the Meuse valley region traded at the fairs of Cologne and in the Rhineland from the twelfth century.

Urban Society and Politics

From the twelfth century, cities began to play an important role in politics. One case in point is the outcome of the political crisis in Flanders (1127–1128). Thierry of Alsace, the pretender who had the support of the cities, won the battle for the succession of the murdered childless count Charles the Good (see p. 78). In the previous period, from c.1000, cities had created institutions that made it possible for certain groups of inhabitants to consult together with the authorities (the bishop or the viscount). Around 1100, so-called sworn communes were founded in some cities (Cambrai, 1077; Valenciennes, 1114; Tournai, 1147). Their members committed themselves by taking an oath to maintain peace and to resolve disputes peacefully.

Aldermen appointed by the count or viscount administered justice. At some point during the eleventh and twelfth century, rulers appointed purely urban aldermen. They were chosen from the families who were, in fact, at the basis of the urban patriciate. In larger cities, merchants started to organize themselves into merchant guilds. A guild promoted mutual solidarity and the economic interests of its members. Guild members offered each other assistance in case of problems with foreign commercial transactions. In the same vein, "Hanses," alliances of merchants' guilds from several cities, were formed to defend common interests abroad. A well-known example is the Flemish Hanse of London, which was active in the thirteenth century.

During the thirteenth century, the merchant guilds, the eligible citizens from whom the aldermen were appointed, and the "sworn commune" merged into one patriciate. In the previous century religious brotherhoods of skilled artisans had come into existence in several cities. Conceptually based on the merchant guilds, they were intended to promote mutual sociability. During the thirteenth century, these artisan brotherhoods developed into formal corporations whose objectives became increasingly economic and political, in addition to their social objectives.

Artisan corporations monitored the quality of the vocational training of future artisans and thus the quality of products delivered and services provided. The regulations of the corporations were laid down by the town council, which was originally composed exclusively of members of the patriciate. In the thirteenth century, economic development led to the emergence of a new economic elite of wealthy entrepreneurs who came from the corporations and therefore, as latecomers, did not belong to the patriciate. In addition to the traditional rivalry between members and families of the patriciate, the pressure from the corporations to have a say in urban government issues also increased political tensions. At the level of a principality, this meant that the relationship between the ruler and a city was no longer limited to prince and patriciate.

City-dwellers distinguished themselves from the rural population by their free status and citizenship. Citizenship was acquired at birth, through marriage, or by purchase. This meant that people were members of the urban community ("commune") and enjoyed certain privileges. "Outsiders" could buy urban citizenship and thus enjoy the rights and benefits attached to it. From the thirteenth century, membership of the artisan corporations was exclusively reserved for burghers. Population growth in cities was largely due to immigration from rural areas. Therefore, first-generation immigrants were condemned to the status of denizen, excluded from membership of an artisan corporation and thereby confined to unskilled and poorly paid labor.

All these provisions and other urban freedoms and obligations were laid down in the urban charter granted by the ruler. In most cases, an urban charter confirmed the existing administrative practice. It goes without saying that, in exchange for the granting of the charter, a city also had to make formal and informal commitments to its ruler. Huy was the first city north of the Alps to obtain such a charter (in 1066). The independent legal status of cities was also reflected through the walls and gates that distinguished them from the countryside.

Within city walls, some buildings and territories were not under the authority of the urban magistrate, such as ecclesiastical immunities or the viscount's castle. On the other hand, urban magistrates often functioned as courts of appeal for the verdicts of rural aldermen. Furthermore, cities obtained privileges from the ruler to regulate or tax certain economic activities in a radius around the city.

Urban identity was further expressed in squares and buildings such as the city hall, the cloth hall and, very typical for the southern Low Countries, the belfry. Belfries were built in the major and even smaller cities of present-day Belgium and northern France. The belfry was at the

Figure 3.2 The Bruges belfry. In some parts of the former Low
Countries, especially in present-day Belgium and northern France,
belfries represented municipal power and prosperity (Unesco World
Heritage, 1999 and 2005)

same time a watchtower (in case of fire or an observation post against the
enemy), a clock tower, with its height and splendor, the symbol of urban
liberty. The early fourteenth century belfry of Ghent, for instance, with
its famous bell, "Roland," measures 91 meters; the famous Bruges
belfrey 83 meters (see Figure 3.2).

Urban populations grew considerably. Around 1300, the Flemish
towns of Douai, Saint-Omer, Ypres, and Lille each counted about
30,000 inhabitants. Bruges and Ghent even had about 60,000. This
population growth meant that an increasing number of provisions had
to be made in public spaces. In addition to urban government and
administration, these spacious facilities cost a lot of money that had to

be raised through taxes, usually excise duties on the basic necessities such as bread, meat, and ale. Consequently, the financial burden mainly fell on the average citizen. As fiscal policy was determined by patrician city councils with little control over expenditure, dissatisfaction and distrust among taxpayers grew.

The large supply of laborers created pressure on wage formation, while food prices rose as a result of increasing taxes and demand. Moreover, competition between woolen cloth production centers increased and, especially in Flanders, as a result of their dependence on English wool, they became victims of international conflicts (see the following paragraphs). The pressure on living standards for artisans caused unrest, first in Flanders and later also in Brabant and Liège. From *c.*1270 onwards, textile worker strikes took place in Flemish cities and violent conflicts between members of the patriciate and artisans occurred. In the county of Flanders, these urban social, economic, and political contrasts were influenced by the changed balance of power between the county and the French king, which in turn also changed internal relations within Flemish cities.

Submission, Revolt and Defeat: Flanders and France (1194–1305)

After the reunification of Flanders and Hainaut (in 1191), the position of the Baldwin family lineage as powerful vassals of the French crown was seemingly restored. In 1202, count Baldwin IX (r. 1194–1206) took part in the Fourth Crusade, but he got involved in the political rivalries in the Byzantine Empire. Baldwin became emperor of the Latin empire of Constantinople (1204) but soon died in captivity after losing a battle. The fact that the count's offspring consisted of two very young daughters created a political vacuum. The French king took full advantage of this opportunity. Johanna (1194/1200–1244) was married to a Portuguese prince who took the fatal decision to side against the king in an international conflict opposing Philip II August, the English king and the emperor. The former's great military victory at Bouvines (in 1214) established French supremacy in Western Europe for more than a century.

Flanders was in fact subjected to the French crown. The count, Johanna's husband taken prisoner at Bouvines, was liberated after a long captivity and the payment of a large ransom. He thereafter acted as a loyal vassal of the French crown. Margaret "of Constantinople" (r. 1244–1278), who succeeded her sister in 1244, was married twice and had male offspring from both marriages. At her accession a dispute immediately arose about her future succession. Both families, the Avesnes and the Dampierre, sought external support, providing potential supporters with every opportunity to claim compensation. As arbitrator, the French king was able to take advantage of the situation. In 1246, he assigned Hainaut to the Avesnes and Flanders to the Dampierre. The King confirmed his arbitration a decade later (*Dit de Péronnes*, 1256). Moreover, in 1299 the Avesnes inherited Holland and Zeeland, thereby creating a personal union between these three counties that would last until 1430. The winner of the arbitration was undoubtedly the French crown. The combined power of Flanders-Hainaut, a potential threat to France, was divided. Moreover, the continuing rivalry between the Dampierre and the Avesnes offered the opportunity to play them off against each other. In assigning Hainaut – formally a fief of the Holy Roman Empire – to the Avesnes, the king confirmed French supremacy in the Low Countries.

Growing economic and social tensions began to affect domestic politics. In 1270 a financial conflict between England and Flanders had huge economic consequences. Without worrying about Flemish dependency on English wool, English goods and ships were confiscated, which led to reprisals and the levying of increased tariffs on the export of English wool. This measure led to price increases, unemployment, and loss of competition for the Flemish cloth industry. This resulted in first-time strikes in cities such as Ypres, Douai, and Bruges. The conflict ended in 1275, but it caused great economic damage and exacerbated social and political divisions.

French involvement in the internal affairs of the county increased in the last decades of the thirteenth century, when Philip IV the Fair ascended the throne. Like Philip II August, he sought to maximize the power of the crown over its vassals. In addition to military means, the king also used the judiciary to further this cause. Philip's main weapon for interfering in the internal affairs of the county was the Parliament of Paris, the supreme court of the kingdom.

Count Guy de Dampierre (r. 1278–1305) tried to increase his authority over the powerful Flemish towns by controlling urban finances more tightly. At first, this was seemingly a response to earlier criticism of the artisan corporations concerning the urban fiscal policy of the ruling patriciate. However, the count had no intention of undermining the power of the patriciate as such. He simply sought to consolidate his power over the city councils by undermining dominant clans within the patriciate. After disturbances in 1280–1281, a number of aldermen in Bruges and Ypres were replaced. Yet at the same time, the count also imposed heavy fines on artisan rioters.

Ghent proved most troublesome to the count. That city was governed by a corporation of thirty-nine aldermen who were recruited from a limited number of families in the patriciate. In 1288, when the count imposed new financial accountability regulations on the aldermen, they appealed to the king. Philip sent a French official, who amended the regulations. In the following years the king constantly maneuvered to undermine the authority of the count, at one point supporting the patriciate and at others making promises to the artisan corporations. He had the Parliament of Paris intervene in conflicts between the count and some Flemish cities. In 1294, Guy was even imprisoned for a time after the Parliament had ruled against him. The count was also forced to observe a French trade embargo against England, which was obviously very detrimental to the cloth industry. By the end of 1296, he finally decided to shift his loyalties to the English camp.

The count's drastic step caused great troubles. Most of the nobles remained loyal to the king, but the patrician elite in big cities was divided. The count sought support from urban corporations. In Ghent, the royal faction was removed from the city council. However, the count's position weakened rapidly. The royal army quietly launched an offensive. Since peace had been established in 1298, the English were unwilling to anger the French and, as such, failed to provide military assistance to the count. Moreover, from 1299 Philip could count on the support of the count of Hainaut whose lands surrounded Flanders. In 1299, Flanders was occupied by the French and, in effect, added to the royal domain. The count and his elder sons were taken to a French prison. A French governor was appointed. In the cities the patrician supporters of the king prevailed and organized harsh repression against the supporters of the count. Two parties were formed: the supporters of the count, *Klauwaarts*, and the supporters of the king, *Leliaards*. The first term referred to *klauw*, after the claws of the lion in the colors of the county, while the second (from *lelie*, or lily in English) alluded to the *lis de France* in the French royal colors.

The French ruled Flanders for just two years. The French governor insufficiently controlled the vengeful policy of the *Leliaards*. Fiscal policy was somewhat arbitrary. The king granted Ghent exemption from a hated tax, while Bruges simply had to continue to pay. This led to great unrest in the latter city. Riots broke out regularly, often led by two artisans: Pieter de Coninck (1250/60–1332/33), a master weaver, and Jan Breydel (dates unknown), a master butcher. In the nineteenth century, both would acquire iconic status as fighters against foreign oppression and for the Flemish emancipation (see chapters 8 and 9). In May 1302, a French army arrived in Bruges to restore order. Fearing repression, the insurgents decided to strike one night. During the famous "Bruges Matins," a few hundred French soldiers were killed and the governor barely escaped. The French military retired and the *Klauwaarts*, supported by the artisan corporations, took power.

Additionally, in other cities, but not in Ghent, regime change took place and corporations were given a role in the urban council. The count's younger sons led the anti-French resistance. On July 11, 1302, the Flemish army, consisting of a few hundred knights and about 8,000 to 10,000 men from the urban militias (so for the most part infantrymen), faced the royal army (consisting of more than 2,000 heavily armed cavalry and some 5,000 infantry) at Kortrijk. The Flemish rebel army made good use of the marshy terrain, which was unsuited for a massive cavalry charge. The battle ended in a disaster for the French. Hundreds of knights and lords were mercilessly killed, among them the commander-in-chief, the king's cousin. This was highly unusual. Normally, the knights of the losing party were taken prisoner and later, after payment of a ransom, released. The "Battle of the Golden Spurs" – some 500 spurs belonging fallen French knights were collected after the battle and were kept and exposed in a local church as a reminder – was a turning point in medieval warfare. For the first time, an army consisting mainly of infantrymen convincingly defeated an army of knights. More important, however, for our subject are the political consequences.

The Flemish insurgents' victory against the royal army had a tremendous impact. In Flemish cities where the *Klauwaarts* prevailed, power changed hands. Everywhere, artisan corporations were involved in the composition of city councils. But the Battle of the Golden Spurs also triggered revolutionary movements outside Flanders. In Brabant, the prince-bishopric of Liège and Utrecht (in the present-day Netherlands), corporations demanded a share of the power. More importantly, in the most economically developed and urbanized principalities, a new view increasingly gained support: a ruler could only count on the obedience of his subjects if he or she took their interests, rights, and freedoms into account.

Contrary to the romantic story of the Flemish victory in the Battle of the Golden Spurs, as it was told in Hendrik Conscience's iconic historical novel, *De Leeuw van Vlaenderen* (1838) ("The Lion of Flanders") (see Chapter 8), the war ended in bitter defeat for both the count and the county. The treaty concluded in 1305 at Athis-sur-Orge stipulated that the county had to pay a large, but monetarily unclearly defined, fine to the king. It also provided that the *Leliaards* had to be compensated for any damages they suffered and that 3,000 inhabitants of Bruges had to go on pilgrimage as penance for the "Bruges Matins." The king took Walloon Flanders, with the cities of Lille, Douai, and Orchies, as collateral. Moreover, the citizens of the rebellious cities had to promise under oath to observe the conditions of the peace and those who perjured were threatened with papal excommunication. Count Robert III de Béthune (r. 1305–1322) had to implement the provisions of this humiliating peace treaty when social and political tension had increased, not only in Flanders but also in other urbanized parts of the southern Low Countries.

Toward a New Balance of Power in an Age of Crisis and Pandemic (Fourteenth Century)

During the fourteenth century, contours of new political relations between rulers and subjects emerged in the most important principalities and cities. Artisan corporations succeeded in enforcing their participation in urban government and administration. These political and social changes resulted from often-changing coalitions between political players and even from civil war. Rulers and patricians usually considered their concessions as temporary and they often tried to recapture lost ground. Consequently, any compromise was fragile, but eventually an internal balance of power was achieved at the urban level. This balance, *mutatis mutandis*, lasted until political revolutions at the end of eighteenth century created an entirely new political system (see Chapter 7). The most important political and social change at the principality level was the widely accepted notion that the legitimacy of rulers was largely determined by respecting agreements with their subjects and respecting their rights and freedoms. In order to gain insight into these political and social developments, we focus on three principalities: Flanders, Brabant, and Liège.

In the prince-bishopric of Liège there were four important political players: the prince-bishop, the Chapter of Saint-Lambert, the nobility, and the towns, especially Liège, the only large city of the principality. The decline of the Imperial Church had weakened the position of the prince-bishops, especially because they were often foreigners. The Chapter of Saint-Lambert elected the prince-bishop but this did not mean that the interests of the ruler and the chapter converged. It was mainly the city of Liège that stressed the urge for political change. During the second half of the thirteenth century, the city council was dominated by the patriciate and the merchant guild. In the years 1253–1255, a member of the patriciate attempted to include the artisan corporations in the urban council to enhance his personal power. This effort failed due to the united resistance of the prince, the chapter, and the patriciate.

In particular, the modalities of taxation caused recurrent political tensions. The spring of 1303 was a confusing period: the bishop's seat was vacant and the patrician aldermen of Liège introduced a new tax, notwithstanding the opposition of the Chapter of Saint-Lambert. With the support of the latter, artisan corporations gained access to the city council for the first time. However, in the following years, the patriciate continued to oppose this division of power. In 1312 this resistance even resulted in an attempt to break the power of the corporations by force. The patriciate's attempted coup ended in a massacre, the *Mal Saint-Martin* (August 4, 1312). The populace's violent reaction compelled the patricians to withdraw into Saint-Martin Church, which was then set ablaze. The civil war ended in 1316 with the Peace of Fexhe. This agreement covered the entire prince-bishopric and was approved by the bishop, the chapter, the patriciate, the city of Liège, and the other cities involved.

The Peace of Fexhe contained two important provisions: first, all were equal before the law and second, the prince had to abide by the law as well. Furthermore, the *Sens du Pays* was established. It was composed of representatives of the clergy (in effect the Chapter of Saint-Lambert), the nobility and the *Bonnes Villes* ("Good Cities") – twelve in 1316 and twenty-two after the incorporation of the county of Loon in 1361. As such, the *Sens du Pays* can be considered as a kind of "States," a representation of the common land. It was a potentially powerful institution, since it was able to change the law. Moreover, no new taxes could be levied without the approval of the states. Gradually, the Peace of Fexhe acquired the status of a kind of constitution, but this didn't happen without struggle.

In 1312–1331, the city of Liège was almost entirely in the hands of the artisan corporations. Many of the surviving patricians had left the city after the *Mal de Saint-Martin*, later joining the nobility. When the Liège corporations began to question the authority of the prince-bishop outside the city, this led to a brief civil war (1328–1331). The prince was victorious. The political power of the corporations was curtailed and an equal division of power between corporations and patriciate was reintroduced (in 1331), but the prince-bishop continued to rule with the consent of the states.

Later the corporations took advantage of the weak position of some prince-bishops to resume the offensive. In 1373, it was decided that the thirty-two Liège artisan corporations would henceforth be the only ones to comprise the city council. Patricians who wanted to participate in the elections had to join a corporation. This looks like a democratic revolution, but it was not. In allowing patricians and merchants to be involved, the corporations became more oligarchic in nature. All the more so because, in the same period, journeymen were excluded from the right to vote and access to the corporations was restricted by higher entry fees. Nevertheless, by the end of the fourteenth century, the city of Liège had about 1,000 adults who were eligible to participate in elections, which is no small number compared to the nineteenth-century electoral census (see Chapter 8).

In the same period, after a brief existence in 1343–1344, the *Tribunal des XXII* was re-established. This court investigated and punished all forms of corruption or abuse of power by the princes' officials. Its composition – fourteen members were appointed by the *Bonnes Villes*, four by the Chapter of Saint-Lambert and four by the nobility – reflects new political relations in the fourteenth century. In the prince-bishopric of Liège, the distribution of power was laid down in texts and institutions, and the prince was one of the four political organs of the common land. Of course, institutional relations were not immutable and some princes temporarily succeeded in imposing their will on their subjects, but the concept that the prince should rule in the interest and with the consent of his subjects, as expressed in the representative institutions, remained in place until the end of the eighteenth century.

In Brabant, political relations also changed, especially as a result of problems relating to the succession of a deceased duke and/or ducal finances. Sometimes the duke was more or less forced to concede, but sometimes concessions were made voluntarily in order to gain support from his subjects. When Henry III died in 1261, he left behind an underage and feeble-minded successor. Through strenuous efforts, the duchess-regent was able, with the support of the cities and thanks to convenient maneuvering, to neutralize both foreign and domestic pretenders to the regency. Moreover, she managed to obtain the consent of both the nobility and the towns for the abdication of her eldest son and to have him succeeded by the younger John I (r. 1268–1294).

As discussed earlier, John I was a very successful ruler, but his exuberant lifestyle and especially his warlike policy of territorial expansion caused major financial and political problems in the long run. The duke had taken out large loans outside the duchy. During the reign of his son, John I's overseas creditors harassed Brabant merchants and their goods were confiscated in an attempt to settle the former ruler's debts. Therefore, in order to pay off the latter, the duke had to rely on his subjects and new taxes had to be introduced. The legitimacy of the duke was not in question, but the requested support was not given without conditions. Cities and the clergy played a leading role in the negotiation process.

In 1312, shortly before his death, John II granted the Charter of Kortenberg. This document confirmed subjects' existing freedoms and privileges and made taxation dependent on the approval of the representatives of the common land. To this end, the Council of Kortenberg was established. Consisting of fourteen members (four noblemen and ten urban representatives of six towns, three from Leuven and Brussels each), it can be considered the forerunner of the States of Brabant. An important factor was the subjects' right to oppose unlawful actions of the ruler. In fact, the charter stipulated that the ruler's policies should primarily serve the public interest, as defined by the cities. When the financial problems persisted, the cities even seized power in 1314. Fourteen-year-old John III (r. 1312–1355) was temporarily placed under guardianship. Until 1320, the ducal finances were managed by the cities, in particular Leuven and Brussels.

The practice of recording agreements between ruler and subjects, the so-called system of "Brabant constitutionalism," reached its zenith in 1356. John III's succession by his eldest daughter Johanna (r. 1355–1406) and her husband, the duke of Luxemburg, was subject to strict conditions. The new rulers took the oath of allegiance to the *Joyeuse Entrée* charter ("Joyous Entrance"). The cities and nobility had stipulated that the unity of the duchy had to be preserved. This provision was mainly directed against the claims of the deceased duke's other sons-in-law. It was further stipulated that public offices could only be held by natives of the duchy, that no taxes could be levied, no currency could be minted and no war could be started without the approval of the "common land," represented by clergy, nobility, and towns. Until the end of eighteenth century, the Joyous Entrance charter was used to legitimize all major conflicts between successive rulers and subjects (see Chapters 4–7).

A striking difference to the Liège developments is the relatively peaceful way in which the Brabant "constitution" took shape. Unlike the Chapter of Saint-Lambert, which considered itself to be the equal of the prince-bishop, the Brabant clergy, represented by a number of abbots, kept to the background. The cities never questioned the duke's legitimacy. A possible explanation for this is the convergence of interests: in exchange for financial support, the duke confirmed the dominant position of the urban patrician and merchant elite and supported them against claims from artisan corporations.

This convergence of interests was particularly evident when the consequences of the political and social revolution in Flanders (in 1302) also made themselves felt in the cities of Brabant. In 1303, artisans in Brussels revolted and the patricians were forced to share power. However, as early as 1306, the patriciate managed to remove the artisan corporations from the city council by military force, with the support of the duke. Later, in the 1360s, when the drapery industry deteriorated, the corporations went on the offensive again, making use of division and rivalry in the patriciate. For example, in Leuven, on the personal initiative of the duke's representative, the corporations were integrated into the city council in order to thwart the former's rivals from the patriciate. The Brussels corporations came into action again in 1360. The result was the emerging of a certain consensus on power sharing between the patriciate and corporations over the next few decades.

However, power sharing at the city level was far from democratic. Within the corporations, only master-artisans had the right to vote; the numerous journeymen did not. Moreover, the relative "weight" of a corporation was not taken into account. Each corporation cast one vote in the urban decision-making process, regardless of its total membership.

The urban charter of Brussels (1421) provides a good indication of the oligarchic nature of the Brabant city councils. From 1421, the urban corporation consisted of three members. The first member, "the Law," consisted of nineteen "officers": ten patricians and nine representatives of the artisan corporations; the second member, the "Large Council," consisted of all the ex-members of the first member; the third member, "the Nations," represented the (roughly) fifty corporations, divided into nine "nations." For a proposal to be approved, it needed a majority in each member. The system was based on checks and balances, but it is clear that the patrician faction had the advantage in the fourteenth–fifteenth century. After 1355, at the level of the duchy, the States as representatives of the country emerged: the clergy, the nobility, and the "third estate" were represented by four capital towns, namely Leuven, Brussels, Antwerp and 's-Hertogenbosch.

After 1302, political developments in the county of Flanders were much more polarizing and violent. Unlike in Brabant and the prince-bishopric of Liège, external factors and economic interests played a greater role in Flanders. In the period 1305–1320, the count was constantly caught between the dissatisfaction of his subjects, with the heavy financial consequences of the 1305 peace treaty and the returning *Leliaards* on the one hand, and the pressure from the French crown to enforce the aforementioned treaty on the other. In 1312, the king even annexed Walloon Flanders (Treaty of Pontoise), which made the financial burden of the treaty of 1305 even heavier for the count's subjects. Shortly before his death, the count submitted to the crown.

Louis de Nevers (r. 1322–1346), the deceased count's grandson, was raised at the French court and had married a French princess. His political line was one of unconditional loyalty to his sovereign. A few years after his rise to power, Louis was confronted with a large-scale uprising of the rural population of the Flemish coast. This revolt was arguably an outburst of displeasure at the extortion and abuse of power of local tax collectors, many of whom belonged to the *Leliaards'* party which returned after 1305. This resulted in a violent civil war. Bruges and Ypres supported the rebellious farmers. Ghent, where the *Leliaards* were in power, remained loyal to the count. Nevertheless the count could not maintain his authority and was forced to flee to France.

The turning point came in 1328, at the death of the last king of the direct line of the Capetian dynasty. The succession was controversial since the English king, Edward III, also believed he had a right to the throne. In this constellation, the Flemish rebels were looking to England for support. Edward held off for the time being, but the uncertain situation about the succession required a swift French intervention. A French army under the personal command of the new king dealt with the Flemish rebels, whose army of peasants and urban militias suffered a crushing defeat (at the battle of Cassel, August 1328) followed by harsh repression. The county was given back to Louis along with an order to punish the rebels and their supporters, confiscate their property, and carry out the financial arrangements made in previous treaties. Therefore, Louis de Nevers was totally bound to French politics.

In the 1330s, during the run-up to the Hundred Years War (1337–1453), the English and French rulers tried to strengthen their influence in the Low Countries, especially in the densely populated and strategically located county of Flanders. To increase the pressure on Flanders, Edward banned wool exports at the end of 1336. The result was an economic crisis and unemployment, which triggered a revolution in Ghent in 1337. A public assembly gave power to five *hooftmannen* (captains). One of them, Jacob Van Artevelde (*c.*1290–1345), a merchant and landowner belonging to the upper class, clearly emerged as the leader. The weavers, who had been excluded from participation in the city council since 1320, were reinstated at his suggestion. He strove for a broad coalition of the patriciate and corporations in Ghent, but also in the county as a whole.

Bruges and Ypres joined Van Artevelde, and the union of the three major Flemish textile centers increasingly defined the political attitude of the county. The three urban corporations were called *scabini Flandriae*, the aldermen of Flanders, thus indicating that a county could best be governed as they did in their respective cities. First, Van Artevelde succeeded in getting Flanders' neutrality recognized by the English and French, allowing the import of English wool to recover and ending the economic crisis. However, the rift between feudal loyalty and the economic interests of the cities caused by the count proved untenable. In 1339, Louis left Flanders and settled in France.

During the following year, a radical breach occurred between Flanders and the French crown. Assembled in Ghent in 1340, the representatives of the Flemish towns recognized Edward III as the rightful king of France and thus as sovereign of the county. Edward promised allegiance to the urban charters and privileges, the discharge of payments to the French crown, the restitution of Walloon Flanders and the re-establishment of the English wool staple in Bruges. Much of what Edward promised was to take place in the future and was therefore highly uncertain. Formally, the legitimacy of the refugee count was maintained by appointing a regent. Most, if not all, decisions were made in the name of the absent count. Between the years 1340 and 1345, actual power in the county was in the hands of the three cities and their leader, Van Artevelde.

The accession of the weavers to the city councils was particularly important for internal political relations in the county. Due to increased competition from other producers, the Flemish cloth industry had been under pressure for several decades. To protect the interests of their own producers, the three cities expanded their influence over the surrounding countryside. Textile production was prohibited in the villages. Small towns were subjugated. Ghent, Bruges, and Ypres sought to divide the county into three *Quartiers* (districts), of which they would be the dominant political, legal, and economic center. Of course, this move provoked resistance. In the cities themselves, the weaver corporation dominated the administration.

The radical position of the three cities provoked opposition from smaller cities, the nobility remaining faithful to the count and the countryside. Furthermore, there were the usual rivalries within the patriciate. Great tensions also existed between weavers and fullers. The former were self-employed; the fullers, on the other hand, worked at a fixed rate on behalf of the weavers and merchants and were therefore more dependent on wages. All these political and social contradictions erupted in 1345. Differences of opinion between the weavers and fullers in Ghent turned into a real battle. The weavers were victorious, after which the fullers were removed from the city council. Shortly afterwards, Jacob Van Artevelde was murdered by a political rival.

The political tide in the county turned when a new count took office in 1346. Louis de Male (1330–1384) was a shrewd and realistic politician. He rejected the three cities' demand to recognize Edward III as his sovereign. He soon began to establish his authority in the county by exploiting to the fullest extent possible the contradictions described above. Moreover, he was able to benefit from a truce between England

and France. In 1349, Ghent was the last city to submit to the count's authority. However, the obedience of its subjects remained conditional.

Unlike in Liège and Brabant, in Flanders political relations between rulers and subjects were not recorded in solemn constitutional charters and institutions. The count and his successors negotiated with the common land represented by the "Members of Flanders," consisting of Ghent, Bruges, and Ypres and, from the end of the fourteenth century, also the "Franc of Bruges," an affluent rural district surrounding that city. Sometimes nobles and/or clergymen also participated in the meetings as representatives of their State, giving that meeting the character of states. However, the role of the "Members" remained crucial. The next chapter discusses how they tried to maintain their dominant position vis-à-vis the ruler. At the urban level, a division of power between the patriciate and corporations emerged in which the position of the weavers next to the patriciate and all the other corporations was particularly striking.

Louis de Male was very successful in his foreign and dynastic politics. He managed to remain formally faithful to the French king and yet look after the economic interests of his subjects by maintaining good relations with England. When his father-in-law died in 1355, after a short and successful war, he was able to gain a substantial part of the inheritance. In 1357, Antwerp and Mechelen came into his possession (via the peace of Ath). The next chapter will discuss how he also succeeded in securing the restitution of Walloon Flanders.

The political and social developments in the three principalities, as outlined above, took place at a time of unprecedented economic and demographic challenge across Europe. From the 1280s, the balance between population and food production became increasingly precarious. Climatological factors also played a role. In 1315–1317, Western Europe suffered from torrential rains and cool summers, resulting in crop failure. Between 1315 and 1322, the whole of north-western Europe was hit by a devastating famine, a real subsistence crisis. One-tenth of the population of Ypres died as a consequence. In the years 1347–1352, the "Black Death" took hold of Europe. Depending on the region, between a third to half of the population died. In the Low Countries, Hainaut was hit hardest, with the loss of about one-third of its inhabitants. The plague remained endemic in the Low Countries until the third quarter of the seventeenth century. The next chapter will elaborate on the social and economic consequences of the late medieval crisis.

Conclusion

The principalities in the "Belgian" part of the Low Countries possessed some aspects of what Henri Pirenne has called a *civilisation commune*: a high degree of urbanization, politically powerful towns, and a contractual relationship between rulers and subjects. However, the range of this common civilization is a matter of discussion. Was there really a fusion of Romance and Germanic civilizations in medieval "Belgium," as Pirenne stated? Maybe at the level of princely courts in the Dutch-speaking part of the southern Low Countries. As far as state formation is concerned, this period showed no development toward a future "Belgian" polity.

From *c.*1000 until the crisis of the fourteenth century, five relatively large principalities emerged in the southern Low Countries: Flanders, Liège, Brabant, Hainaut, and Luxembourg. The following, not yet largely discussed, perspective is relevant for later Belgium's political, cultural, and linguistic contradictions: two languages (Dutch-French or French-German) were spoken in each of these five polities. It is also important to mention that the great majority of Flemish counts were imbued with French culture (literature and music) and had themselves buried in churches and abbeys in Walloon Flanders and Artois.

Personal unions between some principalities arose, either temporarily (Flanders-Hainaut, Brabant-Luxembourg) or permanently (Brabant-Limburg, Hainaut-Holland-Zeeland), between adjacent (Flanders-Hainaut) or far-away (Brabant-Limburg) territories. The creation of these five polities was strongly influenced by political developments in France and the Holy Roman Empire. The most striking of theses is the significant influence of France, from *c.*1200, on Flanders but on the other principalities as well. This kingdom was involved in many issues in the Low Countries, both through direct intervention and through inter-national conflict. As a result, from the end of the thirteenth century, the Holy Roman Empire became a minor player, unless an emperor had an important personal power base (*Hausmacht*). The important role of France will be repeatedly discussed in the following chapters.

From a European perspective, demographic and economic develop-ments in the southern Low Countries were undoubtedly dynamic. Flanders and Brabant had a relatively high degree of urbanization and therefore a high population density. They counted several major cities.

This was less the case for Liège and Hainaut. Luxembourg was large but sparsely populated and had no significant cities. In large areas, agriculture enjoyed a relatively high level of productivity. The textile manufacturing industry, especially the woolen cloth industry, largely determined urban prosperity and the position of Flanders and Brabant as major emporia in north-western Europe.

The high degree of urbanization and the dynamic economy led to the emergence of new social and political relations, particularly in Flanders, Brabant, and Liège, where cities significantly influenced the ruler's position of power. Rulers would only be obeyed if they respected the laws and privileges of their subjects and at least allowed their interests to be taken into account when determining policy. This was clearly a contract between ruler and subjects as equal partners, whether or not laid down in formal (Liège, Brabant) or informal (Flanders) agreements. The constant struggle between rulers and towns over this balance has been called the Great Tradition.

As soon as the cities matured, members of the urban patriciate exercised power in the name of the ruler. As cities grew and developed a more complex socio-economic structure, new groups and their organizations (merchant guilds and artisan corporations) wanted to participate in government. This struggle for power sharing at the urban level has been called the Little Tradition. The power play between ruler, patriciate, and corporations thus became more complex from the end of thirteenth century, mainly due to party and faction formations within the patriciate and the corporations.

In many respects, the socio-economic structure of the urbanized Low Countries is very similar to that of northern Italy. This raises the question of why, contrary to Italy, no independent urban republics such as Venice, Genoa, Milan, or Florence have emerged, even though Flanders seemed to be heading in that direction after the urban revolts of the fourteenth century. A detailed answer will not be formulated here, given the concise character of this book. However, the following elements seem to have been of great importance: unlike Italy, where the nobility and the urban patriciate came together, these remained separate social groups in the Low Countries. The nobility did not settle in the cities. While in Italy one large city dominated a relatively large surrounding area and smaller cities (for instance Venice and the *Terra Ferma*), this was impossible in relatively small Flanders which was characterized by large cities in close proximity to each other. Finally, the Low Countries had to deal with the direct and powerful presence of the most powerful monarchy in Western Europe: France. In the next chapter we will discuss how monarchs from a branch of this French monarchy began to merge all the principalities of the Low Countries and how the cities eventually had to submit to the growing power of the state.

4

Unifying the Netherlands:
The Burgundy–Habsburg Period (1384–1555)

Introduction

In over a century and a half, about fifteen principalities and cities in the Low Countries, from Arras and Luxemburg in the south to Amsterdam and Groningen in the north were unified under one ruler. Burgundy and Franche-Comté in eastern France were also part of this new polity. Dynastic politics were the major factor in the state building. Princes of the French Valois dynasty started this process around 1400, and this evolution was completed by their German-Habsburg successors between 1520 and 1550. The Low Countries (and thus Belgium) became part of the huge Habsburg monarchy.

Around 1350 Europe fell victim to the Black Death, with catastrophic demographic consequences. At the end of the fifteenth century a period of population growth paired with powerful economic expansion began. Antwerp became the most important international trade center of north-west Europe. The expansion of European trade to Africa, Asia, and America played an important part in the growth of the Antwerp market. Lay people desiring a simple, evangelically-based Christianity found the Netherlands to be the perfect breeding ground for the Protestant Reformation that started in the 1520s. The high degree of urbanization, dense population and relatively high quality of human capital created an economic climate that was beneficial to cultural production (painting, literature, and the craft industry) and the propagation of new ideas (Humanism and printing). During the Burgundy-Habsburg period the territories that would constitute Belgium had their greatest international political and economic influence.

The Burgundian Marriage: Alliances, Dynastic Politics and Territorial Expansion

Flanders was the richest and most densely populated principality of the Low Countries. Count Louis de Male (r. 1346–1384) had added Antwerp, Mechelen, and their surrounding territories to his possessions (see Chapter 3). From his French mother he was to inherit the adjacent county of Artois and the Free County of Burgundy. Margaret de Male (1350–1405), Louis' heiress, was therefore an attractive proposition on the matrimonial market. Louis wanted to be both a trustworthy vassal of the French king and a protector of the economic interests of his subjects. He therefore navigated shrewdly between the English and the French during the Hundred Years War.

After lengthy negotiations the Flemish count eventually married his daughter to Philip of Burgundy, a younger brother of the French king, in 1369. Philip was commonly known as "the Bold" (French, *le Hardi*) because of his bravery during the war against the English. Seen from the French perspective, this marriage meant that both the county of Flanders and the factual unification of the duchy and the Free County of Burgundy would be solidly bound to France. Through the marriage of his daughter, the Flemish count was assured of the French crown's support against his often-rebellious subjects. Moreover, Louis obtained the restitution of Walloon Flanders, which had been annexed by the crown in 1312.

After Louis' passing, Philip the Bold (r. 1384–1404) took charge of the Flemish government. One of his first actions was to secure an alliance with count Albrecht of Holland, Zeeland, and Hainaut. In 1385 both rulers confirmed their allegiance to one another by marrying their children to each other (the son and daughter of Philip married the daughter and the son of Albrecht). As one of Albrecht's younger sons became prince-bishop of Liège in 1389, this union only grew stronger.

The relation with Brabant-Limburg proved to be even more important. The childless and widowed duchess Johanna (1322–1406) had been ruling this principality since 1355. Johanna was an aunt to Margaret de Male, and this made the latter or any of her offspring a potential heir to the former. The duchess thoroughly and patiently prepared a Burgundian succession. In 1396 she transferred the small duchy of Limburg to Margaret and Philip. To satisfy the Brabant States, it was agreed that the duchess would be succeeded by one of Philip and

Margaret's younger sons. In 1404 Johanna retired from government in favor of Anthony of Burgundy. At the beginning of the fifteenth century it seemed as if two Burgundian-ruled polities were emerging: Flanders and Brabant-Limburg, with Holland-Zeeland-Hainaut and Liège as allies.

Philip the Bold and his son John the Fearless (r. 1404–1419) were heavily involved in the political developments in France and consequently in the Hundred Years War. The mental illness of the French king resulted in a struggle to exert control over the regency and the royal finances. In 1394–1396 over one-fifth of the Burgundian duke's income came from the French crown. In 1419, the contribution of the French crown to the Burgundian finances reached a staggering 65 percent! Philip the Bold behaved generally as a loyal and cautious member of the royal family. John the Fearless often behaved brutally and recklessly. A civil war between the *Bourguignons* (loyal to John) and the *Armagnacs* (loyal to the king's brother, the duke of Orléans) tore France apart. All this happened while the English enjoyed great military success (e.g. Agincourt in 1415). In 1419 Armagnac opponents murdered John the Fearless.

John the Fearless and Philip the Bold considered their territories in the Low Countries to be extensions to their French power base. However, as the third duke, Philip the Good (r. 1419–1467), rose to power, this dynamic changed. After his father's murder, Philip sided with the English, a decision that, in addition to family honor, was mostly dictated by opportunism. The alliance with the English proved highly beneficial to Philip. In the short term, this resulted in the Burgundians and the English ruling and exploiting a large part of France. In the long run, after the war favored the French, Philip was able to negotiate a good price for his reconciliation with the crown.

Unlike his father, Philip the Good was very present in the Low Countries and continually focused on fortifying his power base. In 1421 the count of Namur, a distant relative, appointed Philip as his heir apparent in exchange for a yearly fee. In 1429, Philip was able to add the small but strategically situated county to his territories (see Figure 4.1).

Complicated political developments were also happening in Holland-Zeeland-Hainaut. In 1417, conflict over the count's succession arose between his daughter Jacoba and his brother John who had been prince-bishop of Liège. Jacoba tried to fortify her claim by marrying her cousin John IV of Brabant (r. 1415–1527). If their union had been

Figure 4.1 Jean Wauquelin presenting the *History of Hainaut* to duke
Philip the Good. Miniature by Rogier Van der Weyden, 1447/8
(Brussels, Royal Library)

successful, the territories of Brabant-Limburg and Holland-Zeeland-
Hainaut could have been joined into a larger second Burgundian polity
in the Low Countries. Alas the marriage of Jacoba and John IV ended in
divorce as John, ignoring his wife's interests, leased Jacoba's land to her
uncle, making him the factual ruler.

Due to a previous succession issue in the 1340s, the cities and nobility
of Holland and Zeeland were split in two camps. The struggle between
Jacoba and her uncle became intertwined with these camps. This provided Philip the Good with plenty of opportunities to intervene in the
conflict. Using money as well as violence, and taking advantage of
Jacoba's political ineptitude, Philip forced the latter to relinquish her
rights. In 1428 Jacoba acknowledged Philip as regent to her territories
(*Zoen van Delft*, or the Conciliation of Delft) and in 1433 she definitively
passed on her sovereign rights to her Burgundian cousin.

The Burgundian Brabant-Limburg polity was short-lived. John IV
(r. 1415–1427) and Philip of Saint-Pol (r. 1427–1430) succeeded their
father Anthony of Burgundy (r. 1404–1415). Since Philip of Saint-Pol

had no legal heirs, his cousin Philip, who had already been appointed heir in 1426, took control of both duchies in 1430. However Philip's succession came with certain restrictions. The new duke swore to the Brabant States that he would strictly respect the rights and privileges as agreed upon in the 1356 *Blijde Inkomste* (French, *Joyeuse Entrée*) (see Chapter 3).

In the 1430s, the tide was turning in the Hundred Years War. The Burgundian–English alliance weakened due to Philip's intervention in Holland, among other reasons. Philip the Good opted for a rapprochement with the king. The Peace of Arras (1435) was quite favorable to Philip. He was personally exempted from paying homage to the king. Philip acquired the adjacent counties of Boulogne and Vermandois, as well as a number of towns in Picardy near the Somme as collateral. These new acquisitions meant that the Burgundian territories in the Low Countries stretched as far south as those of his Flemish predecessor Thierry of Alsace (see Chapter 3).

The expansion of the Burgundian territories in the Low Countries during the reign of Philip the Good was concluded by the acquisition of the duchy of Luxemburg. The childless duchess appointed Philip as regent and prospective heir of her duchy in exchange for a yearly payment. It should also be noted that Philip the Good's power reached beyond his already substantial territory. He succeeded in having appointed two of his relatives as prince-bishops of the most important ecclesiastical principalities in the Low Countries. His nephew Louis de Bourbon ruled over Liège (r. 1456–1482). And one of Philip's numerous illegitimate children, David of Burgundy, served Burgundian interests as prince-bishop of Utrecht (r. 1456–1496).

In about two decades, Philip the Good managed to bring the territories of later Belgium under his direct rule or indirect control. He took every available opportunity to expand his territory and his influence. This resulted in an ever-growing discrepancy between his formal status as a vassal of the French king and the emperor, and his actual position as a sovereign ruler. The only connection between Philip's principalities was his person and his dynasty. It was uncertain, or at the very least unclear, whether the unification of these territories was to be temporary or the start of further expansion. The question remained whether Philip's subjects in these counties and duchies regarded him as anything more than their count or duke. Around 1450, Philip was widely known as "the Grand Duke of the West." This does seem to suggest that a new polity was in the making (see Map 4.1).

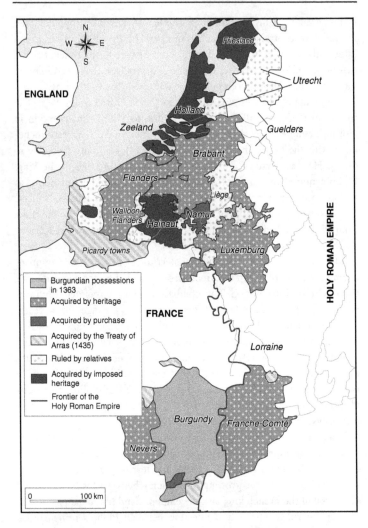

Map 4.1 The Burgundian unification process, 1363–1467. Redrawn based on a map originally published in *Atlas de la Wallonie, de la préhistoire à nos jours*, courtesy of Institut Jules Destrée, Charleroi (© Sofam)

Institutions and State Building

The first three dukes attempted to strengthen their power through both administrative and judicial reform, and also to display their sovereignty over the whole of their lands. Being French princes, they were heavily inspired by French institutions. Following the example of the French *parlements*, they established a council (*Conseil de Justice* or *Justitieraad*) in every principality. These councils were manned by trained jurists and functioned as Courts of Appeal, as well as lawmakers at the regional level. These councils (for instance the Council of Flanders) defended the sovereignty of the ruler. By controlling and limiting for example Ghent's judicial range, the Council of Flanders contributed to the gradual subjugation of the city under the ruler's authority. The councils also ensured that provincial privileges were respected – especially in Brabant, where the Sovereign Council functioned as the highest court.

To manage the ducal domain and to control the financial management of cities and rural districts, *Chambres des Comptes* (Comptroller Offices) were established in Lille (1386), Brussels (1404) and The Hague (1446). Over time the territorial range of these institutions was extended. The *Chambre des Comptes* of Lille, for example, exerted its authority in Flanders and later on also in Hainaut and Namur, thereby enhancing the ducal sovereignty. Monetary policy was cast in the same mold. From 1434, Flanders, Hainaut, Brabant, and Holland all used the same silver coin, the so-called *vierlander* ("Four Countries").

The most important governing body, overseeing all the Burgundian principalities in the Low Countries, was the Court Council consisting of jurists, clerics, and members of the high nobility. The council's daily administration was overseen by the Chancellor of Burgundy, always a member of the lower nobility and coming from one of the duke's French territories. In the course of time, the Court Council was subdivided. The Great Council operated as a supreme court; the Council of Finances discussed fiscal and economic policy and the Privy Council treated administrative and ecclesiastical matters. For a long time the Burgundian polity had no fixed capital; it was wherever the duke resided. Philip the Bold and especially John the Fearless preferred to stay in France for extended periods of time. Philip the Good, on the contrary, often lived in certain northern cities, in order of importance: Brussels, Lille, Bruges, Dijon, and Ghent.

Ruler and Subjects: A Tense Relationship

Between 1379 and 1385, Louis de Male and Philip the Bold were involved in the so-called Ghent War, a conflict that followed the pattern of the Great Tradition (see Chapter 3). Louis had authorized Bruges to dig a canal to the river Lys. Ghent considered this an infringement on her economic interests. The dispute between Flanders' two major cities led to a revolt involving other Flemish towns. A French royal army crushed Ghent's troops in 1382, but the sudden retreat of the French after the battle prevented the city's siege. After succeeding his father-in-law, Philip the Bold decided to compromise. He offered an amnesty for the rebels, as well as the confirmation of the Ghent privileges in exchange for a promise of loyalty. The Peace of Tournai ended the conflict in 1385.

Philip's moderate disposition was mainly tactical. In the long run the Burgundian dukes did seek to bring every city under their control. To reach this goal, they employed different methods and tactics, such as playing city factions against each other, bribing the elite and, when necessary, military violence. The growing army and territory of the Burgundian dukes empowered them to subjugate rebellious cities themselves. As we shall see, mutinous cities without allies were no match for a ruler who disposed of military and financial support of other parts of his dominions.

In the prince-bishopric of Liège, tensions often arose concerning the balance of power between the prince-bishop, the *Sens du Pays*, and the *Tribunal des XXII* (see Chapter 3). These tensions triggered a revolt in 1407–1408. Prince-bishop John of Bavaria called upon his brother, the count of Hainaut, Holland, and Zeeland, and John the Fearless, his brother in law. The combined armies of the three rulers crushed the rebels at Othée in 1408. Liège was overpowered and severely punished by the execution and banishment of rebels and the revoking of urban privileges. As a result, the alliance that Philip the Bold had founded in 1385 proved useful to the ruler's power position.

In 1436 social and political unrest flared up in Bruges. Urban militias were angered by the failure of organization of an expedition to conquer Calais and refused to disband. There was also unease about the deteriorating relations between Bruges, nearby smaller cities, and the Franc of Bruges district. Craftsmen went on strike and a public uprising was triggered. Many foreign merchants in Bruges felt unsafe. Ducal representatives were murdered. Philip tried to restore order, but after entering the city the duke and some of his troops were surrounded by rebels. Philip narrowly escaped. After these humiliating events, the duke came down hard on Bruges. The city was besieged and forced to surrender in 1438.

A decade later, Philip went on the offensive against Ghent, the most powerful city in Flanders. The duke wanted to introduce a *gabelle* – a permanent salt tax in Flanders. If Ghent were to agree, other cities and districts would certainly follow. In spite of many meetings with the Ghent magistrates, the city's Large Council rejected the plan. In retaliation, the duke sought to provoke Ghent by openly violating some of its privileges. Consequently a riot started in 1451, which culminated in a battle between the Ghent militias and the duke's army at Gavere in 1453. The city lost. The former were no longer a match for the duke's increasingly professional troops. A number of humiliating conditions were imposed on the vanquished cities: the formal and solemn subjugation to the duke at some place outside the county, the imposition of enormous fines, and the obligation for urban magistrates and deans of the guilds and corporations to present themselves, bareheaded and barefooted, to the duke at his earliest convenience.

Nevertheless, both the duke and the political elite preferred to avoid violent conflict. For the Burgundian dukes, maintaining good relations with the nobility was of the highest importance, as their patronage networks could prove invaluable at a regional level. To maintain these desired strong bonds, the dukes bequeathed honorable roles to the most prominent nobles, and hosted festivities, tournaments, hunting parties, and so forth. In 1430 Philip the Good founded the Order of the Golden Fleece, which consisted of thirty noblemen he deemed worthy of representing the ideal of knighthood as well as defending the Christian faith. In founding the order, Philip highlighted his sovereign royal ambitions. In the 1450s, Philip took part in a meeting of the diet of the Holy Roman Empire at Regensburg. At this event, the wealth displayed by the duke and his suite confirmed his quasi-monarchal status; it paved the way for the acquirement of a royal title in the near future.

The splendor of the Burgundian court, the maintenance of an extensive patronage network, and the government apparatus itself were very costly. However, the ducal domain did not generate sufficient income to pay for this. Philip the Good therefore increasingly relied on financial contributions from his subjects. In particular, urbanized and relatively wealthy regions such as Brabant and Flanders were eligible for taxation. However, the ruler could not impose taxes unilaterally and was subjected to lengthy negotiations with the states of counties and duchies.

To accommodate these negotiations, Philip the Good introduced the joint gatherings of the states of several principalities. These meetings were held exclusively in the dominions of the Low Countries. For example, in 1431, the states of Brabant, Flanders, Holland, and Zeeland met in Brussels. The first official meeting of the States-General took place in Brussels in 1464. First and foremost, the duke convened the States-General to announce his plans and financial wishes. However, the decision to comply (or not) with these requests was made by the States of the individual principalities and, as such, was subject to discussion and bargaining. In theory, the States-General met on the initiative of the sovereign. However, in times of crisis the States-General often took control, serving as the voice of the common land in opposition to the ruler. Although regional particularism remained strong, the existence of the States-General and the various councils proved that a Burgundian state was developing in the Low Countries.

Economics and Demography in the Fifteenth Century

In the 1470s, the Burgundian Netherlands had a population of around 2.5 million. Of this total, 1.5 million lived in present-day Belgium. Population density varied considerably: 78 inhabitants per km² in Flanders as opposed to 6 per km² in Luxembourg. More than 70 percent of the "Belgian" population lived in Flanders and Brabant. In comparison, England and Wales had about 3 million inhabitants during the same period. In Namur, Hainaut, and Liège a quarter of the population lived in cities, and a third of the population in Flanders and Brabant were city dwellers. The demographic crisis of the fourteenth century (see Chapter 3) resulted in a population decline across Europe. As a direct economic consequence, the concentration of property and income increased among elites and middle classes. There was also a shortage of manpower, causing wages to rise. Generally speaking, it can be extrapolated that in the 1450s Europe had a smaller but more prosperous population than in the 1300s. This was certainly the case in the Burgundian Netherlands.

In the thirteenth century, agricultural productivity in (parts of) Brabant, Hainaut, and Walloon Flanders was on average much higher than elsewhere in Western Europe (see Chapter 3). As the population declined from 1350, the pressure to produce staple food, such as grain, was reduced. Land could be used for animal husbandry. Agriculture and the rural economy in general became more diverse. Better farming techniques increased productivity (crop rotation and better fertilization). Thanks to its network of rivers (the Scheldt and Lys), the major cities in Flanders and Brabant could rely on huge grain supplies from Artois and Picardy. Supply from the Baltic Sea grew increasingly important.

The introduction of innovations was relatively smooth, thanks to the market orientation of many agricultural producers. The rural population increasingly had the opportunity to supplement their income with non-agricultural labor. In the border region between present-day West Flanders and French Flanders, cheaper woolen textiles (new drapery) and lighter woolen fabrics (light drapery) were produced. The processing of flax into linen became an important branch of the industry in parts of Flanders, Hainaut, and Brabant, and a large portion of these cheaper products was exported.

The traditional urban wool centers were facing increasing competition from their own rural industries, Italy, and especially England. The English crown tightly regulated wool exports. This led to higher costs for producers in the Low Countries. In addition, the English began to process their own wool. Traders and cloth producers tried to reduce costs by lowering wages, but the resulting social conflicts led to greater participation of guilds of craftsmen in town councils and therefore made it more difficult to reduce wages. Consequently, entrepreneurs increasingly focused on product innovation and quality control, and the urban textile industry shifted to the more profitable end processes of the production cycle: dyeing and finishing.

Other branches of the urban manufacturing industry focused on the more expensive segment of the market. Objects and artifacts were designed for wealthy customers and institutions – the Church, the aristocracy, various governments, and the upper middle class – both domestically and internationally. Woodcarvings, such as altarpieces (retables) produced in Brabant (especially in Antwerp), were exported everywhere in north-western Europe. Even more important was the production of tapestries. The main production centers were large cities such as Arras, Tournai, Brussels, and Antwerp, but also smaller ones such as Oudenaarde and Enghien. The weaving of these tapestries required highly skilled labor and the use of precious raw materials such as gold and silver wire. From the fifteenth to the beginning of the eighteenth century, these luxury products were exported throughout Europe.

Overland trade in Western Europe had shrunk as a result of the late medieval crisis. Maritime trade, on the contrary, increased in the fourteenth and fifteenth centuries. This growth resulted, in part, from a higher demand for luxury products (spices, silk, fur, etc.) from the Near and Far East. Due to their central location in northwest Europe, the Low Countries enjoyed considerable advantages. The affluent urban middle class was more than a potential outlet for imported luxury goods, but numerous cities also offered a range of high-quality and artistic products for export. Furthermore, the Low Countries were ideally located between the Mediterranean and northern Europe, and also between England and Germany.

As such, it should come as no surprise that, in the period 1380–1480, Bruges was the most important trading city in north-western Europe, and undoubtedly the richest in Flanders. The composition and number of the population involved in foreign trade fluctuated. Some merchants stayed temporarily but many dozens settled there permanently. The Hanseatic League had a permanent *Kontor*, in Bruges through which all trade operations of the Hanseatic towns in the Low Countries passed. Italian merchants were organized in Nations by city (Venice, Lucca, Florence, etc.). The Italians played an important role in money trading and international exchange traffic. All kinds of goods and financial and commercial services were offered in Bruges. The first stock exchange of Europe was developed in that city. The naming of the stock exchange in French (*bourse*), German (*Börse*), Dutch (*beurs*) and English (*burse*, or Royal Stock Exchange after 1775) originated in *Ter Buerse*, a Bruges inn where business was carried out, and local innkeepers such as the Van der Buerse family often acted as brokers (see Figure 4.2).

Many merchants did also business in Brabant, particularly in Antwerp and in the small town of Bergen-op-Zoom, where fairs were held. These events lasted several weeks and attracted many English and German traders. In the late fifteenth century, the cycle of fairs was extended and eventually became permanent. This laid the foundation for the spectacular growth of Antwerp in the late fifteenth century. However, the economic prosperity of the Burgundian state came to an end as a consequence of the stormy political events of the last third of the century.

Figure 4.2 Jan Van Eyck's portrait of Giovanni Arnolfini and his wife (1434) demonstrates both the painter's mastery and the wealth of the Bruges merchant elite (London, National Gallery)

Expansion, Crisis and Survival of the Burgundian State: From Charles the Bold to Maximilian of Austria

In the last years of his long reign, Philip the Good pursued a moderate pro-French policy. Thus he returned (against payment) the Somme towns to the French crown. His son and successor, Charles the Bold (r. 1467–1477), opposed this decision. According to the latter, France, which had emerged victorious from the Hundred Years War, was a major threat to the survival of the Burgundian state. The French king, Louis XI, resumed the politics of his predecessors (see Chapter 3) who tried to subject powerful vassals to the crown. As count of Flanders and Artois and duke of Burgundy, Charles was formally a vassal of Louis. From a French perspective, the Burgundian state was a dangerous rival and a threat to royal power.

Personality also played an important role in this struggle. While he was still crown prince, Louis spent some time at the Burgundian court. Therefore he was well informed about its internal relations and used this knowledge to influence the pro-French policy of the elderly Philip the Good. Louis was a political intriguer of a Machiavellian cut and as such a formidable opponent to Charles. Charles' ambitious project was to become a sovereign ruler and to territorially connect the two parts of the Burgundian lands – the Low Countries and Burgundy, and Franche-Comté in eastern France. This connection implied the annexation of Lorraine. He also wanted to subjugate the prince-bishopric of Liège and the duchy of Gelre and some other territories on the lower Rhine. Should this succeed, Lotharingia, as it existed in the tenth–twelfth centuries, would be restored.

Charles' ultimate goal was the creation of a kingdom that could compete with England and France. His most important ally was the English king Edward IV, whose sister he married. However, the alliance proved to be shaky. At a decisive moment in 1475, when the English and the Burgundians were to advance together against Louis XI, the French king managed to break up the alliance by paying a large sum of money to Edward IV.

Charles' grand schemes could not be put into effect without the necessary finances. Unlike his father, Charles had little patience with the necessity of consulting at length with the States-General or the states of his duchies and counties. The duke was a true authoritarian who increased taxes without the States' consent. In his relatively short reign, Charles collected the same amount of taxes as Philip the Good had done in forty-five years! Charles didn't want to depend on the urban militia or the feudal nobility for his military operations. Instead, following the French example, he founded the *Compagnies d'Ordonnance*, a professional standing army made up of mercenaries. He also spent huge sums on the extension and improvement of the artillery, thereby strengthening his military power.

Charles introduced considerable administrative innovation. Any possible resistance by the States or city councils was nipped in the bud. One of his means of achieving this was the use of the judiciary. He founded a supreme court for all the Burgundian regions in the Low Countries: the Parliament of Mechelen (1473). Brabant, too, was subjected to the jurisdiction of the Parliament, in direct opposition to the *Joyeuse Entrée*. The Comptrollers Offices of Brussels and Lille were abolished and replaced by two new ones, also based in Mechelen. These reforms are examples of Charles' centralization policy. The duke appointed his own creatures to the city councils and he introduced the sale of political offices and functions. The short-term advantages were obvious, but in the longer term this form of privatization undermined the ruler's authority.

Charles did not shy away from using the military means at his disposal, if necessary. Gelre, for example, was subjugated through brutal force. In proclaiming himself protector of Liège, Charles in effect annexed the prince-bishopric, where his cousin Louis de Bourbon had thus far represented Burgundian interests. When the people of Liège rebelled, an extremely violent repression followed. In 1466, Dinant was plundered and many inhabitants were executed. After a number of unsuccessful attempts at reconciliation, it was Liège's turn in 1468. After it was taken, the city was pillaged by Burgundian troops. Thousands of civilians were killed and large parts of the city were systematically destroyed.

Charles the Bold's hard and confrontational politics made him unpopular, as the obedience of his subjects was based on fear and bribery rather than loyalty. The French king took full advantage of his opponent's image by inciting unrest, especially in Gelre and Liège. Accordingly, Charles met with growing resistance abroad. In 1473 he negotiated in Trier for a few weeks with the emperor about the granting of a royal title. The negotiations failed, especially because many German princes, whose opinion the emperor had to take into account, feared Burgundy's expanding power. However, the discussions in Trier ultimately led to negotiations about the marriage between Charles' heiress and the emperor's son.

Charles the Bold's strategy to transform his territories into a sovereign state turned out to be a total failure, due to the duke's stubborn and impulsive personality as well as his tendency to take on too many opponents and to underestimate them. In 1474–1475, Charles came into conflict with the Decapolis, an urban federation in Alsace, and their allies, the Swiss *Eidgenossen*. In 1469, Charles had secured a number of territories in Alsace. When he implemented administrative and financial reforms, this was seen as very threatening by a number of free cities of the Decapolis and their Swiss allies. For the duke, a silver lining in this troublesome period proved to be the conquest of Lorraine in 1475. This acquisition finally connected the two parts of the Burgundian state. However, in 1476 things went wrong: the Swiss defeated the

Burgundian army, led by Charles himself (at Grandson and Morat) twice. The second defeat, during which the whole army camp and equipment were lost, proved especially catastrophic to Burgundian prestige. Lorraine revolted. When Charles tried to turn the tide, he was killed in battle at Nancy in January 1477.

The duke's sudden death and his succession by his unmarried nineteen-year-old daughter plunged the Burgundian state into deep crisis. Charles the Bold's enemies were making themselves heard. Liège and Gelre immediately declared independence. There were uprisings in most other regions of the Low Countries, especially in the cities. These revolts were not directed at the new duchess, Mary of Burgundy (r. 1477–1482), or against the dynasty. The general requirement was to put an end to the high taxes and the blatant disregard of regional and urban privileges. The States-General met in Ghent and demanded Mary's approval of a Grand Privilege that would apply throughout the Burgundian Low Countries. The Grand Privilege stipulated that the monarch had to respect the privileges of regions, cities, and their subjects; that taxation had to be approved by the states; and that the latter had the right to meet freely. Other issues included the curbing of corruption of ducal officials and the agreement that there could be no declaration of war without the approval of the States. It is important to note that the Grand Privilege included a provision that stated that, should the duchess fail to comply, the subjects were released from their duty of obedience.

The Grand Privilege of 1477 was in fact an extension of the Brabant *Joyeuse Entrée* of 1356 to the entire Burgundian Low Countries. It became an important constitutional text that would be invoked later in times of high political tension and revolution (see Chapters 5–7). The Parliament of Mechelen and the new Comptrollers Offices in that city were abolished, while the old Burgundian institutions were restored. Burgundian centralization was not undone, but Charles' endeavours were reversed. Despite the regional and urban particularisms, a moderate form of federalism between the principalities of the Low Countries under the leadership of the Burgundians was apparently appreciated. In exchange for approval of the Grand Privilege, the States-General were willing to grant money to raise an army. This proved urgent because Louis XI, the arch enemy of the Burgundian state, had seized the duchy of Burgundy and launched an offensive in Picardy and Artois.

The Burgundian state seemed to falter and a response to all these threats was urgently required. This culminated in Mary's marriage to the emperor's only surviving son, which was arranged in 1473. Eighteen-year-old Maximilian of Habsburg (1459–1519) took charge of the army and, after a few years, succeeded in stopping the French offensive. However, in the spring of 1482, the young duchess died unexpectedly as a result of a hunting accident. The succession was problematic, as her son, later known as Philip the Fair, was only four years old. Mary of Burgundy had appointed Maximilian as guardian and regent, but this proved to be an unpopular choice, especially in Flanders where he was generally distrusted.

A ten-year period of political struggle and civil war broke out. At the end of 1482, Maximilian was more or less forced by the States of Flanders, Brabant and Hainaut to make peace with France on conditions that were extremely favorable to the latter. His two-year-old daughter, Margaret of Austria, was married off to the French crown prince. Her dowry consisted of Artois, the Free County of Burgundy, and some other Burgundian territories in eastern France. Burgundy itself had been lost in 1477. Consequently, nearly all parts of the Burgundian state that were in present-day France were lost. In the Low Countries, especially in Flanders, a bitter battle arose over the recognition of Maximilian's regency and its practical organization.

Ghent, Bruges, and Ypres demanded the establishment of a Regency Council to oversee Maximilian's rule. The latter had no choice but to accept this de facto division of power. Moreover, as had been the case in the previous century, the three cities began to behave as independent republics, dominating the surrounding countryside and small towns. War became inevitable. Maximilian, the intended successor to the emperor, was even imprisoned in Bruges for several months in 1488. Under pressure from an imperial army, the States-General, in which Flanders, Brabant, Hainaut, and Zeeland played the leading role, reached a compromise with Maximilian. In exchange for his release, he solemnly promised to respect the Regency Council and its privileges.

Immediately after his release, Maximilian rejected the promise he had been forced to make and went on the offensive to restore his authority. In doing so, he exploited the mutual rivalry between cities and regions. Foreign merchants were strongly urged to leave rebellious Bruges and settle in law-abiding Antwerp. This policy would prove to be of great significance for Antwerp's expansion. Between 1489 and 1492, German troops subjugated the rebellious cities and regions and restored Maximilian's authority. In 1493, the projected marriage of Margaret of

Austria and the French king was cancelled. Artois and Franche-Comté were returned. Except for Burgundy, the territorial loss of 1477–1482 was recovered. Maximilian, who had succeeded his father as emperor in 1493, could pass the governance of the restored Burgundian state to his son, Philip the Fair (r. 1494–1506).

Habsburg: A New Dynasty and Its Huge Composite Empire

The marriage of Mary of Burgundy and Maximilian of Habsburg had far-reaching consequences for the Burgundian state, although no one could foresee them in 1477. In the fifteenth century, the Habsburgs ruled over parts of present-day Austria and Alsace, areas that were less populated, less urbanized, and less economically developed than the Burgundian Low Countries. Despite the crisis years following 1477, Maximilian's marriage to the Burgundian heiress proved to be extremely advantageous for the Habsburg dynasty.

The rule of Philip the Fair ended Maximilian's direct influence on the governance of the Low Countries. However, as head of the Habsburg dynasty, the latter was the decisive factor in matrimonial policy. Serving his Italian interests, Maximilian arranged for Philip and Margaret to be married in 1495 to a daughter and the eldest son of Isabella of Castile and Ferdinand of Aragon, the Catholic Spanish monarchs. The Spanish heir died after only a few years, as did his older sister, making Joanna and her husband Philip the Fair the intended successors in the Spanish kingdoms. In 1515, a few years before his death, Maximilian arranged another double wedding that would bring Bohemia and Hungary into the orbit of the Habsburg dynasty, thereby founding what was to become Austria-Hungary.

The government of Philip the Fair (r. 1494–1506) brought political peace and economic recovery after the turbulent period of 1467–1493. The young duke distanced himself from his father by pursuing a "national" policy. Under the influence of Flanders in particular, the relationship with France was improved. Consequently, Philip willingly paid homage to the French king for both Flanders and Artois. He concluded a trade agreement with England that proved favorable to the Brabant textile industry, particularly Antwerp (see p. 130–132). In political and institutional matters, the restoration of Burgundian institutions remained the main point of focus. Thus, in 1504, the Supreme Court was restored as the Great Council of Mechelen but with respect to the privileges of Brabant and Hainaut. In 1504, Philip and Joanna became king and queen of Castile but Philip died unexpectedly in 1506. This more or less repeated the situation of 1482, although this time there was no widower defending the interests of his children, but rather a mentally ill widow residing in Spain.

Maximilian became the guardian of his eldest grandson, later Charles V (1500–1558). Margaret of Austria, Maximilian's daughter (and Charles' aunt), represented him as his regent. She was the first in a long line of Habsburg princes and princesses to govern the Habsburg Low Countries on behalf of an often or permanently absent monarch. Margaret, who had already been married three times by the age of twenty-six, was a competent ruler and diplomat. She continued the peaceful policy of her deceased brother and kept the Burgundian Low Countries out of her father's political ambitions. The young Charles of Luxembourg, the title of the future Charles V, was educated at her court in Mechelen. In 1515 Charles took control of the government. After Ferdinand of Aragon's demise in 1516, Charles left for Spain to take over the crown of Aragon and Castile. Legally, his mentally ill mother was the heiress but Charles factually became king of Castile and Aragon, to which the kingdoms of Naples and Sicily also belonged.

Maximilian died in 1519. Thanks to a great deal of money and diplomacy, Charles was elected Roman-German king and thus succeeded his grandfather as Emperor of the Holy Roman Empire. In 1521, Charles put his brother Ferdinand in charge of the administration of the Austrian Habsburg lands. A few years later Ferdinand would become king of Hungary and Bohemia. Due to these dynastic developments, the Burgundian state evolved, in only two decades, into a rich, but relatively small, part of the huge Habsburg composite monarchy and dynasty of which Charles was the head. During Charles' reign, Spanish conquistadores conquered the empires of the Aztecs and the Incas in Latin America. According to a slightly exaggerated image, "the sun never set" on Charles V's empire.

As the history of emperor Charles V and the Habsburg dynasty falls outside the scope of this book, we will limit ourselves to summarizing the international problems the emperor faced, only to the extent that they are relevant to the Low Countries. Charles V's empire was very large but geographically dispersed and culturally heterogeneous. Unlike

Charlemagne's empire (see Chapter 2), it did not include France, the largest and most populous country in Europe. As France was surrounded by Charles' territories and felt threatened by them, military conflicts were the order of the day. Given the feudal bond between Flanders and Artois, and the French crown, this contradiction was of great importance to the Low Countries.

The second threat to Charles' empire and to Western Christianity in general came from the powerful Ottoman Empire in the Balkan and the eastern Mediterranean. The protestant Reformation was the third major problem facing the emperor. In 1517, Martin Luther published his famous theses, exposing a variety of abuses within the Catholic Church. In 1521, Luther and the young emperor were present at the diet (*Reichstag*) in Worms. Charles presented himself as patron and champion of the Catholic Church, but Luther refused to retract his claims. This formally started the schism in Western Christianity which had far-reaching consequences for political, religious, and cultural relations in large parts of Europe, including the Low Countries.

Territorial Expansion and Constitutional Consolidation in the Low Countries

Despite the many territories requiring Charles' attention, he managed to remain involved in governing the Low Countries. A new phase of territorial expansion began soon after he took office. In 1521 Tournai and the Tournaisis region were annexed. This small territory was important because Tournai was a French enclave and its bishop exercised ecclesiastical authority over a large part of the county of Flanders. Charles also focused on the north and east of the Low Countries. In 1524, he seized Friesland, a free peasant republic in the north of the present-day Netherlands. In 1528, he also formally annexed the prince-bishopric of Utrecht, which had been under the guardianship of the Burgundian state since the fifteenth century.

The annexations of Tournai, Friesland and Utrecht were relatively unproblematic. The duchy of Gelre had been an ally of France, fighting against the Burgundians since Charles the Bold's period. During the 1520s and 1530s, Gelre troops regularly fought a kind of guerrilla war in the northern Low Countries. They pillaged Brabant throughout 1542–1543, eliciting a powerful Habsburg reaction. In 1543 the duke of Cleve, who also ruled over Gelre and Zutphen, was ordered to hand over these territories to Charles V. With these annexations, the Habsburg Low Countries reached their largest expansion. In the numerous royal titles Charles V held, the Low Countries were mentioned as consisting of seventeen territories: the duchies of Brabant, Limburg, Luxembourg and Gelre; the counties of Flanders, Artois, Walloon-Flanders, Hainaut, Namur, Holland and Zeeland; the principalities of Friesland, Groningen, Utrecht and Overijssel; and finally the cities of Mechelen and Tournai. The Low Countries therefore also came to be known as the XVII Provinces. With the exception of the prince-bishopric of Liège, the current Benelux countries came under Habsburg rule from 1543 (see Map 5.1, p. 147).

Like the Burgundian state, the prince-bishopric of Liège experienced an extraordinarily turbulent period in the final third of the fifteenth century. The main issue was the power sharing relationship between the prince-bishop, the States, and – especially – the city of Liège. Both the prince-bishop and his main opponent came to a violent end in the 1480s. From 1492, the prince-bishopric adhered to a policy of neutrality between Habsburg and France, following an agreement between Maximilian and the French king. This political line was respected in name, but was not defended militarily. As a result, in the following centuries foreign troops regularly operated from Liège territory. Both the French and the Habsburgs tried to influence Liège's neutrality to their advantage. In the first half of the sixteenth century, prince-bishop Érard de la Marck (r. 1505–1538) pursued a pro-Habsburg policy, for which Charles V heavily compensated him and his kin. At the same time, de la Marck vigorously defended Liège's independence despite the defensive alliance he had formed with Charles V in 1518.

During Charles V's reign, the government of the Habsburg Low Countries took the form that it would keep until approximately the end of the eighteenth century. The position of the ruler's representative, the regent or governor-general, became permanent. After the regency of Margaret of Austria (1519–1530), Charles appointed his sister, Mary of Hungary (1505–1558) as her successor. She ruled autonomously but followed her brother's instructions. Regents, often siblings or children of the ruler, succeeded one another until the end of the eighteenth century. Mary kept her position for a quarter of a century until Charles' abdication in 1555. As regent she had a royal court, which was established in Brussels in 1531. From that year, with the exception of the

Figure 4.3 *The Coudenberg Palace* (Brussels, *c.*1540/8). Around 1450,
the old castle of the dukes of Brabant was transformed into a palace for
duke Philip the Good. It became the residence of the successive regents
and governors general of the Low Countries. The building was
destroyed by fire in 1731 and replaced by the present-day palace and
parc. Painting attributed to Lucas Gessel (1480–1568) (Brussels,
Museum Broodhuis)

period between 1795 and 1814, Brussels was the capital city of what later
was to become Belgium (see Figure 4.3).

In 1531, Charles V reorganized the government councils. The Council
of State, composed of members of the high nobility and a few jurists,
advised on international politics and other important political issues. The
Privy Council was composed of jurists and functioned as a combination
of the Home Office and Justice Department. Finally, the Council of
Finances dealt with royal finances and economic issues.

Henceforth, the Habsburg Low Countries had a fully-fledged central
government, a slowly growing bureaucracy, a capital, and a regent's
court. At the level of the principalities a permanent representative of
the sovereign also existed: the governor or *stadtholder*, always a member
of the high nobility. Thus, in the Burgundian tradition, the high nobility
was actively involved in national government on several levels. Charles
also aspired to full sovereignty over his territories in the Low Countries,
although Flanders and Artois were fiefs that he held from the French
king. A Burgundian duke paying feudal homage to the French king was
acceptable. But for Charles, wearing no less than nine royal crowns, this
proved problematic.

In the 1520s, Charles waged war with France over the duchy of Milan. In 1525 he achieved a great victory at Pavia, leading to the capture of the French king. In the peace treaties of Madrid (1526) and Cambrai (1529) Francis I eventually agreed to renounce his sovereignty over Flanders and Artois. These treaties also put an end to the jurisdiction of the Parliament of Paris over Flanders and Artois, which formally became part of the Holy Roman Empire. In 1548, Charles pressured the Imperial Diet to merge the XVII Provinces into one Burgundian *Cercle* (the Augsburg Transaction) within the empire. Moreover, this *Cercle* would no longer be subject to the jurisdiction of the *Reichskammergericht*, the Empire's supreme court.

Consequently, the Habsburg Low Countries became de facto a separate political unit. In 1549, Charles V decided that his successors would inherit the Habsburg Low Countries as a whole. The Burgundian–Habsburg state formation process, started over a century and a half before, had reached a critical stage. Since a province is a subdivision of a polity, the use of the term "XVII Provinces" was quite significant: some inhabitants of the individual principalities undoubtedly realized they were part of a larger entity. However, it is important to note that this political construct was not an independent monarchy, like Castile or England. Charles V remained duke of Brabant, count of Flanders, etc. In spite of this ambiguity, the general acceptance of the name "the Low Country" in the sixteenth century signified that it was seen as a geographical unit, both domestically and abroad. However, terminology was still fluctuating. From the sixteenth century it also became common practice to use the terms *Belgium*, *Belgica*, *la Belge*, or *Belgique* as designating the whole of the Habsburg Netherlands. Moreover, its inhabitants (even those from the French-speaking areas) often referred to themselves as *Vlaming* or *Flamand*. In Italy, people living in the Netherlands were called *Fiamminghi*, and the English used the term *Flanders* to refer to the Netherlands as a whole.

The changed balance of power between the Habsburg State and its subjects is nicely illustrated by the development of the Ghent revolt in 1539–1540. At this time, dissatisfaction with the rising cost of living and taxes, and the decline of the wool industry was increasing. In 1538, Ghent was the only city to refuse an increase in taxes because they were meant to finance the emperor's foreign wars. Some Habsburg officials were killed. When Charles was informed, he travelled at a leisurely pace from Spain via France – as there was a brief period of peace – to the Low

Countries. Unlike events in the previous century, there was no warfare. Ghent realized that it was unable to cope militarily with the imperial military. In an almost ritualistic fashion, Charles personally restored order: he ordered the execution of a number of rioters, publicly humiliated the aldermen and deans of the corporations, and imposed a heavy fine. The *Concessio Carolina* stipulated that the city council would be appointed by the monarch and without the participation of Ghent's bourgeoisie and corporations. Times had changed since the fourteenth century, when Ghent positioned itself more or less as an independent republic.

Antwerp and the European Economy

In the second half of the fifteenth century, Europe's demographic expansion resumed after the disastrous crisis of the previous century. The total population of the Habsburg Low Countries increased by 50 percent in the sixteenth century, from 2.5 to 3.7 million. The most spectacular growth took place in Antwerp, from about 30,000 inhabitants in *c.*1470 to about 100,000 a century later. This made Antwerp the second largest city in Europe, north of the Alps. This growth was mainly due to the city's position as the central staple market of Western Europe. Large stocks of all kinds of products prevented steep price fluctuations and thereby the risks of long-distance trade. The presence of numerous merchants generated more efficient financial services. From the perspective of public finances, a high turnover of goods at a central location was very attractive because it could easily be taxed.

Until the fifteenth century, Europe had a multipolar system of equivalent staple markets: Bruges, Venice, Genoa, and Lübeck. In the following century, a unipolar staple market system emerged. Antwerp played the central role in a vast network of international trading centers. Until the end of the fifteenth century, the Mediterranean was the center for European trade. Valuable goods from the Near and Far East reached Western, central, and northern Europe via the Levant, Venice, and Genoa. Two factors upset this system: first, Ottoman domination in the eastern Mediterranean, which threatened the Levant trade; and second, Portuguese explorations along the coasts of Africa and India, and Spanish and Portuguese expansion in the Americas after 1492. Both developments heralded the beginning of an Atlantic economy, with north-western Europe as its center.

The question however remains: "Why Antwerp and not Bruges"? Traditional historiography often mentioned the silting of the river Zwin, linking Bruges to the North Sea. However, political and economic factors were more important. Bruges stubbornly stuck to the defense and protection of its cloth industry against English competition – a lost battle. Antwerp, on the contrary, handled the issue much more pragmatically. Its cloth industry successfully focused on the final processing of English woolen fabrics for export to Central Europe. During the turbulent years of 1482–1493, Bruges had opposed Maximilian of Austria. Antwerp, on the other hand, had been law-abiding and was rewarded with all kinds of privileges by the archduke. Moreover, Antwerp enjoyed a geographical advantage: while being located much more inland, it was still easily accessible for sea traffic. Bruges remained an important economic center but lost its dominant position.

Antwerp's success can be attributed to a fortunate combination of trade flows. The English Merchant Adventurers supplied large quantities of cloth and had them dyed and finished in Antwerp, thereby providing jobs for thousands of craftsmen. The Portuguese chose Antwerp as a major distribution center for spices imported from Asia. The densely populated and urbanized Low Countries provided an ideal outlet for these valuable products, and their central location facilitated their distribution throughout Central and northern Europe. Merchants from southern Germany supplied silver and copperware that the Portuguese needed for their trade along the African coasts and in Asia. The southern Germans exported spices and English cloth to Central Europe. Antwerp also became home to many Italian merchants who were mainly active in silk trading and banking.

The combination of these so-called rich trades with the trade and transport of bulk goods such as wine, salt, grain, and timber was also of key importance. During the fifteenth century, shipping developed rapidly in Holland and Zeeland. Taking into account the climate and the duration of transport, the Low Countries were both the ideal stopover point and outlet for these trades. Antwerp merchants commissioned many of these transports. In the first half of the sixteenth century, Amsterdam, at that time already the largest city in Holland, was still a dependency of Antwerp.

Antwerp also became an international financial center. The large volume of commercial transactions in the city generated a financial market, which proved convenient for businesses and rulers. In 1519,

Charles V borrowed a large part of the money he needed to acquire the title of emperor. Foreign monarchs made use of the Antwerp capital market. For example, Sir Thomas Gresham, the founder of the London Royal Exchange, was based in Antwerp and served as a financial representative of the English crown. Providing loans to sovereigns was attractive because of the, often sky-high, interest rates. However, it was also a risky business, as interest payments and the repayment of sovereign debts were not really enforceable. When Charles' successor Philip II (r. 1555–1598) declared state bankruptcy in 1557 and in 1575, the financial sector in Antwerp was severely hit.

The city's leading role in international trade was an important stimulus for domestic trade and the manufacturing industry. Foreign merchants not only bought products from all over the world, but also from the Low Countries: linen, cheaper woolen fabrics (new drapery), all kinds of mixed textiles (wool, silk, linen, and cotton), different kinds of tapestries from relatively cheap (Oudenaarde) to very luxurious and expensive (Brussels, Tournai), gold leather, etc. This interplay of factors cemented Antwerp's attractive position as a staple market to foreign traders. Although the number of local merchants grew exponentially after 1525, the presence of so many foreign merchants was a liability because they could easily take their trade elsewhere in bad times. The dramatic political developments after 1560 would make this clear.

Arts and Sciences

The Burgundian and Habsburg Low Countries were a fertile breeding ground for art production. Traditionally, the Church and the ruler's court were the main patrons. The Burgundian dukes, especially Philip the Bold and Philip the Good, gained quite a reputation in this respect. Later, when the Low Countries became part of the Habsburg monarchy, royal patronage focused more on the core of the empire. But city councils, corporations, and wealthy citizens also stimulated artistic production, as had been the case in the Italian cities.

The architectural heritage of the Low Countries in the fifteenth and sixteenth centuries is important: in many cities, even those without a bishop or a chapter, churches were built that were as large and as high as the great Gothic cathedrals of England and France. The Saint Lambert Cathedral of Liège, an episcopal church, was home to 4,000 worshipers. The Our Lady Church of Antwerp, a parish church built between

1352 and 1521, was about the same size as the Notre Dame in Paris and boasted a tower of 124 m. Large churches were also built in Ghent, Bruges, Brussels, and Mechelen.

During the fifteenth and sixteenth centuries, city councils spent huge sums on the construction of town halls, whose size and ornamentation expressed their municipal status and prestige. The Brussels Town Hall (1402–1444), for instance, had a tower of no less than 96 m high. Even a modest town like Oudenaarde had a large town hall (constructed in 1526–1536). These edifices were built in flamboyant or Brabant Gothic style. When Antwerp reached its economic zenith, an imposing new town hall was built (in 1561–1564) in pure Renaissance style. Large royal castles such as Hampton Court or Chambord were not built in the Low Countries. However, from *c.*1450 the old ducal palace in Brussels was refashioned into a spacious palace complex in mixed Gothic-Renaissance style, with a Great Hall measuring 40 by 16 m. Charles V abdicated there in 1555.

Painting undoubtedly represents the Low Countries' most prominent cultural feature. The late fourteenth century saw an increasing interest in refined manuscript illustration. The pinnacle of this tradition was the work of the Van Limburg brothers, Herman, Paul, and Johan (*c.*1385–1416). They worked for Philip the Bold and for his brother, the duke of Berry. The book of hours *Les très riches heures du duc de Berry* is considered to be the height of medieval miniature art. Artists were active as book illustrators and painters. This was the background of the Early Netherlandish Painting School, also known as the "Flemish Primitives," founded *c.*1420. "Flemish" refers to artists from all over the Low Countries, including the French-speaking regions. The word "primitive" indicates the new style they developed: a high degree of realism in depicting landscapes and all kinds of details.

The first and most important painters were Jan (*c.*1390–1441) and Hubert (*c.*1385/90–1426) Van Eyck. In 1425, Jan Van Eyck became employed as Philip the Good's court painter and *valet de chambre*. He travelled to Portugal to paint the duke's future wife. During the last decade of his life, Jan Van Eyck settled in Bruges. He painted portraits, triptychs, and polyptychs. In addition to his work for the duke, he painted for high clergymen (*Virgin with child with canon Van der Paele*), government officials (*Madonna of Chancellor Rolin*) as well as wealthy merchants and patricians (*The Arnolfini Portrait*). His most famous work is the Ghent Altarpiece, a polyptych painted for a Ghent patrician couple. Van Eyck's work has a calming feel and is characterized by a faithful observation of nature and exact architectural details of idealized buildings.

The work of Robert Campin (*c.*1375–1444) and his pupil Roger de la Pasture (1399/1400–1464) is characterized by its fierce realism and heavy emotion. Campin worked at Tournai and played an important role in the local guilds. After his apprenticeship, de la Pasture settled in Brussels where he was appointed as the city painter to embellish the new town hall. He enjoyed international fame and visited Italy in 1450. He is best known by his Dutch name, Rogier van der Weyden. Hans Memling (1430–1494), who came from Germany, learned the trade from Van der Weyden and settled in Bruges, where he became an internationally renowned painter. In addition to triptychs with mainly religious subjects, he excelled in portraying wealthy patrons.

Hieronymus Bosch (*c.*1450–1516) spent his entire career in the Brabant city 's Hertogenbosch. His triptychs highlighted his eschatological worldview: human desire and fear, sin and folly, chaos and violence, Heaven and Hell. One of his most famous works is the *Garden of Earthly Delights*. Philip II (see Chapter 5) admired Bosch's work. Starting in around 1500, there was an increasing Italian influence on the work of the Low Countries' painters. The most noted one to visit Italy was undoubtedly Pieter Brueghel the Elder (1525/1530–1569), the first of four generations of painters by that name. Brueghel was the first Flemish Renaissance painter and started the eponymous movement. The influence of his trip to Italy was most notable in his landscapes. Brueghel first worked as an engraver in Antwerp but later settled in Brussels. His short yet highly successful career focused on genre painting of landscapes and peasant scenes. Some of his famous paintings are *Peasant Wedding, Netherlandish Proverbs, Hunters in the Snow, Children's Games* and *The Fight between Carnival and Lent*. His paintings were highly sought after by international collectors. Habsburg emperor Rudolf II (r. 1576–1612) owned at least a dozen.

During the fifteenth and sixteenth centuries, the Low Countries were not only renowned for their painters. Their music and musicians also enjoyed an international reputation. Composers were mostly trained in the choir schools of cathedrals (Liège, Arras, Tournai) or collegiate churches (Ghent, Antwerp, Mons, Bruges). Their position enabled them to renew polyphonic music and dominate the European music world, focusing not only on church music but also writing profane songs and chansons, which were usually sung in French. These composers worked at royal courts (Rome, Paris, Este, Ferrara, Valladolid, Munich). *I Fiamminghi* or the *Capilla flamenca* were established concepts in Italy and Spain. Gilles Binchois (before 1400–1460) served at the court of Philip the Good; Johannes Ockeghem or Hocqueghem (1410/ 1425–1497) worked at the chapel of the French king. Adrian Willaert (*c.*1490–1562) worked for Cardinal Ippolito d'Este in Ferrara and Milan and became *maestro di Capella* of Saint Marco in Venice (1527–1562).

In the literary field, the so-called *Lettres bourguignonnes* are certainly noteworthy. These writings served to glorify the ideal of knighthood and record the chronicles of the royal house. All these works were written in French, the language of royalty and the high nobility. Well-known names are Georges Chastelain (*c.*1410–1475), Jean Lemaire de Belges (1473–1524) and Olivier de la Marche (1425–1502). Besides chronicles and memoirs, they also wrote poetry. They worked for the Burgundian dukes but were also active at the French court.

Rhetoricians were active in many cities. They were citizens who had received a certain education (craftsmen, merchants, patricians, clerks, etc.) and who wrote poetry and/or practiced acting as amateurs. They were organized in so-called Chambers under the formal leadership of a "Prince," usually a person from the local or regional elite who also acted as a patron. By participating as a group in pageants, ceremonies, and inter-city competitions, they contributed to the urban identity of their cities. In times of political and religious tension, their meetings provided an opportunity to criticize or ridicule current events. In her poetry, the Antwerp beguine and rhetorician Anna Bijns (1493–1575) was an ardent defender of the Catholic Church against Protestantism.

Until the first quarter of the fifteenth century, residents of the Low Countries fortunate enough to enjoy higher learning were educated abroad, mostly in Paris or Cologne. Leuven University, founded in 1425, was the only university of the Low Countries until 1559. By 1450, more than 1,000 students attended its courses, and by 1520 this had risen to 2,000. Between 1450 and 1550, Leuven University had more students than any other university north of the Alps and boasted some brilliant professors. Erasmus taught there in 1502–1504 and 1517–1521. The mathematician Gemma Frisius (1508–1555) corresponded with the astronomer and mathematician Copernicus and taught the great geographer Mercator (1512–1594). Brussels-born Andreas Vesalius (1514–1564), the founder of human anatomy, also studied at Leuven

University. Physician Rembert Dodoens or Dodonaeus (1517/8–1585) was trained in Leuven and subsequently enjoyed great fame as a botanist. The university also played a leading role in the field of theology. On November 7, 1519, Leuven theologians were the first to condemn Luther's teachings and took the lead in the Counter-Reformation.

Christian Humanism and Early Reformation

Humanism, originating in Italy in the fourteenth and fifteenth centuries, had a rather worldly tint. Christian Humanism, its northern European variant, focused on the study and writing of classical Latin as a source of Christian purity. In the Low Countries the *Devotio Moderna* (Modern Devotion) was its main spiritual inspiration. A community of laymen and clergy, "Brothers and sisters of the Common Life," shared income, property, meals, and housing. They aspired to a type of Christianity that focused on the believer's direct contact with God but they accepted ecclesiastical institutions and authority. The ideas of this movement were best expressed in Thomas a Kempis' (1380–1471) famous book, *De Imitatione Christi* ("Living in the Image of Christ").

Desiderius Erasmus (1466–1536), the most famous northern Humanist, was educated in the vein of the Modern Devotion. His *Philosophia Christi* aspired to reform and improve both the individual and society as a whole. He stressed the importance of living according to Christ's principles, personal contact with God, and the rejection of superficial and/or formalist piety. He also highlighted the importance of the Holy Scriptures to live as a good Christian.

Erasmus' contemporary, Martin Luther, proclaimed his revolutionary theological theses in 1517. According to Luther, man can only justify his existence through personal faith and the only source for that faith is the Bible. Luther considered the Church to be the community of all believers, making the special status of the clergy obsolete. He unleashed the Protestant Reformation that would permanently divide Western Christianity. The transition of cities, regions, or countries to (a form of) Protestantism took place in different ways. Either a ruler imposed it, or the change was brought about from below – groups of subjects demanding a "reformation" of the Church. The Reformation in the Low Countries followed the second path.

The Low Countries already enjoyed a relatively high degree of literacy and numeracy in the fifteenth century. According to estimates, at least

10–15 percent of the population had notions of reading, writing, and arithmetic. Differences between men and women, and city and country-side were strikingly limited. Schools (particularly in cities) trained young children in reading, writing, and calculating in the local language, often in combination with professional training. In large and smaller towns, the so-called Latin schools even educated children of poor families that benefitted from scholarships or urban charity. The Spanish Humanist Juan Luis Vivès propagated the promotion of Humanist education for girls. His ideas about free education for poor children were applied in Bruges, Ypres, and Antwerp. At the beginning of the sixteenth century, so-called French schools were founded in the larger cities. Their curriculum did not include Latin, but focused on practical subjects such as the mother tongue, French, arithmetic, and bookkeeping.

To promote the new ideas of humanism and reformation, the invention of a movable type of printing proved invaluable. The first printing offices in the Low Countries date from 1473, only two decades after Gutenberg's invention. During the fourteenth and fifteenth centuries, the Low Countries, and especially modern Belgium, were the most important per capita producer of manuscript books in Europe. Until the thirteenth century, the Church was the most prolific producer. In the fifteenth century, demand had shifted to a large extent (70 percent) to rulers, universities, nobles, and wealthy citizens.

Dirk Martens (1446/7–1534) founded the first printing office in his hometown Aalst, and subsequently in Leuven and Antwerp as well. Printers also settled in other cities in the Low Countries. During the fifteenth century, they mostly printed grammars and liturgical works. This changed in the sixteenth century when book production commercialized. The price of books and printed matter in general dropped spectacularly. Dirk Martens, for example, published work by Erasmus and Thomas More, but also Columbus' first letter about his trip to America. After 1520, many pamphlets, psalms, and biblical texts were printed under the influence of Lutheranism, which addressed all believers.

Lutheran teachings proved popular in the Low Countries. By the first half of the sixteenth century there were signs of a relative decline of the Catholic Church. The division of the Low Countries into dioceses was totally outdated (see Chapter 5). The bishops, mostly of noble descent, were more concerned with politics than with pastoral care. Many also criticized the financial privileges of the Church. There are indications that the numbers of priests and monks taking their spiritual vows decreased. Cities provided especially fertile ground for the new doctrine because of their complex political, social, and economic stratification and their many forms of social interaction.

However, the government remained vigilant. In the Low Countries Lutheranism was banned in 1521, and an Inquisition was created to persecute the heretics. The first victims of anti-Protestant repression in Europe were two monks burnt at the stake in Brussels in July 1523, and the persecution of heretics intensified in the 1530s. The Anabaptists, radicalized followers of the Reformation, founded a theocratic republic in the German town of Münster in 1534–1536, abolishing money and introducing common property and polygamy. As a result, thousands of men and women, mainly poor people and artisans from the northern Low Countries, moved to Münster.

The revolutionary behavior of the Anabaptists unleashed a backlash of merciless persecution. About 86 percent of people executed for heresy in Antwerp between 1522 and 1565 were Anabaptists. In 1550, heresy was made punishable by death and the convicted also lost all their possessions. In the Habsburg Low Countries, no less than 1,300 people were executed for heresy between 1522 and 1565. The severity of this persecution had two consequences. Few had the courage to openly practice their new faith. Some held secret meetings in so-called Churches under the Cross. Others emigrated in anticipation of better times, mostly to Germany. From an orthodox Catholic perspective, the fight against "heresy" was successful until 1550.

However, the Inquisition's apparent success caused increasing aversion. Magistrates took offence at the Inquisition, as it interfered with their jurisdiction. The confiscation of the condemned heretic's possessions affected the interests of their family and relatives. Many members of the elite, Catholics who had been educated in the Erasmian vein, were disgusted by the Inquisition's harshness. Clear similarities existed between Luther's criticism of the Roman Catholic Church and the Erasmian *Philosophia Christi*. However, Erasmus remained faithful to Rome because he believed Protestant radicalism would strengthen the hold of Catholic hardliners on the Church. Thus the paths of Luther and Erasmus separated, but Christian Humanism, spreading amongst the higher educated in the Low Countries, would prove very important during the next phase of the Reformation.

Conclusion

Between *c.*1400 and 1550, the Burgundian-Habsburg Low Countries developed into a promising political project: a confederation of approximately fifteen principalities, both large and small, with overarching administrative and legal institutions, a central government, and a capital. However, regional particularism remained very strong and the confederation was only completed in around 1550. Moreover, the Low Countries were but a part, and not even the center, of the huge Habsburg composite monarchy. After 1495, the economy of the Low Countries boomed, especially in Brabant, Flanders, Holland, and Zeeland. However, social inequality increased and trade and the export industries were vulnerable to external shocks. In these uncertain times, new ideas about Church and faith were easily spread in word and print in the densely populated country. When Charles V's successor tried to unilaterally change the balance of power between monarch, aristocracy, and the urban elites, those who felt threatened by this policy change committed themselves to a new radical and militant form of the Reformation. In time, this would prove to have major consequences for the survival of the Habsburg Low Countries as a polity.

The Spanish Netherlands (1555–1700/1713)

Introduction

Until 1555 the Netherlands were part of Charles V's multinational Habsburg Empire. Charles clearly considered the Spanish kingdoms, especially Castile, the core of his monarchy. However, Charles traveled continuously throughout his vast territories and personally participated in many wars, from west and central Europe to North Africa. Despite his long absences, his subjects in the Low Countries accepted Charles as their rightful and "natural" sovereign. His son, Philip II (r. 1555–1598), on the other hand, was born and educated in Spain. During his forty-four-year rule, Philip spent less than five years away from the Iberian Peninsula.

After 1555, the Netherlands became part of the possessions of the Spanish crown. Spain was a "composite monarchy," centered on Castile, with Aragon, Catalonia, Naples, Sicily, Sardinia, Milan, and the Netherlands (including Franche-Comté) as its most important "dependencies." Moreover the Spanish monarchy included colonial territories in America, Asia, and Africa. After 1580, the monarchy was expanded to include Portugal and its colonies. Composite monarchies faced similar problems, namely the difficult communication between the core of the monarchy and the peripheral territories. The geographical distance between the ruler and his subjects proved especially problematic, as rulers could not afford to ignore the interests and political ideas of the latter.

The communication between Spain and the Low Countries was quite difficult, more so than with its Italian dominions. Contact between Spain and Italy via the Mediterranean went rather smoothly, unlike the maritime connection with the Low Countries through the Atlantic, as both

England and France could easily interfere. The fact that the Netherlands bordered mighty and often hostile France posed an additional problem. Moreover, the ruler had to take the strong provincial States and the States-General of the Netherlands into account. Most importantly, in the Low Countries the King had to face the threat of religious divisiveness. This chapter discusses how the political line set forth by the Spanish kings and their ministers caused the disintegration of the XVII Provinces, and subsequently created a proto-"Belgium."

A Problematic Peace (1559)

The peace treaty of Le Cateau-Cambrésis ended over half a century of war between France and Habsburg and confirmed the end of Flanders' feudal tie to France. Apparently, Philip II, who had succeeded his father Charles V in 1555, could safely return to Spain. In reality, the Netherlands were on the eve of a turbulent, even tragic, period.

The return of peace did not stop a decades-long trend of loss of purchasing power and impoverishment for many artisans, laborers, and peasants. The sixteenth century was a time of population growth and price inflation. Food prices increased and those of staple food, like grain, rose more than the price of, for example, meat or wine. As a result, the poor suffered most, having to spend the bulk of their income on staple food.

Monetary factors also contributed to the higher prices. The import of gold and silver from Latin America led to a decrease in the relative value of money. Currency debasement imposed by rulers, thereby hoping to alleviate some of their debts, had the same effect. A major problem with price increases for laborers especially, was that wages didn't follow rising prices or only slightly and after a long period of time. Understandably, this led to unrest and insecurity for many. Of course some social categories and professional groups were able to profit from this price inflation, namely merchant-entrepreneurs and big farmers. But even some of the more affluent population took a financial hit, such as the owners of fixed-rate incomes, like seigniorial rights.

From the perspective of a Catholic king such as Philip II, some threatening international developments arose around 1560. England was ruled by the Protestant queen Elizabeth. In 1555 in the Holy Roman Empire, Lutheran rulers had acquired the right to freely practice their faith and impose it on their subjects. France went through a very unstable period, where factions of nobles, partly based on religious preference, fought each other.

In the Low Countries, too, political relations were tense. Before leaving for Spain, the king had demanded from the States-General a substantial raise of the subsidy and thus an increase in taxes. The war against France had been very costly. Moreover, Philip was involved in another expensive war against the Ottoman Empire. To his great disappointment the States-General, even after months of negotiating, only agreed to a limited increase in taxes. The latter were not prepared to finance the king's war against the Turks. They argued that the Netherlands themselves had suffered greatly during the war with France and, as such, were unable to pay more than they already did.

Before leaving for Spain, the king had appointed his half-sister Margaret of Parma (1522–1586) as governor. During Charles V's rule, government business in Brussels was extensively discussed in the Council of State, giving the high nobility the opportunity to influence policy. This state of affairs had the advantage of implementing government policy more successfully in the territories where they had extensive networks. Philip II, on the contrary, wanted to strengthen his own power by limiting that of the nobility. His ideal government consisted of jurists and bureaucrats without their own base of power, loyally implementing policy as the king saw fit. This difference in vision would result in increasing tensions between the king and part of the political elite in the Low Countries.

Ecclesiastical Reform and the New Dioceses

Equally important to the growing antagonism between the king and part of the population were the position of the Catholic Church and the implementation of anti-Protestant policy. During Charles V's rule, Lutherans and Anabaptists were heavily prosecuted (see Chapter 4). From the 1550s, a new protestant creed, Calvinism, gained popularity in the Netherlands. As will become clear in this chapter, militant Calvinists were not easily intimidated by government repression. They went on the offensive and did not shy away from provocation or violence.

Even members of the Catholic clergy and its associated elite found themselves at odds with the king. The diocesan organization of the Netherlands was completely outdated. There were not enough dioceses in relation to the population. Moreover, all dioceses were subdivisions of foreign archdioceses (Reims and Cologne). So an adaptation of the ecclesiastical structure to the actual polity of the XVII Provinces was quite logical. Besides, to successfully combat the rise of Protestantism, the Church needed to improve its organization. After many years of negotiating, the king and the Vatican finally reached an agreement in 1559. There would be three archbishops and fifteen dioceses and the nomination of archbishops and bishops by the king was to be approved by the Pope.

A fierce level of opposition against the new bishoprics originated from different sources. In order to finance the new dioceses, it was decided that the bishops would have the revenue of one or more abbeys at their disposal. This greatly frustrated the religious orders to which the affected abbeys belonged. In Brabant, abbots of important abbeys were members of the provincial States, and it was feared that the king could use these bishop-abbots to influence the decision making process in the provincial States.

The opposition was mainly directed at the newly appointed archbishop of Mechelen. Nicolas Perrenot de Granvelle (1517–1586) belonged to the nobles of the robe, hailed from distant Franche-Comté. He was a trusted advisor to Philip II and his father had served under Charles V. The Pope made him a cardinal on the recommendation of the king. As a "prince of the Church" the low-born Granvelle came at the top of the aristocratic hierarchy, to the displeasure of the high nobility.

High Nobility in the Opposition (1564)

Granvelle's first-rate position was a thorn in the side of the Council of State's nobles. Margaret of Parma mainly listened to the former's advice, along with a select number of confidants. Meetings of the Council became increasingly formal, to the displeasure of its noble members. William of Nassau (1533–1584) took the lead in the opposition. He was to play a crucial part in the following decades. William was a younger son of the ruler of a small German Lutheran principality. At the age of ten, he became heir to a cousin who met an untimely death and had many properties in both Brabant and Holland. He also became sovereign prince of the southern French principality of Orange. At the Brussels court, William was brought up to be a prominent Catholic nobleman. However, his true religious beliefs were subject to speculation. Contrary to his nickname, "the Taciturn," William was a great conversationalist but rarely showed what he was truly thinking, making the king highly suspicious of him.

In the early 1560s, the policies regarding the persecution of Protestants were an important political and social issue. The so-called Blood Placards (1550) failed to intimidate militant Calvinists. This led to several polarizing incidents: a group of men and women singing psalms, walking the streets of Tournai in protest (1561); men mocking the image of the Holy Virgin Mary; the interrupting of processions and church services, etc. Some also held hedge preachings – sermons in the open air, often outside the jurisdiction of the local magistrates to avoid persecution – these were first addressed to a limited number of people, but as time went by these events drew enormous crowds.

The harsh repression against the Protestants was generally unpopular. In particular, the accompanying societal unrest was frustrating to many local and government officials and the elite. When a plea from William of Orange and several noble members of the Council of State to mitigate the use of the so-called Blood Placards fell on deaf ears, most noble members of the Council abstained from attending its meetings (1563–1564). To appease the nobles, the king finally ordered Granvelle to leave the Netherlands. Later on, this proved to be a simple distraction, as Philip did not ease up on his tough policies regarding Protestants and his plan to impose absolutism. At first, Orange and his colleagues seemed to acquiesce but soon tensions escalated once more.

In 1565, over two hundred petty nobles from different provinces formed a kind of union: the so-called League of Compromise. In the spring of 1566, they marched to the palace of the governor to offer a petition demanding a mitigation of the anti-Protestant laws, and threatening revolt if they were not heard. One of Margaret of Parma's courtiers allegedly compared the protesting nobles to "*des gueux*" (beggars), after which the aforementioned nobles and all who participated in the protest decided to adopt this as a badge of honor, proudly calling themselves "Beggars" (French, *Gueux*; Dutch, *Geuzen*). The great nobles did not participate in the "League of Compromise," but William the Taciturn undoubtedly kept regular contact with them.

Iconoclasm

In the summer of 1566, hedge preaching and protests increased. In August, in the western Flemish village of Steenvoorde, statues in a local church were vandalized after a Calvinistic hedge sermon. According to Calvinistic teachings the Bible, the word of God, was the only true source of faith. The worship of the saints and Mary, certain sacraments, etc. – even depictions of Bible scenes – were to be rejected and therefore destroyed. Some historians think that Iconoclasm was rooted in socio-economic motives. In 1566 food prices had reached a new high and many people lost their job because of a trade conflict with England. It is not unreasonable to see Iconoclasm, partly, as a protest against poverty. However, the general consensus among historians today is that the movement was mainly religiously inspired.

It is important to note that the Iconoclasm was not a spontaneous act, but rather a carefully planned attack coordinated between local, English, and French Calvinists. In some cases, Catholic clerics were abused and their monasteries, mainly their stocks of food and beverages, plundered. In most cases however the "cleansing" of the churches happened systematically and in an orderly fashion. Local authorities generally offered little to no resistance. In some cases they tried to focus Calvinistic efforts on a restricted number of churches, hoping to limit the damage. By offering some churches to the protesters, local authorities intended to stop the hedge sermons and appease the protesters. It goes without saying that the "scandalous behavior" of the Iconoclasts was later widely condemned in Catholic pamphlets.

The government in Brussels was completely surprised by the iconoclastic wave. The governor had no choice but to call upon the high nobility to restore order where necessary. The count of Egmont, *stadtholder* of Flanders, and William of Orange, *stadtholder* of Holland, Zeeland, and Utrecht, played an important part in the restoration of order. The fact that William was actively involved in the repression of violence, despite his suspected sympathies for the Reformation, shows that he kept his political options open. Iconoclasm raged in August and September all over the Netherlands, but the situation differed both regionally and chronologically. It started in the south (West Flanders) and ended in the north (Groningen and Friesland). Iconoclasm touched most parts of Flanders and Brabant, in cities such as Ypres, Oudenaarde, Ghent, Mechelen, and Antwerp, but other important cities like Bruges, Lille, Brussels, and Leuven were spared. In the Walloon region, the movement was limited to Tournai and Valenciennes, the two cities where the first Calvinists had publicly demonstrated in the 1540s. In the prince-bishopric of Liège, only Maastricht was affected (see Figure 5.1; see Map 5.1).

Messages about Iconoclasm bewildered the king and his courtiers. Philip II was the most powerful ruler in Europe. He was known by his

Figure 5.1 *Iconoclasm in the Antwerp Our Lady Cathedral* (1572).
Anonymous engraving

honorary title of "Catholic king" and aspired to either convert or eliminate the Jewish and Muslim minorities in his Spanish territories. Tolerating the mere existence of non-Catholic Christians in one of his territories was unthinkable to him. Therefore, Philip decided that harsh measures were required and Don Fernando Alvarez de Toledo, duke of Alva (1507–1582) was entrusted with the repression of the heretics.

Repression and Revolt

Alva was an experienced general and he had been governor of Milan and viceroy of Naples. Alva's assignment in the Netherlands was threefold: first, punish the iconoclasts; second, cleanse every public authority (magistrates, town councils, etc.) in the Netherlands of those who had behaved weakly or passively during Iconoclasm or the fight against Protestantism in general; third, subjugate the Netherlands to the king's authority once and for all. If successful, the latter measure would enable the king to substantially raise the Low Countries' financial contribution

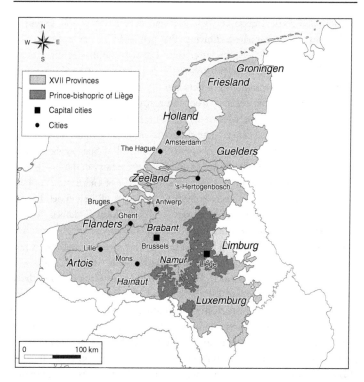

Map 5.1 The Low Countries under Charles V and the prince-bishopric
of Liège, 1549. Redrawn based on a map originally published in *Atlas de
la Wallonie, de la préhistoire à nos jours*, courtesy of Institut Jules Destrée,
Charleroi (© Sofam)

to the Spanish monarchy. To facilitate his plans, the king provided Alva
with a 10,000-strong army. In May 1567, Alva and his troops arrived in
Brussels. The presence of such a formidable foreign army in the
Netherlands marked the beginning of what would become known as
the Spanish period.

Alva established an extraordinary court, the "Council of Troubles"
(*Conseil des Troubles*). The persecuted called it the "Blood Council." As
such, the working of the normal justice system was nullified. Unlike
before, when only the convicted person was impacted by his or her
sentence, the new policy also victimized their families through the
confiscation of their property. Over the years, this new council

pronounced some 10,000 verdicts and had over 1,000 people executed and many more banished. During the propaganda war between the Spaniards and the rebels, the latter would heavily emphasize the cruelty of the "Blood Council." In relation to the population as a whole, the total conviction rate was somewhere between 0.5 and 1.0 percent.

The insecurity that resulted from the restriction of the regular judicial system, as well as the merciless repression, probably had a bigger impact on the political and social climate than the actual number of convictions. At the end of 1567, Alva had two members of the Council of State arrested. The count of Egmont had contributed to an important victory in the war against France in 1558. The count of Horne was *stadtholder* of Gelre and Zutphen, and an admiral. Both men were knights of the Order of the Golden Fleece, which granted them judicial immunity, and were loyal Catholics. After a mock trial, they were executed at the Brussels Great Market. By executing these two noblemen specifically, Alva sent a clear message: nothing would stop him from completing the task the king had entrusted him with.

Had he chosen to remain in Brussels, William of Orange would have certainly been a candidate for the scaffold. In early 1567 he had prevented Antwerp Calvinists from participating in an attack by Beggars on government troops. Orange had kept his political options open and he was certainly unsympathetic to the Calvinistic hardliners. However, he quickly realized how Alva's policies would impact him and left the Low Countries for Germany in a timely fashion. From there, he prepared military actions against the Spanish army. The spring of 1568 signaled the beginning of what would become known as the Revolt of the Netherlands, the Dutch Revolt and the Eighty Years' War. The first year of war ended badly for the insurgents, as the superior Spanish forces easily defeated William's three small armies that invaded the north and the east of the Netherlands from Germany.

After punishing the iconoclasts and disloyal magistrates, and after fighting off Orange's invasion, Alva devoted himself to his third task: the structural increase of royal revenue. He wanted to introduce a new and better performing taxation system that was to be implemented immediately. The design of this new taxation system was highly unusual. Normally, only the provincial States could approve new taxes. Every province had its own taxation system. Moreover, in some cases provincial States even had the right to control how the tax revenue was spent!

The most infamous of the new taxes was the "Tenth Penny," a tax of 10 percent on all commercial transactions. Alva's opponents emphasized its tyrannical and unconstitutional character. From a modern perspective, the new tax seems like an improvement on the existing system, because it meant that all would be taxed equally in equal circumstances. However, early modern society was based on privileges enjoyed by individuals, status groups, and territories and therefore failed to see its merits. So even though the threat of the "Tenth Penny" caused quite a stir, it was never actually imposed. It simply offered Alva leverage to improve the revenue raised by existing taxes. This measure also had an unwanted side effect: Alva's threats incited many loyal Catholics to align with the insurgents.

The revolt of the Netherlands was a layered conflict. It was a religious war between Catholics and Protestants, mainly Calvinists. It was also a conflict between the king and an important faction of the nobility and urban elite. The latter issue mainly concerned the limitations imposed on royal power by the complex system of privileges. In this sense, the insurgence could be considered a civil war. It was also seen as a war of liberation against the Spanish oppressor. Moreover, the insurgence played an important role in international politics, since the Low Countries were a power base for the Spanish-Habsburg monarchy in north-western Europe, thus posing a threat to France, England, and the Holy Roman Empire, and also to Protestantism in those countries. All of these individuals, social categories, institutions, and States followed their own interests during the conflict, but the convergence of some of these interests eventually impacted the outcome of the revolt to a great extent.

Insurgence in Holland (1572)

1572 was a crucial year for the insurgence. Orange had planned a new offensive in collaboration with the French Calvinists. The rebel army attacked the Netherlands from France and conquered Valenciennes and Mons. Cooperation with the French Huguenots, however, fell through as the Catholics massacred them that same year on St Bartholomew's night. Revolts broke out all over the Netherlands. On April 1, the "Sea Beggars," a group of Protestant privateers, occupied the small Holland coastal town of Brielle; this was an event of great symbolic meaning and even greater consequences.

Meanwhile Alva vigorously responded to the rebel attacks. Most cities liberated by the rebel forces were recaptured by the Spanish troops. In some cases soldiers were given a free hand in plundering and the cities' inhabitants were outlawed. Mechelen, Naarden, Zutphen, and Haarlem were plundered and thousands of people were raped, mutilated, and murdered. The purpose of this brutish violence was to set a frightening example to all people tempted by rebellion and to have the outlawed citizens pay the Spanish soldiers their overdue fees. However, Spanish violence proved counterproductive. In Holland and Zeeland, even non-Calvinistic magistrates preferred to open the city gates for the Beggars rather than wait for the Spaniards. Consequently, the parts of Holland and Zeeland that were occupied by the insurgents introduced Calvinism as the official religion. In 1572, the provincial States of Holland and Zeeland recognized Orange as their *stadtholder*, that is, as the king's official representative! One year later, the prince officially converted to Calvinism. The convergence of interests between the high nobleman Orange and the Calvinistic Beggars, with Holland and Zeeland as a territorial base, was the beginning of a long-term alliance.

While Alva's counter-attack against the rebels was successful in the south and the east, it failed in wetland Holland and Zeeland. It became increasingly clear to Philip II that Alva's hardline approach was counter-productive. In 1574, the king recalled Alva and replaced him with his childhood friend Don Luis de Requesens.

Requesens' rule was short-lived. As a gesture of conciliation to the insurgents, he offered a general pardon. The infamous Council of Troubles and Alva's tax reform were abolished. However, negotiations between the king and the insurgents in Holland and Zeeland failed because Philip demanded complete submission from the Calvinists. As a result, anti-Protestant repression was maintained. When Requesens died unexpectedly in the spring of 1576 without appointing a successor, a power vacuum arose. The Council of State seized power and took over as the ruling body.

Pacification? (1576)

The Council was confronted with a most urgent problem: the presence of the Spanish troops. At the end of 1575, the king had announced the bankruptcy of the state. Due to this financial crisis, the Spanish soldiers had yet to be paid. Moreover, there was no commander in chief. The Spanish troops largely retreated from Holland and settled in rich Flanders and Brabant, opting to reclaim their pay from local citizens. On one hand, the Spanish retreat was beneficial to the consolidation of the revolt in Holland and Zeeland. On the other hand, fear of the plundering and murdering Spaniards revitalized resistance in the south. Subsequent events happened in quick succession.

Deliberations between the States-General and the States of Protestant Holland and Zeeland resulted in the Pacification of Ghent (November 8, 1576). This document settled a number of religious and political issues. There was a general consensus that the Spanish troops should leave the country, and that the Netherlands should be governed as they were under Charles V. This meant respect for urban and provincial privileges and the real involvement of the aristocracy and the urban elite in government and taxation.

The arrangement concerning religion was a temporary and shaky compromise. It was agreed that Calvinism would be the official religion in Holland and Zeeland, but that Catholics would have freedom of conscience and thus would be free from persecution. The other provinces were to remain Catholic, but anti-Protestant placards would no longer be observed. Compliance towards a new governor would depend on his willingness to accept the terms of the Pacification. Moreover, the question remained whether the king would agree to such an arrangement. At this point in time the majority of those involved in the revolt, even Orange, aspired to reconcile with Philip II.

A few days before the Pacification was to be signed, Spanish troops invaded Antwerp, the largest and richest city in the Netherlands. The so-called "Spanish Fury" unfolded. The Spanish soldiers raped, murdered, and plundered their way through the city. It has been estimated between 7,000 and 8,000 citizens perished. Hundreds of buildings, including the newly built city hall, were set on fire. More than twenty million guilders worth of money and commodities were stolen by mutinous Spanish troops. It became quite obvious that the Spanish Fury only led to increased radicalization on both sides of the conflict.

In the meantime, the new governor had arrived. Don Juan of Austria was a half-brother of the king and a man of great military prestige. The new governor entered negotiations regarding the provisions of the Pacification. After signing the "Eternal Edict" (May 12, 1577) peace was seemingly on the horizon. The Spanish troops left for Luxemburg, to prepare for their return to Spain. However, agreements concerning religion were open to interpretation. The stipulation that Catholics should be able to practice their faith in Holland and Zeeland proved to be particularly controversial. Less than a month after signing the Eternal

Edict, Don Juan staged a military coup. By the end of the year the Spanish troops had returned.

Radicalization (1578)

In January 1578, a battle between Don Juan's troops and the States-General's army resulted in the former's victory. Bizarrely, both opponents claimed to be fighting in the name of the king. Revolutionary developments in the following months and years made it impossible for the rebels to keep up their fictional loyalty to the king. Don Juan's unreliability caused swift and powerful reactions in Holland and Zeeland. Calvinists went on the offensive, limiting Catholics' rights to a mere freedom of conscience. Churches and monasteries were confiscated and handed over to the Protestants.

In cities like Ghent, Brussels, and Antwerp radicalized preachers, often those that had fled Alva to return later, installed an almost theocratic dictatorship. There was a second wave of Iconoclasm, which was in many cases more thorough than the first. To accomplish their goals the radical Calvinists allied themselves with urban craftsmen against the current administration. Thus forces aiming at a social and political revolution combined with the protagonists of a religious and ecclesiastical transformation. It goes without saying that these radical elements enjoyed only limited support from the population.

Luxemburg, where the Reformation never really took hold, remained loyal to the king. In the Walloon provinces (Hainaut, Artois, and Walloon-Flanders), where the traditional Catholic nobility held strong positions, distaste for the revolutionary trend in Brabant and Flemish cities grew. Don Juan fell victim to the plague at the end of 1578. In contrast to the situation three years previously, his successor was immediately available. Alexander Farnèse (1545–1592), duke of Parma, was the son of the previous governor Margaret of Parma and a nephew of the king. Not only was Parma an accomplished soldier, he was also a gifted diplomat. He was to achieve great success in both these areas. However, more factors than the personal qualities of the new governor came into play.

A truce with the Ottoman Empire (1578) enabled the king to focus on the Netherlands as well as to make additional funds and troops available. In the meantime, Parma did not rest on his laurels. His political strategy focused on exploiting any divide among the insurgents. First, he tried to reconcile the Walloon provinces, which had remained Catholic, with the king by pointing out their mutual distaste for what they called the Calvinistic tyranny in Flanders and Brabant. Parma promised to respect provincial privileges and institutions, and agreed to dismiss the Spanish troops. Based on these conditions, the Union of Arras (1579) was formed and the Walloon provinces promised to be loyal to the king. Parma, having only domestic forces at his disposal, limited military operations to the conquest of Limburg and Maastricht (1579). This conquest enabled him to control the route between Brabant and the Rhineland in Germany.

Holland, Zeeland, and five other northern provinces and cities from Flanders and Brabant formed an alternative political union: the Union of Utrecht (1579). The union focused on expelling the Spanish troops and restoring traditional liberties. When it came to religion, it was agreed upon that every province would be free to choose between Calvinism and Catholicism. There would be a common army and a concerted foreign policy. In practice, they all opted for Calvinism. In fact, the Union of Utrecht created a confederacy; the provisions of the Union operated as the constitution of what was to become the Republic of the United Netherlands, also called the Dutch Republic.

Spain on the Offensive (1579–1590)

In 1580, Philip II took his most drastic step to date. William of Orange, a guiding yet moderating force against the king's policies for decades, was formally accused of high treason and declared an outlaw. With this declaration, the rift between Philip II and William of Orange, and by extension the insurgents, came full circle. The prince responded to being outlawed in a rebuttal that was to become famous, the *Apology*. In this publication, William accused the king, Alva, and the Spaniards in general of being cruel, unreliable, and tyrannical. Besides telling his side of the story, William obviously hoped his *Apology* would intensify anti-Spanish sentiment in his fellow Dutchmen and sway the doubters to his side.

The States-General also took a drastic and revolutionary step in issuing the famous "Act of Abjuration" in 1581, declaring they no longer recognized the king's sovereignty. The arguments established in the Act of Abjuration were along the same lines as the *Apology*, accusing Philip of not behaving in the best interests of his subjects and breaking his oath to respect the privileges of individual cities and provinces as well as violating his subjects' freedom of conscience. The king was depicted as a foreigner and a tyrant who simply did not honor the reciprocity of rights and obligations in the contract between the ruler and his subjects. It was also pointed out that his subjects had, extensively and repeatedly, asked, even begged, the king to reform his policies, alas to no avail. As a consequence, the people were left with no other option than to depose their unworthy Spanish ruler. The Act of Abjuration followed the same reasoning as the 1477 Grand Privilege and the 1356 Brabant *Joyeuse Entrée*: sovereignty of a ruler is not a God-given right; it is, rather, a contract between a king and his subjects, who will obey their lord only if he respects their rights and privileges.

Deposing the king raised the question of which person or institution should be entrusted with sovereignty. The English queen, Elizabeth, was considered, but she declined she did not want to antagonize mighty Philip II. William of Orange hoped for French support. At his suggestion, the States-General appointed the brother of the French king, the duke of Anjou, as Lord of the Netherlands. Anjou was a Catholic. By appointing him, William of Orange hoped to appease the king's Catholic opponents. This proved to be a mistake. Anjou was distrusted in Calvinist-dominated Holland and Zeeland. In 1583 the duke, aided by French troops, attempted to seize power in Flanders and Brabant, but he failed. Thereafter, Anjou returned to France leaving the issue of sovereignty unsolved.

In the meantime, Parma started his offensive. He approached the issue systematically by combining forceful military action with a moderate and financially attractive offer to the insurgents. First, the periphery of a city was looted to stop provisioning. Next, there was a siege. If a city surrendered, it was not plundered and executions were avoided as much as possible. City institutions were restored to how they were before the Calvinists took power. The monopoly of the Catholic Church was also re-established. Protestants who did not wish to recant their faith were given the right to leave the city or country and, most importantly, were given ample time to sell their possessions. Considering the bloody nature of the civil and religious war up until that point, this was a most reasonable offer – mostly for the Catholic majority, but also for the Calvinistic diehards who came to realize that additional resistance was pointless.

After conquering Tournai (1581), Oudenaarde (1581), and parts of what is the north-east of the present-day Netherlands (1580–1583),

Parma succeeded in bringing big southern cities back under the king's authority, first in Flanders (1584: Ypres, Ghent, Bruges) and later in Brabant (1585: Brussels, Mechelen, Antwerp). In particular, the conquest of Antwerp – after a siege that lasted many months and which was a logistical nightmare – gave a powerful signal to the rebels but also to the present and potential enemies of Spain: in August 1585, the main town in the Netherlands, one of the biggest cities of Western Europe and an international trade center, was in Spanish hands once again. The Spanish encirclement of Holland and Zeeland created unrest in the neighboring countries, even more so after the assassination of William of Orange by a hitman in 1584.

The English queen Elizabeth, who up until this point had abstained from acting in the conflict, changed course. From 1585 onwards, she openly supported the insurgents by providing them with troops. Elizabeth's support for the rebels led Philip II to conclude that if he wanted to repress the revolt in the Netherlands once and for all, he had to first eliminate the English threat to his plans. In 1588 he sent the Spanish Armada. The general plan was for the fleet, after the passage of the English Channel, to ship Parma's army to act as an expeditionary force to England. Due to fierce English resistance, insufficient coordination between Parma and the Armada, and bad luck, the whole operation was a calamitous failure.

The failure of the Spanish attack against England enabled the insurgents in Holland and Zeeland to restore their forces and to reorganize their administration, army, and finances. After the Spanish recapture of Flanders and Brabant, delegates from the south abstained from attending the States-General in the north. In 1588, the seven northern provinces decided to exercise sovereignty themselves. A new confederate state, the Republic of Seven United Netherlands, was born. Until 1648, Philip II and his successors refused to formally recognize the sovereignty of the Dutch Republic.

After his failed efforts against England in 1588, the king decided that, rather than attacking the Dutch insurgents, his attention would focus on France. This country had been plagued by religious war and noble factional struggle since 1562. In 1589, Henri III was murdered. His rightful heir was a Calvinist. The Catholic king could not bear the idea that a Calvinist heretic would rule France, the largest country of Western Europe, while Protestants already governed England and large parts of Germany. Therefore he ordered Parma to intervene in the civil war that was ravaging France. He remained active in France until his passing in 1592. This foreign intervention was a godsend to the newborn Dutch Republic. Its impressive military consolidation is illustrated by the capture in 1590 of Breda, home of the ancestral seat of the Orange-Nassaus in the Low Countries, the first of a number of successes in the north and the east of today's Netherlands.

Deadlock between Rebels and Royalists, Catholics and Protestants

Looking back on the quarter of a century between the first iconoclast wave and the 1590s, one is struck by some remarkable developments. The revolt clearly started in the south, the area that would encompass what is currently known as Belgium. However, hardcore Calvinist insurgents sought and eventually found refuge in Holland and Zeeland, which they firmly controlled a decade after William of Orange's first raid. The overwhelming majority of the nobility, urban magistrates, and Catholics in general that rebelled against Philip II's absolutism, in the end willingly accepted the king's hard-line stance on religion in exchange for concessions regarding the style of government.

Many believers, ordinary and educated people alike, were torn between loyalty to the old Church and its traditions and the emotional, intellectual or even just practical appeal of the new faith. This is exemplified in the life of the famous Brabant Humanist classicist and historian, Justus Lipsius (1547–1606), a supporter of Neo-Stoicism and the author of *De Constantia Libri Duo* (1584). He was, consecutively, secretary to Cardinal Granvelle, novice with the Jesuits, and professor in the Lutheran Jena (Saxony) in Calvinist Leyden and eventually in Catholic Leuven, where he himself had obtained his degree. Many ordinary people adopted a low profile and awaited the course of events. To most people, the decisions of the government concerning religious and ecclesiastical matters were essential. For the believers, this was often a practical issue concerning the availability of religious services and the existence of ecclesiastical institutions for charitable purposes. The swift military victory of the Calvinist minority in Holland and Zeeland in the 1570s was an important factor in the rise of the Protestant faith in the Northern Netherlands.

In the southern parts of the Netherlands, many Protestants remained loyal to their faith. To escape persecution they left their homes and went to Germany (Emden, Hamburg, Frankfurt) and England

(London, East Anglia). Most of them however migrated to the northern parts of the Netherlands. In the 1590s a vigorous economic growth started in Holland and Zeeland, in many ways thanks to the contribution of immigrants from the south. The latter's number is estimated at between 100 and 150,000. They were mostly craftsmen and merchants from big cities (Antwerp, Brussels, Ghent, Ypres) and rural areas renowned for their textile trade (West- and Walloon-Flanders, Hainaut), and spoke both Dutch and French. Around 1620 between one-third to two-thirds of the population in big Dutch cities like Leyden, Middelburg, Haarlem, and Amsterdam were of southern origin.

For the Dutch Republic, immigration from the Southern Netherlands was economically beneficial. For the the latter on the other hand, this wave of emigration caused a great loss of human and financial capital. The fact that the population in Antwerp fell from around 100,000 in the 1560s to 40,000 in 1585 illustrates this perfectly. Moreover, the marked rise of the northern provinces intensified the reality of the opposing interests of north and south. After 1584–1585, representatives of the big Flemish and Brabant cities no longer participated in the States-General. In addition, the Spaniards were expelled from the northern and eastern parts of the United Provinces in the 1590s. In a very short time, the States-General became a political institution defending only the interests of the Northern Netherlands.

The Dutch Republic also took military measures designed to affect the south economically. A maritime blockade along the Flemish coast and the Scheldt barred Antwerp from maritime traffic. The fact that these military measures benefited ports in Zeeland and Holland, particularly Amsterdam, was an added bonus. One must also keep in mind that the XVII Provinces of the Netherlands were a fairly recent creation (see Chapter 4). The northern and eastern provinces had been annexed by Charles V as recently as 1524–1543, and had few common interests with the south. In the 1590s, no one could forecast the permanent separation between the north and the south of the Netherlands. The king and the southern Catholics wanted to continue the war to subjugate the rebels and restore the monopoly of the Catholic faith. The Calvinists of the north, whose most radical members were quite often southern immigrants, wanted to free the country from the Spanish oppressor. Over the next decades it would become clear that both opponents chased impossible goals. In the last year of his long reign, Philip II once again changed course concerning his approach to the Low Countries.

Sovereignty for the Habsburg Low Countries
(1598–1621)?

In 1596 the king appointed his nephew, archduke Albert of Austria (1559–1621), as governor of the Netherlands. Albert, the emperor's younger brother, had been raised at the Spanish court from his eleventh birthday. This turned him, de facto, into a Spaniard. He was ordained a cardinal when eighteen, but he only received lower ordinations. After 1583, he gained political and military experience serving as viceroy of Portugal. A few months before his death, Philip II decided that Albert was to marry his daughter Isabella (1566–1633), leaving them the Netherlands as a wedding gift. In fact, the king wanted to relinquish his Burgundian heritage, that is, the Netherlands and the Free County of Burgundy (Franche-Comté) in eastern France (Map 5.2).

By doing so, Philip somewhat acknowledged his inability to defeat the insurgents. He hoped and expected that a sovereign ruler of the Netherlands would have more success negotiating with the north than he ever could have as a Spanish king. Formally speaking, the archdukes were sovereign and behaved as such. A royal court was re-established in Brussels. Foreign ambassadors and envoys were accredited. However, the policies of the archduke remained firmly linked to those of Madrid. As such, Albert played an important part in achieving peace between Spain and England (1604). Practically and legally, the archdukes remained completely dependent on Madrid. The relinquishment agreement stipulated that the marriage of any of their children had to be approved by the Spanish king, and if Albert was to remain childless, the Netherlands would return to Spanish rule after his passing. Furthermore, the agreement specified that Spanish troops were to remain in the Netherlands for a simple reason: the provinces remaining loyal to Spain were not able nor inclined to finance an army large enough to fight the Dutch rebels. Their dependence on Spain was not seen as a hindrance by the archdukes, nor did it imply a lesser status. Saving all of the Netherlands for the Catholic Spanish-Habsburg monarchy was their life's goal.

Albert and Isabella ruled from 1598 to 1621 (see Figure 5.2). This was a time of economic, political, and religious restoration after the destructive civil and religious war. Military actions were rather limited. In 1600, Ostend was the only remaining city and port in the south controlled by the insurgents. That same year the United Provinces for the first time sent a regular army to Flanders to liberate the besieged city of Ostend

Map 5.2 The Spanish Netherlands and the prince-bishopric of Liège, 1621. Redrawn based on a map originally published in *Atlas de la Wallonie, de la préhistoire à nos jours*, courtesy of Institut Jules Destrée, Charleroi (© Sofam)

and push through to Dunkirk, home to the pirates that greatly harmed Dutch maritime traffic and the fishing industry. At Nieuwpoort, this resulted in a battle between the armies of the archduke and the Dutch. The Dutch army ultimately won, but had to retreat immediately for logistic reasons, nullifying any military significance the victory might have had. In 1604, Ostend was taken by the Spanish troops. From then on it was clear that the insurgents were in the north, and the entire south was controlled by those loyal to Spain and the Catholic church.

Albert and Isabella made an effort to revitalize Burgundian traditions and inspire loyalty to themselves, the Church, and the monarchy. The institutions and privileges of the provinces were to be respected, but a potentially dangerous institution such as the States-General was no

Figure 5.2 *Archduchess Isabella of Austria (1566–1633), sovereign of the Catholic Low Countries (1598–1621) and regent (1621–1633), with her husband, archduke Albert.* The inscription below the portrait presents them as *domina* and *dominus Belgy provinciarum*. Workshop of Frans Pourbus the Younger, before 1605 (Versailles, châteaux de Versailles et du Trianon) © RMN-Grand Palais

ALBERTVS·ARCH·AVST
MAXIMILIANVS·IMPERATOR
FILIVS

BELGY PROVINCIARVM
DOMINVS

Figure 5.2 *(cont.)*

longer summoned. For the first time since long, Brussels was home to an authentic royal court. This was important for the archdukes' international prestige. Albert and Isabella were very devout Catholics. They behaved in every way as prototypical counter-reformatory rulers. They continuously showed their devotion to the Catholic Church by personally attending processions and embarking on pilgrimages. Their piety was captured not only in images and in writing, but also in the building of churches and the patronage of the arts.

Even though Albrecht and Isabella profiled themselves as "national" rulers, their government and court were decidedly Spanish. Their courtiers and confidantes were mostly Spanish and Italian, especially at the beginning of their reign. Over the course of time, more "nationals" acquired important positions at court and in government. It has to be noted, though, that the latter were mostly jurists completely loyal to the Spanish monarchy and to royal sovereignty.

Around 1606, both the Dutch Republic and the Spanish-Catholic camp became tired of war, partly due to its enormous financial costs. The Spanish were worried by Dutch commercial and military successes in the Far East, and feared the same could happen in the American colonies. Official peace negotiations were started in 1608. After the Dutch had rejected religious freedom for the Catholic minority as well as the sovereignty of Albert and Isabella, the Spanish eventually yielded. In 1609 the so-called Twelve Years' Truce was concluded. Spain and the archdukes factually recognized the Republic as a sovereign state.

Counter-Reformation

Around 1600 the Catholic Church in the Southern Netherlands was in a deplorable condition. The interiors of many church buildings and monasteries were destroyed. Some dioceses had no bishop and hundreds of parishes were without priests. Restoring the Catholic Church to its former glory was one of the archdukes' main objectives. In 1609, a government edict forbade people to attend any meeting that spoke ill of or contradicted the Catholic faith. Any attempt to practice the Protestant faith therefore became punishable by law. At around 1640, there were virtually no Protestants left in the Spanish Netherlands, these having either converted or emigrated. This religious cleansing contrasted with the situation in the Dutch Republic, where on average and with huge regional and local differences one-third of the population had remained Catholic.

The government carried out the religious cleansing, but the Church itself contributed to it by implementing the rules established at the Council of Trent (1545–1563). The most important task was to improve the education of future priests in seminaries. Henceforth, priests had to be able to properly execute their ministry, to teach their parishioners the articles of faith, to lead their flock, and to meticulously keep records of baptisms, marriages, and funerals. Bishops regularly visited monasteries, abbeys, and parishes to verify priests' devotion to their work and monks' observance of their orders' rules.

The number of religious orders and, correspondingly, their settlements grew. In Brussels, for instance, there were new settlements of Jesuits (1586), Capuchins (1587), Augustinians (1589), Carmelites (1607), Minim Friars (1616), Bridgettines (1623), Oratorian Fathers (1628), etc. The number of monasteries increased from twenty at the end of the sixteenth century to thirty-two in 1633. In Lille, the number doubled between 1588 and 1633. On the eve of the revolt, modern Belgium counted 302 monasteries. An eighteenth-century count mentioned no less than 853. Most noticeable was the prominent role of the Jesuits, especially concerning education. Their numbers grew from around 1,000 in 1610 to over 1,700 in 1671.

Many indications show a change in the religious behavior of the regular churchgoer in accordance with the Church's wishes. Sunday mass was shortened and preached in the vernacular. At around 1630–1640, all children were given religious education. The sacraments were strictly adhered to. All fulfilled their Easter duty. The small number of extramarital births (less than 2 percent) proves that the majority of people adhered to churchly morals concerning sexuality. Publicly showing one's devotion became increasingly important. People went to Communion, even when they were not obliged to. The worship of Mary became increasingly popular, as did the corresponding processions and pilgrimages. Countless charities and brotherhoods were founded to participate in processions and to increase community cohesion. As such, any "weak" individual became part of what the Church referred to as the *Corpus Christianum*, which offered protection against anything that could compromise one's soul. As a beacon for the Counter-Reformation, the Spanish Netherlands transformed into the epitome of a Catholic nation.

War and Crisis (1621–1634)

When archduke Albert passed away in 1621, the Spanish king restored his formal sovereignty over the Southern Netherlands. At the end of the Twelve Years' Truce, that same year, both Madrid and the United

Provinces were once again up in arms. In Madrid, Philip IV (r. 1621–1665) had just ascended the throne. His prime minister, the count-duke of Olivares, wanted to restore Spain's position as the most powerful nation in Europe. To achieve his goal, Olivares was willing and able to go to war on multiple fronts. He counted on the assistance of the king's Austrian-Habsburg cousins. The Holy Roman Empire was in the throes of the Thirty Years' War (1618–1648), a complicated struggle concerning both the balance of power between Catholics and Protestants and the position of the Catholic Habsburg emperor in the religiously divided Empire. Even though the emperor offered little support to the Spanish troops in their efforts against the Republic, many saw the war as a Catholic-Habsburg offensive against Protestant Europe.

The Spanish Netherlands were dragged into a protracted conflict. Between 1621 and 1713 the country was at war for 73 years, that is, three- quarters of the entire period. It was constantly subjected to troop movements, battles, sieges, and quarterings – a heavy toll on both the country and its citizens. During the seventeenth century, many parts of Europe fell victim to war, but none as extensively as the Spanish Netherlands. Originally, the war was successful for the Spanish. In 1625 they recaptured Breda, a feat beautifully depicted in Velasquez' famous painting *Las Lanzas*. However, the tide turned from the late 1620s. In 1629, the Dutch army conquered the Brabant city and surrounding area of 's Hertogenbosch after a lengthy siege. In 1632, the important city and fortress of Maastricht was also taken. The outline of the current border between The Netherlands and Belgium began to take shape.

The loss of 's Hertogenbosch and Maastricht caused great political tension in the Southern Netherlands. Archduchess Isabella, who had remained in Brussels as governor, was faced with increasing criticism of the so-called Spanish ministry and the Spaniards' failing military policies. In 1632–1633, a conspiracy conceived by several nobles came to light. Supported by France, they had planned to trigger an anti-Spanish revolt. The plot failed, but the fact that it was conceived in the first place was telling.

In 1632, the call to summon the States-General to end the war became louder each day. Despite an injunction from Madrid and resistance from the "Spanish ministry," the archduchess had no choice but to give in. The States-General was called and remained in session until 1634.

It started peace negotiations with the Republic but to no avail. The Republic made clear that acknowledging Spanish sovereignty was out of the question. The Spanish demand of freedom of religion for the Catholic minority was equally unacceptable for the Republic.

The increasing awareness, in the deeply Catholic south, that northern Calvinists were unyielding regarding faith, restored Spanish authority and loyalty to the Spanish crown and, more importantly, to the Catholic faith. The States-General was dissolved and would not meet again until the late eighteenth century (see Chapter 7). The crisis years between 1629 and 1634 had lasting consequences for the high nobility, which was excluded from government councils, with the exception of a brief period at the beginning of the eighteenth century. Nobles were henceforth limited to political activities at the provincial or regional level, courtly honorary functions, or a military career. Traditional deliberations concerning taxes remained intact, but they were held bilaterally between the government and the States of each province separately.

More War (1635–1713)

The war intensified after 1635. Until then, France had limited its involvement to financially supporting the enemies of her Habsburg foe. In 1635, she openly joined the war. This was the beginning of a long series of French invasions in the Southern Netherlands. France and the Dutch Republic agreed to jointly attack and, if successful, divide the Spanish Netherlands amongst them. Brabant, Mechelen, Limburg, and Opper-Gelre would become part of the Republic, whereas France would annex Flanders, Artois, Hainaut, Namur, and Luxemburg. This division shows that the fight for the Protestant faith as a motive for war had clearly become less important to the Republic.

Between 1635 and 1640 every party enjoyed successes and defeats. In 1636–1637, the Spaniards even briefly threatened Paris, but in 1637 the Republic recaptured Breda. Dutch hopes that the south would eventually revolt against its Spanish rulers never materialized. The turning point of the war occurred in 1640, when revolts in Portugal and Catalonia hampered Spain's ability to fight both France and the Republic. That same year, the French army began the conquest of Artois.

Spain eventually realized that it was unable to continue the war against both enemies. Only ending the conflict could save honor. Other powers also longed for peace. An international peace conference met in Munster in the German region of Westphalia. France was obstructive at every possible turn in an effort to further weaken its Habsburg enemy. Some factions in the Dutch Republic also wanted the war to drag on too, but the peace party from Holland pressed the issue. In January of 1648, the Peace of Munster was signed. The Spanish king relinquished his sovereignty over the former northern provinces and formally recognized the independence of the Dutch Republic.

The terms of the peace treaty were entirely dictated by the Republic. All areas and cities conquered since the end of the Twelve Years' Truce, even those with an almost exclusively Catholic population, were to remain in the hands of the Republic. This was a humiliating defeat for the Catholic king. His subjects in the Southern Netherlands had to deal with some negative aspects of the treaty. Direct maritime traffic between Antwerp and the North Sea remained outlawed, and tariffs on commodities imported from or via Holland and Zeeland could not be higher than tariffs on commodities that were imported via Flemish ports (Dunkirk, Ostend, Bruges). Considering the dominant maritime position of both Holland and Zeeland, the Spanish Netherlands became dependent on the Republic for a large portion of their international trade.

France and Spain continued their war. Philip IV was only willing to commit to peace if the French agreed to return every conquered area. France rejected this unrealistic proposition. Moreover, Great Britain started a war against Spain. The Franco-British alliance also made incursions in and near the Southern Netherlands, conquering Dunkirk in 1658. Spain had no choice but to admit defeat and signed the treaty of the Pyrenees in 1659. This treaty stated, among other things, that Artois, parts of Flanders, Hainaut, and Luxemburg were to become French territories.

The personal rule of Louis XIV began in 1661. His aggressive foreign policy would lead France to occupy and eventually annex big parts of the Southern Netherlands over the next decades. Two of present-day France's major *départements* (Nord and Pas-de-Calais) consist of territories that were conquered by Louis' armies. The Peace of Aachen after the Devolution War (1667–1668) stipulated that some parts of the conquered territories would remain French, especially important cities like Tournai, Ypres, Lille, surrounding Walloon-Flanders, and smaller places like Nieuwpoort. Moreover, Spanish sovereignty was compromised, as French troops were billeted in a number of cities.

This short Devolution War made it clear that Spain alone was no longer capable of defending its former stronghold in north-western Europe. As a consequence the Dutch Republic considered France no longer as a potential ally but a threat to its economic interests and its survival as a sovereign state. Therefore the Republic became increasingly involved in military alliances designed to protect Spanish rule of the Southern Netherlands' and tried to limit French expansion.

To avenge the Republic's efforts to stymie him in 1668, but also to hamper its dominant position in international trade and transport, Louis XIV started the "Dutch War" (1672–1678), invading the Republic and the Spanish Netherlands. The Treaty of Nijmegen (1678) ended the conflict. Because Spain had been incapable of defending the Southern Netherlands, the latter had to pay the price and parts of Flanders, Hainaut, and Luxemburg became French. At this point, Louis XIV was at the height of his power. In the 1680s, he had French courts seize more adjacent territories. This was purely a show of power. To the Spanish Netherlands, this meant losing an additional part of Luxemburg.

The Glorious Revolution in Great Britain and the replacement of the Catholic and pro-French James II by his Protestant daughter Mary and his son-in-law, *stadtholder* of the Dutch Republic, William III, was a game changer. England, which had thus far abstained from involvement in previous wars or had even taken a pro-French stance, now joined the anti-French alliance. In 1688, war broke out once again. The Republic, England, the emperor, Spain, and some smaller states joined forces against France and the war raged on for nine years, with successes and losses on both sides. The Spanish Netherlands were the primary battleground for the French and allied armies. Economic damage and the number of casualties were enormous. In 1695, for example, the French artillery bombarded Brussels for three days, causing huge destruction (see Figure 5.3). The so-called Nine Year War (1688–1697) ended undecided, with both parties being financially and materially exhausted.

Figure 5.3 *The bombardment of Brussels by the French army* (1695).
Anonymous painting (Brussels, Museum Broodhuis)

For the first time, Louis XIV was unable to expand his territories. According to the Peace of Rijswijk (1697), France was to return all the territories it had conquered since 1679. The Republic was given the right to occupy a number of fortresses in the Spanish Netherlands along the French border. This was a clear proof that Spain factually recognized its military powerlessness. The Spanish Netherlands had actually become a sort of English–Dutch protectorate. It is worth mentioning that none of the inhabitants of the Spanish Netherlands, not even its elites, had any say in all these provisions and treaties.

The Prince-Bishopric of Liège

From 1518, the foreign policy of the prince-bishopric was one of passive neutrality, implying that it was not to be military defended. Moreover, Liège became a toy of foreign powers, as a consequence of its geographical position – surrounded by Spanish-Habsburg territory and forming a kind of corridor along the Meuse River between French and Dutch territory.

From 1581 till 1723 (with the exception of the period 1688–1694) Liège had a prince-bishop who belonged to the Bavarian Wittelsbach dynasty. Moreover, these prelates were at the same time archbishops and electors of Cologne and therefore often absentee rulers. As electors they played an important role in the politics of the Holy Roman Empire. The Bavarian rulers were staunch Catholics and champions of the Counter-Reformation and therefore in theory allies of the Catholic Habsburg emperors. But both dynasties were also rivals. Therefore, the Bavarian rulers in Munich, Cologne, and Liège were much sought-after allies in the international power play between France and Habsburg.

As a consequence of geography and politics, the prince-bishopric was involved in all the wars waged in the Spanish Netherlands. In most cases this involvement consisted of a temporary occupation of part of its territory, the recruitment of soldiers, or the quartering and passage of foreign armies. But at some moments the consequences could be disastrous. In 1688, Liège abandoned its policy of neutrality and declared war on France. The French reaction was fierce: the small town of Huy was set on fire (1689) and Liège itself was heavily bombarded (1691), resulting in the destruction of one-fifth of the city's buildings.

Warfare had economic side effects. Two entrepreneurs are worth mentioning. Jean Curtius (1551–1628) did business on a large scale with the Spanish army in the Netherlands, building a huge enterprise which produced gunpowder. During the Twelve Years' Truce, he started an iron and weaponry facility in Spain. Louis de Geer (1587–1652) of Dordrecht in Holland was the son of an immigrant from Liège who had converted to Calvinism. De Geer was the founder of the Swedish iron and weaponry industry (1618). Both men enabled numerous artisans – about 5,000 for de Geer – to migrate from Liège and other Walloon regions to Spain and Sweden.

The prince-bishopric became an important producer of iron and weaponry. In the first half of the seventeenth century the Dutch Republic and Liège established a mutually profitable economic relationship. All kinds of colonial products were exchanged for weaponry and iron for the Dutch shipbuilding industry. The woolen cloth industry of Verviers and neighboring Limburg began as a distant branch of the huge Leyden drapery industry in Holland but eventually transformed in an important independent manufacturing region. In the 1660s the prince-bishopric built a "New Road" (*Le Chemin Neuf*) linking Liège and Sedan in northern France while avoiding the Spanish Netherlands.

Ferdinand of Bavaria (r. 1612–1650) was a devout and at the same time authoritarian ruler doing his utmost to impose the Counter-Reformation. During his reign, no less than seventy additional monasteries and abbeys were founded in the bishopric. It was said that the city of Liège rivaled Rome in that respect. The relationship of the prince-bishop with the only large city, Liège, was always tense or hostile. In order to raise more taxes to alleviate his financial problems, he decided to subdue the city corporation by quashing its rather democratic election by-laws. His intervention was meant to minimalize the influence of the craft guilds.

A fierce political struggle ensued. The *Chiroux*, mostly patricians, members of the clergy, and the nobility, supported the prince-bishop's policy. The *Grignoux* – consisting of artisans, lawyers, and the new rich – wanted maximal urban independence. The Spaniards and the French tried to influence the struggle between both "parties." In the 1630s and 1640s the *Grignoux* mostly prevailed. Their historic leader, burgomaster Sébastien La Ruelle (1591–1637), supported by the French, was murdered at the instigation of the Spanish. The prince-bishop and his *Chiroux* allies eventually got the upper hand. In 1649, the electoral army occupied Liège and new city by-laws of an oligarchical nature were imposed. As the protector of the so-called German liberties, in fact the conservation of German division, France would support the Bavarian prince-bishops and exert maximal influence throughout the next decades. A cynical reversal of alliances!

"A Century of Adversity"?

The previous pages suggest that the so-called Spanish period was nothing but a time of war, loss of territory, and economic decline. If one compares the economic and political evolution of the Spanish Netherlands with the achievements of the Dutch Republic in its "Golden Century," the image of seventeenth-century "Belgium" is decidedly negative. However, it is important to nuance this image by considering the Southern Netherlands in a broader geographic and chronological context.

The seventeenth century was in general a period of crises and depression. These crises manifested themselves in different areas: in politics (e.g. the English civil war in the 1640s), in demography (stagnation or a decrease in population), and in economics (trade wars, deflation). The crises did not coincide everywhere and their intensity often varied. But despite these differences, one can distinguish an exogenous and an endogenous factor explaining the crisis of the seventeenth century.

The exogenous factor was the climate. The seventeenth century occurred during the so-called mini ice age: colder winters, cool and humid summers, and a slight decline in temperature leading to more crop failures and subsistence crises. In the Low Countries where agriculture was market oriented and where many interregional and international trade networks existed, the effects of the climate crisis were less obvious than in more isolated parts of Europe. It is no coincidence that English Sir Richard Weston, author of the *Discourse on the Husbandry of Flanders and Brabant* (1655), hailed the Flemish crop rotation system as an example for the improvement of English agriculture.

The endogenous factor consisted of the growing pains of the state-building process. The growth of the state apparatus, especially the army and the navy, was very costly. Taxes were not based on financial capability, but rather on tradition. Generally speaking, peasants and craftsmen were disproportionately taxed compared to tradesmen. This seemingly random treatment of taxpayers did not stimulate economic growth. According to comparative research, the average tax burden in the seventeenth-century Southern Netherlands increased at a similar pace to that France, but much less than in the Dutch Republic.

The Scheldt blockade, hindering maritime traffic between Antwerp and the open seas, proved detrimental. While Antwerp lost its position as the central staple market of north-western Europe, being replaced by Amsterdam, it remained an important financial and commercial center. Citizens and inhabitants who had fled the turbulence between 1576 and 1585, returned after the Spanish recapture of the city – among them prominent merchants and even Protestants willing to convert to Catholicism in order to enable their return.

When numerous military operations or embargos impeded commodity trade via the Scheldt, many Antwerp merchants had their goods shipped via Bruges, Ostend, or Dunkirk. Merchants from the Spanish Netherlands were officially excluded from lucrative trade with the Spanish colonies. Nevertheless, a number were able to do business with Latin America by using phony Spanish firms operating out of Seville or Cadiz as cover. The activities of privateers from Ostend and Dunkirk also proved especially lucrative.

Even though the Southern Netherlands no longer played a leading economic role in Western Europe, the human and economic capital they had amassed during previous centuries did not suddenly disappear. Economic recovery after the tragic period of 1566–1600 was remarkable.

Despite the massive wave of migration to the Dutch Republic, the Southern Netherlands remained a densely populated and highly urbanized area with great production potential and important markets. As far as textile production is concerned, the south could hold its own against the north. Semi-manufactured textiles from the Southern Netherlands were finished and marketed in Holland and also exported as Dutch products.

In Bruges, Ghent, Antwerp, Lille, and Brussels the production of light drapery grew considerably. These were mixed fabrics exported on a large scale. Antwerp became a key center for the silk industry. The production of tapestries also remained important. Oudenaarde produced the simplest fabrics, whil Antwerp and Brussels produced the most sophisticated, and therefore most sought after, tapestries for European elites. The production of lace was also expanding, giving jobs to thousands of women and girls. The countryside in Flanders and northern Hainaut became a beacon for the linen industry. Kortrijk damask and Flemish linen became internationally recognized terms.

During the seventeenth century, populations increased in most big cities of the Southern Netherlands, compensating for the demographic losses suffered between c.1570 and c.1600. Antwerp was the only exception. Starting from about 100,000 inhabitants in the 1560s, its population had been halved in the following decades before growing to approximately 80,000 in the final quarter of the seventeenth century. The population of Brussels increased from less than 50,000 to over 80,000 by the end of the seventeenth century. By 1600, the Southern Netherlands counted more cities of over 10,000 inhabitants than Great Britain.

Until the third quarter of the seventeenth century artists from the Southern Netherlands played an important role in European art production. Despite their international success, they continued to live and work in their home country; this proves that an important market for art production and consumption was still thriving there. The economic downturn of the Southern Netherlands unfolded around 1650 and 1660 and was the result of trade wars that were initiated by neighboring powers. Mercantilism was a form of economic nationalism. The implementation of the English Act of Navigation (1651) as well as French protectionist tariffs (1662, 1664), was detrimental to the export of linen, mixed fabrics, tapestries, and lace. Due to the loss of Dunkirk and the Republic's strong position in maritime traffic, the Spanish Netherlands had to depend even more on ports in Zeeland and Holland, which subjected them to even more local tariffs and other transaction costs.

Spanish weakness, French aggression, and military dependence on the Republic and England to protect the Southern Netherlands against French aggression led to economic powerlessness. Tariffs in the Southern Netherlands were considerably lower than in most countries, due to pressure from its three neighbors. Exports dwindled, whereas imports increased, resulting in a gradual decline of urban industries that, in turn, generated unemployment and impoverishment. A good example of this weakness was the genesis and especially the swift repeal of the Eternal Edict (1699), a governmental attempt to introduce some form of protectionism based on the French and English model.

Artistic Flowering and Cultural Activity

The first half of the seventeenth century was an age of a brilliant artistic revival, especially of the visual arts, with Antwerp as its main center. The central figure of the so-called Flemish Baroque painting school was Peter Paul Rubens (1577–1640). His father, an Antwerp alderman, had gone into exile in 1568 to avoid persecution by Alva's Blood Council. Peter Paul was born in Siegen and lived in Cologne (Germany). In 1587 his widowed mother returned to Antwerp and converted to Catholicism. After his apprenticeship in Antwerp, the young painter traveled to Italy, the heart of baroque art and architecture. Between 1600 and 1608 he stayed in Venice, Genoa, Florence, Mantua, and Rome. In 1609 he established his famous workshop in Antwerp.

Rubens excelled in all kinds of drawing and painting. He produced huge religious triptychs such as the *Elevation* (1610) and the *Descent of the Cross* (1612/4) in the Antwerp cathedral; scenes from classical mythology (*The Judgment of Paris*, 1636) and antiquity (*The Death of Seneca*, 1615); hunting scenes; portraits of clients, friends, and family (for instance *Venus in Fur Coat*, an intimate painting of his second wife, 1630/40); landscapes; designs for tapestries; triumphal arches; and self-portraits (*Straw Hat*, 1625). After his return from Italy he became court painter of the arch-dukes Albert and Isabella (1609). Rubens combined a Humanist education and exceptional craftsmanship with business acumen and diplomatic qual-ities. To accomplish his impressive amount of artistic production, he had a number of pupils and assistants in his workshop. He also regularly collab-orated with other renowned painters. In 1628–1631 he was active as a diplomat in Madrid, London, and The Hague.

Rubens worked for foreign rulers such as the English king Charles I, the French queen mother Marie de Médicis, and king Philip IV. In 1629–1635 he painted the canvasses for the ceiling of Banqueting House in the palace of Whitehall (London). In 1622–1625 he made twenty-four paintings about the life of Marie de Médicis and her murdered husband Henry IV for the *Palais du Luxembourg* in Paris. In 1635, Rubens worked on the decoration of the hunting lodge *Torre de la Parada* (Madrid) in collaboration with Jacques Jordaens. Rubens, who was knighted in 1624, had a luxury residence built in the center of Antwerp, inspired by the palaces he had seen in Italy. Until his death in 1640, Rubens occupied the top position of the artistic elite in the Spanish Netherlands.

Anthony Van Dyck (1599–1641) was Rubens' most gifted pupil. Born and educated in Antwerp, he worked under his master's guidance in 1620, painting thirty-nine canvasses for the ceiling of the new baroque Jesuit Church in Antwerp. From 1621 until his death he travelled a lot. In 1621, 1632–1634 and 1635–1641 he stayed in England, and from 1622 to 1627 in Italy. Van Dyck painted religious and mythological subjects but he excelled as a portrait painter for the patriciate and the aristocracy and, especially in England, for royalty. He painted numerous portraits of Charles I and Queen Maria Henrietta and their children (1632–1641). He not only painted friends and colleagues such as Inigo Jones, the famous architect (1635–1636) or the Antwerp painter Frans Snijders and his wife (1621), but also created remarkable self-portraits (*Self-portrait with his Patron, Sir Endymion Porter*, 1635). Charles I knighted Van Dyck in 1632 and appointed him court painter.

Rubens and Van Dyck mostly painted high culture subjects for aristocratic clients. Adrian Brouwer (*c*.1603–1605–*c*.1638), born in Oudenaarde, favored other themes. After a stay in the Dutch Republic, young Adrian returned to the south (Antwerp) where he became known as an excellent genre painter. His subjects were down-to-earth: inns, peasants, fights, smoking, dancing, card playing, and special facial expressions. He died relatively young and poor but was however much respected by Rubens and Rembrandt, who each possessed several of his paintings. Frans Snijders (1579–1657), a pupil of Pieter Brueghel II (1564–1638) (see Chapter 4) specialized in the painting of still life, breakfast scenes, animals, hunting, fish, and kitchen scenes. He regularly collaborated with Rubens. Snijders was a rich man, as was his brother-in-law Cornelis De Vos (1584–1651), a painter of historical and religious subjects and portraits. After Van Dyck's departure for Italy, De Vos was Antwerp's leading portraitist. He also worked as an art dealer and was active in the export business to Spain.

David Teniers I (1582–1649), also from Antwerp and an acquaintance of Rubens' in Rome, painted huge religious, mythological, and historical compositions, landscapes, and village scenes. His son and pupil David Teniers II (1610–1690) painted a wide variety of subjects. The level production at his workshop was prodigious but was sometimes lacking in quality. Teniers Jr. was appointed as court painter and conservator of the art collection of archduke Leopold William, governor of the Spanish Netherlands (1647–1656). Leopold William was a great art collector. In around 1650, Teniers painted the famous *Archduke Leopold William in his Gallery of Paintings in Brussels*. Both father and son were astute businessmen.

Jacques Jordaens (1593–1678) was the leading Antwerp painter after the death of Rubens and Van Dyck. He was greatly influenced by Rubens. He painted portraits, biblical, historical, and mythological paintings, but also humorous pieces based on Flemish proverbs or festivals (*The King Drinks*, 1640; *The Old Sing so the Young Pipe*, 1638–1640) He created many designs for tapestries and worked for foreign rulers (eight paintings for the Queen's House at Greenwich, 1641; *The Triumph of Stadtholder Frederick Henry of the Dutch Republic*, 1651; paintings for the *Torre de la Parada* hunting lodge near Madrid; and a number of paintings for the new town hall of Amsterdam, 1661). In around 1650, Jordaens converted to Calvinism but, surprisingly, continued to live in Antwerp. The authorities fined him but left him unharmed, probably thanks to his status as the leading Antwerp painter.

All in all, the Spanish Netherlands produced visual arts on an impressive scale, both quantitatively and qualitatively – often resulting in international fame. This is all the more striking when one also takes into account the work of many dozens of small masters and the origin of foreign masters, such as the Dutch painter Frans Hals, born in Antwerp, and his French colleague Philippe de Champaigne, born in Brussels. As we have seen, many paintings represented religious subjects destined for churches, chapels, and monasteries whose interior was redecorated after the iconoclast waves of 1566 and 1580–1581. The baroque style – with its emphasis on grandeur, drama, movement, and the contrast between light and dark – perfectly suited the Counter-Reformation offensive of the Catholic Church. Its first purpose was to inspire piety and an understanding of catholic dogma by the ordinary worshipper through overwhelming and effective images.

New churches, chapels, and monasteries were built in the baroque style in Antwerp, Brussels, Bruges, Ghent, Namur, Leuven, and Mechelen. To promote the cult of Mary, the archdukes built a huge basilica in the small town of Scherpenheuvel near Leuven, still a place of pilgrimage today. The interiors of old and new churches were adapted to the new prescriptions of the Council of Trent (1545–1663). Altars, pulpits, confessionals, and Communion banks became more monumental and were richly decorated with elaborated sculptures.

Lucas Faydherbe, a sculptor and architect from Mechelen (1617–1697), was trained in Rubens' workshop and became his protégé. He built churches in Brussels and Mechelen, and created monumental grave memorials and altars, busts, and terracotta and ivory sculptures. Artus Quellinus I (1609–1668) began his career in Rome. In 1640 he settled in his birth town of Antwerp and became the leading sculptor in the Low Countries. Between 1650 and 1664, he was in charge of all the sculptural decoration of the huge new town hall of Amsterdam, "the eighth wonder of the world." Quellinus excelled in sculpting very realistic portrait busts, for instance the leading Dutch politician Johan de Witt (1665), and was given the epithet "Phideas-Quellyn" after the legendary Greek sculptor.

Conclusion

The period between the beginning of Philip II's rule and the end of the seventeenth century was a crucial episode in "Belgian" history. The key element was the splitting of the XVII Provinces in two separate polities. This construct, painstakingly built by the Burgundian dukes and their Habsburg successors during a century and a half, crumbled in less than a few decades. The division had multiple causes: resistance against Philip II's absolutist rule, religious strife and the strength of provincial particularism. The union of the XVII Provinces was recent and therefore still fragile. In the north, a confederate Republic emerged, maintaining provincial and urban particularism, but simultaneously waging a common foreign and military policy and building strong finances. This new state was quite influential internationally throughout the seventeenth century – economically, politically, and culturally. From the 1630s, the Republic became increasingly unwilling to "liberate" the south from its Spanish and Catholic "oppressors." After 1660 it only considered the Southern Netherlands as a barrier against French expansionism.

After the re-establishment of royal authority in the 1580s, monarch and subjects came to an agreement in the Southern Netherlands: the old liberties would be maintained at the level of the provinces and a central government would implement Spanish policy. The Republic was a major player on the international scene, but the Southern Netherlands were little more than a pawn in Madrid's complex game. Spain's involvement in multiple international conflicts and its stubborn refusal to end, first the war against the northern insurgents and then, from 1635, the war against the French, led to a significant decline of its international status. By the end of the seventeenth century the Southern Netherlands were reduced to little more than the territory that was to become Belgium, as a direct consequence of Spain's increasing powerlessness.

Historiography concerning the Spanish period tells a negative story of foreign dominance and decay in many areas. All-in-all, Spanish influence on "Belgian" society was limited with one notable exception: religion. The nearly unbreakable bond between the Catholic Church and the government ensured the success of the Counter-Reformation. Despite city councils' objections to the costs generated by an increasing number of clerics and ecclesiastical institutions, the Catholic Church was undoubtedly infused into every aspect of society.

Why was there such a lack of protest in the Southern Netherlands against the increasingly failing Spanish overlords after 1600 and even after 1630? This is probably due to the deep divide between the Catholic south and the Protestant-dominated Dutch Republic and, consequently, an unwillingness to ask for support from the northern heretics. And since the Spanish rulers maintained certain privileges and liberties at the provincial and urban level, an alternative French absolutist regime was less attractive. Moreover, unlike in the Dutch Republic, the south lacked an elite involved in decision-making on "national" or international matters. As a result, the Southern Netherlands remained loyal to the Spanish-Habsburg monarchy.

The Austrian Netherlands (*c.*1700–1780)

Introduction

In 1700 the last king of the Spanish Habsburg monarchy died. After a turbulent and complex period (1702–1713) the Spanish Netherlands eventually became a possession of Charles II's Austrian cousins. This transfer of sovereignty was the result of a long war, the last one in a series of wars that had afflicted the Southern Low Countries from 1621 (see Chapter 5). The Austrian period in "Belgian" history, presented here, began in 1713 and ended in 1794. In sharp contrast with the previous century, it was a period of peace, with the exception of four years in the 1740's and 1787–1794. The political and social changes leading to the revolutions and the revolutionary wars that ended the Austrian regime, are discussed in chapter 7: they were part of what the British historian Eric Hobsbawm has called "The Age of Revolution" (1789–1848).

The eighteenth century saw many important changes, especially in Western Europe. After decades of stagnation or regression, population growth resumed in around 1720–1740. Almost uninterrupted population growth was made possible through agricultural improvement and the introduction of new crops, especially the potato, in some parts of Europe. Many Europeans continued to experience occasional hunger and food shortages, but subsistence crises and massive mortality became rare.

Demographic growth boosted production, trade, consumption, and consequently economic growth. The consumption of exotic food, beverages, stimulants, and textiles (coffee, tea, sugar, tobacco, cotton), imported from overseas, increased tremendously and became part of the daily life of a growing number of Europeans. A "consumption revolution" was in the making. Growing demand stimulated the substitution of imported Asian industrial products such as cottons or porcelain by European production and led to technical innovation and mechaniza-tion, especially in textile production (cotton) and mining (coal, iron). The Industrial Revolution started in Great Britain. "Belgium" became the first industrial nation on the European continent, as we will see in this and the following chapters (7–9).

The scientific revolution of the seventeenth century (Galilei, Descartes, Bacon, Newton, etc.) and the nascent interaction of Europeans with other civilizations led to a growing criticism of trad-itional values and thinking concerning the Christian faith, the Churches, and social and political order in general. The Enlightenment was a broad philosophical movement. Publications propagating enlightened ideas and ideals, but also their opposites, were widely read by the educated elite and discussed among members of the aristocracy and in learned societies and academies. The work of the French *philosophes* (Voltaire, Rousseau, Diderot, and others) and the great prestige of French literature and culture in general contributed hugely to the circulation of new ideas.

With the exception of Great Britain and some minor powers, royal absolutism was and remained the most widespread political regime, though its character changed. Enlightened absolutism focused on the strengthening of the state through the implementation of rational methods in government where possible. Enlightened monarchs such as Emperor Joseph II (r. 1780–1790) created for themselves the image of "first servants of the State." However, the implementation and range of reforms were not unlimited. Enlightened absolute rulers could not afford to prejudice the interests of the aristocracy and the privileged upper layer of society in general (see Chapter 7).

The War of the Spanish Succession (1702–1713/1714): The Southern Netherlands Occupied and Divided

The succession of childless Charles II posed a major problem for the European balance of power. The Spanish monarchy was weak and the possibility of dividing its numerous possessions in the Americas, Asia, and the Low Countries generated horse-trading between the European powers. Emperor Leopold I, Louis XIV of France and the English-Dutch king-*stadtholder* William III secretly elaborated partition plans from 1697 to 1700.

However, the close family relationship with Charles II gave two rulers a strong claim on the whole of the Spanish succession: Louis XIV for one of his grandsons and Leopold I for his youngest son. In his testament, Charles II eventually bequeathed his crown to Philippe of Anjou, Louis XIV's second grandson. In spite of previous arrangements with the European powers, Louis accepted the testament. Although the testament stipulated that the Spanish and French crowns could never be united, Louis declared that the Pyrenees, the border between France and Spain, no longer existed.

The factual union between the Spanish and the French crowns and the occupation of the Spanish Netherlands by the French army, on a formal basis and with the approval of the new Spanish king, posed a direct threat to Great Britain and the Dutch Republic. In 1702 the War of the Spanish Succession broke out. A Dutch–British–Imperial coalition and some minor powers supported the claim of the Austrian Habsburg archduke Charles, while Louis XIV vigorously defended the Bourbon succession. Military operations took place in Spain, Italy, southern Germany, and the Southern Netherlands. For the inhabitants of the Spanish Netherlands there was little doubt that they were legally part of the Spanish monarchy, but it was unclear to many who the rightful monarch was – Bourbon Philip V or Habsburg Charles III.

The French actually controlled the Southern Netherlands in 1701–1706. French-style administrative reforms were introduced in an absolutist manner. Taxes were raised and the size of the army was significantly increased. The three traditional government councils were abolished and replaced by a single Royal Council. To protect the manufacturing industries, importation from the Dutch Republic and England was temporarily suspended or heavily taxed. Trade with France was encouraged. The government also began constructing a network of paved roads.

Once again, the Southern Netherlands became one of the major theaters of war. It has been calculated that in some periods the combined allied and French–Spanish armies numbered approximately 200,000 soldiers and officers, the equivalent of more than 10 percent of the population. All these men, along with their tens of thousands horses, had to be fed, encamped, or billeted. This put a heavy burden on local authorities and on the population in general, although some, that is, army contractors and their suppliers, fared well. Military operations mostly consisted of marching and shadowing the enemy, but major battles, some very violent (Ramillies, Oudenaarde, Malplaquet, Denain) and sieges (Lille) also took place. In May 1706, a Dutch–British army under the duke of Marlborough won a great victory at Ramillies. In less than two months the allies almost completely conquered the richest and most populous provinces, Flanders and Brabant, while Namur, Luxemburg, and the largest parts of Hainaut remained under Bourbon rule.

Between 1706 and 1713 the Southern Netherlands were divided into two parts. The allies abolished the Bourbon reforms and reinstated the old government in Brussels under the supervision of the *Conférence*, a Dutch–British High Commission. It imposed policies serving the economic interests of the allies. Maximilian-Emmanuel of Bavaria, who had lost his homeland to the Austrians, continued to represent Philip V in the southern provinces, but was in fact a puppet of the French king.

The international political situation changed dramatically in 1710–1711. After the sudden death of the emperor, the Habsburg pretender for the Spanish crown became emperor Charles VI (r. 1711–1740). The European powers could not accept a union between Spain and the Austrian Habsburg monarchy and a restoration of Charles V's empire (see Chapter 4) – a solution as undesirable as a French–Spanish union. A change of government in London in 1711 led to the withdrawal of the British from the allied coalition. A peace conference was convened in the Dutch city of Utrecht in 1712, but the fate of the Spanish Netherlands remained undecided for a long time. The French proposed to offer sovereignty over the whole or part of the country to Maximilian-Emmanuel of Bavaria, but this proposal was eventually abandoned.

In April 1713, Great Britain, the Dutch Republic, France, Spain, and some minor powers signed the Treaty of Utrecht. The Spanish monarchy was divided: Philip V of Anjou kept Spain and its overseas colonies, while most Italian possessions and the Spanish Netherlands were attributed to the emperor. However, Charles VI, who had not participated in the Utrecht Conference, rejected the partition and continued the war for another year. In 1714 he finally made peace with France but not with Spain. Both contenders for the Spanish heritage were dissatisfied with the partition imposed upon them by the British and the French. In the following decades they would try to reconquer the territories that, in their eyes, had been wrongly handed over to the adversary.

The Difficult Beginning of the Austrian Regime

For the emperor the acquisition of the Spanish Netherlands without the other Spanish territories was a kind of poisoned gift. Historically, the

Austrian Habsburgs were more interested in extending their influence in the Italian peninsula. Moreover, since the 1690s they had successfully fought the Ottoman Empire and had extended their territory in Hungary and in the Balkans. From an Austrian point of view, the Southern Netherlands were a distant possession, more a burden than an asset for the monarchy's position in Europe – all the more so as the emperor's hands were bound by burdensome conditions imposed upon him by his Dutch and British allies.

According to the Utrecht Treaty, trade tariffs for the Southern Netherlands had to remain unchanged, unless the emperor and the Maritime Powers reached an agreement. Obviously, Britain and the Dutch Republic were not inclined to comply. The Dutch, in particular, saddled the emperor with harsh economic and financial conditions. This was not unreasonable per se, since they had made great efforts to conquer the Southern Netherlands for the Habsburgs. In order to thwart French expansionism, they had made enormous military and financial efforts. After the Utrecht Treaty, peace, financial stability, and safety from future French aggression were the prime aims of Dutch policy.

To achieve this aim, the Dutch had obtained two important provisions in the Utrecht Peace Treaty. First, the emperor had to equip an army of 15,000 men in the Southern Netherlands. Second, the Dutch Republic could occupy a number of fortifications along the French border. The emperor, in fact his taxpaying subjects, had to pay for these Dutch military expenses. The revenue from import and export duties in the main customs offices of the Southern Netherlands served as a collateral. Moreover, the permanent presence of the Dutch Protestant military was highly unpopular in the Catholic Southern Netherlands. All these provisions of the peace treaty make clear that imperial sovereignty in the Southern Netherlands was quite limited. In practice, the emperor was a caretaker of British and Dutch interests. This put a heavy burden on the relationship between the emperor and his new subjects.

Government: Renewal and Restoration

Restoring an old tradition, the Austrian Habsburg monarchs appointed successive prestigious governor generals to represent them in their new possession: Prince Eugene of Savoy, the famous military leader (1716–1724); archduchess Maria-Elisabeth, the emperor's sister (1725–1741); duke Charles of Lorraine, the empress' brother in law

(1744–1780); and finally the emperor's sister and brother-in-law, the archduchess Maria-Christina and Albert of Saxe-Teschen (1780–1792). The governor general was the formal head of government in Brussels but with the exception of Maria-Elisabeth, this position was foremost representative in nature. The so-called minister plenipotentiary, always an Italian or an Austrian, exercised real executive power as the confidant of the central government in Vienna.

The new Austrian regime replaced the three government councils by a single Council of State (1718–1725). By reintroducing some members of the high nobility into the Council, this reform intended to strengthen the new ruler's political base. However, the experiment failed completely. The high nobility that had been excluded from central government after the failed coup of 1632 (see Chapter 5) was more interested in quarrels with the minister over protocol and privilege than in government affairs. The three Councils were restored in 1725, and were to last until 1787.

Marquis de Prié, a Highly Unpopular Minister (1716–1724)

Eugene of Savoy became governor general in 1716 but never actually resided in Brussels during his mandate. His position as commander-in-chief in the war against the Ottomans prevented him from coming to the Southern Netherlands. As a result, executive power in Brussels was exercised by his Italian deputy, Hercule Joseph Turinetti, marquis de Prié. This excellent diplomat and staunch supporter of absolutism has always suffered a bad reputation in Belgian historiography. His position in the pantheon of villains in Belgian history comes next to the duke of Alva (see Chapter 5). He was accused by contemporaries and also by historians of vanity, tyranny, corrupt practices, cruelty, and even of "being an Italian" (!). However, when looking objectively at the problems he had to solve and at what he actually achieved, a more balanced picture emerges. First, Prié was confronted with the problem of the Dutch garrisons along the French border. The Barrier Treaty of 1715 was strongly criticized, especially in Flanders. The States of Flanders protested against the transfer of some territories to the Dutch Republic. Prié succeeded in reopening the negotiations and achieved the addition of some corrections (second Barrier Treaty, 1716). However, the provision that troops garrisoned at Dutch fortresses had to be financed by the emperor remained unchanged.

Prié's second challenge was the financial weakness of the Austrian Habsburg monarchy and the burden imposed by the Utrecht and Barrier Treaties. Vienna was unable and moreover unwilling to finance the military in the far-away Austrian Netherlands. On the contrary, from the start the Austrian rulers wanted to make the Southern Netherlands a self-supporting part of the monarchy. In the long run this part of their realm was expected to produce a surplus to contribute to the imperial treasury.

This policy led to tax increases that were fiercely opposed, especially in Antwerp, Brussels, and Mechelen, where local manufacturing industries suffered as a consequence of cheap imports from the Dutch Republic and Great Britain. Urban guilds refused to discuss the so-called *bede* (demand) for tax rises and blocked the decision-making process in the Brabant States. Months of negotiations were unable to mitigate the guilds' opposition, forcing Prié to call for the military. A number of guildmasters were arrested and tried. Their most famous leader, Frans Anneessens of Brussels, was found guilty of treason and executed, while others were banished. In 1719 order was restored, that is, States, city corporations, and guilds had some leeway to negotiate taxes, but a flat refusal to comply with a *bede* was henceforth impossible. In the nineteenth century Anneessens was transformed into a national hero and a champion of "Belgian liberties." In 1889, a statue was erected to honor his memory in his hometown Brussels, but in fact he was a stubborn and conservative defender of local and corporate privileges.

The Ostend Company (1722–1731)

Increasing existing taxes was one way to solve the new government's financial problems. Stimulating economic activity, especially trade in easily taxable overseas commodities such as sugar, coffee, tea, tobacco, and spices, could also increase treasury income. Europe's colonial trade boomed in the years after 1715, but fierce international competition put this profitability under pressure. However, in 1714 the new Austrian government started to grant imperial trade licences for the East Indies. In the beginning many shipowners, captains, and sailors were foreigners. The Dutch and English East India Companies accused them of being interlopers. Competition and high insurance costs resulted in disappointing returns for shipowners and investors.

Worried about possible diplomatic implications, the imperial government hesitated for a long time, but Prié finally convinced a number of
investors to participate in a new chartered company. The Imperial and
Royal East India Company was founded in 1722 and registered in
Antwerp. The company's ships would sail from and to Ostend, hence
its common name "Ostend Company." Its capital was completely sub-
scribed in just a few days. Most of the investors were Antwerp capitalists.
The government appointed a board of directors, consisting of Antwerp,
Ghent, and Ostend merchants. The Company unsuccessfully tried to
establish a factory in Bengal, but trade with China boomed. In
1725–1726 about half of total European tea import from China was
delivered by the Ostend Company. Net return on investment rocketed
to about 75 percent.

Other colonial companies felt threatened by their new rival.
Eighteenth-century colonial trade largely depended on military and
maritime power. In this respect, the emperor was obviously disadvan-
taged by his lack of a navy. The Dutch and English companies lobbied
successfully with their governments to eliminate their competitor. The
Dutch Republic was especially hostile to the Ostend Company. France,
always keen on weakening its hereditary Habsburg foe in the adjacent
Low Countries, was willing to oblige its former enemy. A complex
diplomatic situation ensued, especially when the former enemies Spain
and Austria signed a friendship treaty in 1725.

Moreover Charles VI, who had no sons, wanted foreign powers to
recognize his Pragmatic Sanction. This Habsburg family arrangement
stipulated that his daughter Maria-Theresa would succeed him in all
Austrian Hereditary Lands (as a woman, she was ineligible to be
emperor). The legal foundation of the Pragmatic Sanction was weak.
Its recognition therefore offered plenty of opportunities for the powers
to put pressure on the emperor in all kinds of diplomatic matters.

In 1727 Charles VI gave in to Dutch and British demands and
suspended the activities of the Ostend Company. In 1731 its maritime
ventures were ended altogether. Late nineteenth-century nationalist
Belgian historians presented the Ostend Company as a precursor of king
Leopold II's colonial ventures (see Chapter 9). They strongly criticized
Charles' decision to sacrifice "Belgium's" colonial and commercial future
for so-called "purely dynastic interests." However, an objective analysis
makes clear that the Emperor was unable to defend the Company against
combined Dutch, British, and French pressure – even without the

Pragmatic Sanction as a trade-off. Moreover, the Austrian Habsburg monarchy presided over a dynastic state; logically, this meant that the interests and the prestige of the dynasty were paramount.

The Company's discontinuation was not its definitive end: some modest activities went on until 1774. From the 1730s, the government tried other means to improve the economic situation but to little avail. The decline of urban manufacturing industries continued. This slump went hand-in-hand with demographic decline and stagnation in major cities. The population of Brussels, for instance, decreased by about 25 percent in the first half of the century. Spain and its colonies were no longer a substantial export market. For years, the British and the Dutch ignored Austria's request to negotiate a commercial treaty more favorable to the interests of the Southern Netherlands. Finally, negotiations started in 1738 but were suspended in the early 1740s.

Low agricultural prices, due to overproduction, were of course welcomed by urban consumers but not by farmers and landlords. Urban and regional authorities tried to improve and extend the existing road and canal network but without real results. The persisting slump in trade and manufacturing industries impeded traffic growth. Tax and toll returns also stagnated, while the financial burden of these infrastructural investments remained substantial.

The War of the Austrian Succession (1740–1748) and Its Aftermath

On his death in 1740, Charles VI was succeeded by Maria-Theresa (r. 1740–1780). During the final years of his reign, Charles had suffered military defeat in the Balkans and the Mediterranean and had lost important territories (Belgrad, Napels, and Sicily). France and Prussia ignored the Pragmatic Sanction and questioned the legality of Maria-Theresa's succession. In 1739 tensions between Britain and Spain led to a war in the American colonies. In 1740 different alliances resulted in a general conflict opposing France, Spain and Prussia on the one hand and Britain, the Dutch republic, and Austria on the other. For the first time, war was fought on a global scale in Europe, the America's, and Asia. Initially, the Austrian Netherlands stayed out of the conflict, but the French attacked in 1745. The Dutch Barrier, undermanned and in bad shape, could not stop the invasion. Since Great Britain was a guarantor

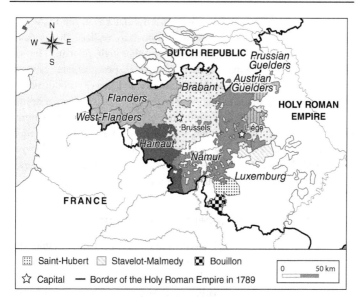

Map 6.1 The Austrian Netherlands and the prince-bishopric of Liège,
1789. Redrawn based on a map originally published in *Atlas de la
Wallonie, de la préhistoire à nos jours,* courtesy of Institut Jules Destrée,
Charleroi (© Sofam)

of the Pragmatic Sanction, it sent an army, but the French beat it twice
(at Fontenoy and Lawfeld), occupying the Austrian Netherlands until
1748. The Peace of Aachen returned the Austrian Netherlands to Maria-
Theresa, whose husband had become Emperor Francis I (r. 1745–1765)
(see Map 6.1).

The French occupation lasted less than four years but had a durable
impact on future political, cultural, and economic developments. The
French imposed new taxes and existing ones were raised without consulting the States. Trade tariffs were reorganized to end the modest
taxation of British and Dutch imports. After taking back control, the
restored Austrian government decided to keep many French reforms.
They also decided to suspend the yearly payment to the Dutch for the
maintenance of the Barrier fortresses since the latter had proved useless.
A general change of government policy in Vienna inspired a more
dynamic policy in Brussels.

After having lost territories in Italy and the Balkans in the 1730s, and rich Silesia in the 1740s, the Austrian monarchy realized that both its government and administration needed a thorough reform. The so-called Theresian Reforms consisted of gradual, practical, and cautious changes to strengthen monarchical authority and power without fundamentally changing the social fabric. For instance, the empress, a devout Catholic, wanted to control the influence of the Roman Catholic Church on civil society, but never contemplated the possibility of granting equal civil rights to the Protestants – as her son would do in the 1780s (see Chapter 7). In short, the Theresian Enlightenment was rather conservative and utilitarian, and was directed at strengthening state power.

Enlightenment in a Backwater?

Around 1740 the French philosopher and writer Voltaire resided for some months in the Austrian Netherlands. In his eyes, both the country and its inhabitants were culturally backward: "a stay of ignorance (. . .) a real country of obedience, without intellect, full of religion." Literary historians have long taken these words for granted – forgetting that haughty and sharp-tongued Parisian intellectuals are seldom indulgent towards less-gifted provincials. However, Voltaire was not entirely wrong. In the first half of the eighteenth century – when Voltaire, Montesquieu, and Leibniz reflected on major political and scientific issues – very little worth mentioning on these subjects originated in the Austrian Netherlands. Few individuals were brave enough to defy censorship, especially during pious Maria-Elisabeth's governorship.

The political and cultural climate in the Austrian Netherlands changed gradually around mid-century. Political, economic, cultural, and ideological transformations were boosted by the presence of numerous French officers and civil servants in 1745–1748 and by the active role played by two enlightened plenipotentiary ministers in the period 1748–1770.

The Southern Netherlands was a profoundly Catholic country. The Roman Church impacted every aspect of civil society. Clerical institutions and their servants were physically omnipresent. In the second half of the eighteenth century priests, friars, nuns, monks, canons, and beguines made up at least 1 percent of the total population (even as much as 1.5 percent in Brabant in 1755), but these clerics were not evenly spread over the country. In large urban centers, between 5 and

7 percent of all adults belonged to the clergy. The public generally appreciated parish priests, teachers, and those who cared for the poor and the sick, but members of contemplative orders and canons were often criticized, and were suspected of leading lives of leisure and luxury.

The Church, a mighty landowner, was immensely rich. According to a financial survey of some hundred abbeys and monasteries in the 1770s, their combined incomes totalled 2.8 million guilders, that is, about a quarter of the total revenue of the central government in the Austrian Netherlands. The accommodation and livelihoods of a few thousand monks and nuns devoured the major part of this huge income. Many people bequeathed or donated goods to the Church. Land thus acquired by the Church remained in the so-called *mainmorte* or "dead hand," meaning that it had left the market for landed property forever. This was highly problematic in a densely populated country that was blessed with strong demographic growth (more on this later). Many people, more-over, thought that the Church managed its landed property badly.

From the 1750s, the Privy Council launched an offensive to curb the Church's power. The asylum right on Church property, invoked by deserters, criminals, and frauds, was curtailed in 1753–1755. Legislation regarding the *mainmorte* (1753) imposed state control and severe limitations on gifts to the Church. The Privy Council revised and extended marital legislation, interfering in a domain exclusively claimed by the Church, marriage being a holy sacrament.

In 1773 the Pope abolished the Jesuit Order. Maria-Theresa person-ally disagreed with the papal decision, but as a pragmatic politician she immediately ordered the confiscation of the Jesuits' possessions. A special *jointe* controlled the order's finances; and its revenue was used to finance a new type of high school replacing the Jesuit colleges. The so-called Theresian colleges introduced a more modern curriculum, no longer exclusively centered on classical languages and religious educa-tion, but also including mathematics, practical sciences, and geography. However, the new schools proved unsuccessful due to a lack of good teachers.

Patrice François de Neny, *Chef Président* of the Privy Council from 1758, was the driving force of clerical and educational policy. He wanted to create an *Église belgique* or "Belgican" Church, in unison with the State and aiming at the general welfare of the community of believers and without undue interference from Rome. These measures were meant to produce well-educated and obedient subjects of the state. Neny and his collaborators in Brussels initiated this bold new policy, rather than the central Viennese government. The empress and her chancelor more than once curbed the enthusiasm of the reformers in Brussels. However Neny and Maria-Theresa both wanted to strengthen state power while strongly rejecting the radical aspects of the Enlightenment. In the 1780s, Neny dissociated himself from the drastic policies of Maria-Theresa's successor (see Chapter 7).

Enlightenment and the spread of enlightened ideas in literature, salons, learned societies, freemasonry, etc., was essentially an urban, aristocratic, and upper-middle-class phenomenon. Freemasonry started quite early in the Southern Netherlands. In the period from *c.*1740 till 1786, some sixty masonic lodges existed for a short or longer period. Originally, membership was overwhelmingly aristocratic. In the 1780s about half of the brothers were members of the (upper) middle class, and 2 percent belonged to the Roman Catholic clergy, notwithstanding the papal condemnation of freemasonry – an odd situation resulting from the government's refusal to publish the papal ban on freemasonry.

The Scientific Revolution was one of the breeding grounds of Enlightenment. Governmental plans to promote experimental physics at Leuven University proved unsuccessful, due to a lack of money. However some noblemen, rich businessmen, and also physicians and pharmacists, were very interested in collecting scientific instruments and objects. The most famous collector was Prince Charles of Lorraine, the governor general. At around 1770, Brussels boasted fourteen private scientific collections, an impressive feat compared with the sixty-odd collections in Paris.

Books were of course the key vehicles for spreading enlightened ideas, but also conceptions opposing the *esprit philosophique*. Censorship existed and was occasionally severe, but generally speaking less so from the 1750s. Notwithstanding pressure from the bishops, the government refused to introduce Rome's *Index* of "blasphemous literature." Forbidden books were readily accessible to those who could afford them.

Research on a few hundred private book collections has established a trustworthy list of the most popular authors: Voltaire, Rousseau, Montesquieu, Hume, Locke, Addison and Steele, Diderot's and d'Alembert's *Encyclopédie*. English authors were read in French translation. One source suggests that no less than five hundred copies of different editions of the *Encyclopédie* were sold in Brussels alone. More detailed examination of private book collections reveals their often ideologically heterogenous composition: Diderot, Voltaire, and Rousseau mixed with reactionary authors such as ex-Jesuit François-Xavier de Feller. The educated and aristocratic classes certainly were intellectually interested in the Enlightenment, but the revolutionary events of the 1780s and 1790s would demonstrate the liveliness of traditional and conservative ideas and forces (see Chapter 7).

Reform of Government Policy

Major political and administrative reforms were introduced from 1749. The government councils were transformed into more efficient Departments of Economy and Finances (Council of Finances) and Justice and Home Affairs (Privy Council). Generally speaking, recruitment and the promotion of ministers and senior civil servants was increasingly based on competence and effort, to the detriment of patronage. Specialized government institutitutions called *jointes* were established to handle issues as the cattle plague, finances of towns and rural districts, grain production, and the promotion of trade between the Southern Netherlands and the Austrian Hereditary Lands, etc.

Central government supported and stimulated the improvement of the infrastructure for traffic in provinces and towns; for instance, the extension of the harbor at Ostend, a canal linking this Ostend and Bruges with Ghent and the Scheldt, a canal between Leuven and Mechelen, etc. The network of paved roads was extended and improved, reaching a total length of 2,850 km at the end of the 1780s, one of the densest road networks in Europe. For the first time since its creation in the beginning of the century, the revenue from turnpikes increased continuously, reflecting growing levels of traffic and trade.

Economic policy was still largely inspired by mercantilistic principles and agricultural interests were subordinate to those of manufacturing and trade. The government handled the monopoly of urban guilds and corporations with great caution, especially in Brabant where guilds indirectly enjoyed a strong position in the states. In some cities, Ghent for instance, the guild privilege stipulated that incoming barges and ships from other destinations had to unload their cargo and transfer it to ships or barges of local shipmasters. Such local privileges were of course at odds with the government's policy of promoting trade and transportation. The central authorities took measures to tackle these and similar situations but guild opposition remained strong. The political struggle to curb guild monopoly continued until 1794, when the French revolutionaries put an end to the guild system altogether.

From the 1750s, central trade policy became more sophisticated by cautiously but continuously adapting tariffs through limited measures, thereby avoiding offense and retaliation from trading partners. In general, commercial policy aimed to substitute import, export, and transit via Dutch ports by trade via Ostend and Bruges. Trade and transport volumes grew and their composition and direction became more varied. This so-called policy *des petits pacquets* ("little packages") generated a higher level income for the Treasury. Public revenue from custom duties increased by 70 percent between 1750 and 1785. Moreover, the new trade policy impacted positively on the economy as a whole.

Reliable statistics are key for the implementation of economic and social policy. The government therefore began to promote the collection of statistics. A general census was held in the duchy of Brabant in 1755. A few years later a general inquiry was made into urban and rural industries. In 1771–1778 count Ferraris produced a remarkable and detailed topographical map of the whole of the Austrian Netherlands, including the prince-bishopric of Liège. Its 275 original maps cover no less than 300 m^2 and its publication in twelve massive volumes was a huge success. In 1784, a general census was held for the first time, reporting a total population of 2,273,000.

Originally, the public finances of the Austrian regime were in total disarray. As a result of continuous warfare before 1713, the country had been flooded by foreign coinage, often of dubious value. The country suffered a negative balance of trade, causing an outflow of precious metals. Local coin production had come to a standstill. In 1749–1755, the government reorganized the mint by issuing new, good-quality coins and concentrating the production of these in Brussels. This policy proved successful.

The central government of the Austrian monarchy could raise loans in the Southern Netherlands on a collateral of taxes paid in, for instance, Bohemia. The repayment of these loans was increasingly and secretly financed by the budgetary surplus of the Southern Netherlands, reflecting the improvement of public financial management. In other words, the Southern Netherlands had become a net contributor to the finances of the monarchy as a whole, unlike the situation in the seventeenth and the first half of the eighteenth century. The level of taxation was about 7.5 guilders per capita per year, varying from 10.4 guilders in the county of

Flanders to about 2 or 3 guilders in Luxemburg. Comparable figures for the United Kingdom and France are 12 guilders and about 8 or 9 guilders per capita respectively.

Demography and Agriculture

The eighteenth century witnessed a period of almost continuous population increase, in spite of regional exceptions. Local and regional population growth figures in the period 1700–1780 vary between 25 and 130 percent. Since no general census was held before 1784, it is impossible to establish a precise general growth figure, but the trend undoubtedly went up. Yet urban and rural demographic growth differed considerably. The populations of major cities such as Brussels, Antwerp, Ghent, Bruges, and Tournai stagnated or recovered slightly after the slump of the first half of the century. Brussels is a case in point: its population dropped from roughly 80,000 around 1700 to 60,000 in 1755, then rose again to 74,000 in 1784. Around 1700 about 40 percent of the Brabantine population lived in the four major cities, but in 1784 the figure declined to 26 percent. In 1690, 13.6 percent of all inhabitants of the county of Flanders lived in Ghent and Bruges; in 1784 the figure dropped to 7.6 percent The Austrian Netherlands clearly suffered from de-urbanization.

In the previous centuries, long-term population growth had been very slow. In the eighteenth century the plague disappeared from Europe. Epidemics became less frequent; they were locally or regionally circumscribed and therefore less catastrophic. During this eighty-odd year period, the country was at peace. Moreover the extreme seventeenth-century weather conditions (see Chapter 5) gave way to a more favorable climate. These developments had a positive effect on agricultural production and nutrition, and famines receded. Good harvests in the 1720s and 1730s generated population growth. Mortality was still relatively high, but with fewer peaks. People married more frequently than before, and declining average marriage ages resulted in more births.

Population growth, initiated by increased agricultural production, impacted the economy as a whole, in the first place on agriculture itself. An abundant supply of agricultural workers kept labor costs low for farmers. The profitability of market-oriented farming increased due to continuously rising agricultural prices in the second half of the century. Population increases also had important consequences for farmland

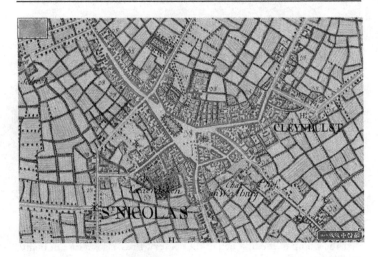

Figure 6.1 In the eighteenth century, Flanders was densely populated, and farmland was intensively exploited, as shown on this topographical map of Sint-Niklaas (East Flanders) and the surrounding countryside. *Count Ferraris, Carte de cabinet des Pays-Bas autrichiens et de la principauté de Liège, 1777* (Brussels, Royal Library)

division. About half of the acreage in the Austrian Netherlands belonged to larger farms (more than 10 ha), essentially situated in Hainaut, Namur, and Luxemburg. In most regions the greater farms seldom represented more than 15 to 20 percent of all farms. An average farm had a surface area of between 2 to 4.5 ha, which is quite small compared to Britain for instance. The government, moreover, stimulated the division of larger farms into units of a maximum of 16 ha (see Figure 6.1).

In densely populated regions of Flanders and Brabant, the number of smallholders, often with less than 1 ha of land, increased dramatically. Life on these minuscule farms was exhausting. Every household member had to work hard and the land was tilled intensively (crop rotation and manuring). Very often, farm income did not match housekeeping expenses. Additional earnings were generated by part-time agricultural work on larger farms, by flax spinning and weaving and, in the southern provinces, by nail production. In some regions with poor soils, division of land came to a halt. If the labour market offered no alternative occupation, people opted for temporary emigration or joined the army.

Permanent emigration occurred in Luxemburg: in the third quarter of the century, some 5,000 people migrated to the Banat, a military border region situated in present-day northern Serbia and western Romania.

The agricultural revolution in Britain was characterized by land enclosure, in some cases the eviction of people, the privatizing of the commons and huge scaling up of farms. Nothing of the sort happened in the Austrian Netherlands, except some privatizing of common land. The rapidly growing population could be fed thanks to the expansion of existing farming methods. The production of wheat increased and spelt was substituted with rye. The per capita consumption of grain diminished as a result of the introduction of a new crop, the potato.

Traditionally, the Southern Netherlands had to import grain for human consumption. In the eighteenth century the government could grant export licences for grain when harvests had been good. Since imported American tobacco could be taxed easily, the government wanted to forbid tobacco growing (1757). This attempt to optimize fiscal revenue failed because of fierce opposition in the States of Flanders. As a result, until the end of the century about one-third of tobacco consumption originated domestically, while two-thirds were imported.

The production of fodder crops that could be fed to cattle in cowsheds stimulated cattle breeding in densely populated parts of Flanders and Brabant. One region, the *Pays de Herve* totally abandoned agriculture and specialized in butter and cheese production. In the final decades of the century livestock diminished in Flanders and Brabant due to increasing agricultural prices relative to meat and dairy prices.

In the second half of the eighteenth century agriculture undoubtedly prospered, but prosperity was unequally spread. Landowners – aristocrats, wealthy town inhabitants, the landed nobility – and wealthy farmers, the *coqs du village*, gained most by increasing trade volumes, prices, and rents, while smallholders, cottagers, and anyone buying their food and paying rent suffered. Enormous hunger for arable land, especially in Flanders, incited or compelled smallholders and cottagers to pay exorbitant rents and endure deteriorating standards of living. This paved the way for the catastrophe of "poor Flanders" in the 1840s (see Chapter 8).

Manufacturing Industry, Trade, and Social Conditions

Traditionally, the Southern Netherlands excelled in textile fabrication. In the eighteenth century, about half of the workforce in the county of

Flanders earned a living as producers of linen. Around 80 percent of all textile workers in the Southern Netherlands were involved in flax production: the spinning of yarn for the weaving of coarse linens and cambrics, mixed textiles, and thread for the production of lace. Linen production, at least doubling in the course of the century, was overwhelmingly concentrated in the county of Flanders and the adjacent parts of Brabant and Hainaut. Ghent and Kortrijk were the main export centers to, respectively, Spain and her colonies and France. Sales abroad soared by 60 percent.

Lace occupied an important female workforce. Thousands of girls and often-unmarried women, widows, or beguines produced all kinds of components for clothing, from basic to very elaborate and expensive. Lace workers were poorly paid but lace merchants traded in highly competitive markets characterized by rapidly changing fashions. Brussels and Mechelen were the main lace producing towns, and their produce was exported all over Europe.

On the other hand, fierce British competition strangled the old urban wool industry of Flanders and Brabant. What remained of this business was concentrated in the east of the country, that is, the duchy of Limburg and the adjacent part of the prince-bishopric of Liège (Verviers and Eupen). These enterprises exported mainly to the Southern Netherlands and nearby Germany. New developments sounded the death knell for the age-old tapestry weaving industry: changed ideas on furnishing, faster changes in fashion, and a general eighteenth-century trend to look for less expensive textiles and alternative wall coverings (wallpaper and textiles).

For some time, cotton yarn had been worked in mixed textiles. From the second half of the seventeenth century pure cottons were imported from India. As a substitute for linens, cottons became very popular all over Europe. In the Southern Netherlands the production of pure cottons started as late as the early 1800s. Cotton printing, that is, the illustration of imported Indian cottons, soared in the second half of the century, starting in Antwerp in the early 1750s, and Ghent and Antwerp became the main production centers. In the 1790s, about twenty cotton-printing plants were in operation.

Except for cotton-printing plants, employing on average thirty to fifty people, textile production remained predominantly small-scale. A myriad of production sites were run by independent masters with one or a few looms, while merchants and entrepreneurs directed dozens of cottage workers in rural areas, or so-called independent masters in cities who were in fact wage workers. Until the very end of the century, spinning and weaving used traditional methods; the flying shuttle, the spinning jenny, the spinning mule, and steam power came later. Consequently, Flanders and Limburg (in particular) were real proto-industrial regions, producing huge quantities of textiles for national or foreign markets under the guidance of capitalist entrepreneurs. This paved the way for a modern, mechanized manufacturing industry; a similar process unfolded for instance in Lancashire and Yorkshire in the late eighteenth and early nineteenth centuries.

While textile industries were mainly situated in the northern part of the country, coal and iron businesses were exclusively located in Wallonia. Coal was extracted in this region from the Middle Ages. From the seventeenth century, it was used for the heating of houses and as an energy supply in different industries (breweries, distilleries, dying works, glassworks, brickyards, limekilns, etc.). The industry was, however, confronted with major problems. The haulage of coal to Flanders and Brabant was expensive. Coal from the western Hainaut basin (Mons) could be transported north by waterways crossing French territory. It was therefore heavily taxed. Coal from the eastern Hainaut basin (Charleroi) had to be transported by road and was also expensive. The Meuse was difficult to navigate and burdened with tolls. On top of this, cheap English coal could be imported easily. The building of railroads and canals in nineteenth-century Belgium would solve these problems, sharply reducing domestic transportation costs.

The coal industry faced another challenge: the drainage of mine galleries. Newcomen's steam pump, an English invention (*c.*1710), was introduced in the Liège basin at around 1720. Forty years later, the components of the machine could be produced locally. In the 1780s, a total fifty-odd machines were used in the four coal basins (Mons, Centre, Charleroi, and Liège). Newcomen's steam pump was the only English technology in the Southern Netherlands before the last decade of the eighteenth century. Capital represented a final obstacle. The installation of steam pumps in order to dig deeper mine galleries (up to 200–300 m below surface) required extensive financial means, the confidence of investors and creditors, and a new business model. Limited liability companies with mine managers and capitalist entrepreneurs replaced small "hand-crafted" companies. In spite of these obstacles, coal production more than doubled in the second half of the century, reaching about

800,000 metric tons in its last decade. This heralded the Industrial Revolution that would make Belgium a major coal producer in the nineteenth and first half of the twentieth century (see Chapters 7 and 8).

The iron industry in the Entre-Sambre-et-Meuse region and in Luxemburg thrived thanks to the rich charcoal resources. It particularly flourished after the imposition of heavy duties on imported Swedish iron. In the last decades of the century, production reached about 25,000 metric tons, that is, the equivalent of a quarter of total French production. Cast iron was processed into wrought iron products: nails, plows, spades, and weaponry (swords, bayonets, muskets, pistols, etc.). The Liège region all but monopolized arms production. The equally important nail production industry was also located there and in the *Pays de Charleroi*. Production methods essentially remained traditional. The most important eighteenth-century innovation in the iron industry, the use of coke (1709), only started in the 1790s. The main export markets for iron were France (cast iron) and the Dutch Republic (nails for shipyards). Weaponry was mostly exported via Holland, among other things to supply the Americans during their War of Independence (see Figure 6.2).

Figure 6.2 Iron production thrived in the eighteenth-century prince-bishopric of Liège. Oil painting by Léonard Defrance, *Interior of a foundry*, 1789 (Brussels, Fine Arts Museum)

The consumption of colonial foods and stimulants exploded all over Western Europe in the eighteenth century. The processing of sugar and tobacco created additional economic growth. About two-thirds of the tobacco processed in the Southern Netherlands was imported from Virginia; the remaining third was produced locally. In 1764, about 160 factories were spread all over the country. While numerous small businesses produced for local markets, some businesses, employing dozens of workers and based on substantial capital investment, were export oriented. The French state monopoly of tobacco made contraband attractive.

Declining molasses prices stimulated demand for sugar. Sugar imports from the Dutch Republic were mostly substituted by production in sugar refineries requiring substantial capital investment. Most of the thirty refineries existing in the 1780s were created in the 1750s. Antwerp, Bruges, Ghent, Brussels, and Charleroi were the main centers. Other new and/or expanding manufactures produced porcelain (Tournai, Brussels), paper (especially Brabant), glass (Charleroi, Brussels, Bruges), and carriages (Brussels).

The authorities tried to divert overseas and transit trade from and to Holland directly to Ostend and Bruges. The Dutch Republic nonetheless remained the most important trading partner of the Southern Netherlands. Exports of all kinds of textiles had declined (France) or all but disappeared (Britain) due to protectionism in these countries, but trade with France became more balanced after 1750. Trade with Spain and (indirectly) its American colonies resumed after a decline in the first half of the century. Commercial contacts with the Holy Roman Empire were negligible, except for the export of woolens from the Limburg-Verviers region. Transit trade between Britain and Lorraine, Switzerland, and Southern Germany increased markedly from the 1750s.

Some interest in colonial trade had also persisted. While the Ostend Company stopped its commercial operations in 1731, it continued to operate as a holding company with interests in the small Swedish, Prussian, and Danish East India Companies. After its final liquidation in 1774, a new "Asiatic Company" was created. Based at Trieste and Fiume in the Adriatic Sea, it was financed by capitalists from the Southern Netherlands, especially from Antwerp. The company traded in India, Burma, and China, and some returning ships unloaded in Ostend. This venture ended prematurely due to discord between the management and shareholders, and the bankruptcy of the company's Paris banker in 1785.

During the American War of Independence, Ostend was declared a free port. The huge increase in shipping in 1780–1783 boosted economic activity. A company run by Brussels merchants engaged in the slave trade and even made plans to acquire an island in the Antilles. Slave ships with imperial passports sailed from Ostend but also from French ports. After the war the Dutch, French, and English companies regained their former position in colonial trade, and the slave trade from the Southern Netherlands stopped. In the 1780s, an attempt to establish trade relations with the United States proved unsuccessful. Ostend faded away and once again became a minor West European port.

There was also a dark side to the generally rosy picture of economic and demographic growth, namely poverty, beggary, and proletarianization. The number of abandoned children increased considerably from the 1770s. In major towns, 10 to 15 percent of the population obtained poor relief, but the real percentage of the needy came closer to 20 to 25 percent. This huge difference can be explained by the lack of means and the selection of the "deserving" poor by authorities. Comparable percentages existed in rural districts. In spite of the extreme division of land, especially in Flanders, many inhabitants were totally dependent on poorly paid wage labor in times of rising prices.

From the 1770s, some magistrates in towns and rural districts started forming plans to tackle the problem of beggary, prostitution, and poverty. Inspired by these proposals, the government facilitated the establishment of correction houses to lock up beggars, vagrants, prostitutes, and other "idle people." However, confinement policy failed for the simple reason that there were too many poor people. Another solution was therefore applied in areas where manufacturers needed a large and cheap labour force, especially in towns and districts with an important textile industry. The so-called deserving poor received minimal outdoor relief under very strict conditions in order to push them into the labour market at minimum cost for the employer.

Conclusion

The War of the Spanish Succession led to an important regime change. The Dutch and British conquerors of the Southern Netherlands handed it over to the new Austrian Habsburg rulers under strict conditions. They imposed a heavy burden, both military, financial and economic. Moreover, the new authorities were confronted by an economic slump, particularly in the urban manufacturing industries. This crisis also caused urban populations to stagnate or even decline. Attempts to improve the situation eventually failed due to weak leadership and insufficient means to throw off the burdens imposed by the Maritime Powers.

Things changed from the 1750s. Maria-Theresa was a shrewd and reform-minded ruler, albeit of the cautious conservative type. A number of reforms made the government and the civil service more dynamic and effective. Moderate enlightened ideas – especially of a rational and utilitarian nature – were hailed in government circles. Ideas of more radical enlightened authors were not, but their writings were not unknown among the educated upper class. While being a devout Catholic, the empress nevertheless asserted the primacy of the state, thus curtailing the power of the Catholic Church in civil matters.

Government policy generally had a positive effect on the upward secular trend and on the trade cycle. Populations and agricultural production increased significantly. In years with good harvests, agricultural surpluses could be exported. In some rural areas, especially in Flanders, the proto-industrial production of linen increased dramatically. In the urban manufacturing industry new businesses such as cotton printing, sugar refining, tobacco processing, etc., substituted declining industries such as tapestry. Coal mining and the iron industry flourished. Transportation and the transit trade increased, thanks to an improved road system.

So the overall economic picture was positive in the four decades after 1750. Furthermore, a conception of "proto-Belgium" began to develop within government circles and the educated classes. The active role of the Brussels central government in policymaking for the whole country, Neny's attempt to create an *Église belgique* or "Belgican Church", the "national" census of 1784, Ferraris' map covering the entire Southern Netherlands (including the prince-bishopric of Liège), and the Gallicization of the upper middle class all contributed to this nascent sense of nationhood in the upper strata of society.

However, this "proto-Belgium" idea was still very fragile. The Austrian Netherlands were, and remained at this time, a confederation of principalities with its own institutions, traditions, and particularities. Bonds of loyalty with one's own town, rural community, or principality continued to be very strong. Relations between the ruler and his subjects, especially the elites, were based on the assumption that the former had to respect the privileges of the latter and the monarch expected his subjects to contribute to his finances and status. In the second half of the century the Austrian Netherlands were indeed a net contributor to the Austrian Treasury.

Maria-Theresa was officially represented as the "mother of her people" (she gave birth to sixteen children!) and Prince Charles of Lorraine, her brother-in-law, was seen as a benign and benevolent governor general. But in fact, the monarch had a rather down-to-earth approach to the place of the Austrian Netherlands within her realm. Plans to exchange the distant Southern Netherlands for nearby Bavaria only failed because other powers, especially Prussia, strongly opposed them. The loyalty of subjects toward their monarch was also conditional, as events at the end of the 1780s would prove (see Chapter 7).

On the eve of the so-called Age of Revolution, the Austrian Netherlands enjoyed a rapidly rising population and a dynamic economy but suffered from an increasing number of needy and poor individuals. Enlightened ideas pervaded the elites and the upper middle class, and a moderately enlightened monarch ruled the country. In spite of this, all the attributes of the Ancien Régime – aristocracy, privileges, estates, hierarchy, and guilds – remained intact, with one exception: the powers of the Catholic Church in civil society were slightly limited. The radical political and judicial reforms of Maria-Theresa's successor would trigger a revolutionary mixture of reactionary and moderate progressive ideas. A few years later, the French revolutionaries would change the fabric of society itself, as the next chapter will show.

The Formation of a New Nation-State (1780s–1830)

Introduction

A Belgian citizen dying in 1840 at the age of eighty lived through a long period of political turmoil. During his lifetime, he or she was the subject of no less than four Austrian Habsburg emperors (1760s–1794), of the French Emperor Napoleon I (1804–1814), of the king of the United Kingdom of the Netherlands (1814/1815–1830), and finally of the first king of the Belgians (1831–). In between, he was also ruled by two non-monarchical systems: an ephemeral independent "Belgian" republic in 1790, and the successive French republican regimes during the years 1794–1804, preceding Napoleon's imperial rule. But underneath the surface of these seemingly volatile political events, lay a coherent pattern of recurring issues. Four crucial questions caused fierce confrontations. Some had existed for centuries, while others were more recent; but during the period under consideration, they all witnessed a decisive breakthrough. After fifty years of dramatic changes, the society and body politic of this small part of Europe had irrevocably changed.

The first question concerned the efficacy of the state apparatus. Throughout this half-century, the successive rulers pursued the modernization of law, institutions, and bureaucracy. Their efforts met with varying success, but in the end this process resulted in the creation of a new and quite efficient set of public instruments and capabilities. The second problem was related to an age-old bone of contention, namely the relations between the state and the Roman Catholic Church. Would one of these actors dominate the other, or would they opt for some sort of mutually recognized autonomy? The third question was no less crucial: autocracy had come under the attack of democratic principles.

The difficult introduction of essential Liberal features such as a modern constitution – as opposed to the ancient "constitutions" or privileges evoked in the preceding chapters – representative mechanisms, and ministerial responsibility, ran like a red thread through these five decades. The first three issues were prominent in many European countries. The fourth, however, even if far from absent in other regions of the continent, was of particular relevance to the Southern Netherlands. The struggle between political centralization and particularistic rule, both on the local and regional levels, had been going on for centuries but now reached its climax.

All these crucial debates were waged against a double background. First, the society and economy of the Southern Netherlands were characterized by rapid and profound transformations. Capitalist industrial production was making its first steps, while the agrarian system witnessed important changes. Both developments went hand-in-hand. Second, the international context was of primary importance. What happened in the Southern Netherlands, and later in Belgium, was of great relevance to the adjacent countries and even to distant monarchies. Far from being passive observers, the foreign states were actively involved in developments taking place in this part of Europe. The outcome was even *shaped* by the Great Powers.

Economy and Society in Transition: Toward the Industrial Revolution

Political mechanisms and institutions changed drastically during the half-century preceding the foundation of Belgium. But during the same period, the transformations of the economy and society were no less profound. In fact, the evolution in both domains was in some ways linked. Changes in the political and the socio-economic field mutually reinforced each other. On the one hand, the modernization of the state and specific policy measures facilitated the transition toward capitalist production. On the other, the rise of new interest groups and sensitivities stimulated the creation of a new public setting.

Like elsewhere in north-western Europe, the population was growing rapidly in the Southern Netherlands, from 2.3 million in 1750 to 3.2 million in 1815. This growth had to be borne by a still predominantly *agrarian* economy. As we saw in Chapter 6, the rate of urbanization had declined in the Southern Netherlands in the seventeenth and eighteenth centuries. At around 1800, whereas 23 percent of total population in England lived in cities of more than 5,000 inhabitants and 37 percent in the Dutch Republic, this proportion was only 18 percent in the Southern Netherlands. Thus, during the eighteenth century in future Belgium, population growth coincided with a relative *increase* in the importance of the countryside.

How was this strain dealt with? As population figures make clear, there was never a dramatic rupture between subsistence and population: the growing number of mouths could indeed be fed. The cultivation of new land was envisaged and, to a certain extent, also stimulated by the authorities; but this extension of acreage was of marginal importance. The main answer to the growing demand for food lay in the intensification and diversification of crops. An accelerated generalization of new farming techniques, coupled with a huge input of labor and fertilizer (e.g. intensive use of manure collected in the cities) explains this steadily growing agricultural output, which was also increasingly market oriented. The introduction of new crops, either for food or for industrial use, was also of great importance. The widespread cultivation and consumption of the potato, in particular, starting in the beginning of the eighteenth century, had tremendous consequences. Growing numbers of people depended on this single product to survive – as would become dramatically clear during the crisis of the 1840s (see Chapter 8).

But the apparently "rich" and thriving countryside of the Austrian Netherlands also produced new social configurations. The growing number of peasants led, in the first place, to a division of farms and, consequently, to a notable decrease of average farm size. The price of buying and renting land increased significantly. Demographic pressure on the land was accompanied by a constant loss of property: a growing number of peasants had to give up their land and became tenants or wage laborers, a process accompanied by a deterioration of their living conditions. Rising rents and increasing prices for land and agricultural products benefited the proprietors, especially the large landowners (including bourgeoisie living in cities), but were detrimental to the growing number of tenants or the landless rural population. However, at the turn of the eighteenth and nineteenth century, the massive exodus from the countryside to the new industrial regions and cities was not yet taking place.

Indeed, one way to cope with the pressure from the growing population and to combat rising or threatening misery was to switch to new forms of activity *in the countryside*. Not only were new crops being introduced; the rural people themselves increasingly and massively turned to cottage industries. The production of linen goods became an essential survival strategy for large parts of the rural population in Flanders. In some areas, the linen cottage industry represented the livelihood of as much as a quarter of all inhabitants. In the Francophone regions, the production of woollen cloth (in Verviers), arms (in Liège) and nails (in the Charleroi region) were organized following the putting-out system and employed many modest people scattered over the countryside.

On the eve of the nineteenth century, therefore, proto-industrialization was thriving in future Belgium. A modern capitalist industry, however, did not essentially originate in this form of activity. It took off in three sectors – cotton and wool textiles, coal mining, and metallurgy – and was located in a few specific regions, one in Flanders and four in Wallonia. Enterprising businessmen introduced the mechanical spinning and weaving of cotton in the Flemish city of Ghent in the opening years of the nineteenth century. One of the very first "Belgian" industrialists, Lieven Bauwens, smuggled the first *mule jenny* out of Britain; in 1801, he opened a factory in Ghent (of which he also became mayor). Other entrepreneurs followed suit; several of them had become rich through calico printing (*indiennes*) in the preceding decades. In a few years' time, this Flemish town grew into a thriving centre of modern cotton production, employing many thousands of factory workers. Although hit by a hard recession at the end of the French regime, the Ghent textile industry managed to survive; during the nineteenth century, it was the only nucleus of a modern, urban industry in Flanders.

In the Walloon city of Verviers, a handful of rich and influential merchant families concentrated the dispersed woolen industry into large factories and introduced mechanical devices to boost activity. Their demand for iron machines stimulated yet another type of capitalist enterprise. The British mechanic William Cockerill, who had emigrated to the continent, met this demand. Only a few years later, his son John was running a large machine construction business, with many other integrated factories. Since the eighteenth century, the Walloon region had already been a large producer of metal products. In 1811, during the French annexation, as much as a quarter of total pig iron and wrought iron output in France originated in future Belgium. But this production was still organized on a small-scale, traditional, and fragmented basis.

At the beginning of the nineteenth century, however, large and mechanized factories, for example blast furnaces essentially located in the Liège and Charleroi regions, became the focus for metal production.

Iron steam engines were indeed in great demand in another thriving business, the coal mining industry. This sector was also undergoing a real metamorphosis. Coal deposits, stretching from the north of France to the western regions of contemporary Germany, cut across Wallonia. These deposits had been exploited on a small-scale, craft basis since the Middle Ages. Traditional legislation, stating that the owner of the surface also possessed the underground, coupled with limited technical capacity, had prevented the development of large-scale exploitation. But in the beginning of the nineteenth century the legal framework, techniques, and organizational structures were all changing rapidly. The French mining legislation of 1801 introduced new and easy procedures to allow coal to be mined (concessions were now granted by the authorities, and not by the many surface proprietors), while steam engines, pumping up the ground water, allowed for deeper mine shafts. New capital associations were set up to ensure large-scale coal production. In only a few years, the regions around Mons (the Borinage), Charleroi, and Liège had become leading coal producers on the continent.

Two other major Belgian towns, Brussels and Antwerp, were initially untouched by industrialization. Brussels developed into a financial and administrative center, while maintaining a dense network of mostly small-scale and poorly mechanized enterprises. The port of Antwerp was a commercial metropolis, but its prosperity fluctuated, to a large extent, with the closing or opening of the Scheldt River. Industrial activities were only developed there from the late nineteenth and early twentieth centuries.

So even before its independence, "Belgium" was taking the lead in continental industrialization. A combination of factors explained this early start: the presence of natural riches, especially coal and iron ore; its geographical position, at the junction of important trade routes in north-western Europe and in the vicinity of large foreign markets; an abundant labor force whose wage levels were lower than in adjacent countries; the effects of the Continental Blockade, sheltering industrial production from British competition during a crucial period; the existence of the British example; and also changes in the rural sector (e.g. the increasing output and commercialization of agriculture).

Finally, the role of public authorities was far from negligible in early industrialization. The successive rulers of future Belgium had all been aware of the country's rich economic potential and had promoted trade and industry, albeit in a specific way. The Austrian emperors were still imbued with traditional mercantilist views. They took interventionist measures to encourage production (monopolies, export or import prohibitions, etc.) and stimulated the building of roads and canals. Due to the turmoil caused by violent regime change, the French authorities were at first less active in stimulating economic activity. But once the situation had stabilized, Napoleon also took several measures to promote economic prosperity (e.g. by stimulating the port of Antwerp, which experienced a boost thanks to the reopening of the Scheldt River). After the creation of the United Kingdom of the Netherlands, King William not only extended the transport infrastructure, but also showed genuine interest in modern techniques and in industry, helping many entrepreneurs set up and maintain their factories. His dream was to link the burgeoning industrial production of the southern, "Belgian" part of his kingdom with the commercial capacities of the northern, "Dutch" part. The new "Belgian" factories indeed profited, for example, from colonial outlets in Java. Nevertheless, it was not easy to reconcile the free-trade attitude of "Dutch" trade interests with the protectionist demands of "Belgian" industry. The Austrian and French regimes had always protected home industries; finally, William also adopted a mildly protectionist stance. Moreover, he created several economic institutions; one of these, the *Société générale pour favoriser l'industrie nationale* (which later became the *Société générale de Belgique*) was to play an essential role in the Belgium's future. Through this initiative, William wanted to remedy the underdeveloped state of banking in the southern part of his kingdom. Although the king was one of its major shareholders, the leaders of the *Générale* sided with the Belgian revolutionaries in 1830 (as we shall see), thereby contributing greatly to the survival of the new state. During the next 150 years, the destinies of Belgium and this financial institution would be closely intertwined, especially through the intimate links the *Générale* established with industry in the nineteenth century.

Revolutions in 1789–1790: The End of the "Old Regime"?

Clearly, "Belgian" society underwent momentous social and economic changes in the fifty years between 1780 and 1830. The accompanying political turmoil was no less pervasive. The first of a long series of upheavals took place in the last decades of the eighteenth century. This was not only due to external factors such as the French Revolution or European wars. It was caused, in the first place, by internal factors. Since the beginning of the eighteenth century, the Austrian Habsburg authorities had been confronted with the difficult task of ruling the peripheral regions of their vast empire. As shown in the previous chapter, they had patiently and cautiously tried to introduce modernizing and centralizing reforms, and to modify the power balance by changing the composition of the States from within. Joseph II's (1741–1790) accession to the throne in 1780 signified a break with this prudent and conciliatory (or dilatory?) policy. The new emperor, a paragon of enlightened absolutism, was imbued with Enlightenment ideas. Appalled by the inefficient structures of his northern territories, he was determined to speed up the pace of reform.

Joseph inaugurated his new policy with religious reform. The Edict of Tolerance (1781) improved the position of Protestants. Many "useless" religious institutions (e.g. several monasteries) were abolished in 1783. Civil marriage was introduced in 1784. Two years later, one imperial General Seminar replaced the existing religious seminaries and theological schools. State authorities wanted to mold, or "domesticate," clerical personnel and turn them into docile actors. The Roman Catholic Church, predictably, fiercely opposed these measures.

Another move, now targeting public institutions, caused a struggle that would be fatal to the reforms in particular, and even to Austrian rule in general. In 1787, Joseph imposed a radical reform of all existing administrative and judicial bodies. The councils, *jointes*, and other central political bodies would be replaced by one single, central governing institution. Moreover, the Austrian Netherlands would be subdivided into nine Circles (*Kreise*) administered by *intendants*, civil servants appointed by the central authorities. Finally, the numerous and scattered jurisdictions would be replaced by a unified and hierarchical court system – functioning on the basis of a projected new legal code. This would mean the end of traditional, regional customary laws.

These measures were far ahead of their time, anticipating the public organization that was to dominate independent Belgium half a century later. But at the end of the 1780s, they were clearly unacceptable for most representatives of the privileged groups in society. The "provincial" States openly defied the Viennese authorities. The confrontation also took to the streets. Agitation spread rapidly, since the opponents to

Joseph's reforms also appealed to popular support. Pamphlets became an essential means of political mobilization. Urban volunteer militias were formed at the instigation of city elites in order to control possible "excesses" of the "populace." The governors gave way to reactionary pressure and immediately suspended the reforms. This was a blow for the emperor, who summoned representatives of the States and other dignitaries to Vienna. He agreed to revoke his administrative and judicial edicts, but not the religious ones. Nevertheless, this move did not stop the growing discontent, and the conflict escalated. Military force was used to curb agitation and to enforce the application of imperial decisions, for example regarding the religious institutions. In 1789, the States of Hainaut and Brabant once again refused to sanction financial aid. The emperor reacted by abolishing the traditional customs of both principalities. A red line had clearly been crossed. In the eyes of traditionalists, the emperor had forfeited his right to rule, since he had violated his oath to respect these old "liberties."

The final decades of the eighteenth century were a period of general upheaval. The successful American Revolution (1776–1783) and the crushed revolts in both Geneva (1781–1782) and the Dutch Republic (1786–1787) showed that profound changes were afoot. In 1788–1789, opposition against the Austrian reforms therefore took on new dimensions. First, some of the leaders of the opposition to Joseph II tried to internationalize the conflict. Henri Van der Noot, a conservative lawyer and spokesman of the Brussels corporations, had fled the country. As the leader of the traditionalists (also called "Statists"), he advocated the retention of the ancient institutions, and unsuccessfully tried to mobilize foreign powers against the Austrian authorities. Meanwhile, the protest movement broadened and radicalized. In the Austrian Netherlands themselves, opposition committees were formed, preparing for armed insurrection against the Austrian authorities. A progressive lawyer, Jean-François Vonck, was one of the leading figures of the democrats opposing Joseph's "tyrannical" attitude. Agitation against imperial rule was no longer limited to traditionalist forces opposing every attempt to modernize politics and society.

In 1789, Van der Noot concluded an agreement with the exiled progressive elements gathered around Vonck; a joint small army of volunteers, assembled in the south of the Dutch Republic, then crossed the border and invaded the Southern Netherlands. Surprisingly, this armed force inflicted a series of defeats on the Austrian troops, which were weakened by desertion. In November, the city of Ghent and Flanders fell into the hands of the rebellious forces. Brussels was taken in December of the same year. The imperial military withdrew completely from the territory of the Austrian Netherlands, except for the southern principality of Luxemburg. How was this power vacuum to be filled?

The traditionalists immediately took revenge and reaffirmed the old status quo. First, each of the nine former principalities (or "provinces") proclaimed the emperor's loss of sovereignty and declared its "independence." Then the representatives of each of the States gathered in the States-General – the first meeting of this institution since the 1630s. On January 11, 1790, they signed an Act of Union founding the *République des États belgiques unis* (Republic of the United Belgian States). This new republic was a *confederal* state in the full sense of the word: several independent political entities agreed to unite their destinies by creating a joint institution to administer well-defined common matters. Defence, diplomacy, monetary policy, and the management of conflicts between the confederated entities were entrusted to a permanent body, the Sovereign Congress (*Congrès souverain*), composed of delegates of the nine States – in fact, the same people making up the States-General. The latter body continued to exist; it could be convened, whenever necessary, when other matters were at stake. The exact competencies of both institutions were not clearly defined. The presidency of the Congress rotated weekly, making a common policy virtually impossible. Executive power lay in the hands of only two people: a minister (the already mentioned Van der Noot) and a secretary of state.

Despite the creation of the new confederal institutions, the old ways and rules had undoubtedly triumphed. Provincial particularism had the upper hand. The position of the privileged groups, expressed in the complex and age-old "representation" mechanisms in the States, had been confirmed. The power of the Church had also been fully restored. The States, founding members of the *États belgiques unis*, had officially affirmed their adherence to the Roman Catholic faith. The clergy, therefore, was a fervent supporter of the new regime.

The progressive and democratic elements, on the other hand, clearly came off worst. Their leaders were eliminated from the top positions in the new state. Some wanted a legislative body comparable to the French revolutionary *Assemblée nationale*, a proposal that was totally unacceptable to the traditionalist leaders, who clung to the ancient system of "representation" of privileged groups. The Statists organized physical attacks on their democratic opponents; their houses were sacked, some were imprisoned, while others managed to flee. Vonck himself found refuge in France, where he died in 1792.

The emperor, Joseph II, embittered by the collapse of Austrian rule in the Southern Netherlands, died on February 20, 1790, only a few weeks after the foundation of the *États belgiques unis*. His brother and successor, Leopold II, initially reached out to the rebellious authorities in Brussels, promising to abolish Joseph's reforms, and even to enlarge the power and autonomy of the traditional institutions of the Southern Netherlands if they accepted the restoration of Habsburg rule. The revolutionary leaders refused this compromise, making a military solution inevitable. Europe's great powers let the new "independent state" down, allowing Austrian troops to move in. The Belgian republic collapsed without much resistance. In December 1790, Austrian troops were back in Brussels, exactly one year after their hastened retreat. The Habsburg regime was restored but Joseph's reforms were definitively abrogated.

In another part of future Belgium, the prince-bishopric of Liège, the existing power structure was also dismantled in 1789. This principality was not part of the Austrian Netherlands and was ruled by the successive bishops of that diocese (see Chapters 3 to 6). However, in some crucial respects, this upheaval did not resemble the Brabant Revolution. For some years, opposition to the autocratic rule of the prince-bishop had been growing. In part, public opinion was influenced by the ideas of the Enlightenment and criticism of the fiscal privileges of nobility and clergy was voiced. In addition, the lower classes suffered from economic difficulties and a dearth of prime necessities. All the ingredients for a revolt against the existing order were present. On August 18, 1789, a popular riot installed a new city government in the town of Liège. The prince-bishop, forced to restore the ancient order, fled a few days later. In other cities of the principality as well, a new municipal authority was installed.

Confrontation now developed between the forces that wanted to maintain the old order, and those that strove for a revolution based on the French model. A *Déclaration des droits de l'homme et du citoyen* was even adopted on September 16, 1789. More radical than its French counterpart, the Liège text stated that sovereignty resided in the *people*, not in the "nation"; and it did not declare that private property was sacred and inviolable. Whereas the Brabant Revolution restored the old order, the Liège upheaval followed the French cue. Traditionally, Liège had close links with France, as we have seen in the previous chapters. Nevertheless, this revolutionary experiment was also short-lived. Having reconquered the Southern Netherlands, the Austrian troops also put an end to the Liège Revolution in January 1791, although the Habsburgs did not rule this territory. The prince-bishop recovered his throne, restored the Old Regime and launched a crackdown on progressive elements. In France, some exiled Liégeois joined with democratic refugees of the former *États belgiques unis* and created a *Comité général des Belges et Liégeois unis* (on January 20, 1792). This development prefigured one of the processes leading to the creation of Belgium in 1830.

The complexity of this episode defies any simple interpretation. Clearly, the 1789 upheaval in the Southern Netherlands was not a copy of the French Revolution. The so-called "Brabant Revolution" did not put an end to the "Old Regime,"; quite the contrary, it saved and restored (for a while) an ancient set of institutions. The truly revolutionary agent was Joseph II, since he had launched a bold but unsuccessful reform program that prefigured future developments. On the other hand, it would also be wrong to reduce the totality of the 1789–1790 events to a retrograde phenomenon. Different currents opposed the conservative Statists. The moderate progressive forces either favored a gradual reform of the old States system or strove for a modern elective mechanism limited to a small elite. Another faction, in fact no more than a tiny minority, was more radical and wanted thorough democratic reforms. But one should not forget the existence of pro-imperial elements that remained loyal to the Habsburgs.

It would also be wrong to limit our view to what happened in the city of Brussels and the duchy of Brabant. In this sense, the term "Brabant Revolution" is clearly a misnomer. Important and decisive developments undoubtedly took place in this central area, but the upheaval was not limited to it. Elsewhere, the situation was different. In some other "provinces," for example, the States were more inclined to reform the old system. Finally, recent scholarly work has also revaluated the significance of the Statists. They were more than just diehard retrogrades. According to their discourse, the emperor had lost his right to reign, since he had violated his oath to respect the ancient liberties. By stressing this element, they promoted the idea of contractual government, which was to play an important role in nineteenth-century political developments. Similarly, the future representation of Belgium as a country based on age-old local liberties and the Catholic faith also went back to the Statists' ideas.

It goes without saying that these events also played a key role in the visions of nineteenth- and early twentieth-century Belgian patriots. In their eyes, the Brabant Revolution and the *États belgiques unis* were a kind of "general rehearsal" or "foreshadowing" of Belgium's creation in 1830. Is this interpretation correct? At first sight, the presence of the term "belgique" seems to prove this continuity. In fact, things are more complicated. First, the origin and significance of the term "Belgium" have to be analyzed carefully; second, one has to gauge the reality and depth of the "Belgian national identity" and its exact role in the upheaval of 1789–1790.

From the sixteenth century, Humanists and other educated people started to use the term "Belgica" more frequently – but only in a geographical sense, not in a political one. The word designated an ill-defined and fluctuating area, but generally referred to the Seventeen Provinces – a synonym for the Low Countries in general. This region was much smaller than the ancient Roman *Belgica* (see Chapter 1); but it was larger than contemporary Belgium, since it also included today's Netherlands and parts of northern France. It is quite revealing that the Dutch equivalent for the extinct French adjective *belgique* was originally *Nederlands*; the Dutch adjective *Belgisch* was coined much later. Moreover, the word "Belgium" was hardly known by the vast majority of people; a fortiori, it did not evoke or arouse any feeling of political or cultural "identity."

But an important development took place from the middle of the eighteenth century. In their struggle against "provincial" particularism, the Austrian authorities started to promote the use of terms such as "*la Belgique*," "*les Belges*," and the adjective "*belgique*." By doing so, they wanted to stress the common elements existing in the territories they ruled, that is, later Belgium (without Liège). For instance, expressions such as "*le droit belgique*" ("Belgican law") or "*l'église belgique*" ("Belgican church"), etc., were increasingly used. Henceforth, the usage of "Belgium" and related words was narrowed down to the area covered, roughly, by the contemporary nation-state (but still without Liège). Moreover, these terms now also acquired a *political* dimension, signifying the common destiny of the Southern Netherlands over and above local particularities. In the 1780s, the adversaries of Joseph's policy also adopted the new meanings of "Belgium" and related terms in order to unite the conservative opposition under a common "patriotic" banner. Admittedly, the conservative opponents to Austrian rule continued to refer to local and regional identities (for instance "*le peuple namurois*," "*la nation flamande*," or "*de brabandsche natie*," etc.). Nevertheless, they also increasingly spread the notion and conscience of a common *Belgian* nation. In other words: despite the continuing importance of local and "provincial" identifications, the uprising of 1789–1790 also expressed and stimulated the growth of mutual bonds over and above the old principalities. In addition, new rhetorical elements and symbols were forged that would re-emerge in 1830. This was the case, for instance, of the future Belgian state's slogan: "*L'union fait la force*" ("Unity bears might"). In 1789, these words indicated that the separate principalities were more powerful when they joined forces.

However, the importance of late eighteenth-century Belgian identity should not be overestimated. The revolution of 1789–1790 and the *États belgiques unis* were not inspired by the desire of "the Belgian people" in its totality to gain its "national independence." A unified public opinion did not (yet) exist; the different social groups involved in the struggle all had different objectives in mind and essentially pursued specific socio-economic and political interests. While a sentiment of "national Belgian identity" existed (mainly in educated milieus), it was not yet widespread, and meant very little to the popular masses. The structure of the *États belgiques unis* of 1790 was also completely different from that of later Belgium. The first was a decentralized polity with old-fashioned institutions, while the second was a modern, unitary nation-state. Finally, Liège was still a separate entity; this principality was not yet part of the "Belgian" dynamic. In other words, Belgium, the state created in 1830, was not an exact copy of the *États belgiques unis* – far from it. Further developments contributed to its modern shape, in the first place the annexation of the Austrian Netherlands by the French Republic.

The Annexation by France Triggers Crucial Ruptures

The Austrian restoration of 1791 was short-lived. Following the Austrian and Prussian attack on revolutionary France, military operations soon spread to the adjacent regions. After their famous victory at Valmy on September 20, 1792, French troops invaded the Austrian Netherlands. A new victory (the battle of Jemappes, November 6, 1792) gave them control over the Habsburg territories and over Liège. An Austrian counter-offensive led to a temporary setback when the French were defeated at the battle of Neerwinden (March 18, 1793). But the second restoration of Vienna's authority was as ephemeral as the first one. Fifteen months later, the French victory at Fleurus (June 26, 1794) put a definitive end to Habsburg rule in this region.

In the beginning, the political fate of the region was unclear. Was this territory to regain the independence it had briefly enjoyed in 1790? In 1792, the victorious French commander-in-chief, general Charles-François Dumouriez, envisaged the creation of a vassal republic, uniting the former prince-bishopric of Liège and the territories previously under Habsburg rule. For most inhabitants of Liège, however, unification with the rest of the former Austrian Netherlands was out of the question. In this region, the idea of becoming part of France enjoyed more support than in the rest of later Belgium, given the age-old links between the former prince-bishopric and the former country.

Finally, this option, annexation by France, also prevailed in Paris. On December 15, 1792, the Convention decreed that the conquered territories would be placed under the "provisional protection" of France. A group of commissioners was appointed to govern the area. All vestiges of the Old Regime would be destroyed. The protests of inhabitants of the concerned region were to no avail: autonomy and self-determination were no longer on the agenda. After the Austrian intermezzo (March 1793–June 1794), the French authorities pursued the same policy. Yet the future of these regions was still a matter of debate in Paris. Some voices called for the creation of an independent state. Others envisaged a fusion with the Dutch Republic, which was conquered by the French in 1795 and transformed into the "Batavian Republic," a vassal state of France. Still others pleaded for the annexation of only the French-speaking parts and the amalgamation of the Flemish-speaking parts with the Batavian Republic. But in the end, on October 1, 1795, the Convention voted for the complete annexation of the former Austrian Netherlands and of Liège to the Republic. In the treaties of Campo Formio (October 17, 1797) and Lunéville (February 9, 1801) the foreign powers recognized France's new boundaries and the annexation of the former Austrian Netherlands.

Two decades of French rule produced profound structural changes in the annexed territories. They are still relevant today, in the early twenty-first century. Annexation logically meant the introduction of French laws. Revolutionary legislation put an end to feudal rights, tithes, corporations, and guilds. The relationship between regional and central authorities was also completely transformed. The age-old institutions of the former principalities were all abolished. They were replaced by nine new *départements*. Provincial autonomy disappeared altogether. Moreover, the spatial configuration of these new subdivisions of the state did not correspond to the (complex) boundaries of the former principalities. Even their names, inspired by geographical features, especially rivers, were meant to erase the memory of the ancient duchies and counties. These new bodies would survive future regime changes: the French *départements* corresponded, roughly, to the provinces of present-day Belgium.

Other crucial domains of public life were also profoundly altered. The way cities and communes were governed was reformed, among others by the creation of a new authority, the mayor. A new judicial system was established, while the Napoleonic *Codes* (1804–1810) introduced radical changes to the public and private life of citizens. Taxes were also completely reorganized. In the field of education, on the other hand, the imprint of the French regime was less profound. In some essential respects, the Belgian school system would diverge from its French predecessor, in particular due to the larger role of the Catholic Church.

Logically, the annexed regions (or *départements réunis*) were also entitled to participate in the *Directoire*'s electoral system. In a census ballot in two rounds, a small elite could elect a whole series of local, departmental, and judicial officials, and also its representatives in the central legislative body in Paris. But this first introduction of the representative system had extremely limited results from a democratic point of view. Moreover, the *coup d'état* by general Napoleon Bonaparte on November 9, 1799 inaugurated fifteen years of autocratic rule. The "legislative" bodies of the Consulate and the Empire were not only powerless; they also counted very few members from the annexed departments. Thus, the French regime had a double impact. On the one hand, it irreversibly transformed essential aspects of public life (in the fields of law, administration, centralization); on the other, it also completely blocked democratic representation and policymaking.

The French period had significant repercussions in two other domains of great importance for future Belgium. As we have seen, state and Church had been struggling for pre-eminence long before the French Revolution. But the latter affected the religious institutions in new and more brutal ways. The harsh confrontation seen in France from 1789 was also exported to later Belgium. In 1795, the clergy had to swear an oath of loyalty to the Republic. Two years later, the clerics had to declare their hate of the monarchy. In 1796–1797, convents and monasteries were abolished and their holdings confiscated. Clerical buildings and large domains, now known as *biens nationaux*, were sold. Many of these properties fell into bourgeois hands. In 1796, the establishment of *l'état civil*, the municipal records office, undermined the dominant position of the Church in the administration of crucial life-cycle events such as birth, marriage, and death. The introduction of the liberty of religious service in 1797 ended the age-old religious monopoly enjoyed by Catholicism. Charity was also taken away from ecclesiastical institutions and entrusted to the municipalities. Catholic educational institutions such as seminars and even the University of Louvain were closed. The opposition of the clergy was severely suppressed. Many priests went undercover; others were imprisoned; some of them were banished to distant and dreadful penal colonies.

Under Napoleon, First Consul and later emperor, the confrontation was toned down. The new ruler concluded a Concordat with the Holy See in 1801. This truce between Church and state essentially confirmed the new power of the latter. The Roman Catholic Church lost its position as the state religion. Faith was now considered a private matter, and all cults were free. The clergy also had to submit to the public authorities, to which bishops and priests had to swear an oath of loyalty. Moreover, these authorities also interfered in the internal affairs of the Church. The spatial configuration of the bishoprics was modified. The First Consul also appointed the bishops, who were then canonically consecrated by the Pope. The choosing of the priests was in the hands of the bishops, but the latter could only appoint persons accepted by the public authorities. Clerical personnel were paid by the State. And last, but not least, the Vatican accepted the dispossession of the Church's huge properties. But tensions between Church and state soon flared up again after the annexation of the Papal States and the arrest of Pope Pius VII. In the "Belgian" departments, some bishops and priests supported the Napoleonic regime, while others were far more critical. Clerical opposition grew, and public authorities responded with the repression and the incarceration of recalcitrant individuals. In short, at the end of the French regime, relations between state and Church were still far from pacified.

Finally, the annexation also affected the linguistic situation. While French was known and often used by elite groups, Flemish was of almost exclusive usage in the northern part of the Austrian Netherlands, both in public and private communication, and in the administration of the area. Only in the central city of Brussels – originally a Flemish town – had French made some headway, especially due to the presence of the governor's court and the central administrative bodies. The new French masters, for their part, had no respect whatsoever for the Flemish language, which was considered to be an obscure Germanic "dialect." The imposition of French, presented as the sublime language of liberty and progress, was an essential tool in their policy of nation building, and would hasten the assimilation of non-French and French-dialectical regions into the *République une et indivisible*. The social and cultural shifts generated by the expansion of French would have important effects in the years and decades to come.

In order to assess the significance of the French period, it is also essential to analyse popular attitudes. Did the inhabitants of the annexed departments accept the new regime? In particular, did they see themselves as citizens of the French State, or did they develop a *specific* national identity? Originally, the military operations and harsh French requisitions bred discontent. The forced introduction of French paper money and the rapidly depreciating *assignats* caused economic hardship. These problems stirred up the hostility of the vast majority of people to incipient French rule. Except for Liège, only a tiny minority of the population, essentially radical progressives, fully approved annexation by France. These faithful supporters of the Republic now occupied many executive offices in the new regime. However, the turnover of political and administrative personnel was quite high and, originally, the French authorities had some difficulty filling all the posts. The highest offices (including bishoprics) were often entrusted to Frenchmen, and not to natives. Conversely, very few "Belgians" occupied high-level positions in Paris.

Opposition to the French regime was essentially caused by two factors. The Roman Catholic faith was deeply rooted in the former Austrian Netherlands. Thus, the anti-clerical measures of 1795–1797 shocked many devout people and created aversion to this impious regime. Military requirements, especially the conscription or forced mobilization of young men, also caused widespread discontent. This latter element, together with economic and social hardship in the countryside, contributed to the outbreak of armed revolts in October 1798, a movement known as the *Boerenkrijg* or "Peasants' War." Bands of hundreds, sometimes even of a few thousand, fighters were formed but major cities were left untouched by these uprisings. It took a few months of severe military repression to restore law and order. By December 1798 most fighting was over, but in some places the unrest persisted into the next year. While some coordination may have taken place between groups, these revolts were in fact poorly led and organized. In many places, the riots were no more than simultaneous local disturbances. The *Boerenkrijg* was only marginally inspired by religious motives, and it was most definitively *not* a "national" (Belgian or Flemish) uprising – although later patriotic interpretations have created this myth.

Initially, therefore, French rule clearly provoked much antipathy in the population. But hostility was neither general nor immutable. After Napoleon's take-over, in particular, several changes could be seen. Relatively few nobles had fled the country, and most of these exiles returned quite rapidly. Contrary to ecclesiastical possessions, the properties owned by aristocrats remained largely intact. Napoleon adopted a conciliatory attitude towards the upper class. Their old privileges were not restored, but he created a new aristocracy, whose members understandably supported his regime. While in the first years of the French regime executive and administrative offices were often entrusted to radical middle-class individuals, more conservative, upper-class people acceded to high office under Napoleon's rule. Moreover, quite a few bourgeois had bought land and buildings confiscated from the Church; they supported the regime that had enriched them. Napoleon took measures to encourage trade and industry; and the years of economic hardship were followed by a decade of relative prosperity, stimulated by the Continental Blockade that banned British goods. The end of the Old Regime was also perceptible in the countryside. Peasants were now freed from feudal obligations and tithes. Finally, the temporary softening of anti-clerical policy also contributed toward a certain appeasement. All these elements explain the relatively calm state of mind in the *départements réunis* in the very first years of the nineteenth century. Many inhabitants of the annexed territories had resigned themselves to being subjects of the Empire.

But during the last years of Napoleonic rule the situation again deteriorated. Anti-French sentiment rose not only as a consequence of renewed confrontation with the Church, but also because of harsh conscription, new taxes, and economic difficulties – all caused by the revival of war in Europe from 1808. This new confrontation between

France and the other powers dealt a fatal blow to the Napoleonic regime. In its final months in 1813, anti-French attitudes were widespread among the population. Finally, after successive disasters in eastern and central Europe, French troops were expelled from the *départements réunis* in January and February 1814. Napoleon's short-lived attempt to restore power from March 1815 ended in the middle of future Belgium, with his defeat at Waterloo on June 18, 1815. The fate of the former Southern Netherlands, yet again, was in the hands of foreign powers.

*

* *

The importance of this period can hardly be overestimated. In less than twenty years, French rule had radically changed the face of many things. The method of raising taxes and spending public money; of handling conflicts and pronouncing justice; of concluding contracts and doing business; of administering municipalities and regions; of handling basic life events such as birth and marriage – all these crucial aspects of public life had been irrevocably transformed in only a few years' time. Age-old obstacles against these reforms were crushed in a spectacular *tabula rasa*. This was done, moreover, with little bloodshed (compared to what happened in some other countries) and with surprisingly little opposition. The future Belgian state was built, essentially, on the foundations laid by French annexation. These foundations also featured, it should be noted, the irrevocable destruction of the autonomy of the ancient principalities and their forced conjunction with the previously separate region of Liège. Finally, the use of French made important headway in public affairs.

Nevertheless, in other respects, the break caused by the French regime was less profound. The power and wealth of the nobility were shaken but not destroyed; aristocracy would remain a fundamental force for many decades to come – even if it had to adapt to a new institutional and socio-economic setting. The Church had certainly suffered a terrible setback, but it had not been destroyed altogether. It had lost much of its public influence and material wealth, but its roots within the population had not been cut off. On the contrary, in the eyes of many believers, its legitimacy was unbroken and even strengthened. Once the Napoleonic regime had come to an end, ecclesiastical authorities intended to regain (at least some of) their previous power. Finally, the French regime had a paradoxical effect on democratic rule. While Liberal political opinions had made new converts due to the French revolution, the political *practice* of successive French regimes had the opposite effect. Autocracy had triumphed, albeit with new clothes. There was no *effective* representative system. Opinions could not be expressed freely, censorship muzzled the press, and political movements were not tolerated. In the years and decades ahead, the drive for democratic reforms would become one among several essential issues. Finally, the French regime encouraged the rise of a new economic structure. All these changes were clearly stimulated by the new rulers through new legislation and appropriate policy measures.

The United Kingdom of the Netherlands (1814–1830)

In the first months of 1814, after the defeat of the French, foreign troops once again occupied the former Southern Netherlands. Initially welcomed by the population in some regions, the new occupants soon made themselves unpopular due to requisitions and the imposition of other hardships. As had been the case in 1789, civic militias were formed in several towns to keep law and order. The Prussians administered the eastern part of the country, while a provisional government, the *Conseil administratif*, ruled the rest of the territory. This body consisted of local notables, nostalgic for the Old Regime, and stood under the supervision of the victorious powers. Clearly, this was only a temporary solution. In the coming months, the fate of these disputed regions had to be settled, yet again. This was an issue of prime importance for the major European powers, since the region was a strategic crossroad. But what did the inhabitants themselves want?

The elites, expressing themselves through public speech and writing, were divided. A few conservatives wanted to restore the traditional, pre-revolutionary "Austrian" situation. But the Habsburgs themselves had made it clear that they were not interested in regaining the Southern Netherlands, so this option was excluded right from the start. Some supporters of the previous regime – essentially people from Hainaut and Liège – preferred to remain a part of France. But the final years of Napoleon's rule had clearly shown that the vast majority of the population opposed the French regime. Moreover, this solution was unacceptable for the victorious powers. A striking feature of this episode is the absence of a pro-independence movement. While the term "*Belgique*" was now used, and the specificity of the region was increasingly stressed (especially in educated and elite milieus), there was as yet no public claim to establish the territory as a sovereign state. The opinions of the popular masses – peasants, artisans and day labourers – remain largely unknown; but there are no indications that they were ardent "Belgian nationalists." On the contrary, in the lower social strata, old loyalties and identifications (to the former principality or to the Austrian emperor) were still quite common. In short, when French rule collapsed, the local population did not ask for an independent Belgium – or for a union with the Dutch. But all in all, most "Belgian" notables favored precisely the latter solution. At the end of the French regime, some influential personalities had already envisaged that option, though their underlying motives were contradictory. Conservative and Catholic elements wanted the restoration of traditional society and institutions. Liberals, on the contrary, hoped that the new authorities of the "Belgian–Dutch kingdom" would definitively break with the Old Regime.

In any case, the opinion of the inhabitants was not the decisive element in deciding the fate of "Belgium." The key decisions were taken by the other nations. And what did the Dutch authorities themselves think of unification with this southern territory? The Batavian Republic, created in 1795 in the wake of the victorious French armies, had given way in 1806 to a short-lived kingdom ruled by Napoleon's brother, Louis Bonaparte. Finally, France had annexed this vassal state between 1810 and 1813. During these eighteen years, decisive institutional changes had taken place in the former Dutch Republic, just as in the *départements réunis*. But when French rule came to an end in 1813, there was no power vacuum as in the "Belgian" departments. Prince William-Frederick of Orange-Nassau (1772–1843), the son of the former Dutch *stadtholder* William V, who had died in exile, returned to the Netherlands once the French had left. He then concocted a constitution for his country and became, on March 30, 1814, the "Sovereign Prince" of the Netherlands. The new monarch, now known as William I, had great ambitions for his kingdom. He conceived the plan of also ruling over the "Belgian" regions, whose political future was about to be decided. Indeed, at that very moment, the Netherlands clearly existed as a nation-state, while "Belgium's" legal status and "national identity" were both uncertain and vague.

After the ousting of the French, things evolved rapidly. First, the Paris Treaty of May 30, 1814 modified France's frontiers and put an end to the annexation of the former Austrian Netherlands, now known as Belgium. Then, on June 21, 1814, through the so-called "Eight Articles," the European powers entrusted the sovereignty over this region to the Dutch monarch. William accepted these clauses on July 21, but, in fact, he had inspired them from the start. He then became the governor general of these territories, ending the rule of the provisional organization mentioned at the beginning of this section. Oddly, in the coming years official terminology often used the words *Belgique* and *Belge* as synonyms of *Nederland* and *Nederlander*, while on other occasions the former terms only designated later Belgium and Belgians in the modern meaning. This shows the still-fluctuating usage of these words.

On March 16, 1815, William was crowned king of this new nation. Strictly speaking, Luxemburg was a distinct polity, that is, a part of the German Confederation that was allotted to William as a Grand Duchy. This special status explains Luxemburg's specific destiny after the Belgian Revolution of 1830 (see Chapter 8). Napoleon's attempt to regain power during *les Cent jours* ("the Hundred Days") had hastened William's royal coronation. Finally, on June 9, 1815, a few days before the emperor's defeat at Waterloo, the famous Vienna Congress, attended by the Great Powers, confirmed the unification of both parts of the former Low Countries. The United Kingdom of the Netherlands was born and internationally recognized. It was essentially conceived as a barrier against France designed to help break, or at least contain, future expansionist plans generated in Paris. Coincidentally, this solution had also put an end to Prussia's plans to extend its direct sovereignty (or influence) in the region. In the decades to come, the latter would remain a centrepiece of Anglo-Franco-German rivalries.

The rapprochement between "north" and "south" – between The Netherlands and Belgium as we know them today – was to be complete and irreversible. The same rules and institutions, based on a new constitution, would govern the whole country. The new kingdom maintained essential parts of its French heritage, notably the fiscal and judicial system, the rule of law (even if the Napoleonic codes were being revised), the organization of regional institutions (now called "provinces"), and the policy of centralization. Policymaking however changed drastically. At least some measure of representative politics was introduced through the creation of a legislative body, the States-General, which consisted of two chambers. The members of the First Chamber were appointed for life by the king, while the Second Chamber was designated through a complicated elective mechanism accessible only to the rich people and that favored nobility. From the start, the Second Chamber was flawed by a geographical imbalance. Both the northern and southern parts of the Kingdom had 55 seats in the Second Chamber. Consequently, the "Belgian" provinces, with 3.5 million inhabitants in 1815, were flagrantly under-represented; the Dutch provinces counted only 2 million individuals (the disproportionate part allotted to the north was justified by their vast and populous colonies). This was one of the causes of displeasure in the southern part of William's kingdom. Moreover, the power of the States-General was limited. When both assemblies had approved a project, the king could either adopt or reject it. Most laws resulted from royal initiative. In addition, several crucial domains were reserved for the king: diplomacy, war and treaties, colonies, monetary policy, etc. He decided these matters with royal decrees and without the intervention of the States-General.

The king was clearly *the* key figure of the body politic. The ministers, appointed by him, were no counterweight. Generally, they were his devoted collaborators and counsellors, rather than autonomous politicians, pursuing their own objectives. All figures deemed to be too independent were sidelined. The Council of Ministers existed but was seldom convened and had no real power. Nor was there ministerial responsibility toward the States-General: the ministers were not held accountable to the electors' representatives, only to the king himself.

In short, the policy pursued in the United Kingdom of the Netherlands was the *king's* policy. This institutional setting certainly corresponded to both William's resolve and his personality. He has often been described as an "enlightened despot," but it would be wrong to assume that his position was similar to that of, for instance, the late Joseph II. However limited, the constitutional and representative dimensions had decisively changed the rules of the game: this was not a "Restoration," but an innovative regime. Certain civil liberties had been inscribed in the constitution, and compared to other continental countries the institutions had, at least, a kind of democratic tint. In the first years of William's reign, the press enjoyed some (modest) degree of freedom – much to the frustration of foreign governments. Even if the Second Chamber had relatively little power, critical voices were in fact raised in this assembly. At certain moments, parliamentary opposition increased to the point of clashing with the royal objectives. In 1826 and again in 1829, for instance, the Chamber rejected the proposed budget.

William could not completely disregard this burgeoning autonomy of political forces; at times, he had to compromise. Although the king could revoke the ministers at will, the latter also played an important role in decision-making, and some of them enjoyed real power. All these elements paved the way for a real constitutional monarchy with ministerial responsibility. But the final step towards a full-fledged Liberal state would not be taken within the framework of the United Kingdom of the Netherlands: the Belgian revolution of 1830 would ruin William's brainchild.

According to traditional nationalistic Belgian historiography, the unification of north and south was from the outset doomed to fail. Both the Dutch and the Belgians had developed into a "nation" many years before, so the story goes; and amalgamating them was by definition unnatural. This view overestimates the depth, width, and strength of the Belgian national identity, and it underestimates the unifying effects of William's policy. The king endeavored to forge both parts of his kingdom into one nation. His effort was multi-faceted and pursued on a symbolic and personal level. The States-General alternately convened in Brussels and The Hague (leading to the regular, costly, and tiresome transport of people and infrastructure). The House of Orange had a palace in Brussels, and the king and his sons regularly resided or travelled in the southern provinces. The royal court was composed of high-ranking personalities and aristocrats from both north and south. Some of William's ministers came from the "Belgian" provinces. Southerners also occupied high-level positions in state administration, and generally staffed the local and provincial institutions in the "Belgian" part of the realm. Nevertheless, "Belgians" were clearly under-represented in the army, and also in both central government and bureaucracy.

William was also especially interested in economic matters. The marriage of Dutch colonies and commercial networks with "Belgian" industry seemed extremely promising. The king took several crucial initiatives to stimulate economic life in both parts of his realm. He built roads and canals (even if the "Dutch" part of his kingdom was given preference over the "Belgian" part in this respect); as we saw earlier, he created new financial and commercial institutions and supported industrialists, etc. The king also intervened in culture, most notably by establishing state universities; in the southern part of his realm, they were established in Ghent, Liège, and Leuven. All these efforts generated support for William in the area: many noble families, magistrates, high civil servants, intellectuals, industrialists, traders, etc., were or became staunch supporters of the House of Orange and the United Kingdom of the Netherlands. They were to form the so-called Orangist movement that opposed the Belgian Revolution from 1830 to well into the 1840s (see Chapter 8).

But this unification policy also met with difficulties, and some key aspects of William's rule ended up stimulating instead of reducing antagonisms between north and south. To begin with, there was no spontaneous and massive enthusiasm for uniting the latter. As we have seen, opinion in the "Belgian" provinces was rather indifferent and/or divided in 1813–1814. Although key elite figures had opted for unification with the Dutch, this opinion was not enthusiastically and generally supported. Conversely, few Dutchmen were enthused by this "reunification" with the "lost brothers and sisters" of the ancient Low Countries. In the Dutch Republic, the Protestants had dominated state and public life for more than two centuries; the Catholics were a tolerated minority. Now, in the new United Kingdom of the Netherlands, Catholics would form the majority of the population. In other words, William's religious policy would be crucially important.

From this angle, the reunification started inauspiciously. Many "Belgian" Catholics, especially leading prelates, feared the rule of a Protestant monarch. They desired, first and foremost, the restoration of clerical power and prerogatives. This would clearly be impossible within the United Kingdom of the Netherlands. Consequently, the Roman Catholic Church opposed the draft constitution of 1815. On the other hand, some "Belgian" Liberals adhered to William's political blueprint because it seemed to guarantee at least *some* constitutional advances and impeded a conservative restoration. But this rather positive attitude on the Liberal side would shift in the future.

William's nation-building policy was indeed confronted with the difficult task of amalgamating a Catholic south and a Protestant north. The king had no intention to achieve this by *imposing* the Protestant creed to the recalcitrant south. His objective was rather to subordinate *all* Churches to civil authority and to control them through the imposition of a legal framework. He had managed to do this for the Protestant Reformed Church as early as 1816. Relations with the Catholic authorities were far more difficult. Tensions between the Roman Church and the state increased due to William's educational policy. To mold the minds of the future generations, public authorities wanted to control the school system, creating their own educational institutions and closing religious schools. In 1825, future priests were even obliged to attend a new state-organized *Collegium Philosophicum* before being admitted to higher clerical seminars. This intrusion into the precinct of the Church was intolerable for clerical authorities. Negotiations to settle the relationship between the Catholic world and the state dragged on for years. Finally, in 1827, a Concordat with the Holy See was ratified. It stipulated, among other things, that the king could veto the nomination of bishops. The conclusion of this agreement was made possible, among other factors, by William's promise to make the attendance of the *Collegium* facultative, a promise kept in 1829. In the end, this contentious institute was closed down in 1830, and religious educational institutions were reopened.

But these belated concessions did not suddenly eradicate all clerical hostility toward William's regime, which had accumulated throughout the years. This opposition percolated through the different levels of the social fabric and most probably influenced many modest believers. It is also important to note that this bone of contention cannot be reduced to a conflict between north and south, or between Catholics and Protestants. Among the anti-clerical advisors of the king were some "Belgians" who were determined to roll back the Church's influence in society. This rift would resurface once Belgium had become an independent state.

William's realm was not only a religiously divided country. A linguistic divide also existed. Approximately 40 percent of his southern subjects exclusively spoke French. A small elite in the Dutch-speaking provinces also used this language, sometimes together with Flemish and Dutch. Finally, there was also a small German-speaking population in Luxemburg. This divide did not immediately trigger opposition from the French-speaking part. Still, the language factor would inevitably play an important role in William's nation-building policy. Between 1794 and 1814, the French had used their language to absorb the *départements réunis* into the Republic and the Empire, replacing not only Flemish but also Walloon dialects; now the king utilized Dutch to consolidate the foundations of his kingdom. He did so in a relatively cautious way, without brutally eradicating French. Dutch was the official language in the army and in central government but, originally, the use of French remained widespread in the administration of the Flemish-speaking provinces. Decisive steps towards Dutch monolingualism in the

Flemish provinces were taken between 1819 and 1823. In the French-speaking parts of the country, however, Dutch was not imposed. French remained the only language, but the knowledge of Dutch (and thus bilingualism) was encouraged. In the central state apparatus, Dutch was the dominant language, even if French was still used on some occasions. Nevertheless, this new linguistic policy was a clear obstacle for all citizens and civil servants who only knew French but strove for a public career. In the face of growing discontent, William once again gave in – just as in the religious conflict. In June 1830, the king restored an important degree of linguistic liberty in the Flemish-speaking provinces.

William's religious and linguistic policy dismayed many Catholics and at least some parts of the French-speaking elites. The concessions made in 1829–1830 in both fields came too late to reconcile these parts of southern public opinion. In the preceding years, opposition to his rule had grown steadily. Not limited to the aforementioned problems, it also had other sources. The conjuncture of these *different* oppositional forces would, in the end, be fatal to William's kingdom.

In the new kingdom, north and south were not treated equally. We have already mentioned two elements. In the Second Chamber, both parts of the realm had the same number of seats, though the southern population by far outnumbered the northern one. In the high executive and administrative offices, the "Belgians" only held a minority of posts. To this under-representation were added other forms of unequal treatment. When the state was founded, the public debt of north and south were fused. The Dutch debt being far greater than the "Belgian" one, common "Belgians" disproportionally repaid bonds overwhelmingly owned by (rich) Dutch creditors. When the new state was founded, the Treasury was in dire straits. In 1821, important fiscal measures were taken. Taxes were introduced on the molding of grain and on the slaughter of cattle; they were especially resented in the south and fueled widespread discontent in broad popular milieus, particularly in the countryside. In 1829, the king repealed the grain tax; but, as with religious and language issues, this concession could not immediately wipe out the hostility that had accumulated over the years.

Finally, the authoritarian nature of William's regime also antagonized other influential sections of public opinion. Since the 1780s, advocates of a measure of democratic representation and responsible government had raised their voices on the "Belgian" political scene. So far, they had not been very successful. They had been defeated during the 1789–1790

Revolution. The French regime had made spectacular reforms, but definitely not in these two crucial domains. In 1814, at the foundation of the United Kingdom of the Netherlands, some Liberals had considered the new system to be relative progress; it had at least prevented the restoration of the Old Regime. The king's anti-clerical and educational policy also met with approval within these circles. But in the end, William also lost much sympathy on this side of the political spectrum. Many young intellectuals (lawyers, teachers, journalists, and junior civil servants), born around 1800, were fascinated by Liberal ideas and increasingly opposed royal autocracy. This hostility was not limited to the southern part of the kingdom. Yet the Dutch Liberals never joined hands with their "Belgian" counterparts. The introduction of a full Liberal system would have meant the numerical domination of the "Belgians" over the "Dutch," and this prospect was clearly unacceptable even for progressive forces in the northern part of William's kingdom. It also threatened to reinforce the position of Catholicism in the kingdom – a bridge too far for many Protestant Dutchmen. In short, faced with "Belgian" demand for political reforms, the Dutch sided with King William.

How were all these forms of opposition in the south voiced – ranging from traditionalist Catholics to radical Liberals? Political and cultural associations sprang up. The press also played an essential role. The diffusion of dissenting opinions was not to William's liking. Journalists were taken to court and jailed, Catholics as well as Liberals. These press trials, in turn, stirred up "Belgian" public opinion. But the expression of opposition was not limited to printed matter. On several occasions, southern representatives voiced their grievances in the Second Chamber. They sometimes acted as a block and even succeeded in rejecting the king's legal initiatives; for instance the already mentioned budgets of 1826 and 1829.

At the end of the 1820s, "Belgian" opposition took on potentially more dangerous forms for William's regime. In 1828, the Liberal and Catholic opposition joined hands, agreeing to tone down their mutual disagreements and to oppose the king in the name of "liberty." This rapprochement was eased by the fact that Catholic Liberalism was slowly emerging: believers began to accept the idea of a representative and responsible government, which was a fundamental Liberal creed. Nevertheless, this so-called *Monsterverbond* ("Gigantic [literally "Monstrous"] alliance") obviously concealed important differences. For the Liberals, the

introduction of "liberty" would *also* signify the end of religious domination in state and society – whereas for the Catholics, this demand was
essentially (but not exclusively) focused on the idea of *religious* liberty.
Freed from governmental interference, the Church would be able to
maximize its presence. These differences in opinion would resurface
once the Belgian state was formed. But for the moment, the alliance
targeted a single and common enemy: the king's policy.

In 1828–1829, another development revealed the growing opposition
to William. Massive and successive petitioning campaigns were organized, urban and rural, and both in French- and Flemish-speaking provinces. On one occasion, as many as 350,000 signatures were gathered,
about 10 percent of the total "Belgian" population! People of different
social categories ventilated a wide spectrum of grievances concerning
taxation, language policy, religion, freedom of the press, etc. Elite figures
such as nobles, clerics, and journalists played an important role in
organizing these campaigns. It is therefore difficult to know whether all
these signatures actually indicated an authentic political consciousness
and, more specifically, a real opposition to the very existence of the
United Kingdom of the Netherlands. We will come back to this when
reflecting on the significance of the Belgian Revolution of 1830.

The Birth of Belgium (1830–1831)

1830 was not a year like any other. First, the winter had been particularly
cold, causing agrarian hardship, rising prices, and a dearth of necessities.
Unemployment was rising in the cities, and the lowest strata of the
population suffered. Political instability spread throughout Europe. In
France, the July Revolution brought down King Charles X. The "citi-
zen-king," Louis-Philippe, came to the throne and constitutional
reforms were introduced. In several Italian and German states, insurrec-
tions were inspired by Liberal ideas, while the Poles rose against Russian
rule on November 29, 1830. William's kingdom did not escape this wave
of unrest.

In the evening of August 25, 1830, a performance of Daniel Auber's
opera *La Muette de Portici* in the Brussels *Monnaie* theatre ended in a
riot. One of the arias, *"Amour sacré de la patrie"* ("Sacred love of the
fatherland") particularly excited part of the audience. They took to the
adjacent streets and loudly claimed their thirst for "liberty." Crowds
gathered and the houses of several officials and of William's partisans

were sacked, but the armed forces did not intervene. The fact that many soldiers were "Belgians" contributed to this hesitation: the authorities feared they might defect. Looting continued the next day; unemployed workers even began to attack factories. As in the chaotic days of 1789 and 1814, an urban militia was formed to maintain law and order. The news soon spread to other towns, both in the French- and Flemish-speaking regions. In several places, militias were also formed to control popular uproar. The official authorities – including the army – had not yet collapsed, but in the main cities new factions, mainly local notables and young intellectuals, came to the foreground through urban militias and committees trying to maintain law and order. These embryonic parallel power structures were to gain in strength in the following days and weeks, especially in Brussels.

Delegations were immediately sent to the king from Brussels and Liège. They asked for political reforms such as ministerial responsibility, freedom of the press, and a better representation of "Belgians" in public offices. William I refused to comply with their demands, but did not state clearly what his intentions were. Simultaneously, he dispatched an army to Brussels to restore the state's full authority. Entering Brussels on September 1 without his troops, the Crown Prince, William of Orange, engaged in negotiations with some leaders of the insurgency and left the city again after a few days. He returned to his father to discuss possible concessions. One solution was an "administrative separation" *within* the kingdom, through the introduction of specific institutions in its northern and southern parts. This suggestion was not unsympathetic to some Dutch, especially the trading elites who would thereby be delivered from the protectionist industrial south. On the other hand, influential business circles in the south opposed the idea since it would damage their own interests. The king wanted to gain time, hoping that things would calm down in the south, and on September 13 he began to consult the States-General in The Hague on future political actions. Surprisingly, most southern representatives ("Belgians") were present and participated in these discussions. Fifty-five members of the Second Chamber voted in favor of separation (forty of them were southern representatives); forty-three voted against (among them, 10 southerners). "Separation" was not the same thing as "complete independence of Belgium"; it was, rather, a form of extensive decentralization. Moreover, this vote also indicates that the possible schism within the realm had partisans and opponents in both the north and south. But when the Chamber adopted this resolution, on September 29, 1830, the pace of events had already accelerated.

Indeed in the meantime, decisive new developments had taken place in the rebellious south. Armed volunteers, for instance from Liège, supported the forces in Brussels, where an elected Public Security Commission was also established, alongside the official city authorities. The radical elements, grouped in yet another body, the *Réunion centrale*, increasingly opposed the moderates who still wanted to reach an agreement with the king. The general mood was deteriorating apace: popular disturbances were continuing, and economic and financial difficulties were growing. It was not clear who really held power in the city. The Public Security Commission and the official town magistrates were rapidly losing all authority, while the *Réunion centrale* claimed a leading role and prepared for military action, even sending emissaries to other "Belgian" cities, where similar bodies had been created.

On September 16, even before the vote of the States-General, William decided to send out troops to restore his authority. By the time they had arrived near Brussels, most rebellious leaders had fled the city. Some radicals were travelling to seek outside support, for example from exiles living in France. But when the royal troops entered Brussels on September 23, they had to fight their way in. The uproar had turned into an armed revolution. A few days of pitched battle took place around the city's centrally located park, where the military bivouacked. About 90 percent of the Belgian fighters were local people; volunteers from other "Belgian" cities represented only a minority. Some leaders who had left the city earlier now hurried back. The insurrection cost several hundreds of lives on both sides. On September 27, 1830, the king's army surreptitiously left the city. The news spread quickly and in other parts of the country, as well, fighting or unrest broke out in the following days. In several cities, official authority collapsed and power was taken over by revolutionary committees.

A Provisional Government was established in Brussels the day before the retreat of the royal troops. The Central Committee, established within this Provisional Government by radical elements, proclaimed the independence of Belgium on October 4, 1830. During these feverish days and weeks, essential symbols were created, notably the national anthem (the "*Brabançonne*") and the Belgian flag (black/gold/red). The fact that this happened *during* and not before the revolutionary events is more than an irrelevant detail. In the beginning, "Belgian" insurgents sometimes used the French flag and the *Marseillaise* as symbols of (Liberal or republican) revolt. It is also striking, but not widely known, that the original words accompanying the *Brabançonne* hymn still referred to the Orange king as the legitimate sovereign, at least if he recognized the legitimate rights of the Belgians. These factors indicate the nascent state of the Belgian national identity, a crucial point analyzed below.

At that point, a compromise with the Orange dynasty was still possible. Moderate southerners started negotiating with Prince William, who resided in Antwerp. They offered him the throne, hoping that this would short-circuit radical plans for a complete break-up of the kingdom. According to these individuals, some mutually beneficial links should and could still be maintained with the north. The prince accepted this offer and even went quite far in his verbal support for the "Belgian" revolt. This attitude was not appreciated in the north. King William, now more determined than ever to crush the secession, recalled his son. After sporadic fighting (for instance in Antwerp, which was still occupied by Dutch troops), his resolve would lead, a few months later, to the Belgian–Dutch War of August 1831. But at that moment, Belgian independence had already been consolidated, both on the diplomatic and on the internal political front. We will examine these developments successively.

In the past, the fate of the Southern Netherlands had always been sealed by international negotiations. In 1790, the European powers had contributed to the downfall of the *États belgiques unis*: they had rejected the existence of this new "nation" and reaffirmed the Habsburg right to rule the territory as part of a larger empire. In 1797, at Campo Formio, they had accepted its integration into the French Republic. In 1815, the Vienna Congress had joined the northern and southern parts of the former Low Countries and created the United Kingdom of the Netherlands. The crisis within this new state once again shook the European order; the Belgian Revolution required careful European monitoring. From November 1830 to June 1831, intense diplomatic talks took place in London between the Great Powers (Great Britain, France, Russia, Prussia and Austria). Their discussions would be of crucial importance for the revolution's destiny. Would they allow the transformation of the geographical notion of "Belgium" into a sovereign state?

The odds were against such a decision. First, the strategic barrier against France had been dangerously damaged, and the recent upheaval in Paris, resulting in a new step towards bourgeois democracy, fuelled doubts concerning possible French expansionism. Second, the Belgian revolutionaries clearly wanted to organize their state according to Liberal principles. They had taken up arms against monarchic authority, an attitude that was unacceptable for the conservative rulers in Vienna, Berlin, and St. Petersburg. Moreover, King William, who was asking for military intervention against the mutineers, had close family ties with foreign dynasties. Nevertheless, things finally turned out in favor of the separatists. A combination of unforeseen circumstances created a unique window of opportunity for the Belgian revolutionaries.

France obviously welcomed the end of the United Kingdom of the Netherlands, which constituted a sturdy obstacle against its own influence. But some French leaders were not pleased with Belgium's independence, because this would rule out, or at least hamper, future annexation of this territory – an idea still very much alive in Paris, indeed far into the coming decades. On the other hand, overt French intervention in Belgium would endanger Louis-Philippe's fragile new monarchy. France, therefore, proposed non-intervention in the Belgian affair. Prussia, worried by the prospects of a European war, stayed aloof, and both Austria and Russia were entangled in their own internal problems. The Polish insurrection of November 29, 1830, in particular, prevented the Tsar from pushing the military option to crush the Belgian mutineers any further. Britain's attitude was crucial. A change in Cabinet favoured the Belgian plans: Wellington's Tory Cabinet left office just a few days after the opening of the London Conference. Grey's Whig government was a partisan of Liberal reforms, both at home and on the European continent, and France's cautious attitude encouraged Great Britain to accept the Belgian *fait accompli*.

Successive protocols adopted by the Conference shaped the diplomatic outcome of the Belgian Revolution. First, all powers exhorted the two antagonists to observe a cease-fire – a proposal rejected by William. Then, on December 20, 1830, the Great Powers recognized the principle of Belgian independence. Later, in January 1831, they agreed upon specific aspects (borders, public debt, etc.). The territorial arrangement raised a difficult question: regions that the revolutionaries claimed to be "Belgian" and that had even participated in the revolt against William would not be part of the new state but would revert to the Oranges (especially the Limburg and Luxembourg areas). Another agreement was to have a crucial influence on Belgium's external position and, consequently, on European politics for almost a century: the new nation was to remain neutral forever. This drastic limitation of national sovereignty would prevent any future change of the balance of power in this strategic corner of the continent. Many Belgian revolutionaries could not accept this status of passive "no man's land." But the Protocol also *guaranteed* the country's independence. If Belgium were attacked, the signatory powers would come to its aid. This clause could (and would) have serious consequences for intra-European relations, and 1914 would prove that this possibility was far from imaginary. Forced neutrality and guaranteed rights would also play a role in internal Belgian politics, particularly in the field of military policy, which was one of the heated public debates of nineteenth-century Belgium.

Between January and June 1831, the international settlement of the Belgian problem lingered on. To the already noted bones of contention was added the delicate question of who would be the future head of the state, an aspect analyzed below. The Great Powers, irritated by Belgian reluctance, had to bring considerable pressure to bear upon the Belgian leaders. In the end, the Protocols formed the base of the so-called Treaty of the XVIII Articles, signed on June 26, 1831 and ratified by the Belgian authorities on July 9. Although King William did not accept it, this act officially sealed Belgium's independence, which was now internationally recognized.

The improvised and weak Provisional Government, created on 26 September 1830 in the heat of combat in Brussels, was faced with a daunting task once the Dutch troops had retreated, that is, the construction of a new state apparatus. Links were established with the revolutionary committees in other Belgian cities; the Provisional Government also imposed its authority in some parts of the country by appointing new executives in many cities. This process of dismantling and replacing the former authorities was not always easy, for the latter sometimes resisted. The Orangists, in particular, opposed the creation of the new state and remained loyal to King William. The revolution in Brussels and the uproar in other parts of the country were nevertheless transformed into one "national" movement, even if the extent and depth of "Belgian" national sentiment varied from one region to another and differed between and even within social groups. The Central Committee created within the Provisional Government and consisting of a handful of persons, now held the reins of power. Urgent action was needed to safeguard their flimsy authority. Financial means were secured through a loan with the Rothschilds and an agreement with the *Société générale*.

This bank, although created by king William himself in 1822, sided with the new Belgian authorities, although many of its leaders were still Orangists. A shaky military force was set up, consisting of deserters of the royal army, volunteers, and foreign adventurers. Measures were taken to stimulate the economy and provide relief or work to the unemployed, who could threaten law and order in this chaotic situation.

Another crucial task was to create a new institutional framework. A National Congress (*Congrès national*) was constituted through nation-wide elections to draft a constitution for the new state. The *vox populi* was however limited to a tiny social elite. Only some 30,000 individuals, the richest taxpayers and the holders of a university degree or a high public office, participated in these elections, which were held on November 3, 1830. The representatives convened in Brussels from November 10, 1830 to July 1831. From their discussions sprang a set of institutions and rules, most of which still determine the political life of Belgians today.

The members of the National Congress created one of the most advanced Liberal political systems of the era (only the United States of America had gone that far). The Central Committee of the Provisional Government had begun to draft the new constitution, but the Congress did most of the work and approved its final version. The very fact that people's representatives gathered to draft a constitution was already quite uncommon. Belgium's fundamental law was not a charter, bestowed by a monarch upon his subjects, as had been the case in France, for example. On the contrary, it was both conceived and approved by "ordinary" persons chosen by their fellow citizens – admittedly, the richest ones. The Belgian constitution, adopted by the National Congress on February 7, 1831, guaranteed an array of liberties: freedom of the press, of opinion, of association, of religion, of the use of languages. Indeed, these demands had been prominent in the struggle against William's autocratic rule. In the coming years, the operationalization of these notions (especially freedom of religion), would fuel fierce political confrontations.

The authors of the constitution also introduced full ministerial responsibility – the absence of which had also sparked opposition to the Dutch monarch. Before coming to office, all future governments (and their individual ministers) would need the approval of a majority of parliamentary representatives. They would also have to resign when losing the latter's support. The people's representatives would indeed play a crucial role in the Belgian political system. Parliamentary elections were to be free and fair, and also *direct*, without intermediary colleges or status groups, as had been the case in the United Kingdom of the Netherlands. Nevertheless, the electorate was restricted to the happy few: only male citizens paying a high amount of taxes had the right to vote – women were completely excluded. In 1831, some 46,000 Belgians (1.2 percent of total population) met these conditions. Under the previous regime, the United Kingdom of the Netherlands, about 60,000 southerners could participate in the ballot. Clearly, the Belgian revolution was not "democratic" from the purely quantitative point of view; it did not grant suffrage to *more* citizens, on the contrary! Some Belgian revolutionaries, the so-called Radicals, were in favour of real democratization, through the extension of voting rights to the lower classes. But this fraction had been rapidly marginalized. Indeed, many of them thought the moderates had "duped" them; "their" revolution had been taken away from them. The regime change of 1830–1831 was "democratic" because of an important institutional reshuffle: henceforth, the propertied elite could freely express its political will through direct elections and ministerial responsibility. But the vast majority of Belgian citizens were still bereft of electoral power.

Nevertheless, even this elitist representative regime frightened many members of the National Congress. To rein in "excessive" bourgeois politics, the authors of the Belgian constitution introduced a check. Alongside the Chamber of Representatives, they also created a Senate. Both assemblies would enjoy the same prerogatives in the legislative process. To become law, a bill had to be adopted by both. Quite remarkably for this epoch, the Senate would not consist of hereditary peers, as in Great Britain. Like the Representatives, the Senators had to be elected and, moreover, by the same constituents. The essential difference between Chamber and Senate resided in the conditions of eligibility. The candidates to a Senatorial seat had to belong to the wealthiest taxpayers. Less than a thousand Belgians could become Senators. *De facto*, the Senate would be a conservative bulwark, dominated by the landed aristocracy.

The authors of the Belgian constitution were also very cautious in choosing a head of state. Some revolutionaries, especially the Radicals, favored a republic. However, partly out of conviction, partly because of tactical reasons, a majority of the National Congress rejected the republican option: Belgium would become a constitutional *monarchy*. This decision would reassure the Great Powers and increase Belgium's chances of survival. But the choice of the future king was also of great importance. In February 1831, carried away by Francophile enthusiasm, a small majority of the National Congress elected the eldest son of the French king, the duke of Nemours. But this proposal was unacceptable for the other foreign powers, as it would place the new state squarely in the orbit of French influence. Other candidates had to be sought. In the meantime, as a temporary solution, a Belgian nobleman, baron Erasme Surlet de Chokier, was elected regent. In the end, the choice fell on Leopold of Saxe-Coburg, a German prince who had been married to Princess Charlotte of Wales, heiress to the British throne. Had she not died when giving birth to a stillborn child in 1817, Leopold would have become the British Prince Consort. Since then, he had stayed in London, and had been looking for opportunities to play a prominent public role. In 1830, he refused the Greek throne. But the next year, he accepted the Belgian offer, swearing fidelity to the Belgian constitution on July 21, 1831 and so becoming Leopold I, the first "King of the Belgians." This symbolic event is, so to speak, the cornerstone of the Belgian nation-state; in 1890, this day was proclaimed the country's national holiday. The monarch was not enthroned as "King of Belgium"; this underlined the contractual relationship between the head of state and the Belgian population (see Figure 7.1).

The position of the Belgian king contrasted sharply with that of William and of most early nineteenth-century European monarchs. The constitution enumerated what the king, the head of executive power, could do: conclude international treaties; declare war; command the army; appoint and dismiss ministers; dissolve parliament; promulgate the laws voted by parliament and make his own executive decrees, etc. But in fact, two fundamental constitutional articles restricted these apparently extensive powers. "The King's person is inviolable; his ministers are responsible" (art. 63). "No act of the King can have effect if it is not countersigned by a minister who, by this very fact, becomes responsible for it" (art. 64). In reality, only the ministers had political leverage. The Belgian king could take no personal initiatives on the public scene. In the coming decades, Leopold would often complain about the constitutional straitjacket into which he was strapped. And indeed, as we shall see, he and his successors would often try to maximize the royal powers and to find unofficial ways of exercising influence.

Figure 7.1 Belgium's first king, Leopold I of Saxe-Coburg, takes an oath on the Belgian constitution, July 21, 1831, on the Place Royale in Brussels. Oil painting by Gustave Wappers, *La prestation de serment du roi Léopold Ier*, 1831 (Brussels, Fine Arts Museum)

How innovative were the Belgian founding fathers? From one point of view, the authors of the Belgian constitution have indeed realized an impressive and long-lasting work. Belgium has been confronted with severe political crises, but the institutional framework itself has never collapsed; the country has never undergone fundamental regime changes, such as those known in France or Germany. Except for two German occupations (1914–1918 and 1940–1944), there has been no interruption or radical reform of the fundamental freedoms, of representative government with a bicameral parliament, of ministerial responsibility, and of constitutional monarchy. The only essential modifications to the original constitution concerned two aspects. First, the electoral system was radically transformed, through successive extensions of suffrage between 1893 and 1921. Second, from 1970 onward, the unitary state has gradually been replaced by a federal system.

But seen from another perspective, the founding fathers of the Belgian state were far less innovative. Indeed, they copied essential institutional arrangements introduced by previous rulers, in particular the French regime. The judicial and fiscal system, law codes, bureaucracy, the centralizing policy and the provinces, etc., all these crucial tools of modern government were, so to speak, ready for use. Almost half of the constitutional articles were taken from the 1815 Constitution of the United Kingdom of the Netherlands. In other words, the new Belgian state inherited many essential reforms of the recent past. The historical credit of the Belgian revolutionaries essentially resided therein: they abolished the obstacles to an authentic Liberal regime still present in William's kingdom, thereby creating the most advanced democratic system on the European continent. Only the fourth fundamental issue mentioned in the introduction to this chapter, the relationship between Church and State, still awaited settlement. It was to dominate Belgian politics for more than half a century (see Chapter 8).

*

* *

Conflicting political opinions, both pro- and anti-Belgian, have profoundly tainted the analysis of Belgium's birth. This does not facilitate a balanced interpretation of these events. According to the traditional patriotic Belgian historiography, still very much alive in the middle of the twentieth century, the revolution of 1830 was the inevitable conclusion of a natural process of evolution. Moved by a burning national sentiment, the "Belgian people" unanimously rose up against foreign oppression with the explicit intention of gaining independence. Another historiographical tradition, inspired by anti-Belgian feelings, expresses a radically different view. Its proponents argue that Belgium was (and still is) an artificial construction. According to one specific interpretation, the only "natural" political structure would be a state uniting all Dutch-speaking peoples, that is, the inhabitants of contemporary Netherlands and Flanders (now still part of Belgium). This so-called "Great-Netherlands" point of view stressed that the United Kingdom of the Netherlands was indeed a viable and beneficial structure; its "accidental" destruction by the 1830 uprising meant the loss of fine opportunities. According to this view, there existed no such thing as a "Belgian national sentiment" and the split between the northern and southern parts of William's realm was imposed upon Flanders by the French-speaking regions. At the opposite end of the Belgian political spectrum, some Francophone Belgians have produced their own interpretation of the events of 1830. Paradoxically, they share some assumptions with their Flemish opponents, interpreting the revolution of 1830 as the victory of the French-speaking population against the Dutch oppressor. Recently, Francophone public authorities have even endorsed this position officially. On September 27, 1830, the (supposedly) "Walloon and Brussels" revolutionaries chased the Dutch troops from the capital. In 1991, this day was proclaimed a holiday for the French Community of Belgium. Some radical Walloons even go one step further. In their opinion, the foreign nations thwarted the Walloons' strongest desire, namely reunification with France. They agree with the Flemish-Nationalists and the partisans of Great-Netherlands on this diagnosis: the Great Powers artificially imposed the Belgian state upon two different peoples, the Flemings and the Walloons.

All these contradictory views have important shortcomings. The simplistic Belgian nationalist interpretation is no longer tenable; the reality was undoubtedly more complex than the Belgian patriots assumed. In the first place, the outcome – the creation of the Belgian nation-state – was far from "inevitable." In fact, the traditional patriotic view *underestimates* the nation-building capacity of the previous regimes. After the annexation of the Southern Netherlands, the French authorities succeeded in radically transforming this region. True, an authentic "French" national feeling was far from widespread in the *départements réunis* before 1814; there was even strong popular hostility toward the anti-clerical and militarist policy. But the French nation-building process was definitely underway; it would just have taken some more time before fully assimilating these northern departments. In less than two decades, French had already replaced Flemish in public life, and large parts of the socio-economic and administrative elites had adopted this language without much difficulty, a process already underway before the annexation by France. Belgium might very well, for instance, have followed the course of the duchy of Savoy. This small, bilingual (Italian and French) frontier region was also annexed by France between 1792 and 1814; then "lost" for four decades, before being re-annexed in 1860. As we shall see in the next chapter, Napoleon III's plans to "re-annex" Belgium failed, while they succeeded in the case of Savoy. This erstwhile independent territory in the neighborhood of Switzerland and Italy is now firmly anchored within the French nation-state. This could also have been the fate of Belgium if war and international diplomacy had taken a different course.

William I also displayed nation-building abilities that should not be underestimated. At the beginning of his reign, very few inhabitants of the southern part of his realm had pro-Dutch feelings. There was no general enthusiasm for being "reunited" with the "brothers and sisters" supposedly lost during the sixteenth century. But William did his best to amalgamate the different parts of his kingdom. He even reaped some successes, for example in the economic field. But he undoubtedly also missed important opportunities to strengthen this objective, especially in symbolic communication, the arts, and the press. Above all, he undermined his own unification policy by clinging to authoritarian decision-making, by opposing the Catholic Church, and by disregarding the indispensable equilibrium between north and south in key domains. Nonetheless, the Orangist regime undoubtedly had supporters in the southern part of his realm, even in the French-speaking regions and especially Liège. As we have seen, many "Belgian" businessmen, aristocrats, and high-ranking officials were quite satisfied with the United Kingdom of the Netherlands because it suited their economic interests and buttressed their social position; some Dutch-speaking intellectuals and men of letters found themselves at ease in a country where their language was used as an instrument of culture and administration.

This brings us to the second weakness of the Belgian nationalist interpretation: it also *overestimates* the depth and width of national identity. To start with, the absence of obvious "Belgian national feeling" at the end of the Napoleonic regime is intriguing. In 1814, very few people (at least publicly) demanded Belgium's independence. Nevertheless, under King William's rule, Belgian national sentiment undeniably increased. Educated middle-class groups such as teachers, lawyers, journalists, students, magistrates, lower civil servants, etc., clearly expressed Belgian patriotic feelings through speeches and writing, often using the typical romantic vocabulary of the time. But were these nationalist discourses the only and/or primal drive for political action against the king? This is doubtful. "Belgian" Catholics were frustrated by William's religious policy. "Belgian" Liberals rejected the king's autocratic rule. "Belgian" peasants and workers suffered from heavy taxation, rising prices, and a lack of jobs. Did all these groups oppose the Orange king because they felt oppressed as "*Belgians*" in the first place? They most likely protested because their particular interests were at stake. The use of Belgian nationalist rhetoric helped to bridge internal differences within the opposition movement. This translation of specific claims into a globalizing nationalist discourse was not necessarily a conscious, "Machiavellian" process; emotional *identity-driven* mobilization is a complex but not uncommon phenomenon when it comes to the defence of concrete interests. Recent research has also shown that educated, middle-class Belgian nationalists – the cutting edge of the movement – were also (at least partially) motivated by specific social aspirations. The destruction of the Dutch state and its replacement with a new Belgian state enhanced their chances of rapidly climbing the social ladder. After their victory, many leaders of the Belgian Revolution indeed saw their aspirations fulfilled beyond their own expectations.

In the past, one would also interpret every form of opposition against the "Dutch" authorities as a craving for Belgian *independence*. In fact, fighting against William's policy did not necessarily imply a genuine will to destroy the existing state. This became clear once the revolutionary process had started. Some leaders of the 1830 uprising did not want to create a new nation-state. We saw that some "revolutionaries" started negotiating with William and tried to agree on some sort of *reform within* the framework of his United Kingdom. Yet they were outmanoeuvred by the Radical fraction, which refused any compromise and deliberately pushed for independence. The Radicals gained the upper hand due to a series of accidental circumstances, among others: the weak reactions of the police and the army when the uproar started; the hesitation of King William and his son; the friction between both of them (at some point, the king was displeased that the prince expressed his ambition to become "King of the Belgians"); the wave of popular discontent; the revolutionary climate elsewhere in Europe; the cautious attitude of the Great Powers, etc. As in every revolution, unforeseen elements and coincidences played a great role in shaping the outcome, which only seems "inevitable" in hindsight.

Finally, it must also be underlined that part of the Belgian population, especially within the elite classes, explicitly *opposed* Belgian independence. High-ranking figures, but also many civil servants, remained loyal to the reigning Orange dynasty and to the existing state. Plain material advantages partly explain their attitude. Officials and nobles lived in the vicinity of the court and did not want to lose their privileged position. Many businessmen opposed the break-up of William's realm because they were afraid of losing markets and profits. During and after the revolutionary months, Orangist conspiracies and troubles broke out in several parts of Belgium. In the end they failed or were suppressed, but they also demonstrated that important parts of "Belgian" public opinion, especially within the elites, opposed the new state. Faced with the sudden existence of Belgium, some entrepreneurs, in particular in the Hainaut province, preferred re-unification with France, rather than an independent Belgian state. A tiny minority of the French-speaking population shared this attitude, especially in the province of Liège.

All these elements show that the Belgian elites were not unanimously driven by Belgian national sentiment and the quest for independence – far from it. But how did ordinary people react – the artisans and shopkeepers, peasants and wage workers? Did they consider themselves "Belgians," in urgent need of political independence? In the present state of knowledge, this seems improbable. Nevertheless, one thing is clear: the urban masses did participate actively in the 1830 revolution, even constituting its driving force. Artisans and wage laborers made up the vast majority of those who fought on the Brussels barricades; most casualties were men from the lower classes. Consequently, still another interpretation of the Belgian Revolution was proposed in the 1930s. Some authors presented it as a "proletarian uprising" that was hijacked by the bourgeoisie. While rightly stressing an important aspect of the process – the decisive presence of the urban masses on the revolutionary scene – this view also delivered a unilateral and truncated view of reality. These masses were not pursuing a specific political or social program. They were reacting against the hardship they were suffering, and rightly or wrongly blamed "*les Hollandais*" (the Dutch) for it; but they didn't take the political analysis much further. Whether they took up arms with a pure sense of "oppressed Belgian identity" is highly questionable.

In short, the standard account of the revolution, as told to generations of schoolchildren, does not correspond to reality. There was no such thing as the unanimous revolt of the Belgian people, rising to gain its independence. The birth of Belgium was the unplanned and accidental outcome of a process with many contradictory forces at work, and where one fraction – the radical Belgians – ultimately won the upper hand and managed to impose its solution. But are the contending Flemish and

Walloon interpretations therefore nearer to the truth? This is also not the case, since they also show important weaknesses and shortcomings.

In the first place, they plainly deny the existence of a Belgian national sentiment. This denial originated in, and is still nourished by, the later crisis of Belgian nationalism and the rise of alternative national identities and movements. However limited and weak, Belgian political identity effectively existed in the 1820s. As we have seen earlier, it was born in the second half of the eighteenth century and reflected the consciousness that this particular region had things in common. During the first decades of the nineteenth century, a growing number of educated middle-class and elite individuals shared this view and acted accordingly on the political scene, even if social and material interests played an important role in the formation of this sentiment, as we have seen. This sense of Belgian identity was certainly less pronounced and crystallized in the lower social strata, but it was nevertheless a reality when the United Kingdom of the Netherlands faced its final crisis.

The idea that the Belgian state was "forced" upon one particular region, especially the Flemish-speaking part, is also incorrect. Belgian patriots, partisans of independence, existed everywhere, even if the insurrectional movement was less vigorous in some parts of the country than in others. Revolutionary committees were also formed in the Flemish-speaking cities, and the volunteers, hurrying to Brussels to fight the Dutch troops, were not only Francophones. Consequently, it would be wrong to say that the Belgian Revolution of 1830 had no roots or even echoes in the Flemish-speaking parts of the country. The Walloon interpretation of the events of 1830, on the other hand, exaggerates pro-French feelings within the French-speaking provinces. Only a tiny minority of the Francophone population wanted reunification with France. The extreme Francophone view stating that the French-speaking people ousted the Dutch because of linguistic reasons is also incorrect. This was only one of the many motives for discontent, and even a relatively minor one. Moreover, most of the men participating in the fighting against the Dutch in 1830 lived in or nearby Brussels (even though many of them were migrants that had settled in the city); for about 60 percent of them, Flemish was the mother tongue. Few fighters came from other parts of the country, for example from Liège. The events of September 1830 certainly were not a "Walloon" or Francophone revolution.

All anti-Belgian interpretations of 1830 are clearly anachronistic when they assume the existence of a "Flemish" and a "Walloon" people. When the revolution broke out, the "Belgian" identity was only budding, and not yet widespread; but the "Flemish" and the "Walloon" identities, for their part, were non-existent. As we shall see in the next chapters, these new national identities were formed *within* the mold of the Belgian state. The Great-Netherlands view, moreover, underestimates the cultural, religious, and economic divides within the United Kingdom of the Netherlands, the discontent in its southern part, and the undeniable forms of discrimination imposed upon citizens who increasingly saw themselves as "Belgians."

Finally, the idea that Belgium was "artificially created" by the Great Powers is also problematic. A Liberal revolt had shaken the European equilibrium, against the will of the main European capitals. The radical solution – Belgian independence – had been imposed upon them. For sure, the end of the United Kingdom of the Netherlands entailed some advantages for London and, above all, for Paris. But neither the British nor the French authorities had planned or provoked the revolt in Belgium. Confronted with this new situation, they just tried to safeguard and promote their own interests. They managed to reshuffle the strategic equilibrium and convinced Austria, Prussia, and Russia to accept this new nation-state. Only in this (restricted) sense did the Great Powers effectively "make" Belgium: without their ultimate consent, especially without the explicit British *fiat*, this new nation-state would not have survived.

Conclusion

In half a century's time (1780–1830), the Austrian Netherlands, also known as the Southern Low Countries, had changed beyond recognition. Signs of these profound transformations were not yet inscribed in the landscape. The seeds of capitalist and industrial development had indeed been sown, but just a few chimneys and factories were visible here and there. Populations increased, both in numbers and density, but the traditional countryside continued to dominate the country's external appearance. Cities were not yet expanding spectacularly, as they would from the second half of the nineteenth century. The metamorphosis transcended the visual order and unfolded on an abstract level. Social and political mechanisms were reshuffled at a startling pace. A conglomeration of age-old principalities had been transformed into a modern and independent nation-state – *Belgium*. This process was realized through a series of spectacular regime changes, accompanied by revolutionary upheavals, and largely determined by the broader European setting. Even if bloodshed did take place (in retrospect and comparatively on a rather modest scale), the country was spared bloody and protracted civil wars. However, the lives of elites and ordinary citizens had been irreversibly and profoundly changed. A new administration, a new judicial system, a new political regime – all labeled "modern" – had been instituted. In this respect, the role of the French annexation was crucial – the famous slogan *"du passé faisons table rase"* was applicable in its full sense. But the importance of the preceding (late Austrian) and following ("Dutch") regimes should not be underestimated in this respect. Henceforth, from 1830, the inhabitants of the new country, the Belgians, theoretically lived in a parliamentary democracy; but voting rights were still limited to a tiny minority. The Belgians would witness spectacular economic growth; but its rewards would be distributed in an appallingly inequitable way. They enjoyed freedom of association, religion, speech, and language use; but all these issues were to be heavily debated in the coming years and decades. The next chapter will examine the ways in which these challenges and conflicts were handled – "resolved" would be an inappropriate word.

The Consolidation of a Bourgeois Regime (1831–1880s)

Introduction

The revolutions sweeping through the old continent in 1830 had many repercussions. One was the birth of a new nation-state, Belgium, which had not gone unnoticed on the wider European scene. As we have seen, the Great Powers had carefully monitored the diplomatic aspects of this process. But even after its creation, this new country still occupied a unique position in the international arena. Of course, small and neutral Belgium could not play an active role on the global stage, but foreign capitals kept a watchful eye on it because it remained an important element in the European balance of power.

Belgium also stood out in the political and economic arena. Between 1845 and 1848, the young revolutionary Karl Marx found refuge in Brussels, where he wrote the *Communist Manifesto*. Drawing on his first-hand knowledge of the realm, he described it ironically as a "'model' constitutional state," a "monarchical Eldorado with the largest democratic base," but where pauperism is "Leopold's greatest vassal" (*Neue Rheinische Zeitung*, August 6, 1848). In *Das Kapital* (I, 3, X and annex X), he also presented Belgium as a "paradise of continental Liberalism" and as "the paradise of capitalists."

Marx's expressions were polemical; nevertheless, he rightly pointed to some essential characteristics of nineteenth-century Belgium. For several decades, it was indeed one of the most advanced Liberal countries on the continent – although suffrage was limited to a tiny, wealthy fraction of the male population. Despite lively political struggles, its institutions actually worked well, and the country was fairly stable. However, the social dimension should not be forgotten. Extreme misery was the lot of large parts of the Belgian population. The way in which the triumphant bourgeois democracy would cope with this (growing and menacing) *"question sociale"* would be of crucial importance. During the first half-century of Belgium's existence, opposition also slowly rose against the unilingual French character of public life and the discrimination of the Flemish language. Both the embryonic social and Flemish movements would reshape the social and political fabric of Belgium from the 1880s onwards. These changes ended the era of the elitist representative regime and of early, unbridled capitalism – the subject of this chapter.

Social and Economic Transformations in the World's Second Industrial Nation

Belgium's consolidation as a nation-state was inextricably linked to its profound social and economic transformation. Belgium became the second industrial nation of the world. The spectacular breakthrough of modern capitalism went hand-in-hand with severe spatial and social disruptions. A demographic explosion was already well underway in the half-century before Belgium's birth. It continued unabated during the decades following independence. The total population grew from 3.7 million in 1831 to 6.7 million in 1900. This increase put heavy pressure onto the countryside, which was no longer able to retain all its inhabitants. Urbanization increased markedly: while only 18 percent of the population lived in cities of at least 5,000 inhabitants in 1800, this was the case for 57 percent in 1910. Four Belgian cities attracted many new inhabitants, especially in the final decades of the nineteenth century. Antwerp, with the fastest growth, more than trebled its population, while Brussels nearly did so. Liège doubled its population, and Ghent came close. But no single city stood out as a megalopolis, towering over all other places; Brussels (with its adjacent communes) only reached the symbolic threshold of one million inhabitants in the course of the twentieth century.

Another specific urbanization pattern was also very important for Belgian history. Far from dwindling, small agglomerations (ranging from 2,000 to 25,000 inhabitants) became more important (48 percent of total population in 1846, 55 percent in 1961). In other words, semi-urbanized communities – not big cities, but not villages either – continued to play a key role in Belgian society. Many citizens were not "uprooted" in the strict sense of the word; for them, the confrontation with occupational and cultural transformation – the so-called "modernization process" – took place within a rather traditional framework. This specific spatial pattern resulted, at least partly, from policy choices. Both public authorities and private organizations, such as the Church and Catholic peasants' associations, helped shape it through a series of policy measures and social actions. Deep local roots thrived through the existence of a dense network of transport facilities. Many wage workers, for instance, continued to live far from their factories because they could afford long and tiresome railway journeys to their workplaces thanks to the low fares introduced by the state railway company in 1870 and extended in 1896. Until this day, intense commuting between home and work remains an essential feature of the Belgian way of life. The persistence of relatively small towns might explain, for instance, the political, religious, and electoral conservatism of large parts of the (especially Flemish) population.

In a country as Belgium, characterized by the existence of two different (and ultimately conflicting) linguistic communities, regional population changes are especially relevant. When Belgium was created, the majority of the Belgian population lived in the Flemish provinces (53 percent). This numerical dominance decreased to 46 percent in 1900, to the benefit of the Walloon provinces and especially the bilingual Brussels area. Tens of thousands of Flemings, impoverished by the rural crisis, left their homes and settled in Wallonia. Most of them rapidly integrated into the Francophone environment. This important population shift within Belgium partly explains why migration flows to foreign countries were comparatively modest. In the course of the twentieth century, the Flemish-speaking provinces, where birth rates were higher than in other Belgian regions, again represented the majority of the Belgian population (today about 60 percent). As we shall see, this relative decline of the population of Walloon caused some concern in the French-speaking part of the country after the Second World War.

During the nineteenth century the Belgian countryside was plagued with continuing difficulties. For farmers, the Revolution of 1830 made little difference, at least in the short run. They were confronted with the same basic problem, before and after the birth of Belgium: how could they feed the ever-growing number of mouths? The main response to the demographic explosion consisted of continuing with strategies already developed from the late Austrian period. Product shifts continued, such as the expansion of the potato crop: by 1846, this plant represented

43 percent of total caloric intake, in comparison to only 10 percent eighty years earlier. Labor input also intensified apace: Belgian peasant families worked harder than ever before, and self-exploitation reached its physical limits. The cottage industry, finally, played an ever-increasing role in the survival strategies of countryside homesteads, at least until the 1840s. Previously sizeable farms were divided into ever-smaller units, and large homesteads were exceptional. Under these circumstances, specialization and large-scale production were impossible; mechanization was marginal in Belgian agriculture before the final decades of the nineteenth century. The growing importance of very small farms went hand-in-hand with increasing proletarianization. An increasing number of farmers had to *rent* the land they tilled. Sharp competition between tenants, eager to have or retain at least *some* access to land, led to rising rents.

In the 1840s, a combination of two elements brutally disrupted the fragile equilibrium of the countryside. The rise of mechanized textile factories had devastating effects on the cottage industry, particularly linen production. Many small producers were unable to survive this competition and lost (part of) their income. On top of that, both the rye and potato harvests failed in 1845–1846 and rising prices of basic foodstuffs threatened the physical survival of many modest inhabitants of the countryside. Like in Ireland, famine made a dramatic appearance in certain parts of Belgium – the last in the country's history. Misery was widespread, especially in the northern regions, where cottage industries had flourished. In only a few decades, the reputation of the Flemish countryside had changed radically. In the second half of the eighteenth century, it was renowned for its prosperity; in the second half of the nineteenth century, it was often described as *Arm Vlaanderen* ("Poor Flanders").

The free trade of agricultural products, introduced in the early 1870s, and especially the massive importation of cheap American grain, put additional pressure on the small agrarian producer. This "agricultural invasion" reduced the basic cost of living for the Belgian population. Both consumers and exporting industrialists welcomed this development: the first enjoyed an increase of their purchasing power, and the second could keep industrial wages low. But this challenge required a new type of response from the agricultural sector itself, which would emerge slowly in the final years of the nineteenth century.

The industrial take-off had preceded the birth of Belgium, but political events could have nipped this process in the bud. Independence in fact impacted negatively on its nascent industries: textile, coal, and metallurgy lost parts of their markets. But these effects were only temporary, and from the 1840s Belgium got back on the track of industrial success. In relative terms, its manufacturing performance even surpassed that of all other continental countries. In the years 1842–1872, the annual growth rate of industrial production in Belgium, averaging 5.2 percent, was higher than elsewhere in Europe (Germany 4.5 percent, Great Britain 3.1 percent). Only the USA did better, with 5.4 percent. This period of formidable expansion was followed by less spectacular performances, when the Great Depression hit the country in the late 1870s and the 1880s. But Belgian capitalism was by then firmly established; it overcame the temporary downturn, and after some adaptations produced new achievements at the end of the nineteenth century.

Belgium owed its position as an industrial leader mainly to coal and metal production. The fact that energy and equipment goods were the main driving forces behind Belgium's industrial success story had several important consequences. First, it explains the high degree of mechanization of Belgian industries, especially thanks to the widespread use of steam engines. Second, the nature of production of booming Belgian industry had an important impact on the country's international position. For sure, coal and metal products were also sold on the relatively small domestic markets, fueled by the expanding railway business and Belgian factories and mines needing huge quantities of iron, steel, machines, and energy. But a substantial part of coal and metal production was sold abroad. This contributed to Belgium's extraordinary success as an exporting nation. Thanks to its industry-driven export-mindedness, the country rapidly gained a lasting, prominent position on the global trade scene. This feat also profoundly influenced Belgian foreign policy, since accessible foreign markets were (and still are) vital for the country, more than for most others.

These general figures nevertheless conceal an essential aspect of Belgian industrial history: its spatial dimension. All the coal mines and the vast majority of metal factories were located in the Walloon region. This was also the case for the thriving glass industry, and the prosperous woolen industry. However, "Wallonia" was still a purely geographical concept, not (yet) a marker of identity, nor a political or institutional reality. Far from being homogeneous, it consisted of two different worlds. Vast areas dominated by a traditional agrarian economy surrounded the modern, capitalist and urbanized "islands." But the latter had clearly taken the lead: the bulk of Wallonia's demographic weight, wealth, and political power were concentrated there. Large-scale capitalist industry was almost non-existent in the northern, Flemish part of the country, itself also far from a homogeneous region. Modern textile factories had only taken root in one city: Ghent. The remarkable demographic growth of Antwerp was essentially due to its booming commercial activities, especially from the 1860s onwards. About 80 percent of total Belgian port activity was concentrated there. The expansion of industry in Wallonia – inextricably linked to imports and exports – largely contributed to the growing international success of Antwerp. In the regional distribution of Belgian industrial activity, Brussels occupied a unique position. It hosted many small and middle-sized industrial enterprises, but its growth was mainly due to the development of central state administration and financial services.

Another specific feature of Belgium's industrial structure had important and long-lasting effects: the early and decisive role of the banks. Soon after independence, the *Société générale*, King William's brainchild, increasingly granted loans to industrial enterprises, essentially coal mines. In 1835, the *Banque de Belgique* was created to counterbalance the mighty *Générale*, which was still suspected of Orangism (i.e. fidelity to the Dutch dynasty). It followed in the footsteps of its competitor by also establishing intense financial links with the nascent mechanized firms. When the latter could not repay their debts, the loans were transformed into capital participation. Already in the late 1830s, the main Belgian financial institutions had developed into mixed banks: Belgium was a pioneer of this type of financial intermediation.

These rapid and fundamental shifts generated, simultaneously, great wealth and appalling poverty. Nineteenth-century Belgium was a country with sharp social contrasts. We have already alluded to the widespread misery in the countryside, especially in the 1840s. But social conditions were also terrible, especially in the four or five largest cities, where thousands flocked together in and around the town centers, which could not accommodate this new population. The poor were packed together in small and filthy houses and lodges, which were hotbeds of disease and – in the eyes of the bourgeoisie – of "immorality" and danger. Typhus and cholera epidemics plagued many cities till the 1870s. In the final decades of the nineteenth century, much attention was paid to public hygiene works, town planning, and the "housing problem" of the workers, but these plans (or realizations) did not always have much effect in the short run.

In fact, as late as the beginning of the twentieth century, the industrial working class was probably worse off in Belgium than in other industrializing countries. Belgium was known as the country of low wages and long working hours. Given the "primacy of exports," Belgian industrialists were obsessed by competitiveness and eager to reduce production costs as much as possible. Wages were one of their essential components, and the industrialists maintained them at very low levels. At the top of the social ladder, a few thousand families lived in opulence. In the first decades of Belgium's existence, land ownership was still the main source of wealth. Many of these proprietors were of aristocratic origin, but nobles had no monopoly on large landed estates. During the second half of the nineteenth century, a growing number of industrialists, big traders, and financiers joined the absolute top ranks of the richest families – while, conversely, aristocratic families increasingly engaged in financial and industrial affairs. It is indeed hard to overestimate the importance of these capitalist dynasties for nineteenth-century Belgian history. They not only constituted the country's wealthiest class, steering the motor of economic expansion, but also dominated social life in their city of origin and played a crucial role in politics. Many of these businessmen held local or national representative mandates, or even exercised executive power, for instance as town mayors or cabinet ministers. They often engaged in philanthropy and quite a few of these wealthy men became patrons of the arts. In short, nineteenth-century Belgium was the European bourgeois nation *par excellence*.

But however fascinating, the glitter of elite power, wealth, and prestige must not drive into historical oblivion the many thousands of citizens who belonged to the lower and higher middle classes. Caught between the mass of poor peasants and industrial wage earners on the one hand, and the elites on the other, these *petits bourgeois* were scattered all over the country, from the deepest countryside to the largest cities. Far from being a homogeneous group, these men and women had a many different occupations, and their social condition stretched from constant hardship to real affluence.

Consolidating a Fragile Nation-State on the International Scene

In 1830–1831, William of Orange lost half of the kingdom allotted to him by the Vienna Congress. He reacted by invading Belgium on August 2, 1831. French troops immediately rescued the young nation, and only ten

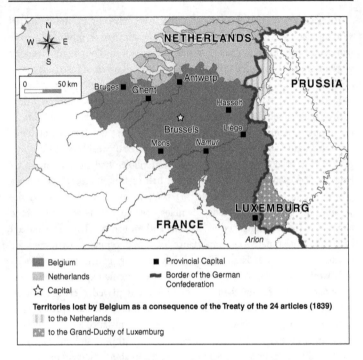

Map 8.1 Independent Belgium, 1839. Redrawn based on a map originally published in *Atlas de la Wallonie, de la préhistoire à nos jours,* courtesy of Institut Jules Destrée, Charleroi (© Sofam)

days later the Dutch army retreated. Belgium's reputation was damaged from the onset, and the international treaty that had permitted the creation of the country was renegotiated. The new agreement, the Treaty of the XXIV Articles (November 15, 1831), was even less advantageous for Belgium than its predecessor. The country, still bound to neutrality, incurred important territorial losses. It had to return the eastern parts of Limburg (as a "duchy") to The Netherlands and to cede the eastern half of Luxemburg as a Grand Duchy to its sovereign, William of Orange. However, in reality, Belgium continued to occupy these regions. When the Dutch authorities finally recognized the existence of Belgium in 1839, the Belgians were forced to evacuate and effectively cede the eastern parts of the Limburg and Luxemburg territories they still occupied, pending the Dutch acceptance of the treaty. Moreover, the Dutch now levied a toll on traffic on the Scheldt River, thus hampering Belgian trade (see Map 8.1).

To foreign observers, it was crystal-clear that Belgium existed by the grace of its two powerful neighbors, France and Great Britain. Other European powers were far from enthusiastic about Belgium's existence. Russia established full diplomatic relations with Belgium as late as 1853. Several leading European politicians were skeptical about the country's future. In the 1860s, for instance, the Prussian chancellor, Bismarck, doubted whether this country was really *lebensfähig* (viable). The opinions expressed in foreign media were no less critical. In 1857, *The Times* still presented Belgium as a "third-rate state." In this rather uncomfortable psychological climate, any major international incident could have had dramatic consequences for Belgium's existence. In 1866, Chancellor Bismarck and Benedetti, the French ambassador in Berlin, agreed upon a draft treaty (which was obviously never realized): France would recognize the unity of Germany; in return, the latter would allow the take-over of Belgium by the former. At about the same time, the French emperor, Napoleon III, undertook some steps to transform Belgium into a satellite state. The final episode of both the German unification process and the French Second Empire – the Franco-German War of 1870–1871 – was fought along the Belgian borders. More than ever, Belgium's existence seemed to be in peril.

But in the end, Belgium survived all these threats, especially thanks to its meticulous respect for the imposed neutrality. The Belgian authorities adopted a low-profile attitude on the international scene. "Neutrality" gradually evolved into diplomatic brokerage; in the next century, the tradition of *bons offices* and consensus seeking would become the trademark of Belgian diplomacy. King Leopold I played a prominent role in Belgian foreign policy. In fact, in this field, he was far more enterprising than the politicians themselves. Having created an extensive network of dynastic and political contacts, he developed an intense level of diplomatic activity. Thanks to his multiple family relations and his tireless activity, Leopold gained the reputation of a "wise man," whose "advice" and opinions echoed all over Europe – not in the least at Buckingham Palace, since he was Queen Victoria's uncle. The conjuncture of both elements – the cautious attitude of Belgian politicians and royal initiatives – helps to explain Belgium's successful record throughout the many international crises that shook nineteenth-century Europe.

The external position of a nation is not only determined by high politics and diplomacy, but also by the mobility of goods and people. The upsurge of migrations that characterized the nineteenth century did not leave Belgium untouched. Between 1847 and 1866, catastrophic social conditions, coupled with the demographic explosion, caused an important net outflow. Belgians mostly settled in adjacent countries such as the north of France. Like so many Europeans, they also crossed the Atlantic, to the United States, but compared with the emigration originating in the Anglo-Saxon, central or south European countries, this destination was rather marginal. Belgian emigration to Canada or to South America was even less important. The relatively modest overseas migration flows from Belgium can be explained, partly, by the importance of internal migration. We have seen earlier that many Flemings settled in Wallonia. Immigration was limited in nineteenth-century Belgium; about one-third of all foreigners in 1890 were Dutch, followed by French and Germans. Among the latter nationalities were many political refugees: revolutionaries such as Karl Marx, opponents of Napoleon III and, from 1871, former *Communards*. In other words, in nineteenth-century Belgium, migratory movements – both incoming and outgoing – were essentially limited to adjacent countries. Distant regions hardly impacted on Belgium, and the Belgian presence in the wider world was rather limited. Apart from the aforementioned settlers, only a handful of daring Belgian businessmen and scientists were present in non-European countries. An exception should nevertheless be made for Catholic missionaries preaching the Gospel in "heathen" countries.

For Belgium's international position, trade was of far greater importance than migrants or refugees. In this small country, with limited home markets, imports and exports played a crucial role; consequently, Belgian politicians, diplomats, and civil servants took commercial policy very seriously. Originally, they favored protectionism; discriminating trade measures sheltered not only agrarian, but also industrial and shipping interests. But around the mid-nineteenth century, free trade gained an ever-growing number of partisans, both in the economic and the political milieus. Belgium concluded successive trade agreements with its direct neighbors: with France (1861), Great Britain (1862), The Netherlands (1863), and with the *Zollverein* (1865). While scrupulously adhering to political neutrality, Belgium wanted to become the central node of the increasing network of trans-European communications and trade flows. The early construction of a railroad network was one aspect of this policy; the abolition of the Scheldt toll was another: it boosted the activity of the port of Antwerp. During the whole of the nineteenth, and well into the next century, the bulk of Belgian imports and exports was oriented toward the four above-mentioned neighbours, accounting for two-thirds of incoming and about 80 percent of outgoing goods. Apart from coal and metal goods, quite a few Belgian products made spectacular breakthroughs in foreign markets (glass, paper, textiles, etc.). Some of them, especially small firearms, even gained a universal reputation.

All the elements mentioned previously – trade issues, emigration, obligatory neutrality and, above all, the active role of the king in foreign affairs – played some part in one specific aspect of Belgium's impact on the global scene, that is, the (absence of) colonial activity. In contrast to The Netherlands, France and Great Britain, it had no overseas connections whatsoever. From the early 1840s, once the country's existence was more or less secured, Belgian authorities and personalities – especially the king himself – therefore started scrutinizing wider horizons, driven by two essential motives: finding new foreign markets, and "exporting" part of the growing pauperized population. In all, Leopold monitored about fifty vague colonial projects, located on the most diverse parts of the globe: the New Hebrides, the Faroe Islands, Cuba, Abyssinia, parts of the Ottoman Empire, Nicaragua, Guinea, New Zealand, etc. Only the attempt at establishing a colony in Guatemala in 1842 (Santo Tomas) is worth mentioning here. Its failure, due to bad management, reinforced the hostility of the Belgian political elite toward colonization projects. Nevertheless, these almost anecdotal episodes were to have one great consequence for Belgian and even international history. Young Crown Prince Leopold was fascinated by his father's colonial projects. This would lead, many years later, to the foundation of Belgium's huge colony in central Africa.

Domestic Political Life: Consolidation Despite the Rise of Political Divisions

In the beginning, and for many years, Belgium was surrounded by countries where the monarch played a decisive role, which was not (or was hardly) hampered by representative mechanisms and ministerial responsibility, Great Britain being an exception. In the 1830s and 1840s, the Belgian political system was ahead of its time, since it had introduced direct and free elections, ministerial responsibility, and the full range of civil liberties. The monarch's authority was limited, and strictly defined by constitutional provisions. But the Belgian representative regime was also clearly elitist. During the period under consideration (until 1893), a key constitutional provision remained in force: only male citizens paying a high amount of taxes had the right to elect parliamentary representatives; women were excluded from voting altogether. The electorate, consisting of a mere 46,000 citizens in 1831 (1.2 percent of the total Belgian population), had grown to about 90,000 (1.6 percent by the end of the 1870s). On the local level, electoral conditions were less stringent: in 1871, about one-quarter of the male population had the right to vote for the councils of cities and communes.

Many essential aspects of the Belgian state apparatus had already been created before the nation's birth, during the French and "Dutch" periods. Belgium's founding fathers made marginal modifications to the basic features of the legal system, taxation, and administrative techniques. Another legacy of previous regimes was the country's division into nine provinces. The smallest administrative units of the kingdom were the communes (i.e. municipalities). In 1830, they totalled 2,498, ranging from small rural villages to large cities. The 1831 constitution had introduced democratic decision-making for both these levels but had not clearly determined their powers. In practice, they had real leverage in areas such as public works, hygiene, and health care, public utilities (water and energy), culture, education, social protection, local police, etc. The central state, or "Brussels," did not have full command of the provincial and municipal authorities, which were emanations of the population and had some measure of autonomy. They could, for instance, raise their own taxes – albeit within certain limits set by the central authorities.

Provincial and, even more, communal mandates were therefore highly coveted. Politicians often built a regional power base at the communal level before jumping to the national level. Once they had been elected a member of parliament, they often continued to cherish and cultivate their local political roots. The notion of *autonomie communale* had always played an important role in Belgian political culture and rhetoric. The "tradition" of the medieval communes was often invoked and local liberties were presented as "typically Belgian." This discourse was anachronistic, but it contributed to the construction of a Belgian identity rooted in a glorious past (more on this below, see p. 268). Undoubtedly, the communes played – and still play – an important role in contemporary Belgium (the provinces less so). Nevertheless, until the final decades of the twentieth century, the country clearly was a *centralized* nation-state. The central geographical location of the capital city, Brussels, also reflected its dominant position in the body politic until the last decades of the twentieth century.

The September Revolution of 1830 had brought to power a new generation of politicians. As we saw, opposition to William's regime was inspired by different and sometimes contradictory motives. Catholics resisted the king's efforts to submit the Church. Liberals fought his autocratic rule. By the end of the 1820s, they had joined forces under the banner of "Unionism." To the surprise of many, this opposition had not resulted in a thorough reform of the existing political structure, the United Kingdom of the Netherlands, but in the creation of an independent state, Belgium. Until well into the 1840s, the new Belgian leaders continued to present themselves as "Unionists." Their program essentially consisted of the defense and consolidation of Belgian independence, but there was no formal organization (or "party") bringing these people together.

This patriotic consensus united them against Belgium's domestic adversaries, especially the so-called Orangists. This strong opposition movement strove for the restoration of the United Kingdom of the Netherlands under the Orange dynasty. It essentially recruited its membership within the higher social strata: businessmen, officers, intellectuals, former civil servants, and members of the old aristocracy. These people mourned the disappearance of William's kingdom for different reasons, ranging from economic interests to cultural affinities, loyalty, and frustrated career opportunities. They founded associations and published many periodicals. Agitation was not limited to pacific means. Groups and individuals nostalgic for the previous regime even launched unsuccessful conspiracies, while Belgian patriots sometimes assaulted Orangists physically and looted their properties. But in the end Orangism gradually disappeared, especially after William I finally accepted the independence of Belgium in 1839. People who wanted reunification with France also questioned Belgium's existence. But these so-called re-unionists were far less numerous than the Orangists and were not organized at all. Since then, and until this very day, the partisans of a Greater France, including the French-speaking regions of Belgium, were limited to a microscopic fraction of the Francophone population. Unionist politicians also successfully excluded from power the radical leaders of the revolutionary movement, who strove for a republic and wider suffrage. In other words, from 1831, Unionist governments not only defended Belgian independence, but also the existing social order and the political supremacy of propertied voters.

But as the domestic and external threats to Belgium slowly receded, the very meaning of Unionism began to change. Political divergences re-emerged and undermined patriotic unanimity. One crucial issue that fueled the political struggle from the eighteenth century (and even earlier) had not yet been settled: the relationship between Church and State. It now became clear that the claim for "liberty" had been an ambiguous *terrain d'entente* between Liberals and Catholics. The former opposed a leading role for clerical institutions in public life. For them, "liberty" meant separation between Church and State and the end of Catholic supremacy in politics. Many Liberals were not anti-religious per se; they still shared the Christian faith and even observed clerical duties. They also considered religion to be an instrument of social cohesion, that is, it maintained discipline and morality in the lower classes. Others were far more imbued with rationalism and sometimes even rejected faith as such. In their eyes, the Church was a pernicious institution, whose influence had to be eliminated or, at least, reduced as much as possible. Originally, only a minority of Liberals defended such ideas; but, during the second half of the nineteenth century, their influence and numbers grew unmistakably.

For Catholics, on the other hand, the notion of "liberty" meant the end of state interference in the clerical sphere. Henceforth, a new Joseph, Napoleon, or William would be impossible! The religious "freedom" granted by the constitution meant that no limitations could ever be imposed on the Church. On the contrary: public authorities had the duty to protect clerical institutions; while, conversely, Catholicism was presented as the cement of the Belgian nation. This new arrangement would guarantee the maximum extension of the Roman Catholic faith and institutions in politics and society. But there was no unanimity in the Catholic world either. Following the Vatican's traditionalist views, the conservative Catholics, or Ultramontanes, opposed Belgium's Liberal constitution. In 1832, the papal encyclical *Mirari Vos* had explicitly condemned modernism. The Liberal Catholics (not to be confused with the Liberals *tout court*), for their part, accepted the constitutional and representative system and the modern freedoms. Within this modern framework, so they thought, the Church could optimize its presence.

The Belgian episcopate sympathized with this tendency and supported the Belgian political experiment, convinced that Catholicism would benefit from it. Until the end of the nineteenth century, both tendencies co-existed, giving rise to frictions and rivalries within the Belgian Catholic world.

In the beginning, neither Liberals nor Catholics had created formal, permanent political organizations, and many politicians could not be clearly defined as belonging to either current. But gradually, the split between Liberals and Catholics became more apparent. The former were increasingly discontented by the growing influence of the Church in independent Belgium. Religious institutions were thriving and regained part of the terrain they had lost during the French and "Dutch" regimes. Several measures, especially in the crucial domain of education, favored the Catholic world. The Liberals also increasingly felt excluded from power. Under the cover of "Unionist" governments, politicians leaning towards the Catholic camp set the tone. The attitude of King Leopold I was important in this respect. Although a Protestant himself, he considered the Catholic Church to be an instrument of social and political stability, and therefore openly supported Unionism with a strong Catholic tint.

In the end, his efforts to prevent the creation of contending political parties failed. In different cities, local Liberal associations were created. Masonic lodges played an important role in this process. In these cenacles, existing since the eighteenth century and constituted through initiation rites, individuals from different backgrounds – but mainly originating within the elites and the higher middle classes – met to socialize and exchange ideas. The Catholic Church deeply distrusted these hotbeds of free discussion and modern ideas. In 1837, the Belgian bishops clearly reiterated the clerical opposition to the Masonic movement: Catholics were forbidden to participate in it. This condemnation annihilated for good the Catholic presence within lodges, which then increasingly adopted anti-clerical positions. It comes as no surprise that these "secret" societies also ended up stimulating Liberal activism and helping to create political associations. A next important step was taken in 1846, when Liberals from all over the country organized a congress in Brussels and founded the Liberal Party. Former Orangists also joined. However, this loosely organized party consisted of two competing currents: the politically and socially conservative wing, the so-called "*Doctrinaires*," opposed the progressive "*Radicaux*" or "*Progressistes*" promoting modest social legislation and an extension of the electorate.

The formation of a modern Catholic party was a protracted and difficult process. Originally, the Church itself served as the organizational backbone for political action. Priests often acted as electoral agents, mobilizing voters and directing them towards the "good," that is, Catholic candidates. This caused much frustration within Liberal milieus. But when the latter began to create their own local associations (moreover supported by an active press), they definitely outpaced the old methods of Catholic political action. The birth of a modern Catholic party was impeded by the diversity of initiatives, opinions, and currents within the Belgian Catholic world. Nineteenth-century Belgium saw a revival of religious activity and proselytism. Processions and manifestations of public devotion were increasing; clerical vocations were on the rise; and orders and congregations grew both in number and strength. In addition, and important from an organizational perspective, many societies were founded to "(re-) Christianize" the working- and middle-class population. Catholic Workmen's Societies, for instance, led by devout bourgeois individuals, were multiplying. In 1878 these local initiatives finally constituted a *Fédération des Cercles catholiques et des Associations conservatrices* – not yet a modern party in the full sense of the word, but the first viable platform coordinating the political action of conservative Catholics on a national level.

Differences in organizational effectiveness partly explain parliamentary and governmental power relations during the first half-century of Belgium's existence. In 1847, the Liberals, galvanized by their recent congress and their propaganda effort, won the elections. Charles Rogier (1800–1885), one of the young leaders of the 1830 Revolution, became the head of the first Liberal government ever. His cabinet lowered the taxation requirements for voting and guided the country "safely" through the eventful months of 1848. In the elections of that same year, the Liberals won an even greater victory. Liberalism was now firmly entrenched in the Belgian political landscape. From 1847 to 1884, Liberal cabinets ruled Belgium for twenty-seven out of a total of thirty-seven years. This domination was only interrupted twice: in 1855–1857, when an unsuccessful (neo-) "Unionist" cabinet took over, and in 1870–1878, when Catholics were in government. In 1878, the Liberals came to power again for a further six years, with an explicit anti-clerical program. This last homogenous Liberal cabinet was led by another prominent figure of Belgian nineteenth-century politics, Walthère Frère-Orban (1812–1896). Its policy sparked off a fierce political struggle that ended in a devastating Liberal defeat in the 1884 elections. For the next thirty years, the Catholics were in power.

Politicians and voters disagreed passionately on the role of religious views, practices, and institutions in public life. After skirmishes in the 1830s, open struggles between pro- and anti-clerical factions started in the 1840s and reached a climax in the 1880s. The conflict was never "settled" once and for all – it would resurface in the twentieth century and still causes some frictions today – but some decisive turns certainly occurred in these decades. This issue had, simultaneously, symbolic, cultural, financial, and organizational dimensions. This complexity made it all the more explosive. Liberals and Catholics confronted each other on issues such as the organization of graveyards and charity, but the main bone of contention was education. Who would organize, or at least dominate, the school system: the Church or the official (secular) authorities? The debate affected all levels of education, from primary classes to university. Before 1830, the "Belgian" educational system was in bad shape. At the end of the eighteenth century, 39 percent of all fathers and 63 percent of all mothers could not write their names under the birth certificate of their child. In the course of the nineteenth century, literacy and schooling gradually increased. In 1866, about one half of the total Belgian population could read and write. In 1845, two-thirds of all children aged seven to fourteen were sent to school, although parents were not obliged to do so. A growing number of young minds had to be molded: it was therefore essential to determine who would fulfil this crucial task, and under what circumstances. In 1847, 60 percent of all secondary schools were Catholic; the municipalities or the state ran the rest, but the clergy was present in 60 percent of these public institutions. From the 1840s to the end of the nineteenth century, successive controversial school laws largely fueled Belgian political struggles. Legislative measures of 1842 and 1879 focused on the organization of primary schools, while the secondary school system was reorganized in 1850. The network of public, non-religious schools gradually expanded, but Catholic institutions remained dominant. The 1879 law, voted by the Liberals and fiercely opposed by the Catholics, caused a real split in public opinion, described as the first "School War" in Belgian history. Important developments were also taking place in the field of higher education: with support from Freemasons, the Free University of Brussels was founded in 1834 to fight the dominance of the Catholic University of Leuven.

Belgian Identity and Culture in the Making

Institutions, foreign relations, or economic activities – however important – do not entirely define the essence of a "nation." Some sort of "identity" seems vital: the members of a "national community" are supposed to share specific cultural traits, attitudes, and beliefs. The previous chapter has shown that a sense of "Belgian identity," although not inexistent, was not widespread before 1830; nor was it particularly well defined. What did it mean, exactly, to be "Belgian"? Which common ideas, cultural codes, and daily practices united the members of this new nation? In the nineteenth century, Catholics often argued that the Roman religion was (at least one of) *the* crucial element(s) defining Belgium – as was the case in Ireland and Poland. But obviously, many Belgians disagreed; the Liberals rejected the idea that *one* particular supernatural belief ran as a common thread through all Belgian minds and hearts.

Language – a potentially powerful tool of nation building – also failed to fulfil this task. French enjoyed enormous prestige in eighteenth-century Europe, and also in the Southern Netherlands. This explains the gradual extension of French in elite (and would-be elite) circles in regions where Flemish was the dominant language. Under the Austrian regime, French was also increasingly used in administrative and political institutions, especially at the central level. But overall, the Austrian authorities did not pursue a deliberate and systematic policy to promote French or to eradicate Flemish. As we saw in Chapter 7, this changed radically under the French regime. To assimilate the newly conquered *départements réunis* into the "Great Nation," standard French was gradually imposed everywhere. When the United Kingdom of the Netherlands was created, William I also used language as a nation-building instrument – but Dutch was now the unifying vehicle.

The wheel turned once again after the foundation of Belgium. In their effort to build a Belgian nation, the new political authorities quite "naturally" turned to French. De facto, only French was used in politics, legislation, administration, education, science, law, etc., although Flemish persisted in some parts of public life, essentially in primary schools and in the lower echelons of administration. Flemish-speakers were not "persecuted" because of their language, and the Dutch language was never "forbidden" in Belgium. But those who adhered to it were clearly discriminated against. To gain access to public offices, or even to communicate with the authorities, one had to master French.

Flemish was also treated as a second-rate language outside the official sphere. In the northern part of the country the autochthonous elite had, generally, adopted French as their everyday language. The powerful attraction exercised by French was not limited to high society. Ambitious people of lower birth who wanted to climb the social ladder also turned to French to obscure their modest origins. In other words: in nineteenth-century Belgium, French was not only an instrument of nation building, but also a marker of social status.

This has important consequences for how to approach Belgium's so-called "language" or "community" problem. All too often, this complex issue is interpreted in an anachronistic or simplistic way. First, the concept of "language problem" falsely implies that it is a matter confined to the cultural sphere. In fact, the social dimension is very important, since language was an instrument of social differentiation, used by the elites *of every region* to reinforce their superiority. Second, the concept of "community conflict" is also inappropriate. There has never been a clash between two spatially distinct "communities," with "the Walloons" oppressing "the Flemings." In the French-speaking parts of the country, small farmers and factory workers also suffered from exploitation and terrible social conditions.

Obviously, Belgians did not share the same language and/or religion; so what did bind them together? Since the cultural basis of national identity was very thin right from the start, the elusive originality of being "Belgian" had to be found elsewhere. In the nineteenth century, the then thriving "*psychologie des peuples*" inspired many popular publications and general discourse. "The Belgians" were said to be industrious, hard-working, rather down-to-earth, and stay-at-home (they did not like adventures and readily stuck to their homestead, sometimes even verging on parochialism). They were also described as somewhat rude in their expressions, hostile to philosophical speculation, but faithful and friendly, with a ready sense of humour and self-derision; they were seemingly attracted to the "good life" and simple and noisy amusements, like the many fairs or *kermesses*. But such impressionistic descriptions clearly did not suffice to define "national identity."

Looking into the past could be far more helpful. Since times immemorial, peoples of distinct origin met and lived together in the territories that would constitute independent Belgium – so the story went. The "Germanic" and "Latin" peoples (or "races"), who were supposed to have fixed characteristics, had created their own nations, respectively

Germany and France, where their specific natures could fully blossom. But in "Belgium" – even if that nation did not yet exist – they had developed a meeting place where intense, peaceful, and fruitful exchanges took place. It was precisely this that made Belgium a special place, and set the Belgians as a people apart. Therefore, neither the country nor its inhabitants could be subsumed into the neighboring big nations. This theory justified Belgium's existence as an independent nation.

These ideas were already present in the second half of the nineteenth century but given their fullest expression – and impressive scientific credentials – somewhat later by the great historian Henri Pirenne, author of the classic *Histoire de Belgique* (1900–1932). In his eyes, Belgium's genesis went back to the Middle Ages and differed from that of most other European nations:

> Contrary to what happened in many other countries, where the monarchy has made the society, where the unity of government has produced national unity, one can say that here [in Belgium] national unity has preceded the unity of government. (...) Elsewhere, the State has often been the cause of a proper national life; here, it seems to have resulted from it.
>
> (Henri Pirenne, *La Nation belge*, Ghent, 1900, p. 4)

Although generally rejected today, Pirenne's vision of the national past was far more nuanced than common Belgian historical perceptions before, during, and even after his lifetime. According to the patriotic view, this rich and coveted territory had been "occupied" by foreign powers for centuries – a long-lasting calamity that made the emancipation of 1830 all the more glorious. Nevertheless, so it was said, the "Belgians" had always been deeply attached to their "liberties," which originated in the medieval cities with their proud belfries. Such anachronistic visions of "national history" – "foreign occupation" or "thirst for liberty" – made it possible to consolidate the labile present by linking it to a prestigious past. Nevertheless, the country's political divides tore up even history itself. Liberals and Catholics disagreed on many aspects of the national past. Interpreting the dramatic sixteenth century, riven by religious strife and the split of the XVII Provinces, was especially touchy. Later, the opposition between Flemings and Francophones would give rise to similar historical dissensions. Constructing a uniform and generally accepted image of the "Belgian" past was therefore far from easy.

Many Belgians were not (well) aware of these intellectual and political polemics. But a certain vision of "national history" nevertheless trickled down to the average citizen. A set of simple images of the past – often more or less linked together in a coherent narrative – was produced and spread through such diverse channels as school textbooks, vulgarized history books, novels, poetry, monuments, statues, paintings, sculptures, theater and spectacular costumed parades, etc.

Some interpretations of Belgian identity even went a step further. According to these, Germanic and Latin elements were not simply juxtaposed and "dialoguing" in Belgium; they were entirely *mixed* and constituted a totally new identity. In 1897, the progressive lawyer, writer, and politician Edmond Picard (1836–1924) couched this view in lyrical terms:

> The Belgian Soul (*l'Âme belge*) (...) proceeds from the Germanic soul and from the Latin soul, the most prominent varieties of the Aryan race. (...) It is a glaring mistake to obstinately believe that our nation is an ill-stitched combination of the Flemish and the Walloon. (...) The historical outcome is better, more intense, and more grandiose. A unique soul, a common soul floats above both apparent groups, and inspires them. They may speak different languages; their physical unity nevertheless dominates all their actions.
>
> (Edmond Picard, "L'Âme belge," in *Revue encyclopédique*, 1897,
> p. 596-598)

When Picard formulated his theory of "*l'Âme belge*", the opposition between the two language communities had already become a rift. This extreme definition of Belgian identity was not really tenable, and therefore rapidly abandoned. But the idea of the "crossroads" as a defining element of Belgian identity persisted. Belgium was and still is commonly defined as the meeting place *par excellence*. The historian Herman Vander Linden, one of Pirenne's pupils, opened his English-language introductory history of Belgium by stating: "(...) it is not paradoxical to assert that one of the characteristics of Belgian nationality is internationalism." In the beginning of the twenty-first century, Belgium is still often presented as the "microcosm of Europe," as the country defined by dialogue and exchange, or as a "laboratory of multicultural contact." This interpretation clearly has profound historical roots. Today, some Belgians carry the paradox even further: confronted with the absence of obvious defining characteristics, they maintain that it is precisely the *absence* of identity that constitutes the essence of "Belgian identity."

The founding fathers of Belgium would certainly disagree on this point. They did not doubt the reality of a "Belgian identity," but they were also aware of the fact that it needed public support to penetrate the hearts and minds of the citizens. Cultural policy was therefore a priority for the new Belgian authorities. Once again, the Belgian state did not start from scratch. Previous regimes had already laid the foundations of a cultural infrastructure, for instance by creating the Academy of Sciences and Letters (1772). Private societies for the encouragement of the arts existed in the premier cities, which also had their own academies for the training of artists. Artistic salons were organized. William I had also founded three public universities (Ghent, Leuven, and Liège). But cultural, artistic, and scientific life had suffered heavily from the many regime changes and the ensuing troubles. Only a few years after the nation's birth, the Belgian authorities therefore undertook an impressive series of initiatives to revive artistic and scientific activity, laying the foundations of Belgian cultural life for the next century and a half. Fine examples of this policy are the Royal Museum of Fine Arts (1842), the Royal Conservatory of Music (1833), the *Commission royale d'Histoire* (1834), charged with publishing important archival sources, and the *Commission royale des Monuments* (1835), entrusted with keeping watch over noteworthy ancient buildings.

In the late eighteenth and early nineteenth century, "Belgian" artistic and literary production had been rather low-key. But after the 1830 Revolution, the active cultural policy of the Belgian authorities rapidly bore fruit, even if most of the mid-nineteenth-century Belgian artists are by now forgotten outside (and sometimes even inside) the realm's frontiers. François Joseph Navez (1787–1869), a former pupil of the great French painter Jacques-Louis David, was known for his many Neo-Classicist portraits and historical and religious scenes. A new generation of painters inspired by Romanticism took over. Painters like Gustave Wappers (1803–1874) and Henri Leys (1815–1869) represented, sometimes with pathos, famous episodes of the glorious Belgian past. Their impact on the formation of a Belgian identity should therefore not be underestimated. The same goes for the sculptor Guillaume Geefs (1805–1883), whose many statues visualized the past and present glories of Belgium. The nineteenth century is known precisely for its "statuomany." Public spaces were increasingly occupied by bronze or stone testimonies of the country's greatness, symbolized by the many outstanding figures of "Belgian" history. However, not every Belgian artist glorified the nation and the reigning powers; significantly, their names still ring a bell today. Constantin Meunier (1831–1905) was a painter and sculptor who represented the world of labor with much empathy; his work echoed far beyond the frontiers of Belgium. The painter and graphic artist Félicien Rops (1833–1898) shocked many contemporaries with his "scandalous" representation of women, sex, and bourgeois or clerical vices and hypocrisy. The *oeuvre* of both artists radiated obvious social criticism. They were forerunners of the new, more autonomous directions that Belgian art would take in the *Fin de Siècle*.

Romanticism was also prominent in literature. One of the most famous works of the Romantic literary school was *De leeuw van Vlaenderen* ("The Lion of Flanders"), published in 1838 by the Flemish writer Hendrik Conscience (1812–1883). His epic novel, narrating the conflict between "the Flemish" and the French king in the early fourteenth century, became a symbol of the glorious past of the Flemish people (see Chapter 3). This work, and the many other historical novels by this prolific author, also proved that the Flemish language was a valuable cultural instrument and not an obscure dialect. Francophone Belgian novelists and poets, for their part, lived in an ambiguous situation. On the one hand, success was achieved and reputations were made or broken in Paris. But on the other hand, Belgian Francophone writers also had to create an original *marque*, distinguishing them from mainstream French creations. This distinctive *cachet* was often found in their so-called "Flemish" roots. It was thought that their specific "Nordic" tint – made of mystery, fantasy, a particular popular mood, idiosyncratic expressions, etc. – set them apart. Until deep into the twentieth century, many French-speaking Belgian writers loudly proclaimed their "Flemish" character, even if they only published in French. In the end, few real Francophone Belgian literary talents emerged by the mid-nineteenth century. Only the progressive and anti-clerical intellectual Charles De Coster (1827–1879) clearly stood out from the rest. His book *La légende d'Uylenspiegel* (1867) narrates, in a truculent way, the tribulations of the lively and witty young man called Uylenspiegel during the bloody sixteenth century, which was marked by violence and religious strife.

Many Belgian cities underwent rapid change in the nineteenth century. Urban patterns of daily life were modified through sanitation works; old buildings, even entire neighbourhoods were torn down, while new ones were erected; and new city districts were created, some destined for the well-to-do, others for the working classes. This frantic building activity was an ideal environment for architecture and architects. This form of artistic creation indeed gained momentum in mid-nineteenth-century Belgium. During his long reign (1865–1909) King Leopold II gave another impulse to urbanism and architecture. He wanted to leave his mark on the urban landscape and even devoted part of his fortune gained in the Congo to spectacular buildings, monuments, and urban planning projects in and around cities such as Brussels and Ostend. The most spectacular stone expression of Belgian architectural ambition is the Palace of Justice, conceived by Joseph Poelaert (1817–1879), but only finished in 1883, four years after his death. This overwhelming and labyrinthine building in the heart of Brussels is an amalgam of different neo-styles and components: Greek, Babylonian, Egyptian, etc. – a spectacular example of architectural eclecticism. It rapidly became one of the emblematic buildings of the country, either admired or abhorred by foreign travellers and Belgians alike (see Figure 8.1).

Musical life also revived after Belgian independence, with – for instance – the outstanding violinist Henri Vieuxtemps (1820–1881).

Figure 8.1 A massive architectural symbol of Belgium's recent independence: the Brussels Palais de Justice (Law Courts) conceived by Joseph Poelaert (1866–1883)

Some of his violin concertos are still regularly performed today. Nevertheless, the most talented of all musicians born on "Belgian" soil, César Franck (1822–1890), lived and worked in Paris and was the author of such masterpieces as "Symphony in D Minor", the "Piano Quintet in F Minor" and the "Sonata for Violin and Piano in A Major." He is considered to be the "father" of a new generation of French musicians. Yet, in Belgium itself, music was also influenced by national identity problems. The composer Peter Benoit (1834–1901) was an ardent defender of the Flemish cause. He devoted himself to musical education (he was said to have "taught the Flemish people to sing") and composed many imposing works, especially cantatas, to Dutch lyrics.

In short, from the cultural point of view, independent Belgium awoke from its previous lethargy. Yet, for many artists and consumers of culture, Paris continued to exert a real fascination and the French capital was considered the ultimate touchstone. Artistic contacts between Paris and Brussels were numerous and diverse. Nevertheless, French artistic production and markets were not unanimously or exclusively accepted. Some artists and writers – among them Flemings – also looked elsewhere for inspiration, models, and contacts. Some producers and consumers of culture, for instance, saw in Germany a fascinating source of ideas and practices. But all in all, this half-century between 1830 and 1880 was only the first, and relatively modest, phase of cultural and artistic revival in Belgium. The golden age of Belgian art – or, better, of art *in* Belgium – was still to come. But the new infrastructural, intellectual, and emotional climate that had been created during this period *indirectly* laid the foundations for the epoch-making cultural blooming of late nineteenth- and early twentieth-century Belgium.

Seeds of Change: Challenges to the Social and Political Order

Contrary to the expectations of some Francophone elites, Flemish did not wither away. Immediately after Belgian independence, a modest reaction arose, which was in the beginning essentially a cultural move- ment. Several Flemish middle-class intellectuals and writers, called *"taelminnaeren"* ("language lovers") essentially promoted Flemish as a cultural language. In this context, linguistic unification was a crucial issue. The "particularists" struggled to maintain a separate identity for the Flemish language(s), as distinct from Dutch, while the "integration-ists" promoted alignment with this already standardized language. Ultimately, the latter point of view prevailed and even succeeded in gaining the support of the Belgian authorities. This seemingly marginal event in fact had far-reaching consequences. Henceforth, the integration of Flemish into the Dutch norm continued step-by-step. This process of evolution led to the adoption of a common standard language in both Flanders and The Netherlands, which was known as "*Algemeen beschaafd Nederlands*" or "ABN" ("Standard Dutch"; literally "general educated Dutch") and which was officially recognized and imposed by the Belgian and Dutch authorities. Local idiosyncrasies in pronunciation, in the use of words and expressions, etc., were and still are banned as "incorrect" or "dialectal." This option reinforced the position of the "Flemish" language (henceforth theoretically identical to Dutch) in the realm of Belgium. However, these vibrant cultural connections did not automatically generate a strong sense of political identity (the so-called "Great-Netherlandic" aspiration and movement), as we shall see in the next chapter.

The early Belgian authorities also showed other signs of interest in the Flemish language, for instance by subsidizing a Flemish private cultural society, which was the predecessor of the Royal Academy of Dutch Language and Literature (founded in 1886). At first sight, governments' favorable attitude toward the Flemish language seems surprising, but this paradox can be explained by referring to Belgium's delicate international position. Far from being repressed, expressions of Flemish culture were encouraged to stress Belgium's multi-layered identity – as being separate from France, the main threat to Belgian independence. Conversely, the early defenders of the Flemish cause did not pursue the destruction of Belgium. On the contrary, they stood out as "Belgian nationalists" because annexation by France would be fatal to the Flemish language. The *taelminnaeren* did not envisage, let alone fight for, the "independ-ence" of Flanders: the concept of a "Flemish nation" had not yet taken shape. They did not strive for reunification with The Netherlands either, even if many of them had (had) Orangist sympathies. One must therefore be wary of an anachronistic view of the "Flemish movement." Its nature fundamentally changed over time. In the 1830s and 1840s, it was still limited to a small group of middle-class intellectuals, and it was very moderate. Two of its present features – broad popular support and the existence of a radical anti-Belgian current – emerged only decades later, at the turn of the nineteenth to the twentieth century.

However, even in the early phases, the *flamingants* (i.e. the defenders of the Flemish cause) did not limit themselves to purely linguistic and cultural objectives, but also demanded political reforms, especially the official recognition of Flemish next to French in public life in Flanders. The Belgian authorities firmly opposed such demands. In their eyes, this would threaten Belgium's future existence as a nation. Formulating Flemish demands was considered unpatriotic. The systematic denial of these modest demands led to the increasing organization and politicization of the Flemish movement. All sorts of associations were created to promote and defend the Flemish cause: students' leagues, cultural societies, theater companies, choirs, literary circles, periodical publications, etc. Some organizations clearly had political objectives, but the clerical/anti-clerical divide tore apart these *flamingant* circles. A pro-Flemish current developed *within* the existing Liberal and Catholic parties, and several Flemish cultural organizations also chose sides in the rivalry between both currents. The *Willemsfonds* association, for instance (created in 1851 to promote the Flemish language and culture, and named after pioneer Jan-Frans Willems), abandoned its philosophical neutrality in the 1860s and adopted Liberal and anti-clerical positions. The Catholics struck back and founded a rivalling association in 1875, the *Davidsfonds*, named after another "founding father" of the Flemish movement, the priest Jan-Baptist David. These opposing views hampered the attempts of the *flamingants* to collaborate beyond party cleavages.

Very few members of the upper classes were pro-Flemish, and the popular masses were not (yet) involved in the struggle against the discrimination against Flemish – although many workers and peasants undoubtedly resented the supremacy of French as one of the many expressions of social injustice and discrimination, and although several progressive frontrunners were in favour of Flemish demands. Most leaders, members, and followers of the burgeoning Flemish movement stemmed from the (lower) middle-class. They were teachers, intellectuals, journalists, writers, small entrepreneurs, artisans and shopkeepers, low-ranking civil servants, or priests – persons with at least some education and enjoying modest to comfortable incomes. Given the elitist nature of the electoral system, it therefore took many years before the voice of the Flemish movement was heard in parliament. Not until 1863 did the first MP swear his oath in Flemish, and the first parliamentary speech in Flemish was given as late as 1888. Endless parliamentary procedures and discussions finally led to the adoption of three laws which imposed the use of Flemish in criminal cases judged in Flanders (1873), in administrative affairs (1878), and in public secondary schools (1883). In reality, the scope of these reforms was limited, and they were not always put into practice. Consequently, they fell far short of *flamingant* expectations. French remained important, even dominant, in official life in Flanders.

The specific pattern of politicization of the Flemish movement in the 1850s and 1860s had long-lasting effects. A specific Flemish party did not (yet) materialize, notwithstanding some short-lived experiments. The *flamingants* who engaged in political action generally belonged either to the Liberal or Catholic party. Their first opponents were fellow party members, namely the elite Francophone politicians ruling both organizations. Pro-Flemish pressure had to be exerted *within* party structures before being able to significantly influence the legislature and government. This had two main consequences. First, Flemish demands reaching the legislative and executive levels were often marked by intra-party compromise and were therefore far more moderate than the claims that would have been formulated by an "autonomous" Flemish party. Second, the slow percolation (or "emasculation"?) of Flemish views through existing party structures, before they reached the decision-making arena, nevertheless produced demands that were, at some point, acceptable to many politicians and likely to be transformed into legislative acts. This situation had a great impact on later developments. From the 1870s, the Belgian state was never impermeable to Flemish demands, but effective steps toward equality for the Flemings were extremely slow. Concessions were often riddled with exceptions and, moreover, badly applied. This process of the piecemeal and gradual dismantling of French dominance in Flanders caused much frustration within the Flemish movement. It therefore contributed to its gradual radicalization and, ultimately, to an internal split. Both effects would occur in the early twentieth century.

*

* *

The popular masses that participated in the fighting of September 1830 had decisively contributed to the creation of Belgium. But once the independent state had been established, the insurgent workers, together with the Radicals, were expelled from the political scene. Yet social and political radicalism did not disappear, manifesting itself in several ways. From 1830 to the early 1880s, the nascent progressive movement never formed a homogenous and well-organized movement. It was a kind of nebula consisting of many different individuals and associations. But despite their diversity, most of them shared several ideas. They wanted social justice, material welfare, and cultural emancipation for working people; they were anti-clerical; and they struggled for democratic reform – especially the introduction of universal suffrage. Many links existed between the constituent parts of this nebula. Upper-middle-class progressives transcended class boundaries and established contacts with artisans and educated working class people; nascent popular associations adhered to the freethinking movement; some democrats defended *flamingant* positions, etc. Individuals and groups of different backgrounds sometimes coalesced; at other times, they formed different organizations and went their separate ways.

Opposition against the bourgeois order and prevalent misery expressed itself in different ways. Radical activists – mostly journalists, students, lawyers, educated artisans, and teachers – created and enlivened clubs and periodicals; at that time, Belgium had an active progressive press. While living in Brussels, Karl Marx and other revolutionary exiles associated themselves with these people and circles. Meetings and popular theater were other ways of voicing discontent. Jacob Kats (1804-1886), a weaver who had become a schoolteacher, became famous for organizing such activities. An anti-clerical and *flamingant*, he is considered to be one of the precursors of the Belgian Socialist movement. Popular protest also took on potentially more disruptive forms, for example the 1846 "Hunger march" on Brussels or the 1839 "Cotton uproar" in Ghent, when the industrial working class made one of its first spectacular appearances on the public scene as an autonomous (but still largely unorganized) actor. Several strikes were bloodily repressed, particularly in Ghent and the Walloon industrial regions in the late 1850s and 1860s.

Step-by-step, Belgian wage earners started to organize themselves. "Labor aristocrats" such as typesetters were pioneers in this process. Their initial self-help societies dated back to the 1820s (one was even created in 1806), but their first real trade union, regrouping the Brussels typographers, was founded in 1842. Workers in modern capitalist enterprises organized somewhat later, the Ghent textile workers being pioneers (1857). Brussels was another cradle of the modern Belgian labor movement, with its mix of self-help societies, freethinking federations (such as *Les Solidaires*, 1857), and political associations (in particular the *Association de la démocratie militante: Le Peuple*, 1860). Many personal and ideological links existed between these organizations. They recruited their adherents among the artisans and wage earners of small enterprises, and maintained contacts with progressive bourgeois individuals, who disagreed with the conservative Liberal Party line. Although not inexistent, this organizational dynamic was somewhat less lively and precocious in other Belgian cities, for example in Antwerp, and especially in the industrial agglomerations of Wallonia.

The foundation of the International Workingmen's Association in London (IWA, 1864) boosted working-class activism. *Le Peuple* became the International's first Belgian branch and other associations soon followed. The active propaganda of the Internationalists caused some anxiety within the upper classes. For the first time, Belgian ruling elites were confronted with coordinated action by the "wretched of the earth." But this radical venture was short-lived. The Belgian section of the IWA disappeared in around 1872 – together with the International as a whole – a victim of both repression and internal disagreement between Marxists and Anarchists. Nonetheless, the seeds of Socialism had been sown in Belgian soil. The small associations that survived in the main cities were isolated and lacked a superstructure to coordinate their action. In the next few years, different attempts were made to remedy this shortcoming. In the second half of the 1870s, regionally based Socialist parties were created in Ghent and Brussels. In 1879, a *Parti socialiste belge* was founded which had nation-wide ambitions. It was a forerunner of the future Labour Party, whose foundation, a few years later, would herald the start of a new era in Belgian history.

In general, Belgian Socialists (like other politicians and social activists) were not theoretically minded, but more attracted by practical initiatives. The flowering of all sorts of organizations – self-help societies, political and cultural associations, etc. – clearly demonstrates the creativity of the early Belgian Socialists. One specific experiment is worth mentioning. In Ghent, a young leader of the Socialist movement, Edward Anseele (1856–1938), organized consumer cooperatives, and in particular the bakery called Vooruit ("Forward"). Breaking with the political neutrality defended by the Rochdale principles, he linked the cooperative societies with the embryonic Socialist movement. The profits of the former were used to finance the propaganda and organizations of the latter. This innovative move was soon successfully duplicated elsewhere in Belgium; it would also serve as an example to other European countries, especially in France and Germany. Seen from this perspective, Belgium did make a modest contribution to the history of international Socialism.

Conclusion

Fifty years after its creation, Belgium had proved that it was not ephemeral. It had withstood dangerous international challenges and not fallen prey to the rivalries and appetites of the Great Powers. This was far from obvious, also given the "advanced" political nature of the young nation. Before 1848, it was a sort of Liberal island amidst a still conservative or even autocratic Europe. After that date, an increasing number of European countries slowly introduced several democratic principles and practices similar to those already guaranteed by the Belgian constitution since 1831. Belgium also drew attention as a spearhead of economic development. Capitalism had struck deep roots in this part of the continent: the "second industrial nation of the world" – a military and diplomatic dwarf – was, first and foremost, an economic giant.

But in the 1880s, young Belgium was also a repository of unresolved issues. Soaring production, export and profits did not automatically generate social benefits. On the contrary, misery was the lot of masses of small people, both in the cities and on the countryside. And about 98% of all Belgians were still excluded from voting. A potentially disruptive "social question" was looming. Within the elites, but also in larger social groups, a fierce struggle opposed the partisans and opponents of Catholic supremacy in public life. This was yet another unsettled conflict. Moreover, it was unclear what it meant exactly "to be a Belgian". The notion of Belgian identity was rather elusive, even if authorities did their best to create and propagate an appropriate ideological and cultural framework filled with "typical Belgian" symbols. Despite these efforts, the weaknesses and ambiguities of this nationalistic "glue" put Belgium in an awkward position within the nineteenth-century context of triumphant nationalism. The first signs of a linguistic divide were already perceptible at the time when the Belgian authorities celebrated, with due pomp and circumstance, the nation's fiftieth anniversary.

The Belgian Nation-State at Its Height
(1880s–1945)

Introduction

While he lived in Brussels between 1864 and 1866, the French poet Charles Baudelaire wrote a pamphlet later known as *Pauvre Belgique!* ("Poor Belgium!"). In this unfinished work, he expressed his aversion for the country and its inhabitants. He presented Belgium as a pretentious *"homunculus"* – an artificially created small human being – that was "the outcome of an alchemical operation of diplomacy." According to him, the Belgians were lazy, avaricious, stupid, and conformist – somewhere "between the ape and the mollusc." This rather harsh judgment may have sprung from his personal frustrations; at that time, he was confronted with financial, personal, and health problems. Nevertheless, the idea that Belgium was an artificial creation was by no means a Baudelairian idiosyncrasy. As we saw earlier, other prominent European personalities – including leading politicians – shared this view.

A few decades later, at the turn of the nineteenth to the twentieth century, Belgium's image abroad had changed dramatically. Another towering figure of European literature, Stefan Zweig, visited the country to meet the Belgian poet Émile Verhaeren, whom he considered "the greatest of our European lyric poets." In a book written in 1910 to glorify his idol, Zweig was also lyrical about Belgium itself, "one of the crossroads of Europe." This small territory was "a multifaceted mirror presenting an abridged version of the multiple universe." According to him, the Belgians were (among other qualities) vigorous, fecund, hardworking and sensual – but at the same time intelligent, creative, and artistic, with a touch of mysticism. In his eyes, this success was due to the fact that the Flemish and Walloon races had not simply collided but had fused into a "new race." Clearly, Picard's theory of *l'Âme belge* and Pirenne's views on Belgian national identity had also gained converts in the rest of Europe.

Of course, foreign perceptions of Belgium cannot be reduced to a few random citations. Nevertheless, these contrasting appreciations undoubtedly reflected a general trend: Belgium's international reputation had indeed improved. Did this change also reflect shifting domestic trends?

Belgian Economy and Society in Transition

The spectacular transformation of Belgian politics, diplomacy, and culture in the late nineteenth and early twentieth centuries was closely connected to changes in the economy and society. The share of farmers in the total active population inexorably declined (31.4 percent in 1896; 13.2 percent in 1947). This was a painful process, with dramatic social consequences. The import of cheap agricultural produce, especially grain from the USA – the famous "agricultural invasion" – threatened the survival of many small producers. Misery, hard work and (self-) exploitation were the lot of many small farmers. Compared to other European countries, Belgium continued to be the "land of small farms," and this extreme fragmentation of farms was detrimental to agricultural productivity. To avoid a complete collapse of rural society, the successive Belgian Catholic governments and the Church stimulated the development of a Catholic farmers' movement. From the 1890s, cooperative societies helped farmers to survive and even to improve their living conditions.

Meanwhile, Belgian industry thrived. As before, it was predominantly export-oriented: foreign markets were crucial for national manufacturing. It was therefore extremely sensitive to global business cycles, such as the Great Depression of 1873–1896 and the crisis of the 1930s. Belgian politicians, however, refused to adopt a policy of full-fledged protectionism. Thick commercial walls could not save the Belgian economy – on the contrary, Belgian foreign policy, soon to be examined, strove to maximize the free flow of goods and services. The main adaptive effort had to come from the entrepreneurs themselves. Several changes indeed proved the vitality of Belgian industry at the turn of the nineteenth and twentieth century.

First, average firm size increased notably, and the *industries à domicile*, or cottage industries, inexorably declined. Second, this growing industrial concentration was accompanied by substantial investment in new technologies. Scientific labor management gradually spread throughout Belgian industry, especially after the First World War, and this accelerated the growth of productivity. Third, this development went hand-in-hand with the emergence of new sectors. Iron and steel, coal, glass, and textiles still dominated the industrial landscape – and this was to remain the case until the middle of the twentieth century – but Belgian capitalists successfully launched businesses in the chemical industry, in machine construction, and in electricity. Fourth, many Belgian capitalists also looked beyond the borders of their fatherland and started to become active all over the world. Belgian enterprises were active in many cities of Latin America, the Middle East, and eastern and southern Europe, creating public utilities and developing urban transport. Huge amounts of Belgian capital flowed into Tsarist Russia, especially into coal mines and iron works. The colonization of the Congo, starting in 1885 – a development analyzed below (p. 286–288) – profoundly influenced the international involvement of Belgian capital. After the First World War, Belgian capitalists invested massively in the Congo, somewhat neglecting the rest of the world. Fifth, the geographical basis of capitalism, finally, also slowly broadened in Belgium itself. The traditional core industrial regions – the Walloon industrial basins and Ghent – gradually lost their monopoly on modern, mechanized production. A growing number of capitalist enterprises were created in Flanders.

However, weaknesses and threats also became apparent during the interwar period. Notwithstanding the rise of the chemical and electrical industries, and machine construction, Belgian exports still focused mainly on partially finished products. This was a dangerous situation, since global capitalism was heading toward new horizons which were dominated by durable consumer products and complex technologies. For instance, on the eve of the Second World War, Belgian industry did not manufacture domestically produced automobile or aeroplane types; it assembled foreign brands. The rigidity of Belgian industry during the interwar years has puzzled many observers. The causes of this relative immobility are not yet fully established, but some analysts have pointed to a particularity of Belgian capitalism: the overwhelming role of four or five mixed banks controlling the bulk of Belgian industry. The *Société générale de Belgique* had developed into the leading financial institution; it commanded a real economic empire, both in Belgium and the Congo. It was difficult to raise capital on the stock exchange to create an independent company. This may explain the growing rigidity of the entrepreneurial structure in Belgium: initiatives taken outside the orbit of the banks (later holdings) were extremely difficult to launch and sustain. The headquarters of a few powerful financial institutions decisively influenced the dynamics of the Belgian economy and narrowed the margins left for autonomous business creativity.

Belgium's First Steps toward Mass Democracy (1880s–1914)

The Belgian political system, originally considered by many contemporaries to be a "model," increasingly lost its "exemplary" character in the second half of the nineteenth century. The key elements of political Liberalism – a representative system, the separation of powers, ministerial responsibility – worked impeccably, but the vast majority of Belgian citizens had no voting rights – including all women, whether rich or poor, in the first place. Meanwhile, neighboring countries had gradually extended suffrage. The contrast was particularly striking in the early 1890s. At that moment, less than 10 percent of Belgian adult males had suffrage, the lowest percentage in Western Europe. Belgium also lagged behind in other crucial domains. There was hardly any social legislation until the mid-1880s; the tax system was outdated and socially unjust, etc. Belgium's bourgeoisie endorsed a *Manchesterian* vision of liberty, staunchly defended its privileges, and it thwarted all plans to reform the unjust fiscal, educational, and social system. The suffrage question therefore became a central issue of Belgian politics and society; this was the precondition for full integration of the popular masses into the fabric of society and for Belgium to adapt to the requirements of this buoyant period.

The struggle for political reform was boosted by the creation, in 1885, of the Belgian Workers' Party (BWP) (*Parti ouvrier belge*), a Socialist party federating a vast number of social and political organizations (coops, self-aid societies, trade unions, local political associations, etc.). In just a few years' time, it grew into a mass movement. Its top priority was electoral reform, and it became the spearhead of the struggle for universal suffrage, although the Socialists were not the only ones promoting this. Agitation was not limited to pamphlets, meetings or large-scale demonstrations. Belgium was also shaken by epoch-making general strikes, especially in 1893, 1902, and 1913, which were organized by the BWP and its affiliated organizations (see Figure 9.1).

Figure 9.1 The army violently represses the 1886 strike in Wallonia.
"*Les Chasseurs du 3ᵉ régiment (...) dispersent par la force les émeutiers qui viennent d'incendier la Verrerie du Hainaut à Roux.*" (Le Monde illustré, April 10, 1886)

A first partial success was obtained in 1893. The ruling elite tried to reduce the unrest by revising the constitution and introducing general male suffrage, though women were still denied the right to vote. However, the ensuing dramatic increase of the Belgian electorate is deceptive, since this seemingly radical step was counterbalanced by the introduction of a plural voting system that preserved the electoral preponderance of the elites: wealthy and educated citizens had two or even three votes. Parliament also replaced the *right* to vote with the *obligation* to vote. The ruling politicians assumed that forcing the moderate, law-abiding housefathers – the "silent majority" – to cast their vote would reinforce the impact of the conservatives. Nowadays, Belgium is still one of the rare countries in Europe (and even in the world) with a mandatory voting system. Another decisive electoral reform took place in 1900. Since the existing majority voting system could lead, in the near future, to an absolute majority of the Socialist party and the partial disappearance of the Liberal party from the parliamentary scene, this system was replaced by proportional representation – almost a première in European history. Henceforth, voter preference was reflected in the attribution of parliamentary seats. These electoral reforms, especially the plural voting system, clearly favored social and economic elites, and conservative Catholic governments stayed in power until 1914.

The rise of mass democracy in Belgium went hand-in-hand with profound changes in the political fabric. The growing success of the BWP ended the traditional bipartisan structure. Many progressive Liberals were attracted by this new movement and left the old Liberal Party. The Socialists also threatened Catholic supremacy within politics. The looming de-Christianization of the masses was a crucial issue. In order to maintain their ideological control of the working population, former *Ultramontane* Catholics created working men's associations, which were "corporations," led by bourgeois figures. Rank-and-file Catholics, however, rejected these patronizing initiatives and developed their own autonomous organizations, which were blessed by Pope Leo XIII's encyclical *Rerum Novarum* (1891). It took decades before this new component of the Catholic world, Christian Democracy, was fully integrated into the Catholic party. While Flanders was the Catholic party's stronghold, the French-speaking part of Belgium became the electoral bastion of the Socialists. A simplistic image of Belgium was created: "conservative and clerical" Flanders was (and often still is) opposed to "Red Wallonia" – forgetting the undeniable existence of numerous Flemish Socialists and Walloon Catholics.

From the end of the nineteenth century, Belgian politics (and society) cannot be understood without the phenomenon of "pillarization." Private organizations of all kinds (mutual benefit societies; trade unions; associations of youth or elderly people; women's and farmers' leagues; cultural or sporting societies; even employers' unions) met with growing success and attracted huge memberships. This was largely due to the competition between Catholics, Socialists and, to a lesser extent, Liberals. Organizations of a different nature but of similar ideology coalesced and formed "pillars" consisting of persons sharing an identical creed, living closely with each other from cradle to grave, but separated from the Belgians of the other ideological "camp." The development of these pillars changed the face of Belgian society and would play a key role until the late twentieth century.

This period was also crucial for the formation of the feminist movement. As in the rest of Western Europe, bourgeois and middle-class women fought for equal political and legal rights, and for educational and professional opportunities. With the support of some feminist men, they created neutral organizations, such as the *Ligue belge du Droit des Femmes* (1892) or the *Conseil national des Femmes belges* (1905). But almost simultaneously, both the Catholics and the Socialists launched their own associations, reaching out to working-class women, or even, in the case of the Catholics, to the wives and daughters of small, self-employed individuals and farmers. These ideologically inspired, "pillarized" organizations were not always in the vanguard of women's emancipation; on the contrary: they often defended a traditional vision of female roles in society. Moreover, the politicization of gender issues slowed down the extension of suffrage to Belgian women: both Socialists and Liberals feared that women, many of whom were supposedly under the influence of the clergy, would predominantly vote for the Catholic party. Despite this deadlock, the feminist movement certainly contributed to the gradual improvement of the juridical and societal position of women, starting in the late nineteenth century. Two individuals symbolized the slowly changing gender relations: Isala Van Diest led the way in obtaining official access to the medical profession (1884) and Marie Popelin was the first woman to graduate from the faculty of Law, Brussels Free University (1888).

Belgium's Position on the International Scene from the 1880s to 1914

By the end of the nineteenth century, Belgium had undoubtedly strengthened its position on the global scene. Its existence was questioned less than before. The young nation-state also reinforced its status through its colonial pursuits, but this development happened rather unexpectedly. Inspired by his paternal example, King Leopold II tirelessly tried to create some kind of overseas enterprise – a commercial company, a "free state," etc. – that would increase both his own fortune and Belgium's prosperity and grandeur. Most of his initiatives were highly unrealistic, and almost all failed, with one notable exception: his activities in the Congo River mouth and basin. In the wake of the European intrusion into the heart of Central Africa, he set up several shady private organizations from 1876 to obtain, in his words, "a piece of the cake." Originally, his initiatives met with skepticism or even hostility from the Belgian public authorities, but thanks to his vast personal fortune and astute diplomatic manoeuvres he managed to create the

Congo Free State, which was recognized by all foreign powers in 1885. Against all odds, this bizarre polity survived: a colony without a motherland, and autocratically ruled by a European monarch. After years of difficult military campaigns, it established its authority over the entire Congolese territory. The Belgian state supported this enterprise indirectly by granting loans and allowing Belgian volunteer officers and soldiers to be seconded to the Congolese administration or armed forces. Nevertheless, in the early 1890s, the Congo was on the verge of financial collapse. However, the worldwide rubber boom saved Leopold's brainchild. The king forced the local population to collect as much wild rubber as possible. Moreover, parts of public land were conceded to private companies that also pressured the Congolese. Villages were burnt, hostages taken, people massacred – all this to maximize the income of the state and the private companies. It is unclear how many Congolese lost their lives, but between 1885 and 1920 the population probably declined by 500,000 to several (at the most five) million people – a decrease caused by violence, disease, malnutrition, and falling birth rates.

These ruthless methods indeed saved Leopold's Congo from bankruptcy, but they also sparked a wave of international protest. After alarming accounts by Protestant missionaries and a devastating eyewitness report by the British consul Roger Casement, the Congo Reform Association was founded by Edmund Morel and other activists in 1904. Through public meetings and publications, this humanitarian lobby group denounced the cruelty of Leopold's rule in the Congo. The campaign also had diplomatic repercussions. Voices were raised to summon an international conference that might seal the Free State's fate. In Belgium, opposition to the king's policy also grew, particularly from Socialists, progressive Liberals and some Catholics. Protracted discussions finally led to the annexation of the Congo as a Belgian colony in 1908.

Although the terrible abuses and the many shortcomings of the Free State were gradually abolished, coercion and repression remained the hallmark of the Belgian colonial regime, as of all others. Recurring revolts and unrest were firmly suppressed. Many Congolese adult males were forced to work in plantations or mines. Obligatory labor was also introduced to create and maintain infrastructures, or to cultivate cash crops that were sold on world markets. In the 1920s, Belgian capital exports to the colony soared, making the Congo one of the world's largest suppliers of primary products such as industrial diamonds, copper, tin, uranium, gold, palm oil, and cotton, etc. From the interwar period onwards, the authorities started to expand primary schools, extend medical help throughout the country (essentially realized through religious missions), and regulate the recruitment of labourers. Some big private companies promoted both mechanization and a paternalistic workforce policy, thereby alleviating the unbearable pressure on rural communities. Belgium – originally somewhat of a "reluctant imperialist" – had joined the select club of colonizing powers and firmly controlled – and fully exploited – one of the richest natural reserves on the planet.

From the 1880s, Belgium also reinforced its international position in other, more peaceful ways. Belgian legal and administrative expertise was highly valued in countries that shunned the intrusion of superpowers. Belgians played an important role, for instance, in the creation and functioning of a modern legal system and civil service in Siam and Persia (respectively, modern Thailand and Iran). Attracted by the growing reputation of its universities and technical colleges, many foreign students came to Belgium. Global religious missions also increased, and Belgian Jesuits, Franciscans, Scheutists, etc., evangelized parts of India, the Philippines, North America, Mongolia and, of course, the Congo. Belgium was also heavily involved in international cooperation and held a disproportionate number of economic, social, administrative, scientific, and cultural conferences. In 1912, 105 international organizations (out of 437) had located their seat in the small kingdom; France and Germany came second and third, with 92 and 84 seats respectively. This top-ranked position was due to many factors. Despite its new status as a colonial power, Belgium remained a neutral country that was devoid of hegemonic ambitions. It was located at equal distance from three European superpowers, and it benefited from an excellent transport and communications system. Prominent Belgian scientists, social activists, and civil servants also invested heavily in the development of international networks. Their organizational and intellectual capacities, their sense of compromise, and (sometimes) their linguistic skills made them ideal presidents or secretaries of associations that refused to be linked to a powerful country. The conspicuous position of Belgians in international organizations became a kind of tradition which persisted into the interwar period and the second half of the twentieth century. These efforts at promoting international cooperation did not go unnoticed. Of the eleven Belgian Nobel Prize Laureates from 1901 to 2020, three were winners of the Peace prize before the First World War.

World exhibitions and fairs, another nineteenth-century invention, were also regularly organized in Belgium.

Undoubtedly, Belgium's international position was somewhat more comfortable than before 1870, when Napoleon III's expansionism openly threatened its survival. The country was nevertheless doomed to keep the main powers at equidistance. Cultivating privileged relations with one or another neighbor might jeopardize its neutrality and turn it, once again, into a battlefield. Economic relationships could also have dire consequences. If Belgium were to overdevelop its relationship with *one* particular neighbor (e.g. through a commercial treaty) it could become a satellite state, which could have dreadful political consequences. Belgian military strategic planning also had to avoid the impression that one of its neighbors was *a priori* targeted as a future invader; the latter would interpret this attitude as a grave violation of neutrality, and Belgium's alleged "partiality" could thus "justify" a preventive invasion.

Dragged into the First World War (1914–1918)

Despite all these difficulties, the Belgian authorities succeeded in maintaining the balance between the Great Powers – until the First World War broke out in August 1914. Against its will, the Belgium was dragged into the conflict. Once again, it was the focal point of intra-European rivalry. The Schlieffen plan, drawn up by the German High Command, provided for an attack on Paris through Belgium. On August 2, 1914, the authorities categorically reasserted Belgium's neutrality and rejected the Kaiser's ultimatum requesting safe passage for his armies. The invasion began two days later. The 200,000 to 240,000 Belgian troops could not resist the German army, which consisted of about one million men, and the state-of-the-art forts around Liège surrendered on 16 August. Four days later, the invader entered Brussels. During their advance, the Germans destroyed many villages and towns (most notably Leuven) and massacred about 5,500 civilians in several locations. These acts of violence sparked off a worldwide wave of indignation: "poor (or brave) little Belgium" had fallen prey to "Teutonic barbarism." On October 6, the bulk of the remaining Belgian forces abandoned the stronghold of Antwerp – which was defended by a series of massive forts – and retreated further west. The Belgians finally clung to a tiny, north-western part of the national territory on the left bank of the Yser River, between the North Sea and the French border. The voluntary inundation of the adjacent countryside stopped the German advance in October 1914. For the next four years, this area constituted the frontline, where Belgian and allied troops faced the invader.

France and Great Britain, as guarantors of Belgian neutrality, immediately sent in troops. The unexpected Belgian resistance considerably slowed down the advance of the German troops; this delay helped both countries check their common enemy. Allied, particularly British, troops were deployed on the small fringe of Belgian national soil. Many people all over the world only know Belgium because of the bloody battles of the First World War. Many tens of thousands of soldiers from Great Britain, Australia, New Zealand, and other places, lost their lives in Flanders' fields, for example at Ypres or Passchendaele. For the first time in human history, combat gas was used on these battlefields. However, the Belgian authorities, for their part, never joined the allies in futile offensives that hardly changed anything on the ground and only resulted in massive casualties (see Figure 9.2).

The German invasion of August 1914 generated an unprecedented wave of Belgian patriotism. Politicians also closed ranks. Both the

Figure 9.2 The city of Ypres was completely destroyed by the fierce combats opposing British and German troops (1914–1918)

Catholic government and the opposition gave absolute priority to the defense of the fatherland. Even the pacifist and internationalist Socialists now supported the war. Political dissensions were muted in front of the enemy and the main opposition leaders were appointed as Ministers of State (a purely honorary title) in 1914, and as cabinet ministers in 1916. The government lived in exile near the northern French port town of Le Havre. Quarrels between personalities, currents, and parties persisted behind the scenes, but front-stage patriotic unanimity was well and truly preserved until 1918. King Albert I (1875–1934) played a key role in these events. As his predecessors did, he interpreted quite literally the constitutional article stating that the king was the head of the army; so he effectively exercised military command throughout the war. He established his personal headquarters in De Panne, a small coastal resort located in free Belgium, which was only a few kilometres behind the frontline. This earned him, both at home and abroad, the reputation of the undaunted "*Roi chevalier*" (the Knight-king).

In 1914 and subsequent years, about half a million people lived as refugees in the countries adjacent to Belgium, often in difficult material conditions. Some found jobs in their guest countries, while still others joined the Belgian troops, but most Belgians endured an occupation that was hard to bear. The stopping of trade and the disruption of domestic agriculture caused by the war would inevitably lead to famine. Elite members of the financial and economic sector took action to save the population from starvation, creating the *Comité national de Secours et d'Alimentation* – a nation-wide organization coordinating social initiatives for those who needed help. A massive importation of food was made possible through the creation of the *Commission for Relief in Belgium*, led by the talented and enterprising US engineer (and future president) Herbert Hoover. In fact, the *Comité national* was much more than a purely charitable body. Hierarchically organized, it was led by prominent personalities from different milieus, including Socialists. It exercised considerable influence on the daily life of Belgians and became a sort of "shadow authority" in occupied Belgium.

But real command over the occupied country was in German hands. The occupying forces exercised many administrative duties in Belgium – a huge and complex workload which was poisoned by the hostile attitude of most Belgians. The occupation regime was harsh indeed. The necessities of life were hard to procure and other products were expensive. The Germans also raised heavy war impositions and carried out large-scale pillage of economic goods and infrastructures. Many enter-prises temporarily closed their doors and massive unemployment hit the working population. Deportations, which began in 1916, were particu-larly hated and feared. No less than 160,000 men were put to work in Germany, and 60,000 more were confronted with forced labor at home. On top of these miseries came bureaucratic harassment, censorship, and the merciless repression of expressions of Belgian patriotism and resist-ance, especially the publication of pamphlets and periodicals, the gathering of intelligence for the allies, the organization of escape lines, and the sabotage of infrastructures. Some of these clandestine opponents to German rule were captured and executed, and later hailed as martyrs by the Belgian authorities and the populace. Armed resistance, on the other hand, was non-existent – this was a striking contrast with the occupation between 1940 and 1944.

To facilitate control over the conquered territory, the Germans imple-mented the *Flamenpolitik*, an adroit strategy that exacerbated the ten-sions between Flemings and Francophones. Existing linguistic laws were scrupulously enforced, but new measures were also introduced. In 1916, a Flemish university opened in Ghent under the aegis of the Germans. Only a minority of radical *flamingants*, the so-called "activists," wel-comed the German policy. Following a German plan developed in 1916 to foster administrative separation within Belgium and to create a "representative" body for the Flemings, these "activists" created the *Raad van Vlaanderen* (Council of Flanders) in February 1917. The occupying power imposed the administrative separation between Flanders and Wallonia in March 1917; but in December of the same year, the *Raad*, which represented only a small minority of the Flemish movement, went a step further and proclaimed the "complete auton-omy" of Flanders, a decision not endorsed by the German authorities because it complicated their position in possible future peace talks.

Flemish frustrations were also expressed in the ranks of the Belgian army. About 60 to 65 percent of the soldiers were Flemings, but the command language was generally French. *Flamingant* soldiers first created cultural associations, which also started to criticize this discrim-ination. The military and political authorities, afraid of sedition and anxious to preserve a flawless Belgian patriotism, repressed this so-called "Frontist" movement. Some of its leaders were punished and sent to disciplinary battalions, but the movement continued clandestinely and increasingly expressed *flamingant* political demands.

Finally, after four years of hard trench warfare, the Belgian army participated in a victorious offensive launched in September 1918, together with the French, British, and American troops. The armistice of November 11, 1918 was greeted with a wave of patriotic joy.

The Interwar Period Profoundly Modifies Belgium's Domestic and International Politics (1918–1940)

The end of the First World War also caused a major turn in domestic politics. Frightened by post-war revolutionary dangers, the elites finally accepted the "one-man-one-vote" system in 1919. Women were still excluded from national suffrage, although they could vote for municipalities from 1921. This electoral reform, combined with proportional representation introduced in 1900, was a crucial game changer. Henceforth, no party was ever able to win a majority of parliamentary seats single-handedly; homogenous cabinets, consisting of a single party, definitively belonged to the past (the only exceptions – the Catholic absolute majorities of 1950 and 1958 – will be discussed in Chapter 10). The epoch of coalition cabinets had begun. During the interwar period, two types of coalition dominated. Generally, Catholics and Liberals joined hands to form a conservative cabinet. But in times of severe crisis, they formed a "National Union" government with the Socialists to face daunting challenges such as the post-war reconstruction effort (1918–1921), a severe financial crisis (1926–1927), then global economic disruption and finally the menacing war (1935–1940). A short-lived, progressive cabinet, consisting of Christian Democrats and Socialists (1925–1926), ended in failure due to opposition from the elite classes and the financial world.

Belgium could no longer be ruled without striking complex preliminary deals, since no party could impose its views unilaterally. Parliamentary majorities in support of successive governments had to be constructed through (often difficult) negotiations. The "sense of compromise," often presented as an innate, almost genetic characteristic of "the Belgians," is the outcome of a specific set of electoral rules, combined with an increasingly fragmented public opinion. The tradition of compromise runs like a red thread through recent Belgian history. It often slows down decision-making; and the results (sometimes) appear to be overly complicated or even shaky.

The crucial electoral reform of 1919 also changed the party landscape. The Socialist party largely benefited from the one-man-one-vote system:

in both electorate and parliamentary representation it nearly equalled the Catholic party, which retained the top position. The latter's prominence was made possible by the integration of the Christian Democrat movement. Originally, these progressive Catholics had only marginal leverage, but in 1921 they organized themselves into the *Algemeen Christelijk Werkersverbond* (General League of Christian Workers), which became one of the components of the internally still-divided Catholic party. The Liberal Party, however, was downgraded to the position of a third, smaller contender. But new parties also emerged. One newcomer was the Flemish-Nationalist Party, to be analyzed below (p. 299). On the far left, radical elements broke with the "reformist" Socialist party and founded the Belgian Communist Party (CP) in 1921. However, this obedient follower of Moscow only escaped marginality after the 1936 general election and during (and a few years after) the Second World War. Despite its limited parliamentary representation, the CP nevertheless generated a "red scare," both in the BWP and in the conservative parties. Belgian public opinion also became radicalized on the opposite side of the political spectrum. In 1936, extreme right-wing dissidents of the Catholic party formed a new party called Rex that developed into an outright fascist organization on the eve of the Second World War. The effects of these new parties on Belgian politics and society varied. Except for the late 1930s, their electoral audience was negligible. From 1919 to 1932, their cumulative number of seats in the Chamber of Representatives fluctuated between five and twelve (on a total of 186 and 187 seats, respectively). None of these political outsiders ever succeeded in acceding to power. Nevertheless, their actions and mere existence changed the outlook of domestic politics. They raised new issues, fueled political passions and attacked the established order, thereby indirectly influencing the agenda and behavior of the three main parties.

Belgium's victory in the First World War, together with that of the allies, also brought about important changes in the country's international position. The Versailles Peace Agreement of 1919 transferred from Germany to Belgium a modest territory in the east of Belgium consisting of some thirty communes; they formed the new cantons of Eupen, Malmedy, and Sankt-Vith. Later known as the *Cantons de l'Est*, this region officially became part of Belgium in 1920. Originally belonging to the Austrian Netherlands, it had been allotted to Prussia by the 1815 Vienna Congress. Belgium therefore claimed sovereignty over it and its 60,000-odd German-speaking inhabitants. However, the population was generally far from enthusiastic about the prospect of embracing the new Belgian citizenship. A significant number of people wanted to be reunited with Germany. The irredentist party, the *Heimattreue Front*, linked with the German Nazi Party, won 45 percent of the votes at the 1939 parliamentary elections.

The post-war settlements also provided for the dismantlement of the German colonial empire. In this context, Ruanda and Urundi, two small African kingdoms in the Great Lakes region, which were formerly controlled by the Germans, were given to Belgium as mandate territories by the League of Nations. This was a "reward" for the successful actions of Belgian colonial troops in German East Africa between 1916 and 1918. But next to important German reparation payments, the most important consequence of the Versailles Treaty for Belgium undoubtedly was the abolition of obligatory neutrality. The country could now choose its allies in full sovereignty. Originally, strong ties were established with France, but this rapprochement came to a full stop in the 1930s. In 1936, Belgium *voluntarily* chose to remain aloof from Great Power rivalries, hoping to escape the looming Second World War. Moreover, the Belgian authorities were also exploring new ways of managing foreign relations. Belgium joined and actively participated in new world organizations such as the League of Nations and the International Labour Organization. But other steps seemed necessary to stabilize turbulent international relations. In 1921, Belgium and the Grand Duchy of Luxemburg created an economic union, the *Union économique belgo-luxembourgeoise* (UEBL). In the 1930s, economic and diplomatic links were also established with other small European powers, especially The Netherlands and Scandinavian countries (the Ouchy Convention, 1932; Oslo Convention 1930; Arrangement of The Hague, 1937; Oslo Declaration, 1938). All these efforts in favor of trade, international cooperation, multilateralism, and peaceful relations, largely supported and even inspired by Belgium, failed – at least provisionally. In fact, they anticipated the intra-European rapprochement which started in the 1950s, a process in which Belgium, once again, would take a leading role. But as in 1914, scrupulous neutrality was to be of no avail. On May 10, 1940, German troops once again invaded Belgium.

The Growing Rift within Belgium

Belgian national sentiment was at its height in the decades preceding and following the First World War. Many inhabitants of the country were proud to be Belgians and did not question the "self-evident" nature of this viewpoint, which was constructed and propagated by ceremonies, monuments, discourses, teaching, school books, and so forth. Yet, at the same time, this centralized nation-state came under increasing *internal* pressure. In these years, Belgium's fault line became more and more apparent, thus contradicting the theory of the successful mixing of the "German" and "Latin races."

The social, cultural, and political dominance of the French language in Belgium was increasingly challenged in the Flemish part of the country. This growing discontent was fueled by different causes. As we saw earlier, modern industry gradually took root in Flanders from the first decades of the twentieth century – a prelude to the massive changes that would take place after the Second World War. The growing riches of Flanders, and accompanying social transformations, contrasted with the second-rate position of the Dutch language in public and private affairs. The two-step democratization of suffrage, in 1893 and in 1919, transformed the political context. Henceforth, the voice of the ordinary Flemings could be heard on the political scene. Finally, the efforts of the first generation of *flamingants* gradually bore fruit. They had "rediscovered" the value of the Dutch language and the Flemish culture, and had generated symbols, works of art, and manifestations that echoed throughout the population.

These changes fundamentally transformed the social basis of the Flemish movement that, in the beginning, mainly consisted of educated middle-class people. From the end of the nineteenth century, it also attracted small Flemish farmers, shopkeepers, artisans, working men, employees, civil servants, and even employers. These individuals were frustrated by persisting discrimination against their language and culture and often resented the resulting lack of upward mobility, since language still acted as a social barrier. The Flemish movement not only became a mass movement; it also transcended the borders of social groups, which ranged from budding capitalists to the most humble citizens.

These transformations boosted the audience and activity of the Flemish movement. Existing associations increased their membership, while many new organizations were formed before and after the First World War. Mass demonstrations and meetings were held; public mass singing events were organized; *flamingant* newspapers, books, and pamphlets were published and widely distributed. The growth of the Flemish movement profoundly affected the "sense of belonging" of people living within Belgian frontiers. When Belgium was created, a specific "Flemish identity" did not exist. Far from being "defeated" by the Francophone leaders of the 1830 Revolution, this identity was, in fact (and somewhat paradoxically), their unwanted child. As we saw earlier, the first *flamingants* were Belgian patriots; by opposing the domination of the French language and culture they (also) wanted to defend Belgium's independence against France's expansionism. But by the end of the nineteenth century, a "Flemish identity" had well and truly taken shape. It encompassed *all* Dutch-speaking territories in Belgium and transcended the many local or "provincial" senses of belonging that existed (and continue to exist) in the northern part of the country. Flemish cultural symbols enjoyed growing popular success: the yellow flag with a clawing lion; the anthem entitled *De Vlaamsche leeuw* ("The Flemish Lion"), composed in 1847 and gradually adopted by the *flamingants* as their rallying cry; a series of great historical events and figures that embodied the Flemish virtues, etc. This sense of belonging to a specific and "united" group was fueled by persistent discrimination against the Dutch language.

But the outcome of this process was rather complex. People defining themselves as Flemings were not necessarily opposed to Belgium *as such*. Most of them saw no incompatibility in being, at the same time, "Belgian" and "Flemish." The vast majority of Flemings who fought for the Flemish cause did not *per se* want to destroy the Belgian nation-state; they only wanted to change the way it worked. But in the end, the slow pace of change in Francophone-dominated Belgium disgusted a growing fraction of the Flemish public and militants. By the beginning of the twentieth century, more specifically during and after the First World War, they broke with the moderate *flamingants* and adopted a radical stance. One of their slogans was rather explicit: *België barst!* ("Belgium, burst!" or "Belgium, go to hell!"). Their political alternative was either an independent Flanders, or reunification with The Netherlands. Cultural cooperation between Flanders and The Netherlands was already envisaged and (moderately) practiced in the nineteenth century, but the concept of *Groot-Nederland* (Great-Netherlands) as a *political* goal essentially emerged in the wake of the Great War. According to this creed, the Flemish and the Dutch should live in one and the same nation-state, since they shared a common history, language, and culture. But this vague idea remained rather marginal. It was a sentimental dream that some extreme *flamingants* shared with a handful of Dutch "blood brothers." Great-Netherlandism lacked a concrete political project, and it was firmly rejected by the main political forces in Belgium and the Netherlands.

The growth of the Flemish movement also generated another development in Belgium's complex history of "identities." At the end of the nineteenth century, it indirectly and unwillingly triggered important changes in the Francophone part of the country. Civil servants, in particular, felt threatened by the (modest) first linguistic laws that did justice to the Dutch language and the Flemish people. They feared the imposition of bilingualism (or even Dutch unilingualism) in the administration of Flanders and the capital city. Other Francophones, not only these "threatened" civil servants, also resented the possible "ousting" of French culture from Flanders, a region they considered "theirs" as much as the southern, unilingual French part of the country. They claimed that the disappearance of French would strike a fatal blow to Flanders; the adoption of Dutch as the only official language would cut the Flemings off from the flux of cultural progress and emancipation. Even more, Flemish demands were considered as an attack on the Francophones, who therefore felt they had to defend themselves against the obtrusive Flemings.

This led to the birth of the Walloon movement. Although the word "Walloon" (both as an adjective and a noun) was already used sporadically earlier, probably from the late fifteenth century, the term "Wallonia" – denoting a (projected) political entity consisting of people with a specific socio-cultural identity – clearly dates from the second half of the nineteenth century. Gradually, some inhabitants of the Walloon provinces and, originally, also some Francophones living in Brussels, began to define themselves as "Walloons," a quality that, in their eyes, was easily compatible with being Belgian. Only a tiny minority wanted to be reunited with France. From the end of the nineteenth century, the awareness of being "Walloon" (over and above the many local identities) manifested itself – rather modestly – through several means. Associations were created; cultural and political congresses held; artistic exhibitions organized; books, pamphlets and periodicals published. All these initiatives helped shape and spread the new Walloon identity. The so-called "*wallingants*" created their own symbols as early as 1913: they adopted a flag (a red clawing rooster on a yellow background); constructed a specifically "Walloon" history; and looked for an anthem and a commemorational feast, etc. But overall, the Walloon movement was far less important than its Flemish counterpart.

In short, the creation of Flemish identity was born as a reaction to the Belgian identity; the Walloon identity, in turn, originated as a response against the former. These interlocking processes ultimately shaped the complex identity structure that still characterizes Belgium today. They also impacted the political scene. Within each of the three traditional parties, the *flamingants* expressed themselves in a more vocal way, but they had to struggle with the Francophone leaders *within* their own parties. In some cases, Catholic, Socialist, and Liberal *flamingants* joined hands to further their cause, for example to lobby for the creation of a Flemish university. But attempts to transcend traditional party boundaries were short-lived. Moreover, the action of *flamingant* Catholics, Liberals, and Socialists was always contained *within* the perimeter of the existing nation-state. Their aim was to *change* Belgium, not to destroy it.

Finally, some *flamingants* became weary of this gradualist and politically fragmented approach. They now plainly *rejected* the Belgian state as the ultimate touchstone; they also prioritized Flemish identity over ideological divisions. In their eyes, the *flamingant* struggle not only needed drastic action, but also a *specific* political mouthpiece. The First World War gave this political current a historic impetus. The radicalization of *flamingantism* resulted from the actions of two elements. On the one hand, a tiny fraction of *flamingants* responded enthusiastically to the German *Flamenpolitik* in 1914–1918 (see above, p. 292). With the help of the occupying authorities, they tried to realize some essential demands of the Flemish movement (e.g. the creation of a Flemish university). On the other hand, certain Flemish soldiers, fighting in the Belgian army, were increasingly committed to the Flemish cause; as we saw, they started the so-called *Frontbeweging* ("Front Movement") which demanded the equal treatment of Flemings and Francophones in and outside the army. Both developments led to a crucial change once the war was over, namely the creation of a specific Flemish-Nationalist party. The *Vlaamsche Front* (also known as *Frontpartij*) disappeared after a few years, but in 1933 the *Vlaamsch Nationaal Verbond* (VNV, "Flemish National Alliance") took its place. This extreme right-wing party not only fought for the destruction of the Belgian nation-state, but also for the establishment of a "New Order." A radical fraction of the VNV openly sympathized with Nazi Germany. Despite the party's virulent criticism of Belgium and its "rotten parliamentary system," it ran for the national elections and in 1936 it conquered no less than 16 of the 202 seats in the Belgian House of Representatives.

Due to the intense political pressure created by the Flemish movement, the position of the Dutch language gradually improved in Belgium. The first linguistic laws passed in the 1870s and early 1880s, fragmentary and badly applied, dissatisfied most *flamingants*. In the following years, new pro-Flemish measures showed that the ruling Francophone elites were not impermeable to Flemish demands. A Flemish Royal Academy of Language and Literature was created in 1886. In the subsequent years, Dutch was used on coins, banknotes, and postage stamps and in the official newspaper, the *Moniteur belge* (now also *Belgisch Staatsblad*). The so-called *Gelijkheidswet* or Equality Law of 1898 was a symbolic milestone. It recognized Dutch as an official language with full legal status. But these and other changes were extremely slow. Consequently, by 1914, the gap between *flamingant* expectations and practical realizations was wider than ever before. Frustrations grew accordingly. As we saw, some *flamingants* therefore rejected the Belgian framework altogether. But the vast majority remained loyal to the existing nation-state. This was also the case when the fatherland was attacked and occupied by the Reich. During the Great War, the moderate, patriotic *flamingants* accepted the domestic political truce (*Godsvrede*). In theory, all the issues dividing the Belgians were toned down in front of the enemy. These *flamingants* were also called "passivists," in contrast to the "activists" who collaborated with the Germans. The former hoped that their demands would be met once the war was over. The king himself made such promises.

But after the armistice, the *flamingants* were disappointed yet again. While the other contentious matter – electoral reform – was swiftly dealt with in 1919, Flemish demands were disregarded. However, the unrelenting pressure of the *flamingants* within the three traditional parties finally bore some fruit. A first law, passed in 1921, made Dutch obligatory in all public administrations in the Flemish provinces, but several provisions weakened the effect of this measure. These equivocations occurred amid growing agitation. Meetings, demonstrations, and ad hoc committees maintained constant pressure on Flemish public opinion. These tensions were also felt in parliament and government, and they finally led to important breakthroughs. In 1930, French was completely banned from the University of Ghent. After decades of struggle, Dutch higher education was realized at last. Two statutes of 1932 reformed the linguistic situation in public administration and in primary and secondary schools; the judicial system and the army followed in 1935 and 1938 respectively. The basic principle of all these laws was *Streektaal = voertaal* ("The language of the region = the official language"). The territory, rather than the person, was the guideline. This stopped the mechanism of Gallicization in most parts of Flanders. Henceforth, most *fransquillons*, who were born in a Flemish milieu and had switched to French for reasons of social convenience or ambition, had fewer, if any, reasons to abandon their mother tongue. In a few decades' time, the Francophone minority in Flanders began to gradually disappear.

The linguistic laws of the 1930s decisively influenced the course of Belgian history in two respects. First, they created a model of political action for the moderate *flamingants*. It took a great deal of time, patience, and nerve to convince the Francophones to accept their demands; but in the end, the moderate *flamingants* realized their so-called minimalist program. In their eyes, the Belgian nation-state was well and truly *amendable* – through constant dialogue with the Francophones. This attitude would determine *flamingant* tactics and strategies in the next decades, when the tensions between the two national communities would resurface. The Flemish-Nationalists, for their part, had not participated in the reform process – at least not *directly*. They nonetheless played the role of the whip. Their uncompromising radicalism probably spurred the moderate *flamingants* to persevere. The polarization of Flemish public opinion may also have incited Francophone politicians to negotiate a deal with the "reasonable" Flemings who still accepted the Belgian framework. In this whole process, the Walloon movement hardly played any role; it had not (yet) created an autonomous Walloon party.

Second, the interwar linguistic reforms definitely put Belgium on a specific historical track. In the final decades of the nineteenth century, the Belgians were at a crossroads – probably without knowing it consciously. At that time, the Flemish claim for equality could have been answered in two different ways. Either Belgium could become a completely bilingual country, with Dutch and French as the official languages in *all* parts of the country. Or each region could officially become unilingual, with Dutch in Flanders and French in Wallonia (and a bilingual regime in Brussels). The first option was totally unacceptable for the Francophones. They were not prepared to introduce Dutch to public services in Wallonia, although many Flemings had migrated and settled there. When the Francophones were confronted with the Flemish demands, their initial response was to "accept" bilingualism in one part of the country (Flanders), while refusing it in the other (Wallonia). This solution clearly violated the equality principle and was therefore not tenable in the long run. This rejection of general bilingualism therefore paved the way for the second option: Belgium was irreversibly on the way to the formation of *two linguistically homogeneous and administratively separated communities.*

Nevertheless, the linguistic laws of the 1930s also contained the seeds of new problems. These new rules were not always strictly applied. In practice, Francophones continued to occupy most of the top administrative jobs and French also remained the main language in the heart of the state. Very few Francophone politicians (especially from Wallonia) knew Dutch, while all their Flemish colleagues were bilingual. In the long run, this asymmetry would remain a source of frustration for the Flemings. In the eyes of the *flamingants*, the linguistic reforms of the 1930s had another crucial shortcoming. Rules applicable to specific areas potentially undermined the hard-won official unilingualism of Flanders, mostly in communes located along the linguistic frontier. And in Brussels and its adjacent municipalities, Dutch was increasingly losing ground. In other words, interwar linguistic legislation had not solved all the problems identified by the Flemish movement and had even created new sources of friction.

The Explosion of Cultural Creativity in *Fin de Siècle* and Interwar Belgium

Belgium's founding fathers had expected art and culture to promulgate national glory, both in Belgium itself and in other countries. These hopes remained largely unfulfilled: few Belgian patriotic and academic works of art became known abroad. In the 1880s, things suddenly changed in a rather paradoxical way. A new generation of Belgian artists rapidly gained an outstanding international reputation, but largely outside the academic canons. One of them was the poet Émile Verhaeren (1855–1916), who became widely known all over Europe. He sympathized with the Belgian Workers' Party and its struggle for social justice. The symbolist writer Maurice Maeterlinck (1862–1949) – the only Belgian yet to obtain the Nobel Prize for Literature (1911) – enjoyed great international fame from his late twenties. He revolutionized the way theater was conceived and practiced; his drama *Pelléas et Mélisande* inspired the music of composers such as Debussy, Fauré, Sibelius, and Schoenberg. Painting also flourished in *Fin de Siècle* Belgium. The fascinating symbolist paintings of Fernand Khnopff (1858–1921), bathed in a dream-like atmosphere and often representing hieratic, mysterious ladies, influenced artistic creations outside Belgium; members of the Viennese avant-garde, such as Gustav Klimt, admired him. Impressionism and neo-impressionism inspired skillful painters, for example Théo Van Rysselberghe (1862–1926) and also the so-called "luminists" of the "First school of Latem" – which was named after a beautiful village on the banks of the Leie (Lys) near Ghent – represented idealized rural scenes with stunning light effects. But the towering figure in visual arts was undoubtedly James Ensor (1860–1949). The hallmark of this enigmatic and isolated personality was the representation of masked figures, skeletons, and grotesque caricatures, often in a carnival-like and satirical setting. His fascinating *oeuvre* mixed "classic" social critique and the symbolic depiction of human destiny in general.

Far greater still was, and is, the reputation of the Belgian architects of the late nineteenth and early twentieth centuries. Victor Horta (1861–1947) contributed to the creation of the world-famous *art nouveau* style. Characterized by an innovative way of organizing space and by the use of new building materials such as iron, this movement also conceived the building as a *Gesamtkunstwerk*. Decorative elements, furniture, and practical objects were not considered mere accessories; they were essential parts of the aesthetic environment and were carefully designed by the architect. Easily recognizable by their elegant yet complex plant-like motifs in façades and decoration, *art nouveau* buildings – whether the private homes of rich bourgeois families or public edifices such as warehouses – marked many cityscapes, most notably in Brussels. The architect and decorator Henry Van de Velde (1863–1957) worked for many years in Germany, and contributed greatly to the development of architectural modernism and design arts in the early twentieth century.

At that time, Belgian culture also witnessed another major development: Dutch-language literature finally came of age. A new generation of poets, novelists, and playwrights gathered in cultural circles and founded literary periodicals like the influential review *Van Nu en Straks* ("From Now and Soon," 1893–1894 and 1896–1901). Rejecting Romanticism, sentimental verbosity, and academism, these writers experimented in search of new ways of expression. No longer interested in the heroic Flemish past, they were haunted by contemporary themes. Some of them focused on the social problems of the day, for instance the naturalist writer Cyriel Buysse (1859–1932) who described the hardships of country life and the decay of individuals stricken by heredity and hit by social and psychological misery. The Flemish countryside – both its beauty and its miseries – formed the core of Stijn Streuvels's work (1871–1969). He described the tragic fate of the small peasants confronted with the impassive forces of nature and social problems. Other creators felt more attracted to introspection and the analysis of complex emotions, such as Karel van de Woestijne (1878–1929) – one of the main figures of the Symbolist movement. He set new standards in Dutch–Flemish poetry.

In so-called modern art, avant-gardes rapidly replace one another, and artistic Belgium was no exception to this rule. Just before and after the First World War, Futurism, Dadaism, expressionism and surrealism all had their Belgian representatives – although some of these movements developed there somewhat later than abroad, due to the vitality of Belgian (neo-) impressionism and symbolism. The young Dadaist and expressionistic Flemish poet Paul van Ostaijen (1896–1928) resided in Berlin between 1918 and 1921 and became one of the main figures of the literary avant-garde in Flanders. Many Belgian artists were attracted to the French capital; some stayed there for good; others returned to Belgium after some time. In painting, the graphic arts and sculpture, two interwar avant-garde currents left an indelible mark on Belgian twentieth-century art. The expressionists, sometimes influenced by primitive and "negro" art, produced robust and sober representations of common people and rural landscapes. Among the leading figures of this movement were three Flemish artists: Constant Permeke (1886–1952), Frits van den Berghe (1883–1939), and Gustave De Smet (1877–1943) – members of the so-called "second school of Latem," which referred to the obviously inspiring village near Ghent.

The other great artistic avant-garde movement in interwar Belgium gained a much greater international reputation: surrealism. This group of artists emerged in the second half of the 1920s. The Belgian surrealists rejected key attitudes of their French colleagues, such as the importance given to the subconscious and the technique of "automatic writing," and their explicit political engagement in favor of the Communist Party. Many of the Belgian surrealists indeed harboured extreme-left sympathies and were even fellow travelers of the Communist Party, but their artistic *oeuvres* kept a distance from open political activity. The Belgian surrealists nevertheless wanted to "subvert" the established order. In their works – be they paintings, collages, drawings, engravings, pictures, photographic montages, texts or three-dimensional objects, – they explicitly or indirectly criticized society's established powers; they ironically questioned the "obvious" nature of things and situations; and they introduced banal objects in unusual contexts; they combined seemingly contradictory elements into highly original representations that debunked reality. These approaches characterize, most notably, the paintings of René Magritte (1898–1967). Always graphically simple, they convey a dream-like and vaguely threatening atmosphere that puzzles and even provokes the observer's mind. Today, cultural and tourist authorities have turned this "discreet provocateur" into a merchandizing trump card, who is honoured by his own museum in Brussels. However, he was only one of a large group of creators who pursued their vocation well after the Second World War. The other great Belgian surrealist painter, Paul Delvaux (1897–1994), did not really belong to the hard core of the Brussels surrealist group. He disagreed with them on several aspects, for instance their political attitude, and pursued his career in his own way. His highly recognizable, dream-like and fascinating paintings often represent nude women walking or lying in nocturnal Greco-Roman ruins, or in train stations, and accompanied by impeccably dressed bourgeois men. He adopted his peculiar style in the late 1930s and early 1940s, but his production continued well after the Second World War. He was not alone: Belgian surrealism was very lively until well into the second half of the twentieth century. The concept itself was ultimately watered down and gained a popularity extending far beyond the realm of art. Belgians like to use the term to ironically denote the seemingly absurd and complex situations of their country. In this sense, Belgium is *the* home country of surrealism.

Belgium and the Second World War (1940–1944)

Growing international tensions in the late 1930s all pointed to the imminence of war. The Belgian army was mobilized in 1938, during the Munich crisis, and again in September 1939, when the Phoney War broke out. As in 1914, the Reich had chosen neutral Belgium as the central theater for their attack on France. The invasion started on May 10, 1940 and was even more devastating than the previous offensive. A total of 600,000 Belgian troops now faced 3,000,000 German soldiers.

The new and supposedly "impregnable" fort at Eben-Emael, in the east of Belgium, fell within hours. The Panzers rolled right through the Ardennes and smashed the French defense lines at the French border town of Sedan on May 15. The German advance in the northern part of Belgium was also unstoppable. On May 28, King Leopold III, supreme commander of the Belgian army, ordered the end of fighting and personally surrendered to the Germans. This decision had a crucial impact on the conduct of the war. The French and British authorities felt betrayed and heavily criticized Leopold's decision. The British expeditionary forces hastily re-embarked to the British Isles; the French signed an armistice June 22. The blitzkrieg ended in a crushing German victory.

Leopold's decision also caused a dramatic domestic political crisis. Following in the footsteps of his late father, King Leopold III had personally taken command of the Belgian troops and cared little about the government's opinions. In fact, both branches of executive power had already clashed long before the war. Leopold dreamed of a new regime based on strengthened royal prerogatives. This divergence, absent in 1914–1918, exacerbated tensions between the government and the king once military events took a dramatic turn. With the Belgian army on the verge of collapse, ministers asked the king to leave the country and continue the war at the side of France and Great Britain. Leopold refused and then capitulated. The government went into exile in France to pursue the struggle against the Germans – even if there was no Belgian army left. After the French defeat and many other tribulations, some ministers went to London to continue the fight against the Germans. Originally, the exiled cabinet looked like a rump government, but it slowly managed to restore its credibility and capacity to rule. The Belgian authorities built, from scratch, a small military force consisting of Belgian volunteers who had fled the country. However, the break with the king could not be mended because of the monarch's stubbornness. Leopold considered the ministers of the exiled government to be "traitors" and refused any contact with them and with the allies. Moreover, he tried to make a deal with the German authorities. Although officially a prisoner of war, he envisaged the installation of an authoritarian regime. Several members of the Belgian political and business elite supported his initiatives. A meeting between the king and Adolf Hitler himself, in November 1940 in Berchtesgaden (Germany), did not yield the results the monarch had hoped for, namely the Führer's authorization to undertake domestic reforms. The Führer had not yet decided what to do with Belgium. He thereby unwittingly spared Belgium the dreadful experience of a collaborationist government *à la Quisling* or *à la Pétain*. This would cause a major political crisis in post-war Belgium, as we shall see in the next chapter.

In May and June 1940, many Belgians thought the Germans were behaving "correctly." The mass exodus of May 1940 was only temporary: most of the people who had fled Belgium in panic soon returned to the country. The group of exiled Belgians was far less numerous than during the First World War. Disruption of social and economic life was also less than in 1914. After their blitz victory, the Germans immediately installed a military government or *Militärverwaltung*, thus avoiding their error of 1914–1918: they left as much administrative business as possible to the Belgians. They dismissed "dangerous" and unreliable Belgian high officials and replaced them with reliable members of the Flemish-Nationalist party VNV or of Rex. These collaborators were zealous agents of German policy. An important minority of the Belgian population indeed welcomed the German victory or was not radically opposed to it. Flemish-Nationalists hoped that their "German blood brothers" would help them to realize their emancipatory dreams, while Francophone fascists linked to Rex dreamed of a new political and social order. Both groups had no qualms over collaboration with the occupant. They accepted the positions the Germans offered them and also engaged in military collaboration. Both Flemish and Francophone volunteers enlisted in the German police force to maintain Nazi law and order, or joined the army to combat bolshevism. Intellectual and artistic collaboration also occurred. But besides having meteoric careers or temporary fame, the Flemish-Nationalists, the Rexists and their acolytes reaped very little reward from the occupant. The Germans made some efforts to please collaborating *flamingants*, for instance liberating Flemish POWs (whereas Francophones were kept in captivity). However, the German authorities made no move to dismantle the Belgian state and to bring Flemish independence (or Great-Netherlandic reunification with the Dutch) any closer. Rexist hopes for a new, fascist political regime also remained unfulfilled. The German-speaking part of Belgium was however reunited with the *Heimat*. The young men of the former Belgian *Cantons de l'Est* were therefore drafted into the German army.

Indeed, the Nazis were mainly interested in securing their own short-term interests in the occupied country and the exploitation of its economy was among their top priorities. The blitz conquest of May 1940 had left most infrastructures and factories undamaged; and the Reich coveted Belgium's riches and production capacity. Belgian authorities and businessmen, for their part, wanted to avoid the collapse of economic activity and the dramatic supply problems of 1914–1918. Many Belgian enterprises therefore kept on producing for and trading with Germany. Belgian men were forced to work in Germany from 1942 onwards. The Germans did not pay for all their purchases but amassed a huge debt, to the country's detriment, and indeed pillaged Belgian wealth. Famine was avoided during the occupation, but prices of foodstuffs rose steeply, and the black market flourished. Necessities were hard to get, despite official rationing.

The second German occupation was harsher than the first. The Belgians were ruled by a fascist dictatorship that was far more brutal than the repressive and authoritarian regime of 1914–1918. Opponents were hunted, tortured, and executed by the Gestapo and other German police forces. Some 16,000 Belgian political prisoners were sent to German concentration camps, where 6,000 to 7,000 lost their lives. In common with all other countries conquered by the Nazis, Belgium also endured their ruthless anti-Semitic policies. First, Jews were discriminated against, excluded from public life, and pillaged; then they were systematically hunted down. Large-scale raids took place from the summer of 1942 onwards, capturing Jews and Roma who were sent directly to the extermination camps. Of the 25,000 Jews who were deported, 95 percent never came back. Around 5,000 Jews, who were present on Belgian territory before the war, but who had fled or been expelled, were deported from the French camp of Drancy. Only 300 or so survived the ordeal. Some Belgian authorities, such as communal administrations and the police, assisted the Germans in their anti-Semitic policies – as happened in most European countries; but other Belgians refused to comply or courageously helped Jews to escape or hide.

Helping this persecuted group was but one aspect of growing anti-German attitudes within the Belgian population. "Resistance" encompassed many different realities. Some forms were already practiced during the occupation of 1914–1918: clandestine pamphlets or periodicals; shelters and escape lines for prisoners or allied soldiers; espionage for the allies. Sabotage was also practiced on a wider scale and *armed* resistance emerged. Undaunted Belgians resorted to violent action, killing Belgian collaborators and German soldiers and officials, or robbing banks to finance clandestine activities. Some even retreated into the *maquis*, in the Ardennes, and fought the occupant on a permanent basis. There is no clear definition of what a "real resistance" is: small, individual, or passing acts of hostility or disobedience to the Germans were no doubt numerous and widespread. Nevertheless, the total number of resistance fighters has been estimated at 2 or 3 percent of the total population aged between 16 and 65. The resistance increased its influence and its actions in 1943–1944, but never really threatened the hated regime. Far from being a unified movement, the Belgian resistance was in fact profoundly divided along political and ideological lines – ranging from right-wing and conservative, to communist organizations.

The Nazi German occupation lasted for fifty-one months. Three months after D-Day (June 6, 1944), the allied troops liberated Belgium in September 1944. The small corps of Belgian volunteers, having fled occupied Belgium, participated in this successful and rapid operation, but their presence was rather symbolic. The main thrust was realized by British, Canadian, and American troops. Hitler's desperate gamble on the Western front – the von Rundstedt offensive in December 1944 and January 1945 – also took place on Belgian soil. The famous and bloody "Battle of the Bulge," fought in the southernmost part of the country in the middle of a harsh winter, still evokes vivid memories in many hearts, especially in the USA.

Conclusion

In 1880, at the age of fifty, the small European kingdom of Belgium had, so to speak, come of age. From then on, its existence was generally accepted on the international scene, even if diplomatic and military threats persisted. Belgium also increased its presence in the world. Quite unexpectedly, through the annexation of the Congo, it became a colonial power. Belgian entrepreneurs and engineers were doing business in global markets. Obviously, this commercial and financial expansion was linked with thriving economic activity at home. After the early start of the Industrial Revolution, Belgium continued to forge ahead on the path of capitalist development. Despite (or because of?) sharp and persisting social contrasts, Belgium was indeed the "rich country" that caught Zweig's attention, as noted in the introduction to this chapter. Moreover, its foreign prestige was not limited to down-to-earth, material factors. In the 1860s, Baudelaire still complained that there was not one single artist in Belgium, except his friend, the "rebellious" Félicien Rops, mentioned in Chapter 8; but only three or four decades later, a whole generation of Belgian painters, architects, and writers belonging to Europe's creative avant-garde, had established a widespread and durable reputation.

Undoubtedly, the Belgian nation-state experienced a climax from the 1880s to the middle of the twentieth century. It had established its own "brand" in the outside world. On the domestic scene, a sense of Belgian identity flourished as never before. Patriotism was boosted during and after the First World War, one of Belgium's major ordeals during this period – the other calamities being the crisis of the 1930s and the Second World War. But the zenith of the Belgian nation-state, far from being a golden age, did not just coincide with these painful external shocks that caused so many human dramas. During the belle époque, from the 1880s to the First World War, the social and political fabric of Belgium underwent drastic changes which were generated by long but largely peaceful confrontations. Social movement organizations boomed and henceforth dominated the daily life of many Belgians. The political landscape also changed drastically, together with the rules of parliamentary and governmental life. All these developments led to the emergence of mass democracy and laid the foundations of the post-war welfare state. This process cemented a widespread consensus in an otherwise increasingly divided country. Indeed, while Belgian national feeling reached a climax, anti-Belgian opinions, or at least the forces opposing the centralized and Francophone nation-state, were also developing – paving the way for the new institutional and psychological changes of the second half of the twentieth century.

The Metamorphoses of a Nation-State (from 1945 to the Present Day)

Introduction

Among the many buildings that attract the tourist's attention in Brussels, the Law Courts (*Palais de Justice*) is, one might say, the star of the show. The work of the architect Joseph Poelaert, referred to in Chapter 8, dominates the urban landscape. Its colossal size and labyrinthine structure perfectly symbolize the Kafkaesque aspects of the legal system. But this building may also inspire other metaphors. Restoration and development works have been going on for decades. Some of the scaffolding has even rusted and become impossible to dismantle; paradoxically, it has, as it were, become part of the whole. Furthermore, the functionality of this stone colossus has been called into question. Is it still adapted to current needs? Should it not be abandoned altogether?

It is easy to draw a parallel with Belgium today. This once unitary nation-state has been undergoing transformation for five decades, and the process has not yet been completed. For half a century, the institutional scaffolding has been an integral part of the Belgian political landscape. A maze of institutions has been created whose complexity certainly is impressive, but in which citizens (and even more, foreigners) easily get lost – just as they lose their way in the numerous rooms and corridors of Poelaert's *Palais de Justice*. Some even suggest simply abandoning Belgium, a construction considered to be outdated, and replacing it with new nation-states. The extent and duration of Belgium's institutional "construction site" is intriguing, well beyond its borders. However, the country's recent history cannot be reduced to the process of federalization. Important social, economic, political, and diplomatic developments also took place, all of which profoundly reshaped this small West European nation.

Economic and Social Challenges and Changes

After the Second World War, the Belgian economy underwent profound changes. Between 1958 and 2001, the proportion of agricultural labor in the total working population fell from 8.1 to 1.4 percent. Rural activities became marginalized in the overall economic structure. But industry also faced a severe decline (from 47.2 to 25.5 percent), while profit and non-profit services soared (44.6 to 73.1 percent). Clearly, Belgium did not escape the basic trends of all advanced capitalist societies, that is, deindustrialization and the boom in tertiary activities. However, it also exhibited specific features.

Throughout the past seven decades, the country continued to be one of the world's top exporters in relative terms. The open character of the Belgian economy forced investors, often helped by public authorities, to modify the fabric of the economy. Manufacturing industries not only receded in the long term; in addition, new types of production also replaced ageing or disappearing methods. Since Belgian plants and infrastructures had suffered comparatively little from the war, economic activity rapidly resumed from 1945 – contrary to most West European countries. But this "Belgian miracle" was short-lived. At the start of the 1950s, economic performance slowed and the country joined other European stragglers such as Great Britain. The shortcomings of the Belgian economic structure, mentioned in Chapter 9, now became obvious. The old sectors that had fueled Belgium's amazing nineteenth-century developments – the coal, metallurgical, glass, and textile industries – still formed the backbone of the national economy and this threatened Belgium's position as an industrial leader.

However, towards the end of the 1950s the Belgian economy recovered, and growth resumed in the following decade. Massive investments by foreign multinationals rejuvenated the industrial base, especially in automobile construction, (petro-) chemical and electrical products, advanced machinery, and durable consumer goods. But there was also a gloomy side to this seemingly bright picture. Coal mines were closing one after the other, together with a growing number of factories geared toward traditional, unsophisticated metallurgical, textile, and glass products. The glories of Belgium's First Industrial Revolution disappeared in frightening tempo. From the 1970s to the 1990s, the protracted global crisis created new mutations that are still underway. Several multinationals shut down their plants in Belgium and reopened them in the European periphery or on other continents. Deeply transformed by new technologies, manufacturing now focused on ICT, biotech, pharmaceuticals, and the like. These enterprises produced impressive levels of value added but offered few jobs. Luckily, the formidable expansion of trade, transport, logistics, finance, personal care, and public services compensated for this shortcoming, triggering the spectacular shift in employment mentioned above.

These changes went hand-in-hand with two factors that are key to understanding contemporary Belgium. First, the uneven spatial distribution of sectorial transformations. Flanders' share in the Belgian gross national product (GNP) grew from 51.6 percent in 1966 to 57.6 percent in 1984, while Wallonia's and Brussels' shares fell from 30 to 27 percent and 18.4 to 15.1 percent respectively. The declining industries were essentially located in the Francophone part of the country. By contrast, many modern plants were established in the Flemish part. Foreign multinationals were attracted (among other things) by public aid programs specifically designed to combat Flemish "underdevelopment." The remodeling of the Belgian economic space had several crucial effects. *Social* effects, to begin with: henceforth, unemployment rates were much higher in Wallonia than in Flanders, and social conditions were less advantageous. Then, effects on *perceptions*: Belgium's image was radically transformed, both inside and outside the country. In the 1870s and 1880s, observers often contrasted "poor Flanders" with "prosperous Wallonia." These labels were dramatically reversed a century later. In recent years, Wallonia has been slowly catching up. In 1960, Flemish and Walloon annual growth rates were respectively 7.7 and 2.5 percent, while in 2011 this gap narrowed to 2.1 and 1.8 percent. But in that same year, Flanders was still producing 83 percent of Belgian exports, a clear sign that the economic disparities between the Flemish and Francophone parts of the country lingered on. Finally, these contrasts also generated major *political* effects, precipitating the end of the unitary state – a crucial aspect discussed below.

Second, the very notion of a "*Belgian* economic structure" is being increasingly overtaken by events. Many large companies that were predominantly or exclusively owned and/or controlled by Belgian capitalists have disappeared over the last two or three decades or have been taken over by foreign capitalists. This has happened not only in industry (for instance in the steel industry), but also in "strategic" sectors such as energy, finance, and transport. The dismantling of the *Société générale* was particularly notable in this respect. This powerful private holding company, once controlling huge parts of the Belgian economy, was taken over by a French group in 1988, and disappeared altogether in 2003. Holding companies still exist in Belgium, some of them in the hands of capitalists from the Flemish- or French-speaking part of the country, but the days of large-scale *domestic* corporate control are long gone. The privatization of formerly publicly owned enterprises has accelerated this loss of national control. On top of that, Belgium has relatively few important multinationals, among them Solvay (chemistry industry), Umicore (formerly *Union minière*, precious metals and materials technologies), and AB-InBev (a brewery which is only partly in Belgian hands). A list of the top 2,000 multinationals compiled by *Forbes* in 2008 mentions only twelve Belgian companies, whereas The Netherlands and Switzerland, two countries of similar size, boast twenty-four and thirty-seven enterprises respectively. In other words: while capitalism still thrives *in Belgium*, it is increasingly difficult to speak of *Belgian* capitalism.

Still, amid all these important changes, social conditions generally improved, especially in the first three decades following the end of the Second World War. Two innovations were especially important in this respect. Both were prepared by the 1944 "Social Pact," a path-breaking agreement concluded clandestinely by representatives of employers' organizations and trade unions while the country was still occupied by the Nazis. The first change was the introduction of social security. Social insurance had developed on a voluntary basis since the end of the nineteenth century, but the modest and incomplete arrangements still left many workers un- or ill-protected. Following the guidelines of the Social Pact, post-war governments introduced a protective system funded by compulsory contributions by both employees and employers. From 1945, all salaried workers were entitled to unemployment benefits, old-age pensions, family allowances, protection against sickness and invalidity, paid holidays, and compensation for accidents at work. Gradually, other categories, such as independent workers, also benefited from social protection. This specifically Belgian variant of the welfare state, largely based on private associations such as trade unions and mutual benefits societies, still exists today.

The second post-war innovation pioneered by the Social Pact profoundly modified the relationship between employers and employees. The authorities not only encouraged bargaining between capital and labor; they also created a legal framework with which to shelter social dialogue. Employers were willing to pay good salaries and grant attractive working conditions (in terms of holidays, shorter working hours, protective provisions, etc.) in exchange for intensive and efficient work from their employees. In order to settle pending social issues, strong labour unions (Christian, Socialist, and Liberal), representing no less than 50 percent of the total work force in 2018, engaged, on a regular basis, in negotiations with employers' associations at the national, sectorial, and plant level. In relatively short time, Belgian labor and capital well and truly developed a neo-corporatist culture of compromise that strongly contrasted with the Manchesterian attitude of nineteenth-century Belgian capitalists. However, dialogue did not preclude conflict: for instance, the general strike of the winter of 1960–1961 left a deep imprint on public and private memory, especially in Wallonia where clashes with law enforcement forces led to casualties.

Both developments greatly improved the social condition of the Belgian population. First, through relatively generous unemployment benefits, affordable health care, and so on, the welfare state contributed to the retention of purchasing power for people confronted with hardship. Second, while Belgium previously enjoyed the unenviable reputation of being the "country of low wages," things radically and quickly changed after 1945, largely thanks to the bargaining system. Since then, Belgium has ranked among world leaders in terms of purchasing power. High wages are compensated (indeed, made possible) by high productivity – a field in which Belgium still holds a leading position today. In the 1950s the authorities, intent on stimulating incomes through reinforced state intervention, also introduced Keynesian economic methods. Moreover, the population of Belgium also stands out due to its saving rates and its level of property ownership, both of which are high – two other crucial (auto)protective devices. Finally, income distribution is somewhat more equal in Belgium than in neighboring countries.

From the 1980s, however, the social and political context changed. Successive governments broke with Keynesianism and adopted comparatively mild neo-Liberal precepts. Budgetary austerity, the reduction of social spending, control of wage costs, and the privatization of public companies were henceforth prioritized, leading to tensions with trade unions and social non-profit organizations. These measures, aimed to reduce state expenditure and public debt, as well as deregulating the economy, were also undertaken to achieve the macro-economic objectives of the European Union, with a view to the introduction of a single currency, the euro, in 2002. The neo-corporatist bargaining system came under strain, especially during lean periods and crises, and strikes were far from unknown in late twentieth-century Belgium. The overall architecture of the welfare state was maintained, but cracks became visible. Social provisions were curtailed, following restrictive budgetary policies; the costs of social security rose; compared to other countries, legal old-age pensions are relatively low; nowhere is the ratio between the working population and the total population as small as it is in Belgium; waiting lists for youth protection, mental health care and help for the disabled are growing; and last but not least, poverty is increasing. In short, in the first decades of the twenty-first century, Belgium's protective system has been suffering from undeniable shortcomings.

The Metamorphoses of the Social Fabric

Societal changes in post-war Belgium were not limited to occupational shifts and material conditions. Like its neighbors, this small West European country has also been confronted with other spectacular transformations of its social fabric. First, massive schooling. The number of pupils in secondary schools increased from 118,000 in 1948–1849 to 845,000 in 2008. Obviously, this extraordinary expansion required enormous investments in human and material resources (teachers and buildings). As we shall soon see, education became the subject of a fierce political battle between partisans of the Catholic and official (secular) school networks. The explosion in secondary education was closely followed by a major breakthrough in higher education. In 1954–1955, Belgium had barely 22,000 university students, but this number increased tenfold to 206,092 in 2016–2017. To these figures must be added the number of students in non-university institutes of higher education (e.g. 67,000 in 1970–1971 and 210,000 in 2009–2010). Access to the top tier of education was indeed democratized, but working-class children remained under-represented in university education. This trend occurred in all Western countries, but if we subdivide Belgium's global results by language community, it is striking to see the extent to which Flanders has "caught up." The first Dutch-speaking university was not created until 1930 (see Chapter 9). This cultural "backwardness" – one of the main battlegrounds of the Flemish movement – was still perceptible after the Second World War. While the

Flemish population represented more than 60 percent of the country's total, Belgium had less Flemish than French-speaking university students (34,979 compared with 40,409 in 1970–1971). This imbalance was rectified over the following decades: in 2016, the figures rose to 108,683 and 97,409 respectively. It is easy to understand that universities also became a crucial issue in the struggle between Flemings and Francophones, yet another subject that will be tackled below (p. 339).

Second, post-war Belgian society was also characterized by a striking improvement in conditions for women and, more generally, by deep and lasting changes in gender relations. The first wave of feminist activism, starting at the end of the nineteenth century (see Chapter 9) had already somewhat enhanced the position of women by abolishing flagrant legal discriminations (for instance, women gained access to higher education and the professions). However, traditional gender roles had largely remained intact, both in the public and the private sphere. This immobilism was targeted by a second feminist wave from the 1960s onwards. A new generation of organizations – one of them defiantly called itself "*Dolle* [= frenzied] *Mina's*" – mobilized young and vocal women who (had) often enjoyed higher education. This was yet another effect of increasing access of women to secondary and higher schooling. According to these new feminists, "emancipation" was not just a matter of legal reform. Real and lasting advances in the condition of women implied so much more: control over their own body, sexuality and procreation; equality in performing domestic tasks; changes in everyday male perceptions and attitudes; access not only to so-called "male" jobs, but also to higher positions in all enterprises, institutions and organizations, etc.

A precondition for the latter demand was broader access to the labor market. Women's salaried work had been declining since the late nineteenth century, for several interrelated reasons (legislation discouraging formal female jobs, discriminatory practices by employers, voluntary or forced retreat into household work after marriage, etc.). This trend was dramatically reversed from the 1960s onwards. Women increasingly chose to start or continue salaried or independent work after marriage. In 1953, only 30 percent of all women over fifteen years of age were part of the active population; in 1999 this percentage had risen to 45 percent (the male percentages were respectively 78 and 60 percent). But the growing labor market participation of women did not suddenly smash the "glass ceiling." It was only from the final years of the twentieth century, for instance, that some (though few) women become CEOs of large enterprises or organizations. In politics, changes were also slow to come. Women were finally granted the right to vote for parliament in 1948, but Belgium had to wait until 1965 before a woman occupied a ministerial office – unsurprisingly Family and Housing. Significant female participation in high-level politics only emerged in the final years of the twentieth century: four different women were cabinet members between 1960 and 1979, fifteen between 1980 and 1999, and twenty-seven between 2000 and 2019. A symbolic landmark was the appointment, in 2019, of the Liberal politician Sophie Wilmès as the first Belgian female prime minister.

Third, Belgian society was also profoundly marked by growing immigration – this was a spectacular contrast with the nineteenth century, when emigration predominated (see Chapter 8). After the First World War, Belgium hosted a mere 100,000 non-Belgian individuals (less than 2 percent of all persons living in the country). The first significant wave of immigrants, in the interwar period, consisted of foreign coal mine workers hired because Belgians were no longer eager to toil underground. This experience was repeated on a far larger scale in post-war Belgium. From the late 1940s, Italians – working in Walloon collieries and metal factories – were the first to arrive. Then, in the mid-1960s, the Belgian authorities concluded treaties with Morocco and Turkey, organizing the recruitment of "guest workers," also mainly for the coal mines. Originally conceived as a temporary "stopgap" arrangement that mobilized single adult males who would return home after years of hard work, this system rapidly gave way to the permanent settlement of a growing number of families of, essentially, Mediterranean origin. During the crisis of the 1970s the Belgian government decreed a stop to labor immigration, but this measure did not end the growing influx of foreigners. Their number grew from 367,000 in 1947 to 696,000 in 1970 (7.4 percent of the total population) and 870,000 (8.7 percent) in 2005. It is important, however, to stress that in 1996, EU citizens represented not less than 61 percent of the total non-Belgian population.

This impressive growth was due to a variety of factors: clandestine immigration; family reunification; asylum for refugees, essentially at the turn of the twentieth and twenty-first centuries; about the same period, intra-EU regulations facilitating labor immigration from Eastern European countries; and finally, the fact that many large enterprises and international organizations established their headquarters in or around Brussels – the EU and NATO being only the most conspicuous examples. Unlike other former colonial powers, Belgium hosted relatively few immigrants from formerly dependent territories (the Congo, Rwanda, and Burundi). Moreover, they came comparatively late and were not "workers" in the first place, most of them being students or political refugees fleeing the Mobutu and Kabila regimes. While numerically significant in some parts of the country, especially in specific Brussels neighborhoods, the Congolese community was and still is outnumbered by the Turkish and Moroccan population.

The uneven spatial distribution of immigrants is also striking. They originally and predominantly settled in Walloon industrial areas and Brussels. Only gradually did they also establish themselves in Flanders (first, around the Limburg coal mines and later also in large cities, especially Ghent and Antwerp). In 2005, non-Belgians represented 4.9 percent of the total population in Flanders, 9 percent in Wallonia, and 26.5 percent in Brussels. However, the official number of "foreigners" underestimates the presence of persons born outside the realm, since many newcomers meanwhile obtained Belgian nationality. For instance, between 1988 and 2007, 600,000 originally non-Belgian men and women became Belgian citizens; logically, statistics no longer counted them as "foreigners." Nevertheless, their geographical and cultural roots lay elsewhere – even if many of them adopted, in varying and contrasting ways, local language(s) and habits.

From the 1970s, this raised the issue of "integration" and "identity," two hotly debated issues in contemporary Belgium, as in so many other European countries. In some regions, particularly in Brussels, diversity and "multiculturalism" now predominate. For some, this is an asset, creating all sort of mutually enriching exchanges and boosting the economy, an otherwise declining demography, and associational life. Others present the loss of "ethnic homogeneity" as a real threat – a source of crime and anomy, and even the harbinger of the decline of Western civilization. Paradoxically, this negative discourse is heard most loudly in Flanders, where foreigners or "new Belgians" are comparatively less numerous. While latent, or open xenophobia, or even plain racism are also present in the Francophone parts of Belgium, this discourse is propagated on a much wider scale in the northern part of the country, due to the presence of a strong extreme-right party with Flemish-Nationalist roots that has a long tradition of advocating "identity politics" and (racial and cultural) homogeneity (see below, p. 329). This matrix is absent in Wallonia and Brussels.

Fourth, Belgian post-war society also underwent profound religious changes. Chapters 2 to 6 have amply shown the importance of Catholicism to this country's history. This brand of Christianity deeply shaped "Belgian" society from Frankish times. As a result of the religious wars of the sixteenth and seventeenth centuries, the Southern Low Countries distinguished themselves from the henceforth Protestant and independent Northern Low Countries by their fidelity to Rome. However, the regimes successively led by Joseph II, the French *Directoire*, Napoleon, and William I shattered the complete identification with Catholicism and "Belgian" society and politics, since they affirmed the state's prominence over the Roman Church. After the creation of Belgium, the constitution of 1831 provided for a (mild) form of separation of Church and state, but Catholic influence in daily life and politics remained paramount. Catholic politicians even proclaimed that Catholicism was Belgium's defining characteristic. From the 1830s, the Liberals, later joined by the Socialists, challenged this assumption, and fought to limit the public dominance of the Church (see Chapters 7 to 9). While this struggle continued in the second half of the twentieth century, for instance in the field of education (see below, p. 327–328), the decades following the Second World War also brought about a decisive change in the relationship between Catholicism and the Belgian population.

From the late nineteenth century, the southern, French-speaking part of Belgium had increasingly embraced secularization, while in the northern, Flemish region, Catholicism continued to predominate. Hence, "declericalized" Wallonia was often contrasted with deeply religious Flanders – a rather fallacious comparison, since it failed to consider the strength of Catholicism among many Walloons and the lively presence of free thinking in Flanders. But one of the most striking changes in the past few decades has been the rapid decline of organized religious practice, not only in the French-speaking region but also in Flanders. While 52 percent of all Flemings attended weekly mass in 1967, this percentage dropped to 11.2 percent in 1998. In Wallonia, the corresponding figures are 33.9 and 9.3 percent, and in Brussels 24.3 and 6.3 percent. Other religious rites, such as baptisms, clerical marriages, and funerals are also declining in all parts of the country. This does not mean that religion is "disappearing" – certainly not in the face of the growing presence of Muslims in post-1960 Belgium, resulting from the immigration we just mentioned. In 2017, their number is estimated to be between 600,000 and 850,000 (respectively 5.5 or 7.4 percent of the total Belgian population). These immigrants (or persons who have recently adopted Belgian nationality) are generally more prone to conform to religious beliefs and practices. The increasing visibility of Islam in Belgium – through mosques, the observance of rites such as fasting, or the headscarf for women – added a new dimension to the anti-immigrant stance adopted by the extreme-right Flemish party, since it also embraced an overt anti-Islamic discourse (see below).

The declining influence of the Catholic Church on the population of Belgium had other crucial effects on Belgian society at large. First, it facilitated important ethical changes. After making abortion a legal right in 1990, Belgium was among the first countries in the world to legalize same-sex marriage (2003) and to authorize same-sex couples to adopt children (2006). In 2002, parliament also introduced legislation allowing people to request euthanasia under well-defined circumstances. Clearly, religious imperatives no longer influenced the majority of Belgian legis-lators, and these changes were readily accepted, and even welcomed and demanded, by most Belgians. Second, both secularization and the waning influence of Social Democracy (due to improving social condi-tions) loosened the attractiveness of the vast network of ideologically linked associations known as "pillars" (see Chapter 9). Empty churches and disappearing *Maisons du Peuple* (People's houses, i.e. local gathering places and pubs for Socialists) symbolize the growing "de-pillarization" of Belgian society. This process, accelerating in the final decades of the twentieth century, transformed electoral behavior and undermined party loyalty, as we will soon see.

Cultural Highlights in Post-War Belgium

Cultural production in the strict sense of the word, that is, in literature, the visual arts, music, etc., thrived as never before in post-war Belgium. More than just a few Belgian artists and creators acquired fame abroad. But the very meaning of the word "Belgian" has to be questioned in this domain, as in others. Francophone Belgians very rarely come in contact with cultural products in languages other than French: they almost exclusively consume Francophone Belgian and French media; they read newspapers, magazines, and books in French; foreign films are often dubbed. In other words, first-hand contact, in the original Dutch language, or even in translation, with cultural products made in Flanders is extremely rare in the French-speaking part of Belgium. The situation is slightly different in Flanders, Dutch/French bilingualism being more widespread (although the mastery of French is also declining among Flemish youth). But overall, Belgium consists of two different, even separated, cultural scenes with few bridges between them.

Only a few leading creative figures could boast quasi-equal renown north and south of the linguistic frontier – and some of them also gained world fame. One is Hergé (the pseudonym of Georges Remi, 1907–1983), the Francophone father of the comic-book hero Tintin, who is also popular in Flanders as Kuifje – the young reporter whose exploits are eagerly read all over the world by millions of people "from 7 to 77 years old." Hergé is only one of the talented Belgian creators of comic strips who made "the ninth art" an outstanding Belgian specialty. Another figure bridging both language communities is guitarist and harmonica player Jean-Baptiste "Toots" Thielemans (1922–2016), who established an extraordinary reputation on the international scene, playing with the greatest jazz musicians all over the world: his legendary performances touched both Flemish- and French-speakers.

The notion of "Belgianness" in the cultural field is also debatable from another point of view. In the Francophone literary world, many famous writers born in Belgium have spent parts, even most, of their lives outside their motherland. Georges Simenon (1903–1986), from Liège, wrote hundreds of books, in particular the police investigations conducted by Inspector Maigret, and is one of most widely read Belgian authors worldwide. For many years, he lived outside Belgium, in France, the United States, and Switzerland. Other Belgian-born writers who conquered a place in the annals of French literature also left their country, mostly attracted by the Parisian literary scene (Félicien Marceau, Henri Michaux, François Weyergans, Conrad Detrez, etc.). The Brussels-born *chansonnier* Jacques Brel (1929–1978) – a poet in his own right – also established his reputation on the Parisian musical scene, but many of his songs referred to his Belgian origins (one of his most famous compositions evokes "*ce plat pays qui est le mien*" – "My flat homeland" – although he did not speak Flemish). The situation is different on the Flemish literary scene. The two most important writers of the second half of the twentieth century, Louis-Paul Boon (1912–1979) and Hugo Claus (1929–2008), both lived and worked in Flanders, even if the latter also resided some for years in Paris and Italy.

The first produced a rich *oeuvre* describing the social reality experienced by the working class and their social movements in (semi-) urban Flanders. The second authored, among many other works, the novel *Het verdriet van België* (1983, *The Sorrow of Belgium*), an essential text of contemporary Flemish literature, painting an uncompromising picture of rural and semi-urban Flanders between 1939 and 1947, and seen through the eyes of a young boy from a Flemish nationalist and collaborationist environment. While Claus' book has also been widely read – in translation – in Francophone Belgium, Boon's work is hardly known south of the linguistic frontier, despite the fact that he (like Claus) was often cited as a potential Nobel Prize Laureate.

Cinema reveals yet another story. In Belgium, quality fictional filmmaking emerged relatively late. The films of André Delvaux (1926–2002), dating from the 1960s, some of which were inspired by novels from both Flemish and Francophone Belgian writers, bathe in a so-called "magical realist" atmosphere. The work of leading Walloon movie directors, brothers Jean-Pierre and Luc Dardenne (b. 1951 and 1954 respectively), on the other hand, is clearly rooted in the grim climate of industrial Liège. However, their portrayal of the difficult social conditions of ordinary working people manifestly enchanted international audiences, as demonstrated by the highest awards they repeatedly obtained at the Cannes Film Festival. In Flanders, filmmaking also flourished from the 1970s onwards, but with several talented directors who unfortunately do not enjoy the same international renown as their above-mentioned French-speaking colleagues.

Finally, the "identity" issue lost all meaning in the fine arts. Contemporary art became a global movement that freed itself from the framework of nation-states. A revealing symptom of this internationalization was "Cobra," a fertile artistic movement, characterized by its cross-border dynamic, which several leading Belgian artists joined. Its very name is revealing, because it is the acronym for COpenhagen – BRussels – Amsterdam, the three places where it was founded in 1947. Cobra anchored its roots in surrealism (and made no secret of its leftist, even revolutionary, political opinions), but quickly developed its own experimental visual language, thanks to figures such as the painter Pierre Alechinsky (b. 1927) and Christian Dotremont (1922–1979), famous for his "logograms," poems written in an idiosyncratic "script". Actual Belgian surrealism – which had already taken off in the 1920s – continued on its trajectory after the Second World War, with artists as

René Magritte and Paul Delvaux, already mentioned in Chapter 9, and Marcel Mariën (1920-1993), whose writings, collages, graphics, and other works often breathe a subversive flavor. The peculiar and complex personality of Marcel Broodthaers (1924–1976), a great driving force behind conceptual art in Belgium, also deserves special mention. Influenced by figures such as the Frenchman Marcel Duchamp, he produced a protean body of work comprised of films, collages, graphic works, installations, and even simple, apparently "banal" objects which he subtly transformed into "something else." The most famous of these artifacts is a cooking-pot of mussels painted in the Belgian national colours – both a mischievous nod to and a caustic questioning of the illusory "Belgian identity."

Domestic Politics from 1945 to the 1970s

The fundamental rules of Belgian politics witnessed little change after the end of the Second World War except for the gradual dismantling of the unitary state, a crucial theme examined separately at the end of this chapter. The only substantial modification – granting women the right to vote in general elections (1948) – had no *immediate* impact on Belgian political life. As we saw earlier, feminine presence in high public offices increased only gradually.

From 1945 to the mid-1960s, the political scene, occupied by only a few contenders, was rather simple. The extreme-right parties that had collaborated with the Nazi occupier – both Rex and the Flemish-Nationalist VNV – disappeared once the war was over. The extreme-left, on the other hand, enjoyed a brief breakthrough, thanks to its role in the resistance and the prestige of the Soviet Union. The Belgian Communist Party obtained 12.7 percent of the votes in the 1946 general election. It even participated in several post-war government coalitions, but was ousted from power in 1947 in the context of the Cold War. The Belgian Communists then suffered a continuous decline before disappearing from parliament after 1985. As a result, the three so-called "traditional" parties dominated the post-war political scene – as they had done in the interwar period. In 1945, the Catholic Party transformed itself into a centrist, Christian Democrat formation, with both a progressive and a conservative wing. For decades, this new *Parti social chrétien / Christelijke Volkspartij* was the leading organization. The Belgian Socialist Party followed closely. It was also created in 1945, on the ruins of the BWP that had been disbanded when the Germans invaded the country in 1940. The Liberal Party occupied third place but succeeded in winning votes after a successful reorganization in the 1960s. It reached out to Christian and popular voters by stripping itself of its old anti-clerical and bourgeois clothes.

As explained in Chapter 9, the combination of universal suffrage and proportional representation almost inevitably prevents any party from winning an absolute majority of votes and, hence, of parliamentary seats. A coalition between at least two parties is therefore unavoidable. This "rule" has only been broken twice. In 1950, the Social Christian Party enjoyed a unique electoral triumph: with 47 percent of the votes, it won 108 out of 212 seats in the Chamber of Representatives. This enabled the Christian Democrats to rule without a coalition partner between 1950 and 1954. In 1958 a comparable victory (46.5 percent and 104 seats) allowed them to form a (short-lived) homogenous minority government, from June to November. But except for these instances, all post-war Belgian governments were based on interparty compromises. In the immediate post-war years (1944–1945) reconstruction paved the way for "national union" cabinets, involving all parties, including the Communists. Coalitions between Socialists, Liberals and Communists followed between 1945 and 1947. But after this brief intermezzo, bipartisan coalitions – a common formula in the interwar period – re-emerged. With the sole exception of the above-mentioned homogeneous Christian Democrat cabinets, all governments between 1947 and 1973 consisted of two traditional parties. Between 1947 and 1999, the Christian Democrats participated in all of them, and they always took the lead, that is, held the office of prime minister – with only two exceptions: between 1954 and 1958, the Socialists and the Liberals joined forces to form an anti-clerical cabinet amid a severe political crisis which we will examine shortly. And in 1973, a short-lived tripartite was led by a Walloon Socialist. In the 1960s and early 1970s, a coalition between the Christian Democrats and the Socialists, the so-called "*travailliste*" (or progressive) option predominated.

Between 1945 and 1950, Belgian political life was essentially dominated by the heritage of the Second World War. Once the country was liberated in September, the authorities started prosecuting collaborators of the Nazi regime, or those suspected of sympathy with the occupant. Until 1949, legal authorities opened more than 400,000 "treason" cases, but only 57,000 of them led to legal proceedings. In the end, some

53,000 people were given various sentences. The death penalty, pronounced in almost 3,000 cases, resulted in 242 actual executions. Furthermore, many public and private institutions implemented "purification" operations (*épuration*), aimed at removing or simply punishing individuals whose attitude during the occupation had been questionable.

The German-speaking region, annexed by Nazi Germany in 1940, returned to Belgium once the war was over. The prosecution of collaboration was quite a challenge there because it was far from easy to distinguish real and active sympathy for the Nazi regime from forced commitment, for instance through enlistment in the *Wehrmacht*. The Belgian courts opened no less than 15,623 cases, relating to 25 percent of the total population, whereas the corresponding percentage in the other parts of the country was "only" 4 percent. Many inhabitants of the *Cantons de l'Est* were traumatized by these dramatic events and never really came to terms with this dark wartime episode and its aftermath. An irredentist movement, however, did not re-emerge in the post-war era, and the German-speaking inhabitants of Belgium generally did not question their Belgian citizenship. From the 1970s, when Belgium gradually evolved toward a federal state structure, this would largely facilitate the official recognition of this region as a full-fledged cultural community with some measure of autonomy (see below, p. 340).

The war created another important political fall-out, the so-called "Royal question," which was caused by King Leopold III's attitude during the German occupation of 1940–1944. As we saw in Chapter 9, he chose, as the commander-in- chief of the Belgian army, to stop the fight against the Nazi invader on May 28, 1940, against the will of the government. As a prisoner of war, he had to refrain from any political or other public activity. Leopold nevertheless tried to establish an authoritarian political regime in occupied Belgium. An unsuccessful meeting with Hitler in November 1940 thwarted his plans: the Führer had not yet made up his mind as to Belgium's political future. During the rest of the war, the captive king refused any rapprochement with the Belgian government in exile and also with the allies. Since the Germans had abducted him to Germany when retreating in 1944, Leopold was not present in Belgium when legal authorities took back control of the country. Parliament therefore appointed his brother, Prince Charles, as the regent, or acting head of the state. But when American forces liberated Leopold in 1945, his return to Belgium was unacceptable to a large part of the Belgian population. The Communists, the Socialists, and many Liberals considered him to be a traitor and a danger to democracy, and therefore refused to allow him to simply resume his royal duties. Most Catholics, on the other hand, favored his immediate return. This deadlock lasted five years and resulted in opposition between anti- and pro-Leopoldists. In the end, a popular consultation, held on 12 March 1950, showed that Belgium was deeply divided. Fifty-seven percent of all Belgians voted in favor of the king's return. This result also revealed a fracture between the northern and southern parts of the country, since 72 percent of Flemings voted for the king, compared with only 42 percent of Walloons and 48 percent of the inhabitants of Brussels. The Christian Democrat majority in parliament voted for the end of the king's inability to reign. His return, on July 22, 1950, immediately triggered a wave of protest, especially in Walloon left-wing circles. Belgium seemed to be on the brink of civil war. To prevent a regime crisis, Leopold III abdicated a few days later, delegating his powers to his son, the royal prince Baudouin, then barely twenty years old (1930–1993, r. 1950–1993). This passion-ridden episode in Belgian politics had an important effect in the long run: the new monarch and his successors, his brother Albert II (b. 1934, r. 1993–2013), and his nephew Philip (b. 1960, r. 2013–) were less involved in political activity than the first members of the dynasty (Leopold I, Leopold II, Albert I, and of course Leopold III himself). However, this general trend admitted some exceptions. Baudouin himself, for instance, was actively engaged in the decolonization of the Congo and its aftermath, as we shall see below (p. 333).

Another bone of contention that deeply divided politicians and public opinion in the 1950s was the so-called "school question." Since the nineteenth century, the public role of the Catholic Church had been hotly debated, especially in education (see Chapter 8). The absolute majority of the Christian Social Party between 1950 and 1954 opened unexpected possibilities for the defenders of denominational education. Within the context of the rapid growth of secondary education (see p. 316), the homogeneous Catholic government passed several measures in favor of the Catholic schools' network, while penalizing the official network. This provoked protest from the Liberals and the Socialists, who took revenge after the 1954 elections. The Christian Democrats then lost their majority, and their opponents formed an anti-clerical government that forced their common enemy into opposition. This time, restrictive provisions on the Catholic network accompanied a battery of measures favoring official schools. The Catholic pillar was mobilized and organized demonstrations, petitions and so on. But in 1958, electoral fortune – known for its fickleness – shifted yet again. The Christian Democrats returned to power with a minority government. But instead of unilaterally imposing its point of view, the cabinet invited the opposition parties, both Socialists and Liberals, to settle the question once and for all. A tripartite conference led to the conclusion of the 1958 "School Pact," a long-term agreement favoring compromise over confrontation. Both clerical and anti-clerical forces agreed to meet the fundamental demands of their opponent. Since then, rivalry and friction between public and Catholic schools (and, more generally, between clericals and anti-clericals) has re-emerged from time to time, but the previous fierce tone of the confrontation has been reduced by the School Pact – this is one telling example of the "pacification politics" also skilfully applied by Belgian political elites in other domains.

Domestic Politics from the 1970s: Increasing Fragmentation and Complexity

From the mid-1960s, voter preferences and, hence, party dynamics, were profoundly shaken by growing tensions between language communities. Two changes succeeded each other in time. First, clashes between Flemings and Francophones engendered new parties specifically focused on these issues. The Flemish-Nationalists still existed, despite the disappearance of their pre-war mouthpiece, the fascist VNV. Deeply resenting the judicial repression of the Flemish collaborators, they mistakenly claimed that the Belgian state took revenge on the Flemish people for expressing their rightful demands. In reality, the courts also pursued Francophone collaborators in a proportionate way. The frustration of Flemish-Nationalist public opinion concerning this "unjust" treatment came on top of a lingering dissatisfaction concerning the ramshackle state of linguistic legislation that still discriminated against the Flemings in public life (see below, p. 336). To express their dissatisfaction, the Flemish-Nationalists founded a party of their own, the *Volksunie* (VU) (People's Union), in 1954. After modest beginnings, it managed to attract about 16.3 percent of all votes cast in Flanders and Brussels at the end of the 1960s. This revival of *flamingant* activism in turn stimulated the fears of a growing number of Francophones of being cornered and even "oppressed" by Flemings. Moreover, industrial decline in Wallonia, which was causing much social hardship, also fueled demands for Walloon (economic) autonomy. This resulted in the formation, in 1968, of a *wallingant* party, the rather short-lived *Rassemblement wallon* (which disappeared in 1985). In 1964, Francophones living in Brussels founded the *Front démocratique des Francophones* (FDF) to defend the specific interests of the French-speaking inhabitants of the capital against the so-called "menacing" demands of the *flamingants*. Subsequently, these growing tensions also tore the three traditional parties apart. Flemings and Francophones were no longer able to come to terms within the unitary party structure. Between 1968 and 1978, the Christian Democrats, the Liberals, and finally the Socialists successively split into two new formations. As a result, no less than ten parties competed in the Belgian political arena at the end of the 1970s. But the (henceforth six) "traditional" parties were generally still larger than the newcomers.

However, the process of fragmentation continued. During the 1980s, a growing awareness of the threats posed by human activity to the environment led to the creation of a Francophone and a Flemish green party, respectively *Ecolo* (1980) and *Agalev* (1981, now *Groen*). Following tensions within the Flemish-Nationalist party VU, a dissident, extreme-right faction formed a new and radical party, *Vlaams Blok* (renamed *Vlaams Belang*, "Flemish Interests" in 2004) in 1979. Cultivating xenophobia, racism, and Islamophobia on top of an uncompromising demand for the independence of Flanders, this party managed to attract between 10 to 20 percent of the electorate in the northern part of the country between the 1990s and 2010s. Meanwhile, the ailing VU still faced internal struggles, before eventually disappearing altogether. In 2001 a new, center-right Flemish nationalist, the *Nieuw-Vlaamse Alliantie* (N-VA), finally emerged from these chaotic events. In the 2010s, it enjoyed resounding electoral successes, becoming Flanders' and even Belgium's largest party. Finally, the elections of the late 2010s also witnessed the revival of a communist party, the *Parti du Travail de Belgique – Partij van de Arbeid* (PTB-PVDA), Belgium's only unitary political formation.

To sum up, in the second decade of the twenty-first century, no less than twelve parties are represented in the Belgian parliament: two Christian Democratic parties, two Socialist parties, two Liberal parties, two green parties, one extreme-right and "populist" Flemish nationalist party, one center-right Flemish nationalist party, one communist party, and one Brussels Francophone party. Moreover, the majority are middle-sized organizations, each mobilizing around 10 per cent of the electorate. The Belgian party system has obviously reached a pronounced state of fragmentation. Several factors contributed to this problematic outcome: increasing tensions between both language communities; the rise of new societal issues such as ecology and immigration; the personification and mediatization of politics (charismatic personalities play an increasing role); growing distrust of ordinary citizens towards the body politic; and last but not least, the erosion of the "pillars." As a result, the Belgian electorate has become more volatile than ever.

The disintegration of the political landscape obviously has an impact on the way the country is being governed. Since the mid-1970s, the monopoly of the three traditional parties on government formation definitively belongs to the past. First, Belgian political life was dominated by increasing tensions between Flemings and Francophones. The so-called "linguistic" parties (VU, RW, FDF) attracted a growing number of voters and could no longer be ignored or marginalized. One element was of particular importance: amending the constitution, in order to realize a thorough reform of the state, was impossible without a two-thirds majority in parliament. This explains why these parties were, on some occasions, included in the cabinet. However, the six traditional parties (or at least four of them) still formed the axis of cabinet formation. Then, from the end of the twentieth century, new and complex issues were added to "classical" language community problems, while party fragmentation increased. The Christian Democrats, Socialists and Liberals managed to attract and retain fewer voters than ever before. This explains why the Green parties also acceded to power (first in 1999–2003, and again from 2020). Henceforth, political elites were forced to display an unheard-of inventiveness and sense of compromise in cabinet formation. Successive government formations dragged on for longer and longer periods of time. Between 1946 and 1966, it took an average of twenty-seven days to form a cabinet; between 1968 and 2003, this time span had more than doubled to sixty-six days. In the 1980s, some formations merrily broke the symbolic barrier of 100 days – figures that were largely beaten in the first decades of the twenty-first century. Government formation required 225 days in 2007, an appalling 541 days in 2010–2011 and no less than 493 days in 2019–2020. Belgium unfortunately counts among the world record holders of government formation duration. In the long run (1945–2020), it appears that *all* possible combinations between parties were tried out – the only exception being the permanent exclusion of the extreme-right party *Vlaams Belang*. Given its racism, all other parties agreed, in the early 1990s, never to govern with this formation (the so-called *"cordon sanitaire"*). Likewise, the new Communist Party PTB has not (yet?) been part of government, but it only broke through very recently. All the other Belgian parties have acceded to power, at least once.

But does coalition politics *à la belge* necessarily condemn the executive to instability? No less than forty-nine different governments have led Belgium since the end of the war until the end of 2020, that is, an average of one government every 567 days (or almost nineteen months). In reality, the image is considerably more complex. Some periods were particularly unstable. The difficult post-war years (1945–1949) saw the succession of no less than seven coalitions; three decades later, in the middle of a linguistic and economic crisis, eight governments passed on the torch between 1977 and 1981. But at other times, Belgian governmental life had an exemplary level of stability. Several cabinets managed to stay in power for a complete term, that is, four years. The continuity of political staff also helped guarantee the permanency of the country's management, passing incidents aside. Between the end of 1981 and the beginning of 2008, so for almost thirty years, Belgium only had three prime ministers: the Christian Democrats Wilfried Martens (1981–1992) and Jean-Luc Dehaene (1992–1999), then the Liberal, Guy Verhofstadt (1999–2008). Other politicians also held key posts during long ministerial careers.

Belgium in the Post-War World: Between Presence and Dilution

Compared to previous issues, foreign policy was rather less divisive. This was also the case, for instance, regarding colonization. Although the Socialist Party and some Liberals had unsuccessfully opposed the take-over of King Leopold's Congo Free State by the Belgian state, they aligned themselves with the pro-colonialists once the annexation was realized in 1908. Ruling a huge territory in the heart of Central Africa was a source of patriotic pride for Belgian political authorities. Its status as a colonial power unexpectedly increased Belgium's prestige on the international scene. In the eyes of foreign public opinion and authorities, the memory of the rubber atrocities gradually receded without disappearing altogether, and this incited the Belgian colonial authorities to do their utmost to present the Belgian Congo as a "model colony." After 1945, extensive primary schooling and health care were presented as unique achievements in Black Africa, and a Ten Years' development plan (1949–1959), fueled by huge investments, boosted the modernization of the colony. But in a certain sense, Belgian politicians also fell victim to their own propaganda. Even in the mid-1950s, they genuinely believed that the "winds of change" would spare their magnificent colony, and that their obedient Congolese subjects were happy to live under the paternalistic rule of Belgium – anti-colonial activism, essentially voiced by the small Communist Party, was rather weak.

In fact, the authorities did not perceive (or interpreted wrongly) the state of mind of both the rural and urban masses. During the Second World War the Congolese had worked hard, often on a compulsory basis, since the Belgian Congo was a key supplier of raw materials for the allies. Dire social conditions and physical exhaustion had triggered unrest among the Black population between 1941 and 1945, but these uprisings, great and small, were brutally crushed. Syncretic religious movements voiced African discontent, and Congolese men and women also expressed their grievances through informal and infra-political means such as music, proverbs, unruly daily behavior, and so on. But as a growing number of Congolese enjoyed better material conditions after 1945, and the authoritarian and repressive practices gradually eased, open and "modern" (or "Western-style") and/or openly violent opposition to colonial rule was slow to develop. However, things suddenly changed at the end of the 1950s, when the small group of so-called *évolués*, or "Westernized" Congolese, having benefited from a secondary and technical education, engaged in a frenzy of "modern" political activity. They founded one nationalist party after another, all demanding independence at very short notice. The unprepared Belgian authorities were taken by surprise: decolonization now had to be rushed. The Belgians unanimously excluded the military option of restoring the crumbling colonial order; dialogue with Congolese nationalists was therefore the only option. In January and February 1960, the Belgian government convened the "Round Table Conference" in Brussels, which was attended by the three Belgian traditional parties and all the Congolese political forces, fragmented into a dozen or so factions. The participants rapidly agreed on the date of Congolese

Figure 10.1 King Baudouin reviews Congolese troops on his arrival in Léopoldville (June 29, 1960) for the independence ceremonies taking place the next day. The king, in white uniform, is accompanied by President Kasa Vubu and Prime Minister Patrice Lumumba, on the far right. Unknown photographer, Congopresse agency

independence – only four months later, on June 30, 1960 – and managed to draw up a constitution for the new republic. During this process, and in the final years of colonial rule, King Baudouin played an active role; he tried, for instance, to become the head of state of independent Congo – a plan rejected by the Congolese (see Figure 10.1).

But while the Round Table Conference seemed to have wrapped up decolonization smoothly, crisis was looming on the horizon. From the start, the Belgian authorities manoeuvred to retain some sort of control on "independent" Congo, since huge economic interests were at stake. "Business as usual" after June 30 was to be taken quite literally. Subservient Congolese leaders, "counseled" by Belgian assistants, were therefore considered essential instruments in this process. The charismatic nationalist leader Patrice Lumumba certainly did not fit the job description the Belgians had in mind, but his *Mouvement national congolais* emerged as the single most successful party during the May 1960 general elections. He therefore became the Prime Minister of the Congolese Republic – and at once an object of distrust and even hatred on the part of the Belgian (and US) authorities, who considered him a dangerous Communist (which he was not). The apparently successful transfer of power ended in tragedy just a few days after the official ceremonies. The Congolese army, disappointed by the lack of concrete changes, rebelled on July 4. On July 10, the province of Katanga seceded, helped by Belgian officials and private interest groups, especially the powerful mining company *Union minière*. King Baudouin showed sympathy for the rebellious province and its leader, Moïse Tshombe. The province of Kasaï, renowned for its diamonds, followed suit. The ensuing chaos triggered a Belgian military intervention that was officially designed to save and evacuate Belgians, but also aimed to protect crucial Belgian economic interests. This unilateral measure hastened the rupture with the Congolese legitimate authorities led by Lumumba and these events turned the Congo into a Cold War proxy battlefield. When Lumumba, who felt that the USA and the UN were letting him down, turned to the Soviets for help, he definitively became *l'homme à abattre* in the literal sense of the word. In September 1960, a coup, inspired by Western powers, removed him from power and in January 1961 he was handed over to his worst enemies, the men in power in Katanga, who promptly murdered him. The Belgian authorities were not only well aware of this, but even facilitated the assassination.

It took several years before Congolese unity was restored and some sort of normality re-emerged out of bloody civil wars that were also repressed with direct and indirect Belgian military and political help. Clearly, Belgium was still very much involved in the internal affairs of its former colony. This was also the case after the 1965 coup that brought general Mobutu to power. This kleptocratic dictator pillaged his country for more than three decades, but Western powers, including Belgium, supported him, fearing that the Congo would fall into chaos or into Communist hands if he lost power. Meanwhile, Belgian economic interests were waning. While Belgium certainly does not have the will, let alone the capability, to mould the destiny of twenty-first-century Congo, it remains very much involved in the diplomatic ballet around Central Africa's most important country.

Belgium lost its status as a colonial power altogether in 1962, when its trusteeship over Rwanda and Burundi also came to an end. But its position on the international scene also changed drastically in other respects. The Second World War paved the way for more international cooperation and multilateralism, but also for the Cold War. Far from opting for neutrality, Belgium took pole position in these processes. It firmly anchored itself in the "free world," becoming a founding member and faithful ally of NATO (even if its military expenditure was comparatively modest). A Belgian volunteer corps fought in the Korean War (1950–1955). However, faithful Belgian alignment with the USA did not prevent Belgian diplomacy from fostering detente with the Soviet Union, as exemplified by Foreign Minister Pierre Harmel's efforts in the late 1960s and early 1970s. Belgium was also a convinced and active member of the UN – with, however, one notable exception: when the organization criticized colonialism and intervened, with an armed force, in chaotic Congo, the Belgian authorities were utterly opposed to the UN's scrutiny and peace enforcement. This ultra-nationalist episode aside, Belgium often positioned itself as an "honest broker" in international relations (for instance when it was a member of the UN Security Council).

Belgium devoted even more efforts to developing *transnational* cooperation. In September 1944 Belgium, The Netherlands and the Grand-Duchy of Luxemburg created Benelux. This agreement first abolished domestic customs tariffs, and then evolved towards more advanced forms of economic cooperation, heralding comparable projects on a European scale. Belgian diplomacy, particularly under Foreign Minister Paul-Henri Spaak (1899–1972), one of the "Fathers" of the European unification process, played an important role in the creation of the European Economic Community (Treaties of Rome, 1957). Since then, Belgian authorities have always belonged to the advocates and even architects of the extension of European unity. Several leading politicians played a key role at the highest levels of EU politics. Prime Ministers Leo Tindemans, Jean-Luc Dehaene, and Guy Verhofstadt devoted major efforts to European unification. Belgium's traditional pro-European stance and compromise-prone attitudes undoubtedly also contributed to the appointment of Prime Ministers Herman Van Rompuy and Charles Michel as President of the European Council (respectively 2009–2014 and 2019–). The choice of Brussels as the seat of the European institution is another telling indication of Belgium's profound involvement in the EU's destiny.

(Language) Community Tensions and the Gradual Construction of the Federal State

In the 1950s and 1960s, the Belgian unitary state came under increasing pressure. A growing number of Flemings were disgruntled by the fact that Dutch was often still treated as a second-class language. The language laws of the 1930s had certainly improved things for the Flemings (see Chapter 9), but they were not always consistently applied. In the 1950s and 1960s, French was still firmly entrenched, not only in central administration, but even in the heart of Flanders. For instance, diplomacy essentially consisted of French speakers and the Flemings were often under-represented in the upper echelons of administrative hierarchy. Moreover, French continued to be the common language spoken in many large enterprises located in Flanders – a problem not yet tackled by legislation. While many Flemish speakers had some knowledge of French, most Belgian Francophones had no mastery (even passive) of Dutch. Very few of them had taken the trouble to learn the other national language and some even openly displayed their contempt for "Flemish," which was presented as a "dialect," that was devoid of prestige and international influence. When Belgians from different language communities met, the conversation was (and still is) almost automatically conducted in French. In other words, despite undeniable advances the language situation still caused frustration in Flanders. This was of course the case for diehard *flamingants*, but also for a growing number of moderate Flemings, ordinary people as well as rank-and-file party members and leaders of the traditional parties.

The Flemish movement also criticized a specific part of the interwar legislation that had introduced unilingualism in official affairs in Flanders and Wallonia (respectively Dutch and French) and bilingualism in the Brussels area: the boundaries of these regions were not yet defined, and the linguistic status of communes could be changed. If a future linguistic census showed that 30 percent of the population in a commune belonged to the other language community, public life would automatically switch to bilingualism. This extension of bilingual areas, to the detriment of the unilingual Flemish area, was far from imaginary – especially along the language border, that is, the *de facto* demarcation line between Dutch-speaking and French-speaking populations, and also around Brussels. An increasing number of French speakers settled in the communes near the capital, and many Flemings continued to adopt the still-dominant French language. This so-called "*olievlek*," or expanding "oil stain," threatened the Flemish character of Flanders and a growing number of Flemings wanted to stop it altogether. Mounting Flemish activism expressed itself through a wide variety of channels: the numerous existing Flemish cultural associations were joined by newly founded

Figure 10.2 A Flemish demonstration in Brussels (October 14, 1962) demands the definitive delimitation of the "linguistic border"

action groups, professional lobbies (uniting Flemish academics, lawyers, doctors, students, etc.) and, last but not least, Flemish politicians, from the communal to the national level. Brochures and pamphlets were published, protest meetings held, and marches organized (especially in the capital, see Figure 10.2).

On the French-speaking side, dissatisfaction was also growing. From the 1950s, the *wallingants* essentially focused on economic grievances. The painful decline of Walloon industry (and its population) fueled criticism of "*l'état belgo-flamand.*" According to an increasing number of French speakers, the Flemings (especially the Catholics) dominated the Belgian state and neglected or even undermined the interests of the southern part of the country. *Wallingantism* acquired a leftist and

337

working-class dimension through the *Mouvement populaire wallon*, an organization created in 1961 in the wake of the great strike of 1960–1961. As we saw earlier, a new political party – the *Rassemblement wallon* – was founded in 1968. Economic autonomy, one of its main demands, would enable the Walloons to control their own destiny and restore prosperity in its ailing industrial centres.

In 1962–1963 the national parliament passed two important laws that would deeply influence later reforms. With hindsight, they can be described as the precondition for Belgium's later federalization – although this option was not yet (fully) envisaged at that time. The law of November 8, 1962 fixed the linguistic frontier. North of this line, the official language would definitively and exclusively be Dutch; to the south it would be French. In future, it would no longer be possible to change the linguistic status of the communes, even those located right on the border. However, taking into account the linguistic composition of the population at that very moment, some communes were transferred from one linguistic regime to the other – a source of future friction, as we will see. The law of August 2, 1963 determined the linguistic status of the capital, Brussels, and its adjacent eighteen communes: only these nineteen communes would enjoy official bilingualism. No other neighbouring Flemish commune would, henceforth, switch to this regime. Clearly, both laws fulfilled one of the Flemish movement's dearest wishes, namely the immutability of the linguistic border. The Gallicization of Flanders was stopped, once and for all – or so it seemed. Yet the legislator had also introduced a provision that satisfied the Francophones and, consequently, would generate new conflicts. A special regime, the so-called "facilities" system, was introduced in specific unilingual communes along the linguistic border and around Brussels. The inhabitants of these communes who belonged to the "minority" language community could, on their specific request, receive official documents in their own language, and educational and cultural infrastructures would also be available in that tongue. In other words, the unilingual nature of these communes was softened – or, as the *flamingants* claimed, dangerously undermined. In 1962–1963, German was also recognized as an official language in Belgium, a decision presaging the acknowledgment of the German-speaking community as an equal partner in the federalization process starting in 1970.

Despite their importance, the linguistic laws of 1962–1963 were unable to stop the increasing tensions between Flemings and

Francophones. They even fueled the flames of discontent through specific provisions originally intended as a compromise. The inhabitants of some communes that were switching from one linguistic regime to the other protested loudly. One case became a toxic obsession: the commune of Fourons, with a significant minority of French-speakers, had been transferred from the Walloon province of Liège to the Flemish province of Limburg. Although they enjoyed linguistic facilities, these Francophones wanted to return to Liège. This agitation lasted for decades and even triggered cabinet crises. Francophones also insisted that Flemish communes near the capital with a significant French-speaking population would become part of bilingual Brussels. In some cases, Francophones even constituted a large majority of officially Flemish communes. Flemings, on the other hand, fiercely opposed these demands. In their eyes, the linguistic frontier was intangible. They also saw the facilities as temporary and destined to fade out – while the Francophones claimed that this system was definitive.

Other issues also inflamed linguistic passions. The universities are a case in point. Since bilingual Brussels only had a French-speaking university, the Flemings demanded a separate Dutch-speaking institution. The split came in 1969. The bilingual Catholic university in the Flemish city of Leuven even triggered huge demonstrations, fueled an outright (Flemish) student revolt, and led to the fall of a government. In 1966–1968, the Flemish rallying cry was *Leuven Vlaams/Walen buiten* ("Leuven Flemish/Walloons out"), which was considered by many Francophones to be a shocking slogan. In 1970, a separate Catholic, French-speaking university was indeed created, to be located in Louvain-la-Neuve – a new city in Wallonia. On top of that, economic problems causing opposition between Flemings and Francophones also persisted and even escalated (for instance when ailing sectors needed public financial support). From the last decades of the twentieth century, *flamingant* discontent with existing Belgium increasingly focused on economic and financial issues. The Flemish-Nationalists particularly criticized the financial drain from the northern to the southern part of the country. Part of the tax revenues and social contributions generated in Flanders were spent in Wallonia, where economic and social conditions were less favorable. Radical *flamingants* stated the message rather bluntly: "rich, dynamic and thrifty" Flanders subsidized "poor, lazy and wasteful" Wallonia. Needless to say, the Francophones considered this framing insulting.

In short, the unitary nature of the Belgian state could no longer be maintained. *Specific*, decentralized institutions were to be created to tackle the *specific* needs of each language community. Decisions could no longer be taken at the central level only, and Belgium therefore engaged on the long road toward federalism. Until 2021, Belgium underwent no less than six state reforms, five of them realized through a revision of the constitution: 1970, 1980, 1988–1989, 1993, 2001 and 2012–2014. This process is probably still incomplete, and, more importantly, it was not planned from the onset. There was no such thing as a unique "federal blueprint" that guided legislators over the decades. Reforms came gradually, sometimes in a rather haphazard way, as a response to suddenly emerging problems. Indeed, the language communities remained mobilized over the years and passions often erupted at certain moments. Among the recurring disputes were the previously mentioned Fourons question, and the bilingual electoral district of Brussels-Halle-Vilvorde, which the Flemings wanted to split and while the Francophones insisted on retaining. Foreigners often have difficulties grasping the importance of such conflicts focusing as they do on local or seemingly minor issues. They are nevertheless relevant, since they became symbols of identity and crystallized passions on both sides. It took intricate negotiations and complex compromises to overcome these blockages and to reach the successive agreements that gradually changed Belgium's architecture.

One element runs like a common thread through all these events: the *dual nature* of Belgium's new state structure. The three power levels created in 1831 – the communes, provinces, and the central state – were retained. But from 1970, two new, but "parallel," levels were added. On the one hand, Belgium consists of three cultural and linguistic *communities*: the Dutch-, French- and German-speaking community (which is now officially recognized as a discrete entity within Belgium, with autonomous policy instruments). They deal with matters linked to *individuals* (culture, media, education, social care, etc.). This level was originally conceived to meet Flemish demands for cultural autonomy. On the other hand, the nation is henceforth also composed of three *regions*, Flanders, Wallonia and Brussels-Capital. They handle issues relating to the *territory* (infrastructure, transport, economy, etc.), and were created to satisfy Walloon demands for economic self-determination. Person-linked and territory-linked issues were not entrusted to a single decentralized level, since communities and regions do not have the same spatial boundaries. Most notably, Flemings and Francophones are mixed in the bilingual territory of Brussels-Capital, and the 78,000 German speakers live in the territory of Wallonia. In the new Belgian state structure, the notions of "communities" and "regions" do not simply refer to, respectively, identity groups and spaces; they also designate constitutionally defined public entities (see Map 10.1).

Due to the existence of communities and regions, side by side, the number of institutions proliferated. Each community and region was (and still is) endowed with its own legislative body (i.e. a parliament), its own executive (i.e. a government composed of ministers) and its own administration (ministries). Including the national level, Belgium therefore counts no less than six parliaments and six governments, each with its own representatives and ministers (the Flemings decided to merge Flemish regional and community institutions into one single body). Besides, Flemings and Francophones in Brussels also have their own parliament and executive.

This somewhat chaotic impression was reinforced by the gradual and possibly still incomplete nature of the process. The first attempt at reforming Belgium's unitary state structure, in 1970, was soon considered unsatisfactory. After difficult negotiations and multiple cabinet crises, the legislator started all over again in 1980. During this stage, the basic architecture of communities and regions was established, each with specific executive and legislative bodies (though the latter were composed of national representatives, not of specifically elected members). Moreover, the competences entrusted to them were rather limited and their own financial means were very scarce (their budgets were essentially funded by the central state). The next stages of the reform process therefore focused on two crucial aspects: first, the increasing transfer of new competences from the central state to the decentralized bodies; and second, the allocation of new specific fiscal revenues to the latter, to enhance their financial capabilities, autonomy, and responsibility – a key element in stopping the "north–south" financial drain criticized by the Flemish-Nationalists. This would also allow each region and community to take full control of its destiny. Important new competences were entrusted to the communities and regions in 1988–1989, especially in educational and economic matters. In 1989 the Brussels-Capital Region was officially created – some years after the Flemish and Walloon

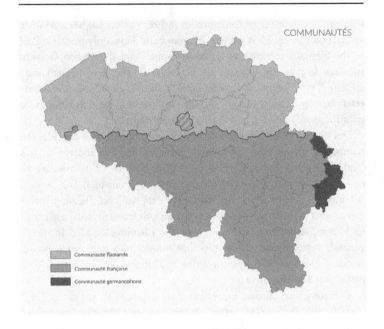

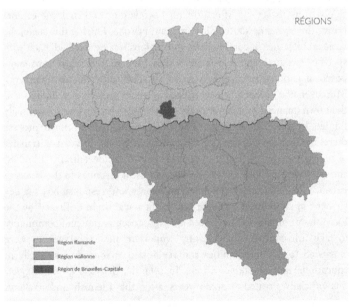

Map 10.1 The communities and the regions in the contemporary Belgian federal State (source: official website of the Belgian federal government)

regions. The Flemings had long opposed this step, since they feared that Brussels and Wallonia would coalesce against Flanders. In 1993, Belgium was officially declared a federal state, and the members of the communities' and regions' legislative bodies (henceforth called parliaments) were elected directly by the population. In the following stages, still more competences were successively transferred from the national (henceforth "federal") level to the communities and regions, for instance (aspects of) environmental policy, foreign trade, agriculture, labor market policy, child allowances, etc.

Half a century after the start of Belgium's protracted institutional metamorphosis, several key questions still remain unanswered. Which level of state authority is doing what, exactly? Is this complex institutional network working smoothly? Are all competences logically and efficiently distributed among the different levels? For sure, many ordinary Belgian citizens have difficulty understanding how this multi-layered structure works. It sometimes even takes specialists to map the intricacies of this or that specific domain. The 2020–2021 Covid crisis, for instance, revealed that eight different ministers (at the federal, regional and community levels) handle matters of public health. Other policy issues are confronted with similar problems of fragmented and/or conflicting responsibilities: labor management, environmental management, transport, energy, etc. Clashes between the federal government, regions, and communities are not uncommon. This begs a crucial question: Has the federalization process gone too far, or not far enough? Or does Belgium need a complete overhaul, on a completely different institutional basis? While radical Flemish-Nationalists declare that total independence of Flanders is the only solution, other, more moderate, *flamingants* ask for further transfers of competences. They demand, in particular, that social security should be taken from the central authorities and entrusted to the regions and communities. This idea is strongly opposed not only by the Francophones (who would be confronted with important financial losses), but also by moderate and left-wing Flemings who argue that solidarity between all Belgian citizens is not only a moral duty, but also a precondition for the country's very survival. Whether the latest, sixth, state reform (2012–2014) will be followed by other reshuffles is of course impossible to predict. But one thing is certain: at the beginning of the 2020s, Belgium's institutional structure is still hotly debated – to the point that its future existence is itself questioned.

Conclusion

Without revolution or bloodshed, Belgium has undergone an institutional metamorphosis, spread over fifty years. This spectacular process was accompanied by broader economic, social, and cultural changes that are no less important, but which are unfolding on a Europe-wide scale. However, some of these changes have a specifically Belgian tint. The Belgian welfare state, for instance, is characterized by the strong involvement of private social organizations. Relations between employers and workers take place within a rather strong neo-corporatist framework. Both elements, the welfare state and the neo-corporatist compromise, have come under severe strain for two or three decades and have moreover become an issue in the Belgian community struggle. As in most West European countries, economic changes have led to a marked decline of manufacturing industries but in this case the decline also contributed to the disappearance of specifically "Belgian" economic levers. Foreign groups now control crucial parts of the Belgian economy – a feature that contrasts with neighboring countries. This evolution has further contributed to the waning of the Belgian "identity."

Belgium did not only remodel its internal structure ; its international position was also radically transformed. Since the Second World War, the country has had to reconsider its position and role on the world stage. In 1960, Congolese independence shattered the illusive dream of imperial greatness. A standalone position on the international stage – some Swiss-like and splendid neutrality – seemed impossible. Belgium therefore engaged in the construction of various international organizations and alliances, an option almost unanimously supported by both public opinion and political leaders. Belgium has even held a leading position in the construction of the European Union, not hesitating to transfer a growing number of competences to supranational authorities. This leads us to the surprising conclusion that the Belgium nation-state is draining itself both "upwards" (especially toward Europe) and "downwards" (toward the communities and regions). Will it drain itself to the point of losing its very reason for existing and ultimately disappear altogether? This is precisely the core issue of the internal Belgian political debate, which is still underway in 2020–2021.

Which scenarios lie ahead for Belgium? No one expects the historian to predict times to come: a regular "concise history" should stop at this point, and not speculate about the future. However, reviewing the last seven decades inevitably invites one to consider possible forthcoming developments. The first scenario, a return to a unitary structure, is purely theoretical. Nowadays, only a tiny minority of Belgians reject federalism and dream of returning to the status quo ante. The second scenario involves the scission and, hence, disappearance of Belgium as we know it. This is certainly not the option promoted by the French-speaking side. Only an insignificant minority of Walloons want either the independence of their region, or its attachment to France. Some parts of Flemish opinion, on the other hand, retain the dream of full-fledged independence for Flanders which has existed since the beginning of the twentieth century, though for decades it only enthralled a tiny minority. In the last twenty years or so, however, this idea has seduced a growing number of Flemings. It is not impossible that in future general elections the extreme-right and the center-right Flemish-Nationalist parties could, together, collect 50 percent or more of the Flemish vote. Even if part of this electorate opts for these parties for other reasons than Flanders' independence, such a victory could trigger a formidable institutional crisis.

However, a complete scission of Belgium is far from easy. On the contrary, it involves many uncertainties and difficulties. No one has ever "calculated" the human, political, diplomatic, and even financial "costs" of the disappearance of this nation. Clearly, the divorce between the two language communities of which Belgium is composed would not be one of "mutual consent" – at least in the present circumstances. The separation would be imposed unilaterally on the overwhelming majority of French speakers, by a *narrow* majority of Dutch speakers. Furthermore, the Brussels-Capital Region remains an enormous complication in any divorce, whether amicable or not, between Flemings and Francophones. What would become of this small but densely populated area, totalling one-tenth of the total Belgian population and representing an enormous economic and political asset? Even if they may not openly admit it, radical Flemish-Nationalists have difficulty in adopting a clear stance on the subject. Should Brussels be part of an independent Flanders? This option has little chance of being accepted by the 80 to 85 percent majority of French-speaking inhabitants, many of them moreover of foreign nationality or origin. Supposing this city was indeed made part of a new Flemish state, the presence of a large non-Flemish population would render the existence of a unilingual Dutch-speaking Flanders – which is precisely one of the Flemish national movement's key dogmas – impossible. Or could Flanders "cut Brussels loose," abandoning to their fate the 100,000 to 200,000 Flemings living there? This idea has few followers, even within radical Flemish nationalism. In short, the Brussels-Capital Region remains a link between the country's two communities – a bridge that helps to maintain Belgium.

The third scenario involves one or more institutional reforms. The dual structure of regions and communities could be replaced by a simpler architecture. Or the internal efficiency and mutual coordination of the existing institutions could be enhanced. Do the regions, the communities, and the federal state work hand-in-hand? Do the different levels of power have logically constituted competences and adequate financial resources? Are the tasks rationally shared between central government and the federated entities? When all is said and done, these issues raise a question of an existential nature for the nation-state: in the end, what is the *specific* vocation and the "added value" of the federal level, that is, of Belgium itself? This question still remains open.

General Conclusion

Despite (or due to?) increasing globalization and intensifying trans-national links, nation-states still dominate both the political scene and people's minds. In a not-so-distant past, observers and scientists alike had written off this phenomenon, but the recent surge in nationalistic ideology, activism, and policy has proven these claims to be false or at least premature. Far from becoming irrelevant, nation-states are still alive and strong. However, their structural flaws are also undeniable. One is a lack of internal coherence – and here Belgium offers an interesting case in point. In the first decades of the twenty-first century, important European nation-states struggle with serious "domestic" problems: Spain, for instance, vetoes Catalonia's independence, while the United Kingdom of Great Britain and Northern Ireland is confronted with Scottish nationalism and the Ulster problem. But no EU member experiences such existential threats as Belgium. Chapter 10 pointed out that its very survival is a matter of serious political debate, not just of theoretical speculation. Top politicians, opinion leaders, scholars, and ordinary citizens – all wonder whether this country, torn apart by unrelenting struggles between language communities, will be able to celebrate its two hundredth anniversary in 2030.

At first sight, Belgium therefore appears a weak, unrepresentative example of what a nation-state fundamentally is, or should be. Its relatively short history as an independent, unified, and modern polity; its striking deficit of "national identity;" and its current institutional instability all seemingly converge to make this country a maverick in the club of "real," sturdy nation-states. And, yet, paradoxically, one could also argue that Belgium's peculiarities – or weaknesses – precisely reveal,

347

in an extreme way, the contingent nature of nation-states in general. This country's tribulations in the long run vividly demonstrate that nations are not self-evident, "natural" and eternal entities, and that national borders are not fixed once and for all. A bird's-eye view of two millennia of "Belgian" history can help to clarify these points.

A political fault line, running from Frisia and the estuaries of the Scheldt, Meuse and Rhine rivers in the north of continental Europe, to the Alps (and beyond) in the south, slowly emerged at the end of the Frankish era. It separated the regions that would gradually coalesce into France, and those that eventually constituted unified Germany. At the end of the Carolingian period, these "regions-in-between" formed a separate polity first called *Francia Media*, ruled by Charlemagne's grandson Lothar I, and then Lotharingia, the part inherited by his son Lothar II and stretching from the North Sea to the Alps. This entity, however, disappeared rapidly and was broken up into a series of (quasi-) independent territories, some small to minuscule, others larger and mightier. This was also the case in the northern part of late Lotharingia, that is, the modern Benelux countries (Belgium, The Netherlands and Luxemburg). Ironically, the French-speaking principalities gravitated to the orbit of the overwhelmingly German-speaking Holy Roman Empire, while a key Flemish-speaking region, the county of Flanders, was bound to France through feudal ties. At that time, vernacular language was not a relevant driver of power and politics. No clear political project emerged during the medieval period, which was characterized by constant friction and recurring wars, often due to personal and dynastic competition – but sometimes leading to personal unions between otherwise rival principalities. Local autonomy, claimed and fiercely defended by the rich cities that emerged in this region, completed this chaotic and shifting picture.

Before unfolding the chronological thread of political developments, we must stress the importance of the geographical setting of *Francia Media*'s northern regions. Consisting of plains and moderate hills, and irrigated by important rivers flowing into the North Sea, this open space not only easily bridges the east and the west of the continent, it also offers a convenient stepping stone to lands beyond the maritime horizon. This location also facilitated economic development. Agriculture thrived there from Carolingian times, practiced by both large domains and small independent peasants; since the beginning of the second millennium, textile and metal industries flourished and fueled commerce. These joint developments gave rise to the many proud and powerful cities we have mentioned. From the start, the medieval principalities, later known as the "Low Countries," were therefore entangled in a complex web of foreign relations. Powerful neighbours, that is, France, England, the Holy Roman Empire, and later Germany, were always focused on, and heavily involved in, this part of north-western Europe. These principalities' riches made them all the more attractive to adjacent powers, but they also reinforced their autonomous capacities: they could not be subdued easily. These features persisted through the centuries, until the present era: later "Belgium" was (and still is) a crossroads facilitating communication, production, and commerce; in past times, and until the middle of the twentieth century, its location also invited armies to confront each other in pan-European struggles, and tempted mighty countries to bring it into their sphere of influence or to annex it, as France repeatedly did or tried to do.

From the late fourteenth to the late fifteenth centuries, a major development dominated political life in the "regions-in-between". The rulers of Burgundy, one of the principalities located between the crystallizing French kingdom and the still profoundly divided German-speaking polities, generated an ambitious project to build a state that would more or less resurrect bygone Lotharingia. For decades, the audacious Burgundian dukes were quite successful. Astute diplomacy, carefully planned marriages, and sheer force engendered an impressive series of personal unions that turned them into the rulers of a vast array of principalities which, taken together, formed a quasi-uninterrupted land mass stretching from the North Sea to the Alps. However, Charles the Bold's royal dream was shattered due to his recklessness, causing his numerous possessions to head toward different political futures. The small Swiss polities, combined in successive fluctuating confederations since the end of the thirteenth century and for some time menaced by Burgundian expansionism, decisively contributed to Charles' defeat in 1477. They managed to maintain their autonomy, and ultimately founded the modern, multilingual, and federal nation-state of Switzerland in 1848. However, most of the Burgundian dukes' southern ("French") possessions lost their autonomy: while Franche-Comté remained under Habsburg sovereignty until 1678, heartland Burgundy was fully integrated into France, and Alsace and Lorraine remained bones of contention between France and the Holy Roman Empire, later Germany, until 1945 – when they were, once again, integrated into the French Republic. The northern "leftovers" of the late Burgundian state-in-the-making – the Low Countries, that is the future Benelux together with two of modern France's most populous departments, Nord and Pas-de-Calais – for their part, continued to exist as nominally distinct principalities.

But the Burgundian century had irrevocably changed their destiny. Due to fortuitous dynastic and political circumstances, one and the same monarch would henceforth rule them all simultaneously (with the exception of the prince-bishopric of Liège). After the death of the last Burgundian heir in 1482, the common sovereign of the southern ("Belgian") principalities would always be a member of the Habsburg dynasty – first its Spanish branch until 1700; then, from 1713, its Austrian branch until 1794. These successive rulers did not just passively wear the title of duke or count of such or such polity; like their Burgundian predecessors, they also tried to impose some kind of unity upon their possessions, despite (or rather, because of) the latter's visceral attachment to their local traditions and administrative autonomy, known as "liberties." Not all the Habsburg rulers were very active in this regard (the Spanish kings Philip IV and Charles II, for instance, did not leave indelible marks), but several strong monarchs – first Charles V and his son Philip II, and later the cautious Austrian empress Maria-Theresa followed by her more brusque son Joseph II – definitely wanted to impose more centralization upon their rich but heterogeneous and often unruly territories. Philip II's centralizing policy, inclining toward absolutism, was moreover coupled to the religious intolerance ignited by the struggle between Protestants and Catholics. This explosive cocktail led to a long and bloody war that ultimately split the Low Countries. The slowly emerging but still fragile common destiny of the so-called XVII Provinces was destroyed.

On the one hand, a new and dynamic confederal state was created, dominated by the Protestants: the Republic of the United Provinces, the direct ancestor of the modern Netherlands. On the other, nothing really changed for the age-old principalities still governed by the Catholic Spanish Habsburgs. These Southern (or Spanish, later Austrian) Netherlands – one might call them, somewhat irreverently, the "remnants of the post-Burgundian leftovers" – lost even more of their surface area in the course of the seventeenth century, since the northern part of Brabant was integrated within the United Provinces, and vast regions on its south-western flank were annexed by France (to become the already mentioned later *départements* of Nord and Pas-de-Calais). These "remnants," however, maintained their specificities and age-old institutions, even if their respective and successive sovereigns were one and the same person. For sure, the inhabitants of these territories shared, to some extent, a common destiny resulting not only from comparable social, economic, religious, and cultural contingencies and structures (from the medieval period onwards), but also from identical top-down monarchical policies (from the early fifteenth century). However, ordinary people spontaneously defined themselves, first and foremost, as *Liégeois* (inhabitants of the still autonomous prince-bishopric) or *Namurois*, or Flemish (i.e. inhabitants of the *county* of Flanders), or Brabantine, etc. – or they expressed a vague loyalty to the Spanish or Austrian monarch. Only from around the middle of the eighteenth century did some groups – essentially higher middle-class and lettered individuals – express this sense of common destiny as an explicit "Belgian" identity. In other words: the many dramatic political changes in the Low Countries and, later, the Southern Netherlands were not driven, bottom-up, by a sense of "Belgianness"; they rather resulted from international rivalries, that is, from forces completely alien to any form of (even embryonic) "national identity." In spite of the image created by nineteenth-century patriotic Belgian historiography, the "oppressed Belgians" never opposed or drove out a "foreign" ruler and his "occupying" authorities – because these rulers were considered legitimate as long as they respected the traditional "liberties," and because authority was partly exercised by local institutions managed and staffed by local elites.

Only as late as 1789 did "Belgian" claims play a role in regime change. However, the former Austrian masters rapidly crushed the independent United Belgican States. Strikingly, the "Belgian" element played no role whatsoever in the ensuing political developments. Both the annexation of the Southern Netherlands by France, and their subsequent amalgamation into the United Kingdom of the Netherlands (a sort of resurrection of the XVII Provinces), were realized without any notable Belgian protest. Even the Revolution of 1830, founding the Belgian nation-state, offers a complex picture. In the 1820s many members of the elites were obedient subjects of the Dutch king, William I (and many were to remain faithful to him even years *after* Belgium's creation); in addition, important leaders of the revolt tried to negotiate a compromise with the reigning monarch. They wanted more autonomy for the "Belgian" provinces, not independence. Only radical revolutionaries opted for the extreme solution; namely full-fledged independence. Their plan eventually succeeded through a series of fortuitous events. The support of insurgents from the lower classes was crucial in helping them realize their project, but popular protest was far from being inspired by "pure Belgian sentiment" – if such a thing actually exists – because many ordinary armed men took to the streets to violently express their social disgruntlement.

At this crucial turn in Belgian history, the international dimension again enters the picture. Belgian independence clearly resulted from a domestic dispute within the United Kingdom of the Netherlands, fueled, among other things, by an incipient sense of Belgian national identity. It was not "invented" nor "imposed" by the foreign powers. Still, their role was indeed decisive, since they ended up accepting the birth of this new European country. As with all its predecessors, Belgium was and remained an important crystallization point of intra-European rivalries. In the early nineteenth century, the (former) Southern Netherlands were still an unsettled diplomatic issue. The Habsburg rulers in Vienna were no longer interested in these northern possessions. Even during the course of the eighteenth century, they had tried to "get rid" of them. Since Louis XIV, France certainly aspired to annex these regions, but this solution was unacceptable to the other powers. Because the United Kingdom of the Netherlands, a resurrection of the ancient Low Countries, also failed, the creation of an independent Belgium was a final option, on the condition that no Great Power would take advantage of it: neutrality was therefore imposed on the young kingdom.

This solution saddled the country with a serious liability, since its diplomatic wings were clipped. It could choose neither friends nor foes. Even after this humiliating provision had been lifted in 1919, Belgium quickly returned to *self-imposed* neutrality – but to no avail. Geographical location obviously molds diplomacy and strategy: Swiss-style neutrality was manifestly unsuited for the country. A German army invading France (or vice-versa) will most likely not cross the Alps, but rather the flat country separating both age-old contenders. And British supremacy at sea is not threatened by forces stationed at the shores of Lac Léman, but rather by a navy harbored on the North Sea coast, or in Antwerp. This had twice resulted in invasion and occupation (1914–1918 and 1940–1944), with a French army and a British expeditionary force coming to the rescue, though with varying degrees of success. Even apart from military intervention, Belgium was subjected to informal political, economic, or cultural influences dragging it into the sphere of influence of one of its mighty neighbors. This was yet another threat to its existence as a nation.

Belgium's inevitable entanglement in international competition as a passive rather than an active subject finally led its political leadership to promote multilateralism and even supranational political construction, with its pioneering role in European unification as the most striking example. This option was all the more logical given the economic context. Since the early nineteenth century, Belgium had spearheaded capitalist industrial development, fueling a thriving export economy thanks to its position as a logistical and transportation hub. In other words, the central theme of pre-nineteenth-century "Belgian" history – the crucial role of adjacent powers in shaping it – continued to dominate the fate of the independent nation. However, one fundamental change is obvious: from the middle of the twentieth century, Belgium traded its passive, instrumental role for an active one. Henceforth, it took the lead in efforts to thwart a key threat to its very existence – that is, intra-European nationalistic and hegemonic policies – even at the cost of abandoning parts of its sovereignty.

*

* *

These observations amply demonstrate the complexity of its singular historical trajectory. Belgium, as we know it, *might very well never have existed*. Admittedly, "what-ifs" are vain thought experiments; but they nevertheless help stress the many historical contingencies in "Belgian" history. And in this case, counterfactual perspectives indeed abound. First, Burgundian state building – from the North Sea to the Alps – was not automatically destined to fail. Second, the Low Countries, combining the three modern Benelux states, could also have become a viable polity if the struggle between Protestants and Catholics had turned out differently in the sixteenth and seventeenth centuries. Third, if Napoleon had curtailed his pan-European warmongering in the early nineteenth century, the Southern Netherlands could well have remained part of France, with Flemish in the long run "enjoying" a status similar to that of Breton in the modern Fifth Republic. Finally, the United Kingdom of the Netherlands (1815–1830) was not doomed from the outset, and, on the contrary, not all the "Belgians" rejected it. Clearly, coincidences and accidental events – but most of all, as we have stressed, international political and military confrontations and arbitration – cut off these paths leading to political outcomes that were far different to modern Belgium.

But on the other hand, Belgium *could also have taken shape earlier than 1830*, the date of its actual birth. If – yet another "if"! – archdukes Albert and Isabella had been blessed with a male descendant, a (semi-) independent realm very similar to modern Belgium could have been created in the early seventeenth century. Moreover, as we have underlined earlier, the Spanish/Austrian Netherlands were indeed subjected to identical political, social, economic, religious, and cultural determinants from the late sixteenth century. This inevitably generated a common destiny and, ultimately, also some undeniable sense of "Belgian identity," even if it was late, weak, and unevenly distributed among the social classes. As we have seen, Belgium was not an "artificial" state, fabricated from scratch by the Great Powers in 1830, as its contemporary Flemish-Nationalist opponents often claim. And unlike what happened, for instance, in the case of Czechoslovakia or Yugoslavia in 1918, it most certainly was *not* the "forced marriage" of pre-existing peoples, the Flemings and the Walloons, because these "identities" were not yet forged – contrary to, for example, the Catalan or Scottish cases that can boast a long historical tradition. While reinforcing the feeble *Belgian* sense of identity – a sentiment reaching its zenith around the turn of the nineteenth and the twentieth centuries – the Belgian national authorities also unintentionally contributed to the birth of two competing identities; first Flemish, then Walloon. A sense of common belonging of all the Flemish speakers, on the one hand, and of all the French speakers on the other, did not exist before the nineteenth century, just as a "Belgian" identity was non-existent before the eighteenth. Ironically, both alternative and competing identity formations had something in common: they emerged as movements opposing injustice, real or imagined. Flemings opposed the blatant discrimination of their language in the Gallicized Belgian state, while French speakers reacted when the former gradually obtained equality before the law – an evolution that some Francophones saw as threatening their position in the Belgian nation-state.

This generated and gradually reinforced two new identities within Belgium, a sense of belonging to a unified "Flemish (or Walloon) people" that allegedly but mistakenly existed for ages. But despite this evolution, (sub-) regional attachment also persisted in modern Belgium. Being *Liégeois, Montois, Carolo[régien], Borain, Ardennais*, etc. (being born or living in, respectively, the cities of Liège, Mons, Charleroi, or the regions Borinage and the Ardennes) was and still is important in people's everyday lives and the in self-definitions of the Francophones. Likewise, in Flanders, the inhabitants of cities such as Ghent, Antwerp and Bruges, or regions such as Limburg and the coast, are all profoundly impregnated with their local dialects, traditions, and even material interests that differentiate them from the other Flemings and sometimes even cause them to oppose the latter. Contrary to the monolithic definition of "identity" often propagated by nationalistic ideology, this notion is a multi-layered phenomenon *par excellence*. It allows men and women to feel and present themselves at the same time, or in different contexts, as a Belgian, as a Fleming (or a Walloon), and as a proud inhabitant of this or that city or region.

The century-old attachment of the inhabitants of the Southern Netherlands to their ancient principalities and their "liberties" may, at least partly, explain the persistence of such regional affinities. It undoubtedly also accounts for the lasting importance of municipalities as a power base in modern Belgian politics. Whether this age-old tradition also facilitated the gradual dismantling of the central state is not only less clear, but also far from certain (no research has yet been conducted on this subject). But one thing is unquestionable: the growing struggles between the language communities finally induced the transfer of an increasing number of competences from the unitary state to the newly created sub-national institutions, and the communities and regions (Flanders, Brussels, Wallonia, and the French- and German-speaking communities). This still ongoing process represents more than a quarter of Belgium's history as an independent nation-state! It was moreover preceded by a conflict that lasted for decades and was, originally, essentially fueled by Flemish demands for equality, followed by Walloon claims for economic autonomy. A remarkable feature of this process was (and still is) its entirely peaceful nature. Apart from a few isolated deadly incidents (most notably the shooting of a Flemish student by police in a forbidden march in 1920, and the death of a Francophone militant following an electoral scuffle with Flemish-Nationalists in 1970), Belgium's protracted and otherwise often-passionate language conflict produced no fatal bloodshed.

This aspect is certainly worthwhile emphasizing from an international perspective. Are the profound institutional changes of the Belgian nation-state in some ways relevant or "instructive" for similar transformations of other modern nation-states? How can different cultural communities co-exist in an all-encompassing political framework? How can profound social, economic, and political changes be managed without violence but rather through compromise? Answering these questions obviously goes beyond this book's scope but delving into Belgian history certainly helps to clarify some key issues. Such interrogations are also highly relevant for the future of the European Union – a nascent body politic confronting these same questions. Strikingly, the gradual dismantling of the unitary Belgian state was not only realized by transferring competences to sub-national entities (the above-mentioned communities and regions), but also by reinforcing the supranational level, that is, the EU. In other words, as "Brussels" (the capital of unitary Belgium) became less powerful, "Brussels" – the capital of the Flemish community, next to other subnational entities – grew more important, together with "Brussels," the seat of the EU. Politics is, for a good deal, the art of exercising the fitting competences at the appropriate spatial level. The nation-state is only one variant of the levels, next to regions, large urban areas, etc. In this respect, modern Belgium has indeed accumulated some experience – by trial and error, and for better or for worse.

Appendix: List of Rulers, Sovereigns and Heads of State (1419–Present) and of Governors General (1507–1794) of the Southern Low Countries and Belgium

Burgundian Dynasty (1419–1482)

1. Philip the Good, b. 1396, r. 1419–1467
2. Charles the Bold, b. 1433, r. 1467–1477 (son of 1)
3. Mary of Burgundy, b. 1457, r. 1477–1482 (daughter of 2)

Habsburg Dynasty (1482–1555)

4. Maximilian of Austria, b. 1459, regent 1482–1494 (spouse of 3)
5. Philip the Fair, b. 1478, r. 1494–1506 (son of 3 and 4)
6. Maximilian of Austria, regent 1506–1514
   a. Margaret of Austria, b. 1480, governor general 1507–1514 (daughter of 6)
7. Charles V (I in Spain), 1515–1555 (son of 5)
   a. Margaret of Austria, b. 1480, governor general 1519–1530 (aunt of 7)
   b. Mary of Hungary, b. 1505, governor general 1531–1555 (sister of 7)

Spanish Habsburg Dynasty (1555–1700)

8. Philip II, b. 1527, r. 1555–1598 (son of 7)
   a. Margaret of Parma, b. 1522, governor general 1559–1567 (half-sister of 8)
   b. Don Fernando Alvarez de Toledo, duke of Alva, b. 1508, governor general 1567–1574
   c. Don Juan of Austria, b. 1547, governor general 1576–1578 (half-brother of 8)
   d. Alexander Farnèse, duke of Parma, b. 1545, governor general 1578–1592 (nephew of 8)
   e. Ernst of Austria, b. 1553, governor general 1593–1595 (nephew of 8)
   f. Albert of Austria, b. 1559, governor general 1595–1598 (nephew of 8)
9. Albert of Austria, b. 1559 (nephew of 8) and Isabella of Austria, b. 1566 (daughter of 8), r. 1598–1621
10. Philip IV, b. 1605, r. 1621–1665 (grandson of 8)
    a. Isabella of Austria, b. 1566, governor general 1621–1633 (aunt of 10)
    b. Ferdinand of Austria, "Cardinal-Infante," b. 1609, governor general 1634–1641 (brother of 10)
    c. 1641–1647: Francisco de Melo and the marquess of Castel-Rodrigo
    d. Leopold-William, b. 1614, governor general 1647–1655 (2nd cousin of 10)
    e. 1656–1664: don Juan of Austria and the marquess of Caracena
11. Mariana of Austria, b. 1634, regent 1665–1675 (spouse of 10, mother of 12)
    a. 1664–1674: the marquess of Castel-Rodrigo and the count of Monterey
12. Charles II, b. 1661, r. 1675–1700
    a. 1674–1691: the duke of Villa-Hermosa, the Prince of Parma, the marquess of Grana and the marquess of Castanaga
    b. Maximilian-Emmanuel of Bavaria, b. 1662, governor general 1692–1706 (1713)

Bourbon Dynasty (1700–1713)

13. Philip V of Anjou, b. 1683, r. 1700–1713 (greatgrandson of 10)

Austrian Habsburg Dynasty (1713–1794)

14. Charles VI, b. 1685, r. 1713–1740 (2nd nephew of 10)
    a. Prince Eugene of Savoye, b. 1663, governor general 1716–1724 and his representative Hercule-Louis Turinetti, marquis de Prié, b. 1658, minister plenipotentiary 1716–1724
    b. Mary-Elisabeth of Austria, b. 1680, governor general 1726–1741 (sister of 14)
15. Maria-Theresa, b. 1717, r. 1740–1780 (daughter of 14)
    a. Charles of Lorraine, b. 1712, governor general 1744–1780 (brother-in-law of 15)
16. Joseph II, b. 1741, r. 1780–1790 (son of 15)
    a. Mary-Christine of Austria, b. 1742 and her husband Albert of Saxe-Teschen, b. 1738, governor general 1781–1792 (respectively sister and brother-in-law of 16)
17. Leopold II, b. 1747, r. 1790–1792 (brother of 16)
18. Francis II, b. 1768, r. 1792–1794 (son of 17)

French Republic (1794–1804)
Consulate and Empire (1804–1804)

19. Napoleon Bonaparte, b. 1769, r. 1799–1804 as "First Consul," 1804–1814 as Emperor

Orange-Nassau dynasty (1814–1830)

20. William I, b. 1770, r. 1814–1830

Kingdom of Belgium (1831-Present)

21. Erasme Louis Surlet de Chokier, b. 1769, regent 1831
    Saxe-Coburg-Gotha Dynasty
22. Leopold I, b. 1790, r. 1831–1865
23. Leopold II, b. 1835, r. 1865–1909 (son of 22)
24. Albert I, b. 1875, r. 1909–1934 (nephew of 23)
25. Leopold III, b. 1901, r. 1934–1950 (son of 24)

26. Charles, count of Flanders, b. 1903, regent 1944–1950 (brother of 25)
27. Baudouin I, b. 1930, r. 1950–1993 (son of 25)
28. Albert II, b. 1934, r. 1993–2013 (brother of 27)
29. Philip I, b. 1960, r. 2013–present (son of 28)

The complete list of Belgian governments since 1830 (including the names of all ministers and their party affiliations) is to be found on the database Belelite, which is hosted by the Royal Historical Commission (www.commissionroyalehistoire.be/belelite/index.php)

Further Reading

N.B.: publications in English have been privileged.

General Works

Bibliographie de l'histoire de Belgique, 1952– (yearly), available at www.rbph-btfg. be/fr_biblio.html and at http://biblio.arch.be/webopac/Vubis.csp? Profile=BHBBGB&OpacLanguage=fre (2008–).

Algemene geschiedenis der Nederlanden (General history of the Low Countries), Utrecht–Zeist–Antwerp: De Haan–Standaard Boekhandel, 1949–1958, 12 vols.

Algemene geschiedenis der Nederlanden (General History of the Low Countries), Haarlem: Fibula-Van Dishoeck, 1977–1982, 15 vols.

Arblaster, Paul. *A History of the Low Countries*, Houndmills: Palgrave Macmillan, 2006.

Bairoch, Paul, Batou, Jean, and Chèvre, Pierre. *The Population of European Cities from 800 to 1850*, Genève: Droz, 1988.

Bitsch, Marie-Thérèse. *Histoire de la Belgique. De l'Antiquité à nos jours*, Brussels: Complexe, 2004.

Blampain, Daniel e.a. (eds.). *Le français en Belgique*, Brussels: Duculot, 1997.

Blom, Johan C.H. and Lamberts, Emiel (eds.). *History of the Low Countries*, New York: Berghahn, 2006.

Boone, Marc and Deneckere, Gita (eds.). *Ghent: A City of All Times*, Brussels: Fonds Mercator, 2010.

Decavele, Johan (ed.). *Ghent, in Defence of a Rebellious City: History, Art, Culture*, Antwerp: Fonds Mercator, 1989.

Dumoulin, Bruno (ed.). *A Cultural History of Wallonia*, Brussels: Fonds Mercator, 2012.

Dumoulin, Bruno and Kupper, Jean-Louis. *Histoire de la Principauté de Liège*, Toulouse: Privat, 2002.

Hasquin, Hervé (ed.). *Histoire et historiens depuis 1830 en Belgique*, Brussels: Revue de l'Université de Bruxelles, 1981/1–2.

——*Historiographie et Politique. Essai sur l'histoire de Belgique et la Wallonie*, Charleroi: Institut Jules Destrée, 1981.

Janssens, Paul. "Taxation in the Habsburg Low Countries and Belgium 1579–1914," in Yun–Casalilla, Bartolomé, O'Brien, Patrick, and Comin Comin, Francisco (eds.), *The Rise of Fiscal States: A Global History 1500–1914*, Cambridge: Cambridge University Press, 2012, pp. 67–92.

Lejeune, Carlo (ed.). *Grenzerfahrungen. Eine Geschichte der Deutschsprachigen Gemeinschaft Belgiens*, Eupen: GEV, 2014–2019, 5 vols.

Morelli, Anne (ed.). *Les grands mythes de l'histoire de Belgique, de Flandre et de Wallonie*, Brussels: Vie ouvrière, 1995.

Pirenne, Henri. *Histoire de Belgique*, Brussels: Lamertin, 1900–1932, 7 vols. (reprint in four volumes, 1948–1952).

Pye, Michael. *The Edge of the World*, London: Penguin Books, 2014.

Smolar-Meynart, Arlette and Stengers, Jean (eds.). *La région de Bruxelles: des villages d'autrefois à la ville d'aujourd'hui*, Brussels: Crédit communal de Belgique, 1989.

Stengers, Jean (ed.). *Bruxelles: croissance d'une capitale*, Antwerp: Fonds Mercator, 1979.

——"Le mythe des dominations étrangères dans l'historiographie belge," *Revue Belge de Philologie et d'Histoire*, 59 (1981): 382–401.

Stengers, Jean and Gubin, Eliane. *Histoire du sentiment national en Belgique des origines à nos jours*, Brussels: Racine, 2000–2002, 2 vols.

Verhulst, Adriaan (ed.). *Agriculture in Belgium: Yesterday and Today*, Antwerp: Fonds Mercator, 1980.

Verhulst, Adriaan. *Précis d'histoire rurale de la Belgique*, Brussels: Éditions de l'Université de Bruxelles, 1990.

Wangermée, Robert and Mercier Philippe (eds.). *La Musique en Wallonie et à Bruxelles*, Brussels: La Renaissance du Livre, 1980–1982, 2 vols.

Willemyns, Roland. *Dutch: Biography of a Language*, Oxford: Oxford University Press, 2013.

Wils, Lode. *Histoire des Nations belges : Belgique, Wallonie, Flandre : quinze siècles de passé commun*, Brussels: Labor, 2005.

Witte, Els (ed.). *Histoire de Flandre: des origines à nos jours*, Brussels: La Renaissance du Livre, 1983.

Chapter 1

Brulet, Raymond (ed.). *Les Romains en Wallonie*, Brussels: Racine, 2008.

De Laet, Siegfried. *La Belgique d'avant les Romains*, Wetteren: Universa, 1982.

Mariën, Marcel-E. *Belgica Antiqua. L'empreinte de Rome*, Brussels: Fonds Mercator, 1980.

Nouwen, Robert. *De Romeinen in België (31 v.C.–476 n.C.)*, Leuven: Davidsfonds, 2006.

Warmenbol, Eugène (ed.). *La Belgique gauloise: mythes et archéologies*, Brussels: Racine, 2010.
Wightman, Elisabeth. *Gallia Belgica*, Berkeley: University of California Press, 1985.

Chapters 2–6

Aerts, Eric e.a. (ed.). *Les institutions du Gouvernement central des Pays–Bas habsbourgeois (1482–1795)*, Brussels: State Archives, 1995, 2 vols.
Blockmans, Willem–Pieter. "Princes conquérants et bourgeois calculateurs. Le poids des réseaux urbains dans la formation des états," in Bulst, Neithard and Genet, Jean-Philippe (eds.). *La ville, la bourgeoisie et la genèse de l'état moderne (XIIe–XVIIIe siècles)*, Paris: CNRS, 1988, pp. 167–181.
Boone, Marc and Prak, Maarten. "Rulers, Patricians and Burghers : the Great and Little Traditions of Urban Revolt in the Low Countries," in Davids Karel and Lucassen Jan (eds.). *A Miracle Mirrored. The Dutch Republic in European Perspective*, Cambridge: Cambridge University Press, 1985, pp. 99–134.
Derville, Alain. *Villes de Flandre et d'Artois (900–1500)*, Villeneuve–d'Asq: Presses universitaires du Septentrion, 2002.
De Vries, Jan. *European Urbanization 1500–1800*, London: Methuen, 1984.
Dubois, Sébastien. *L'invention de la Belgique. Genèse d'un État-Nation 1648–1830*, Brussels : Racine, 2005.
Gelderblom, Oscar. *Cities of Commerce. The Institutional Foundations of International Trade in the Low Countries, 1250–1650*, Princeton-Oxford: Princeton University Press, 2013.
Israel, Jonathan. *The Dutch Republic. Its Rise, Greatness, and Fall 1477–1806*, Oxford: Clarendon Press, 1995, Part I (1477–1588), pp. 9–230.
Nicholas, David. *Medieval Flanders*, London and New York: Longman, 1992.
O'Brien, Patrick (ed.). *Urban Achievement in Early Modern Europe. Golden Ages in Antwerp, Amsterdam and London*, Cambridge: Cambridge University Press, 2001.
Prak, Maarten, Lis, Catharina, Lucassen, Jan, and Soly, Hugo (eds.). *Craft Guilds in the Early Modern Low Countries: Work, Power and Representation*, Aldershot: Ashgate, 2006.
Le Réseau urbain en Belgique dans une perspective historique (1350–1850). Actes du 15e colloque international 1990, Brussels: Crédit communal de Belgique, 1992.
Simons, Walter. *Cities of Ladies. Beguine Communities in the Medieval Low Countries, 1200–1565*, Philadelphia: University of Pennsylvania Press, 2001.
Van Houtte, Jan Arthur. *An Economic History of the Low Countries, 800–1800*, London: Weidenfeld and Nicolson, 1977.
Verhulst, Adriaan. *The Rise of Cities in North-West Europe*, Cambridge: Cambridge University Press, 1999.
Xhayet, Geneviève. *Réseaux de pouvoir et solidarités de parti à Liège au Moyen Âge (1250–1468)*, Genève: Droz, 1997.

Chapter 2

Devroey, Jean–Pierre. *Économie rurale et société dans l'Europe franque (VIᵉ–IXᵉ siècles) : Tome 1: fondements matériels, échanges et lien social*, Paris: Belin, 2003 (see also other works of this author, available online at http://difusion .ulb.ac.be/).

Dierkens, Alain. *Abbayes et Chapitres entre Sambre et Meuse (VIIᵉ–XIᵉ siècles) : contribution à l'histoire religieuse des campagnes du Haut Moyen Age*, Sigmaringen: Thorbecke, 1985 (see also other works of this author, available online at http://difusion.ulb.ac.be/).

Faider–Feytmans, Germaine. *La Belgique à l'époque mérovingienne*, Brussels: La Renaissance du Livre, 1964.

Ganshof, François–Louis. *La Belgique carolingienne*, Brussels: La Renaissance du Livre, 1958.

Verhulst, Adriaan. *The Carolingian Economy*, Cambridge: Cambridge University Press, 2002.

Chapter 3

Boone, Marc. *À la recherche d'une modernité civique. La société urbaine des anciens Pays–Bas au bas Moyen Âge*, Brussels: Éditions de l'Université de Bruxelles, 2010.

Brown, Andrew and Dumolyn, Jan (eds.). *Medieval Bruges: c.850–1550*, Cambridge: Cambridge University Press, 2018.

De Roover, Raymond. *The Bruges Money Market Around 1400*, Brussels: Koninklijke Vlaamse Academie, 1968.

Dumolyn, Jan and Haemers, Jelle. "Patterns of Urban Rebellion in Medieval Flanders," *Journal of Medieval History*, 31 (2005): 369–393.

Lambrechts, Pascale and Sosson, Jean–Pierre (eds.). *Les métiers au Moyen Âge. Aspects économiques et sociaux*, Louvain-la-Neuve: Institut d'Études médiévales, 1994.

Lejeune, Jean. *Liège et son Pays. Naissance d'une patrie (XIIIᵉ–XIVᵉ siècle)*, Liège: Faculté de Philosophie et Lettres, 1948.

Murray, James (ed.). *Bruges, Craddle of Capitalism, 1280–1390*, Cambridge: Cambridge University Press, 2005.

Nicholas, David. *The Metamorphosis of a Medieval City. Ghent in the Age of the Arteveldes, 1302–1390*, Lincoln and London: University of Nebraska Press, 1987.

Sosson, Jean–Pierre. *Les travaux publics de la ville de Bruges, XIVᵉ–XVᵉ siècles. Les matériaux. Les hommes*, Brussels: Crédit communal de Belgique, 1977.

Chapter 4

Blockmans, Wim and Prevenier, Walter. *The Promised Lands: The Low Countries under Burgundian rule, 1369–1530*, Philadelphia: University of Pennsylvania Press, 1999.

Boone, Marc and Prevenier, Walter (eds.). *Drapery Production in the Late Medieval Low Countries. Markets and Strategies for Survival (14th–16th Centuries)*, Leuven and Apeldoorn: Garant, 1993.

Cauchies, Jean–Marie (ed.). *À la cour de Bourgogne, le duc, son entourage, son train*, Turnhout: Brepols, 1998.

Haemers, Jelle. *For the Common Good. State Power and Urban Revolts in the Reign of Mary of Burgundy (1477–1492)*, Turnhout: Brepols, 2009.

Howell, Martha. *The Marriage Exchange. Property, Social Place and Gender in Cities of the Low Countries, 1300–1550*, Chicago: University of Chicago Press, 1998.

Lecuppre-Desjardin, Élodie. *Le royaume inachevé des ducs de Bourgogne (XIVe–XVe siècles)*, Paris: Belin, 2016.

Prevenier, Walter and Blockmans, Wim. *The Burgundian Netherlands*, Cambridge: Cambridge University Press, 1986.

Schnerb, Bertrand. *L'État bourguignon 1363–1477*, Paris: Perrin, 2005, 2nd ed. (1999).

Soly, Hugo (ed.). *Charles V 1500–1558 and his Time*, Antwerp: Fonds Mercator, 1999.

Stabel, Peter. *Dwarfs Among Giants. The Flemish Urban Network in the Late Middle Ages*, Leuven and Apeldoorn: Garant, 1997.

Stein, Robert (ed.). *Powerbrokers in the Late Middle Ages: The Burgundian Low Countries in a European Context*, Turnhout: Brepols, 2001.

——*Magnanimous Dukes and Rising States: The Unification of the Burgundian Netherlands, 1380–1480*, Oxford: Oxford University Press, 2017.

Van der Wee, Herman. *The Growth of the Antwerp Market and the European Economy. Fourteenth–Sixteenth Centuries*, The Hague: Martinus Nijhoff, 1963, 3 vols.

——(ed.). *The Rise and Decline of Urban Industries in Italy and in the Low Countries (Late Middle Ages–Early Modern Times)*, Leuven: Leuven University Press, 1988.

——*The Low Countries in the Early Modern World*, Aldershot: Variorum, 1993.

Vaughan, Richard. *Philip the Bold. The formation of the Burgundian State*, London: Longman, 1979.

——*John the Fearless. The Growth of Burgundian Power*, London: Longman, 1979.

——*Philip the Good. The Apogee of the Burgundian State*, London: Longman, 1970.

——*Charles the Bold. The Last Valois Duke of Burgundy*, London: Longman, 1973.

Chapter 5

Carter, Charles H. "Belgian 'Autonomy' under the Archdukes, 1598–1621," *Journal of Modern History*, 36 (1964): 245–259.

Craeybeckx, Jan, Daelemans, Frank and Scheelings, Frank (eds.). *1585: On Separate Paths. Proceedings of the Colloquium on the Separation of the Low Countries held on 22–23 November 1985*, Leuven: Peeters, 1988.

Duerloo, Luc. *Dynasty and Piety: Archduke Albert (1598–1621) and Habsburg Political Culture in an Age of Religious Wars*, Aldershot: Ashgate, 2011.

Duke, Alistair. *Reformation and Revolt in the Low Countries*, London and New York: Hambledon, 2003.

Everaert, John. *De internationale en koloniale handel der Vlaamse firma's te Cadiz 1670–1700. Avec un résumé français : Le commerce international et colonial des firmes flamandes à Cadix (1670–1700)*, Bruges: De Tempel, 1973.

Hasquin, Hervé. *Louis XIV face à l'Europe du Nord. L'Absolutisme vaincu par les libertés*, Brussels: Racine, 2005.

Janssens, Paul (ed.). *La Belgique espagnole et la principauté de Liège 1585–1715*, Brussels: La Renaissance du Livre, 2006, 2 vols.

Kamen, Henry. *The Duke of Alba*, New Haven and London: Yale University Press, 2004.

Marnef, Guido. *Antwerp in the Age of Reformation: Underground Protestantism in a Commercial Metropolis, 1550–1577*, Baltimore: Johns Hopkins University Press, 1996.

Parker, Geoffrey, *Imprudent King: a New Life of Philip II*, Hew Haven and London: Yale University Press, 2014.

Parker, Geoffrey, *The Grand Strategy of Philip II*, New Haven and London: Yale University Press, 1998.

——*The Army of Flanders and the Spanish Road 1567–1659: the Logistics of Spanish Victory and Defeat in the Low Countries' Wars*, Cambridge: Cambridge University Press, 2004² (1972).

Raeymakers, Dries. *One foot in the Palace. The Habsburg Court of Brussels and the Politics of Access in the Reign of Albert and Isabella, 1598–1621*, Leuven: Leuven University Press, 2013.

Stradling, Robert A. *Spain's Struggle for Europe*, London: Hambledon, 1994.

Thomas, Werner and Duerloo, Luc (eds.). *Albert & Isabella, 1598–1621. Essays*, Turnhout: Brepols, 1998.

Chapter 6

Bruneel, Claude. *La mortalité dans les campagnes: le Duché de Brabant aux XVII⁵ et XVIII⁵ siècles*, Leuven: Nauwelaerts, 1977, 2 vols.

De Peuter, Roger. *Brussel in de achttiende eeuw: sociaal–economische structuren en ontwikkelingen in een regionale hoofdstad*, Brussels: VUB Press, 1999.

Hasquin, Hervé. *Une mutation. Le "Pays de Charleroi" aux XVII⁵ et XVIII⁵ siècles. Aux origines de la Révolution Industrielle en Belgique*, Brussels: Éditions de l'Institut de Sociologie de l'Université Libre de Bruxelles, 1971.

——(ed.). *La Belgique autrichienne, 1713–1794: les Pays-Bas méridionaux sous les Habsbourg d'Autriche*, Brussels: Crédit communal de Belgique, 1987.

Lottin, Alain and Soly, Hugo. "Aspects de l'histoire des villes des Pays–Bas méridionaux et de la principauté de Liège," in Poussou, Jean–Pierre e.a. (eds.), *Études sur les villes en Europe occidentale (milieu du XVII⁵ siècle à la veille de la Révolution Française)*, vol. 2, Paris: SEVPEN, 1983, pp. 213–306.

Mendels, Franklin. "Agriculture and Peasant Industry in Eighteenth Century Flanders," in Parker, William N. and Jones, Eric L. (eds.). *European Peasants* and their Markets, Princeton: Princeton University Press, 1975, pp. 179–204.

Moureaux, Philippe. *Les préoccupations statistiques du Gouvernement des Pays-Bas autrichiens et le dénombrement des industries dressé en 1764*, Brussels: Éditions de l'Université de Bruxelles, 1971.

Vandenbroeke, Chris. *Agriculture et alimentation dans les Pays-Bas autrichiens*, Leuven and Ghent: Centre belge d'Histoire rurale, 1973.

Chapter 7

Blanning, Timothy. *Joseph II*, London and New York: Longman, 1994.

Craeybeckx, Jan and Scheelings, Frank (eds.). *La Révolution française et la Flandre. Les Pays-Bas autrichiens entre l'ancien et le nouveau régime*, Brussels: VUB Press, 1990.

Fishman, J.S. *Diplomacy and Revolution. The London Conference of 1830 and the Belgian Revolt*, Amsterdam: CHEV Publisher, 1988.

Hasquin, Hervé (ed.). *La Belgique française: 1792–1815*, Brussels: Crédit communal de Belgique, 1993.

Judge, Jane. *The United States of Belgium: The Story of the First Belgian Revolution*, Leuven: Leuven University Press, 2018.

Lebrun, Pierre e.a. *Essai sur la Révolution industrielle en Belgique 1770–1847*, Brussels: Académie royale de Belgique, 1979.

Lis, Catharina. *Social Change and the Labouring Poor. Antwerp 1770–1860*, New Haven and London: Yale University Press, 1986.

Polasky, Janet. *Revolution in Brussels 1787–1793*, Brussels: Académie royale de Belgique, 1985.

La Révolution liégeoise de 1789, Brussels: Crédit communal de Belgique, 1989.

Tamse, Coenraad and Witte, Els (eds.). *Staats-en natievorming in Willem I's koninkrijk (1815–1830)*, Brussels: VUB Press, 1992.

Witte, Els. *La construction de la Belgique*, Brussels: Le Cri, 2010.

——*Le Royaume perdu: les orangistes belges contre la révolution: 1828–1850*, Brussels: Samsa, 2016.

——*Belgische republikeinen. Radicalen tussen twee revoluties*, Kalmthout: Polis, 2020.

Chapters 8–10

Berg, Christian and Halen, Pierre (eds.). *Littératures belges de langue française. Histoire et perspectives (1830–2000)*, Brussels: Le Cri, 2000.

Coolsaet, Rik. *Histoire de la politique étrangère belge*, Brussels: Vie ouvrière, 1988.

Deprez, Kas and Vos, Louis (eds.). *Nationalism in Belgium: Shifting Identities, 1780–1995*, New York and London: St. Martin's Press-Macmillan, 1998.

Gubin, Eliane e.a. (eds.). *Histoire de la Chambre des représentants de Belgique 1830–2002*, Brussels: Chambre des représentants, 2003.

Halleux, Robert (ed.). *Histoire des sciences en Belgique: 1815–2000*, Brussels: Dexia Banque, 2001, 2 vols.

Helmreich, Jonathan. *Belgium and Europe: A Study in Small Power Diplomacy*, The Hague and Paris: Mouton, 1976.

Hermans, Theo, Vos, Louis, and Wils, Lode (eds.). *The Flemish Movement: A Documentary History 1780–1990*, London and New York: Bloomsbury Academic, 2015.

Janssens, Valéry. *Le franc belge. Un siècle et demi d'histoire monétaire*, Brussels, 1976.

Kossmann, Ernst H. *The Low Countries 1780–1940*, Oxford: Clarendon Press, 1978.

L'industrie en Belgique: deux siècles d'évolution 1780–1980, Brussels: Crédit communal de Belgique, 1981.

Laureys, Véronique e.a. (eds.). *L'histoire du Sénat de Belgique de 1831 à 1995*, Brussels: Racine, 1999.

Mabille, Xavier. *Histoire politique de la Belgique. Facteurs et acteurs de changement*, Brussels: CRISP, 1986.

Mommen, André. *The Belgian Economy in the Twentieth Century*, London and New York: Routledge, 1994.

Nouvelle histoire de la Belgique, Brussels: Le Cri, 2008, 6 vol.

Palo, Michael. *Neutrality as a Policy Choice for Small/Weak Democracies. Learning from the Belgian Experience*, Leiden: Brill, 2019.

Palmer, Michael. *From Ensor to Magritte: Belgian Art 1880–1940*, Brussels: Racine, 1994.

Stengers, Jean. *L'action du roi en Belgique depuis 1831: pouvoir et influence*, Brussels: Racine, 2008.

Stouten, Hanna e.a. (eds.). *Histoire de la littérature néerlandaise (Pays-Bas et Flandre)*, Paris: Fayard, 1999.

Van den Eeckhout, Patricia and Vanthemsche, Guy (eds.). *Sources pour l'étude de la Belgique contemporaine, 19ᵉ–21ᵉ siècle*, Brussels: Commission royale d'Histoire, 2017, 2 vols.

Van der Wee, Herman and Blomme, Jan (eds.). *The Economic Development of Belgium Since 1870*, Cheltenham: Edward Elgar, 1997.

Van Goethem, Herman. *Belgium and the Monarchy: From National Independence to National Disintegration*, Brussels: University Press Antwerp, 2010.

Vanthemsche, Guy. *Belgium and the Congo, 1885–1980*, Cambridge: Cambridge University Press, 2012.

——(ed.). *Les classes sociales en Belgique: deux siècles d'histoire*, Brussels: CRISP, 2017.

Witte, Els, Craeybeckx, Jan and Meynen, Alain. *Political history of Belgium: From 1830 onwards*, Brussels: Academic and Scientific Publishers, 2009.

Witte, Els and Van Velthoven, Harry. *Languages in Contact and in Conflict: The Belgian Case*, Kalmthout: Pelckmans, 2011.

Chapter 8

Draper, Mario. *The Belgian Army and Society from Independence to the Great War*, Basingstoke: Palgrave Macmillan, 2018.

Laqua, Daniel. *The Age of Internationalism and Belgium, 1880–1930: Peace, Progress and Prestige*, Manchester: Manchester University Press, 2013.

Van Ginderachter, Maarten. *Le chant du coq. Nation et nationalisme en Wallonie depuis 1880*, Ghent: Academia Press, 2005.

——*The Everyday Nationalism of Workers: a Social History of Modern Belgium*. Stanford: Stanford UP, 2019.

Chapter 9

Conway, Martin. *Collaboration in Belgium: Léon Degrelle and the Rexist Movement, 1940–1944*, New Haven and London: Yale University Press, 1993.

De Schaepdrijver, Sophie. *La Belgique et la Première Guerre mondiale*, Brussels: PIE-Peter Lang, 2006.

Gérard–Libois, Jules and Gotovitch, José. *L'an 40. La Belgique occupée*, Brussels: CRISP, 1971.

Hogg, Robin. *Structural Rigidities and Policy Inertia in Inter–War Belgium*, Brussels: Koninklijke Vlaamse Academie van België, 1986.

Stengers, Jean. *Une guerre pour l'honneur: la Belgique en 14–18*, Brussels: Racine, 2014.

Van der Wee, Herman and Verbreyt, Monique. *A Small Nation in the Turmoil of the Second World War: Money, Finance and Occupation (1939–1945)*, Leuven: Leuven University Press, 2009.

Verhoeyen, Étienne. *La Belgique occupée. De l'an 40 à la libération*, Brussels: De Boeck, 1994.

Chapter 10

Conway, Martin. *The Sorrows of Belgium: Liberation and Political Reconstruction, 1944–1947*, Oxford: Oxford University Press, 2012.

Deschouwer, Kris. *The Politics of Belgium. Governing a Divided Society*, Houndmills: Palgrave Macmillan, 2012.

Elias, Willem. *Aperçu de l'art belge après '45*, Ghent: Snoeck, 2008.

Kesteloot, Chantal. *Au nom de la Wallonie et de Bruxelles français: les origines du FDF*, Brussels: Complexe, 2004.

Schrijvers, Peter. *Liberators: The Allies and Belgian Society, 1944–1945*, Cambridge: Cambridge University Press, 2009.

Smeyers, Kristof and Buyst, Erik. *Het gestolde land. Een economische geschiedenis van België*, Kalmthout: Polis, 2016.

Von Busekist, Astrid (ed.). *Singulière Belgique*, Paris: Fayard, 2012.

Witte, Els and Meynen, Alain (eds.). *De geschiedenis van België na 1945*, Antwerp: Standaard Uitgeverij, 2006.

Index

Index

CPSIA information can be obtained
at www.ICGtesting.com
Printed in the USA
LVHW051217140323
741585LV00009B/402